The
Story
of
Judaism

The Story of Judaism

BERNARD J. BAMBERGER

Third, Augmented Edition

SCHOCKEN BOOKS · NEW YORK

To

𝔓resident Julian Morgenstern

IN GRATITUDE AND AFFECTION

This edition is published by arrangement with
Union of American Hebrew Congregations

Library of Congress Catalog Card No. 64-16463
Manufactured in the United States of America

Table of Contents

Part 6. Era of Hope

Part 7. The Road to the Abyss

Part 8. Problems and Opportunities

Part 1.
The Foundations

At Meeting

THIS BOOK is not for the scholar, but for the general reader. It is bulky, no question, but then the story it tells is a long one—it began over three thousand years ago, and is still not ended.

This is not a history of the Jews, or of Jewish literature, but of the inner content of Jewish life. Each of these three topics, of course, involves the other two. The Jewish religion cannot be understood apart from the experience of the Jewish people and their preoccupation with many books. The comment of a mystical writer that "God, Israel, and the Torah are one and inseparable" is in this sense literal fact. But though we shall take constant note of political, economic, and social forces, and of the vast Jewish literature in many languages, our attention will be centered on religious ideas, observances, and institutions.

What is Judaism? Instead of starting with a rigid definition and forcing our material into the mold, we shall let the answer emerge from the story itself. The author firmly believes that the core of Jewish experience is religious: the God idea, the concept of man and of humanity, the moral law, the future hope, the two foci of synagogue and home, the system of study, prayer, and observance. Nevertheless, room has been found in our account for elements that are neither theological nor ceremonial, and yet belong somehow to the inner life of the Jewish people. Moreover, the secular Jewish philosophies now current constitute a challenge to Jewish religion and must be considered (at the very least) for this reason.

The attempt to write a comprehensive yet popular history of Judaism was both quixotic and presumptuous, especially since much scholarly spade-work is still to be done. This volume can be justified only in terms of present need: the need of Jews engaged in the task of self-comprehension, the need of Christians to understand the background

I

of their own faith. It seeks to display, however incompletely, the richness, vitality, and relevance of the Jewish spiritual heritage.

Both these needs have become sharper in the dozen years since this book first appeared. Many young Jews, especially university students, are in revolt against what they consider the superficial, conformist Judaism of their elders, and they complain that the Jewish education they received in childhood offered them little that was relevant or important. Such strictures are by no means unjustified. But the recognition that Jewish education has often been ineffective does not justify the conclusion that Judaism is without content or contemporary significance. It should lead rather to a more adult quest for knowledge of the Jewish heritage. For this purpose, the present volume provides at least a sketchy introduction.

Many a present-day Christian likewise finds himself ill prepared for living in this "ecumenical" age. He would like to arrive at a better understanding of his Jewish neighbors, but he realizes how little he knows about contemporary Jewish realities and their historical background. Histories of the people and religion of Israel written by Christian scholars usually end with the destruction of the Temple by the Romans in 70 c.e., and they present the New Testament as the direct and logical continuation of the "Old Testament." Few Christians have even a vague notion about Jewish experience and Jewish spiritual creativeness in the last two thousand years.

A motorist driving along Route 47 comes to a fork in the road. If he wants to stay on 47, he must bear left; if he goes straight ahead, he will find himself on Route 191. (Of course, the Highway Commission could have reversed the numbering.) Similarly, Christians have assumed that the development recorded in the Hebrew Bible is directly continued in Christian scripture and church history, while the subsequent evolution of Judaism is a byway that leads nowhere in particular. For Jews, on the other hand, Judaism is the main road and Christianity the turnoff. Without debating which view of the matter is correct, we can certainly agree that both roads are of interest and worth exploring.

I am deeply grateful to all who helped me to prepare and publish this book, and subsequently to correct some of its errors. In this new edition there have been substantial revisions, and two more chapters have been added to bring the story—for the moment—up to date.

Bernard J. Bamberger

1.

Seeds and Roots

ACCORDING TO FAMILIAR TRADITION, THE JEWISH RELIGION BEGAN
with Abraham and reached its full development with Moses. The
well-loved story tells that God revealed Himself intimately, personally, to Abraham, a Babylonian whose family had settled in Syria.
Under direct divine guidance, Abraham went to Palestine, where
God promised him that the land should be the heritage of his descendants. The Patriarch transmitted the worship of the one God
to his children; some relapsed into idolatry, but through Isaac and
Jacob the true faith was kept alive.

The fourth generation of the tribe settled in Egypt, where in a few
centuries they grew into a people of some six hundred thousand souls.
The envious Egyptians reduced them to slavery, and dealt so cruelly
with them that they turned to their God for help. Moses, of the tribe
of Levi, was sent as their divinely chosen deliverer, and brought them
out of Egypt with "signs and wonders."

Under Moses' leadership, the people came to Mount Sinai in the
wilderness. There God displayed His power in thunder, earthquake,
and the sound of a wondrous horn; and all Israel heard His voice proclaiming the laws by which they were to serve Him. A solemn covenant was sealed. Israel promised to obey God's commandments, receiving in turn the assurance of His protection and guidance. The
basic laws heard by all the people were supplemented by a much
fuller and more specific body of legislation revealed to their leader.
Part of this was written down at once to form the "Five Books of

Moses." But even bulkier was the revelation, supplementary to and explanatory of the Written Law, which Moses transmitted to later generations only by word of mouth.

The entire body of doctrine and commandment, written and traditional, constitutes the Torah, the literally divine rule for Jewish religious life. It is complete and perfect. Nothing can be or need be added to Judaism. Later Jewish teachers, Biblical and otherwise, merely explain or reemphasize the lessons of the Torah. Such small modifications as changing times require were already implied in the original revelation. The Judaism of today is the Judaism of Sinai.

This account of the matter has been current for many centuries; but to many moderns it is no longer satisfying. The miracles to which former ages pointed as the most conclusive proof have the opposite effect on us: they rouse our doubts. True, such episodes as the dividing of the Red Sea may be the legendary embroidery of an essentially historical narrative. But our difficulties go deeper. We can no longer conceive of God speaking in an audible voice to the multitudes of Israel, or dictating the very words of the Torah.

Besides, the Bible as we have it contains elements that are scientifically incorrect or even morally repugnant. No amount of "explaining away" can convince us that such passages are the product of Divine Wisdom. Above all, it is hard for us to accept the notion of a completely changeless religion. The concept of historical development is strongly established in our minds; we know that ideas do not come abruptly into existence and then remain static. Ideas grow, change, evolve; and we should expect this to be true also of religious ideas.

Actual analysis of the stories and laws of the Torah has fully justified these contentions. The early Biblical books are not a consecutive and consistent narrative, but a highly complex compilation. The inner discrepancies and contradictions of the Pentateuch * make it clear that its various parts were written at different times, and reflect different social and intellectual backgrounds. The religion of Israel has gone through a long process of evolution. Its ideas, attitudes, and practices have often been modified; only by degrees have they reached their full magnificence.

But to trace the development of Judaism from its origins is no small undertaking. It was comparatively simple for modern scientific stu-

---

* Five Books of Moses, Torah.

dents of the Bible to undermine the traditional views. But to reconstruct what actually happened in the history of the people of Israel and their religion, especially in the earliest periods, is not so easy. The problems are thorny, the materials for their solution limited and fragmentary. It is not surprising that scholars disagree sharply on many crucial questions.

During the nineteenth century many Biblical critics went to radical extremes in refashioning the early history of Israel. The authenticity and correctness of many Biblical documents were denied without sufficient reason. This trend has now been reversed. The critics have been criticized in their turn. In particular, archeological discoveries have indicated that the narratives of the Pentateuch contain a substantial kernel of historic fact. But where history ends and legendary embellishments begin is something which no one can yet decide with complete assurance.

* * *

At the earliest period when we can with certainty detach history from legend and folklore, we find the Hebrews as a group of tribes but recently settled in Palestine. Previously semi-nomads in the desert regions to the south and east, they had forced their way into the country and gained control of a large part of it. Many localities remained for a long time in the hands of the earlier inhabitants.

Despite ties of common blood, language and culture, the tribes had little sense of unity. There was no national government and there was no central religious authority. Each tribe had its own holy places, sacred objects, and priestly leaders.

Yet the religious cult of all the tribes was substantially the same. It was the worship of a deity called YHWH (probably pronounced Yahweh, though this is not quite certain).

The tribes also shared certain historic memories and traditions. They had not always worshipped Yhwh. Their fathers had "dwelt of old time beyond the River Euphrates . . . and they served other gods." The people also recalled living for a time in Egypt, where the ruling power oppressed them. They escaped under the leadership of a man named Moses; and it was he who formally inducted them into the religion of Yhwh. At Mount Sinai the people and God had become partners to a solemn covenant. Israel promised to give Him their exclusive and faithful worship and to obey the laws He imposed on them. Yhwh in turn undertook to guide, protect, and prosper them, and to bring them to a land "flowing with milk and honey." These traditions are so clearly attested in all our sources that we cannot doubt their historic truth. Especially do the covenant at Sinai and the compelling leadership of Moses influence the whole subsequent development of Judaism. The figure of Moses looms up magnificently through mists of popular fancy that blur its outlines. Generation after generation idealized him, and attributed to him not only the foundation of Judaism, but all the advances and elaborations which later ages produced. No other prophet, they believed, had ever risen or could rise to his level; his very face had shone with an unearthly radiance.

After we make due allowances for the adornments and exaggerations of legend, the greatness of Moses still remains clear. The Hebrew tribes had an extraordinary sense of a common destiny, of a dynamic role which they were to play in the economy of the world, and of a brotherhood which their tribal divisions could not efface. These convictions, on which the later development of Judaism was based, must have come to them from a greatly inspired and inspiring personality. If we knew nothing about Moses, we should have to assume that some such man existed.

We shall perhaps never succeed in distinguishing sharply between the Moses of history and the Moses of Jewish tradition. For this great figure became the symbol of Israel's highest idealism, the model teacher, leader, and good shepherd. His importance consists both in what he actually was and did, and in what later ages thought about him. In both senses, he has been for subsequent generations *Mosheh Rabbenu*, Moses our teacher.

How did the Hebrews worship God? The cult as we find it in the early Palestinian period includes two elements, already closely intertwined. Certain features reflect the life of the desert dwellers. There were few formal shrines: a bare rock at some central spot served as a sacrificial altar; heads of the clans acted as priests. One of the chief observances was the spring festival called *Pesach* (Passover); at this time the firstlings of the flocks were sacrificed to God.

But the wanderers from the desert soon gained a foothold in the fertile districts of Palestine and became farmers. Before long, their religious observances began to reflect the conditions of agricultural life. Three festivals in particular acquired an important place in the calendar of Israel. The beginning of the grain harvest (which in

Palestine occurs in the spring) was marked by the Feast of *Matsos* (Unleavened Bread). It fell about the same time as the nomadic Passover, and the two were eventually combined into one observance. Seven weeks after Passover, the end of this first harvest period was celebrated by the Feast of *Shovuos* (Weeks). The vintage and fruit harvest, which marked the completion of the agricultural year, culminated in the Feast of *Sukos* (Tabernacles). In early times, the New Year Day, observed by rites of purification, was probably celebrated at the close of this autumn festival.

These holidays, celebrated at each village shrine by animal sacrifices and offerings of crops, by songs of thanksgiving and ritual dances, were not unlike the observances of other agricultural peoples, ancient and modern. It was something new, however, when the Israelites (from an early date) began to give their feasts an historical significance. The Pesach-Matsos festival was regarded as the anniversary of the deliverance from Egypt; the Feast of Tabernacles, as a memorial of Israel's desert wanderings. But the Feast of Weeks was not connected with the giving of the Torah at Sinai until post-Biblical times.

A unique feature of Israelite religion was the Sabbath. This institution must have arisen * after Israel entered the land; for under desert conditions, the shepherds must care for their animals every day. Sabbath observance was only possible after the Israelites had settled down as farmers. Some other Semitic peoples, notably the Babylonians, had an observance which bore a similar name; but it was quite different in character. The Babylonian *Shapatum* was an unlucky day, on which certain official persons were forbidden to work (like "Friday the thirteenth"). Quite different was the Israelite Sabbath: it was a day of universal rest even for slaves and work-animals; and this rest was not a device to ward off evil fortune, but a commandment of God. Later on, the tremendous social and religious implications of the Sabbath were more fully developed; but this unique observance shows us how, even in its very early stages, the religion of Israel was already something new and distinctive.

It is true that in some ways the Yhwh-cult reminds us of other Near-Eastern religions. Its intent was to secure large flocks and plentiful crops, health, children, and victory. The chief means to these ends were offerings of animals and cereals to the Deity. Yhwh was thought to possess human form and feelings. Though all agreed that

---

* Or, at least, evolved fully.

He had an exclusive claim to the worship of Israel, it was widely believed that other nations had gods just as (or almost as) real and useful to them.

Nevertheless, the differences that marked off Israel's religion from that of its neighbors are far more striking than the resemblances. In these differences lay the seeds of sublime and revolutionary advances. First, Yhwh had no female consort. The cruder physical attributes ascribed by many peoples to their deities did not apply here; the gross sexual myths so common in ancient religion were never associated with the God of Israel.

But we can go further. The religion of Israel had no myths at all. Other peoples told not only of the loves and marriages of the gods, but of their battles with each other and with monsters and titans, of their banquets and festivities, of their rivalries and intrigues. All this was alien to the spirit of the Israelite religion. Yhwh was austere, apart, and subject to no mortal weaknesses.

Third, the Israelite cult was, generally speaking, imageless. In the earlier period, it is true, household gods and other objects of veneration were not entirely unknown; but the dominant trend, which grew stronger all the time, was to prohibit pictures or statues of the Deity. This helped enormously in educating the people up to a more lofty concept of God.

Again, most Semitic deities were thought to have a sort of family relationship to their worshippers. The god was therefore obligated to look out for his people, no matter how much they displeased him, as a father must still care for a disobedient child. But Yhwh became the God of Israel at a particular time and through a formal covenant. He and Israel had, so to speak, entered into a partnership on the basis of specific terms. Violation of this law would not only arouse God's wrath: it would dissolve the partnership. Thus the relation between God and Israel took on a fundamentally ethical character; Israel had Yhwh as its Protector only so long as it observed His Law.

Finally, the religion of Israel, even after the tribes had taken root firmly in Palestine, always retained something of its desert, pastoral tone. As civilization advanced, as increasing prosperity brought increasing social problems, as the multiplication of luxuries led to a weakening of moral fiber, the ancestral faith struck a wholesome note by recalling the stern simplicity of desert days.

Out of these unpretentious but significant beginnings the great structure of Judaism was destined to rise.

2.

Growth of a National Religion

THE LOOSELY FEDERATED TRIBES OF ISRAEL HAD A LONG HARD TIME
establishing themselves as masters of the land of promise: they might
never have succeeded had not the Canaanites been divided among
themselves. While the Israelite invaders were conquering and settling
the country, they must have been considerably influenced by the
culture of the older inhabitants. The Hebrew language of the Bible
closely resembles that of the Phoenicians, the survivors of the Canaanites.

Culture, of course, included religion. The observances of the agricultural year as practiced in Israel were, to a considerable extent, borrowed from the old settlers. The local shrines, where each village
performed its sacrifices, were no doubt the holy places where the
Canaanites had worshipped.

But at times the influence went much deeper: many Israelites were
tempted to adopt the entire Canaanite religion. This was a pagan
nature cult. Prominent among its deities were Baal, who represented
the masculine principle and the sky; Astarte, the mother goddess,
symbol of the fertile earth, and their son Tammuz (also called
Adonis *), the personification of the annual crop. This fertility religion, with its dramatic myths and its sexual orgies, was doubly
appealing to the newcomers because its adherents believed it to be
indispensable for success in farming. Attempts were made to intro-

---

* i.e., The Lord, *Adon* (Hebrew *Adonoi*, My Lord).

duce Baal rites into the Israelite religion, and sometimes Yhwh and Baal were identified. But the loyal adherents of Yhwh fought sturdily against these trends, and ultimately overcame them.

In the political insecurity of those early days, several tribes were absorbed by larger and more powerful groups, losing their separate identity. The tribe of Levi, to which Moses had belonged, acquired a special status. It seems never to have possessed a territory of its own; yet its members, scattered through the country, remained a distinct group. They served as priests at the various sanctuaries, and survived as a priestly caste, influential despite their dispersion.

Three forces helped to bring the Israelite tribes into a national union: foreign enemies, the genius of David, and the influence of the prophets.

The Philistines, invaders from the Mediterranean islands, established themselves on the seacoast and, forming a powerful confederacy, subjugated the entire land. The Hebrews came to realize that they must combine or perish. It was David, the brilliant soldier and statesman, who freed the country from Philistine rule and established a national government.*

From that time (roughly 1000 B.C.E.) the tribes began to think in national terms, both about public affairs and about their religion. Jerusalem, a well-nigh impregnable fortress in ancient days, was still in the hands of a Canaanite tribe: David captured it and made it his capital. The mountain of Zion had not yet been associated with the religious practice of any Israelite tribe; thus it could become the site of a national shrine without stirring tribal jealousies.

Here David set up a sacred tent, in which he gathered many holy objects hitherto venerated at the tribal sanctuaries. He also planned a permanent temple, which was built during the reign of his son Solomon. Thus began the process by which Jerusalem at length became the Holy City of most of the civilized world.

But Solomon's Temple was not at first the beloved and revered sanctuary of later years. The more pious clung to the original spirit of the desert religion; this imposing structure with its elaborate ritual seemed to them foreign and even idolatrous. And to some extent, they were right. The Temple was built by Phoenician architects, who followed the models with which they were familiar. No doubt the ritual included some imported elements. Solomon's foreign wives—

---

* The first Israelite king, Saul, did not succeed in establishing a firm union.

whom he had married in order to extend the diplomatic and trade relations of his kingdom—seem to have had chapels for their ancestral gods within the Temple area. Only by slow degrees did the new and expensive edifice capture the hearts of Israel.

The union effected by David was imperfect, for a strong spirit of tribal self-consciousness and jealousy undermined it. The more advanced and prosperous groups in the central and northern parts of the country were constantly irritated because the king belonged to the relatively backward pastoral tribe of Judah. Even during David's lifetime there were several serious revolts, and after Solomon's death the northern tribes seceded and formed a separate state.

This Kingdom of Israel was far larger in area and population, greater in wealth, and more advanced in civilization than the Kingdom of Judah which remained under the rule of David's family. But after about two centuries, the Northern Kingdom was conquered and swallowed up by the great Assyrian Empire. Only a small part of our Biblical literature comes from the Kingdom of Israel, so we do not know the full details of its religious development.

The trends in both countries seem to have been parallel. Israel was perhaps more susceptible to foreign influences. In the ninth century, Jezebel, a queen of Phoenician birth, led a militant attempt to introduce the worship of her ancestral god, the Tyrian Baal; but popular opposition, roused by the famous prophet Elijah, finally blocked the undertaking.

A significant distinction between the two kingdoms grew out of the special Judean attitude toward the dynasty of David. This great popular hero was adored in his lifetime and reverenced after his death by all the members of his tribe. Soon the belief arose that the Davidic family had been divinely selected for rulership. God had promised to maintain their throne forever. The immediate result of this belief was the comparative peacefulness of Judah's internal affairs. Whereas the Northern Kingdom had a bloody history of civil wars, usurpations, and palace revolutions, the family of David reigned over Judah from the beginning to the end of its national life. When, as happened several times, a hated king was assassinated, some other member of the family was always chosen as his successor. This growing belief in the divine appointment of the Davidic kings was to have a profound effect on Jewish religion later on.

* * *

The Biblical authors speak about two types of inspired religious leaders in early Israel. One, called a "seer," was a soothsayer or diviner, who did such humble tasks as finding lost property and giving advice for the future. The other type was called *novi*. The word means spokesman, or "mouthpiece"; it may come originally from a root meaning "to pour forth." The *n'viim* were ecstatic individuals who roamed the country in bands. By music and other exercises they wrought themselves and those about them into a state of religious-patriotic frenzy. They may thus be compared to the dervishes of Islam or to the American revivalists. Sometimes in their ecstasy they would break into spontaneous utterance; and then they were thought to be speaking words "put into their mouth" by God.

Gradually the two types of visionary seem to have fused into one, bearing the name novi, which our English Bibles regularly translate as *prophet*. These prophets used their gifts less and less for individual clients, and more and more for the guidance of the whole people. The first move toward national independence and unity was made by the prophet Samuel, who commissioned Saul to lead a revolt against the Philistines. When this general of his choice disappointed him, Samuel selected and inspired David to make the attempt. The latter was subject all his life to the influence of prophets; one of them, Nathan, was among his closest advisers.

Throughout the history of the divided kingdom we meet constant reference to the prophets. Sometimes they spoke as individuals on matters both religious and political. Sometimes they assembled in bands to practice their ecstatic rites; some of them had disciples, "the sons of the prophets." During periods of national disaster, they were fiery champions of resistance to foreign domination. They were equally fierce in their resistance to foreign idolatries, and called the people back to the old desert loyalties. Several times during the centuries after Solomon, the prophets led successful movements of religious reform, designed to purify the religion from alien contaminations, and to simplify it in harmony with its austere pastoral spirit.

Most remarkable was the disposition of the prophets to befriend the victims of social injustice and to maintain high standards of public morality. King David became enamored of Bathsheba, the wife of one of his soldiers. When he had matters arranged so that the husband Uriah died in battle, his courtiers may have shrugged their shoulders cynically. But the prophet Nathan rebuked David to his face for the sin, and wrung from the king himself a humble admission of guilt. In few oriental courts of the time would such an intrigue have been so vigorously condemned; in still fewer would the despot have accepted the rebuke instead of killing the rebuker.

Equally dramatic was the case of Elijah and King Ahab of Israel. The latter had caused the judicial murder of one Naboth, in order to secure a piece of landed property which Naboth was unwilling to sell. In the name of God Elijah publicly denounced Ahab's crime. Such episodes plainly foreshadow the mission of the great literary prophets. The early n'viim sustained the national Israelite spirit, as expressed in the struggle for political independence and in adherence to the ancestral cult. Their work was admirable, but it is chiefly important as the prelude to the work of the later prophets. This last is in sober truth a miracle, which we must now approach with awe.

3.

The Great Revolution

WHERE SHALL WE FIND WORDS TO EXPRESS THE MIRACLE OF THE prophetic movement that swept through Israel? Suddenly mankind attained its spiritual majority. This happened in a small obscure people, much less advanced in material culture than the great nations around it. The native Hebrew religion, even in its earliest forms, contained unique possibilities of growth, which we have already noted. But it flowered with startling suddenness. Amos, the first great literary prophet, marks an abrupt and tremendous advance over all his predecessors of whom we have knowledge.

This man was a shepherd from a little village in the Judean hills. It seems unlikely that he had any formal education; his home was off the track of the great caravan routes, over which ideas flowed as well as goods. Nor was he trained in the usual prophetic traditions. He repudiated indignantly the suggestion that he was a prophet by occupation. Yet this inspired rustic gave to his generation and to posterity a religious and ethical doctrine of sublimity and power far in advance of anything that had ever been produced before; and he couched his message in fiery, poetic, yet measured eloquence that still leaves the reader spellbound. That this extraordinary genius should have been followed (during a period of over two centuries) by a whole company of seers, as great as himself, some perhaps even greater, is one of the incredible facts of human history.

Before Amos, men had thought of God (or the gods) as powerful beings who must be placated and pleased. Amos did not deny God's power, but found the supreme reality in God's righteousness. God is not only bigger and stronger than man, He is the Source of moral values. As an ethical Being, God ceases at once to be bounded by national limits. He will destroy the nations round about Israel, not because they are the enemies of His people, but because they have broken the moral law—by violating treaties, cruelty in war, and so on. By the same token He will not tolerate moral evils in Israel, the nation which had learned His power and righteousness through their redemption from Egypt. On the contrary, they will be held the more strictly to account just because of God's prior mercies. Israel has no more claim to favoritism than the Ethiopians; and if they do not return from their present sinfulness, God will destroy them.

Amos (about 760 B.C.E.) lived in a period of prosperity such as the nation had not known since its division. The Arameans who had harried the Northern Kingdom for over a century were crushed by Assyria; for the time this great power came no further west, so that Israel was enabled to enlarge her boundaries and expand her commerce. With the new prosperity, new social problems arose. Great landed estates worked by slaves absorbed the holdings of the small farmers and sent a propertyless horde into the rapidly growing cities. The social injustices resulting from these dislocations were attacked by Amos and his successors with a bitter power that has never been surpassed. Extremes of poverty and wealth, exploitation and speculation, profiteering in foodstuffs, judicial corruption and palace intrigue—the prophet tells the harsh truth about them all. He has no patience with the pampered daughters of the rich, "kine of Bashan * . . . that oppress the poor . . . that say to their lords: Bring, that we may feast." The cry for justice to suffering humanity finds classic expression in the words of the prophets: "What mean ye that ye crush My people and grind the faces of the poor?"

But defects in the social structure were not the only concern of the prophets. They were equally troubled by the breakdown of personal morality, which they blamed on the growing ease of city life. Some of them also attacked pagan religious practices which were still common in the land, whether survivals of the old Canaanite observances, or more recent and fashionable importations from other countries.

But they were equally dissatisfied with the legitimate Yhwh-cult. To them, God was not a national ruler to be placated, but the right-

---

* i.e., well-fattened cows. The cattle of Bashan were famous.

eous and loving Father of all men. In the service of such a God, ritual and sacrifice are unnecessary. The prophets were not content, however, to dismiss ceremonial religion as superfluous and irrelevant: they attacked it vehemently as harmful and dangerous. For as long as the people were convinced that they could win the divine favor by sacrifices and ritual observances, they would not realize the need for the radical inner change that the prophets demanded.

God's favor depends on the practice of personal and national righteousness—this is the corollary of the prophetic doctrine that God is an ethical Being.

So we read constantly:

> "Seek good and not evil, that ye may live,
> And so the Lord of Hosts will really be with you."

> "Cease to do evil, learn to do well,
> Seek justice, relieve the oppressed,
> Judge the fatherless, plead for the widow."

> "It hath been told thee O man, what is good,
> And what the Lord doth require of thee:
> Only to do justice, and to love mercy,
> And to walk humbly with thy God."

Each of these ringing utterances—and there are many more like them —follows an attack upon the sacrificial cult.

Amos' doctrine of a universal God of Justice, who is served by obedience to the moral law, was greatly deepened and enriched by his successor Hosea. He lived about a generation later in the Northern Kingdom, when the brief prosperity was giving way to outward and inward decline. Hosea strikes the ethical note as austerely as Amos; but he also tells of a God whose redeeming love tempers His justice. Comparing the relation between God and Israel to that of husband and wife, Hosea declares that the faithless wife must be punished for her infidelities; but this punishment does not imply the end of the husband's love. Rather does it evidence the deeper love that chastens and purifies. The downfall of the nation, which Amos had predicted as the inevitable result of Israel's sinfulness, is also foreseen by Hosea; but he looks forward to a final redemption of a people taught by suffering that only faithfulness to God can bring security and peace. A note of tenderness runs through the poetic, though at times obscure, sentences of Hosea. In the speeches of Amos, God thunders; in the verse of Hosea he pleads:

> "I desire love and not sacrifice,
> And knowledge of God rather than burnt offerings."

Here we stand upon one of the great heights of human experience—the realization that God is Love. Never before had the Divine spoken to man in the accents with which Hosea announces the future redemption of Israel:

> "I will betroth thee unto Me forever;
> Yea I will betroth thee unto Me in righteousness and in justice,
> And in lovingkindness, and in compassion.
> And I will betroth thee unto Me in faithfulness;
> And thou shalt know the Lord."

4.

The Great Revolution

(*continued*)

HOSEA'S WRITINGS REFLECT THE BREAKDOWN OF MORALE IN THE Northern Kingdom during the second half of the eighth century. Palace revolutions and assassinations caused frequent changes of dynasty. The Assyrian power swept westward, and Israel became a vassal state. But Egypt was constantly tampering with the small nations of western Asia, using them as catspaws in her struggle with the Assyrian enemy. Israel was divided into two camps, one counseling submission to the conqueror, one relying on promises of Egyptian aid in case of revolt. Tragedy had to follow. Ultimately the country was ravaged by Assyrian armies and the capital, Samaria, was razed. The leaders of the people were deported to distant parts of the empire, and other colonists, torn from homes equally remote, were settled in the partly depopulated areas.

Henceforth the "Ten Lost Tribes" become the theme of popular legend, and in more recent times of theorizing no less fantastic. Would-be scientists have discovered the Lost Tribes in the British, the Japanese, and the American Indians. Actually the fate of the Northern Kingdom is in no way mysterious. Not all the inhabitants of Israel were deported. The exiles were absorbed in a few generations by the peoples among whom they lived and disappeared from history as a separate group. Those who remained either attached themselves to Judah, or amalgamated with the foreign settlers to produce the "Samaritans."

Judah survived the debacle of the Northern Kingdom in part for geographic, in part for internal, reasons. This rugged hill country was difficult of access and poor in resources. Armies and caravans passed the country by, following the seacoast which was still in Philistine hands. Moreover, the government of Judah remained comparatively stable through its fidelity to the family of David, and so could deal more effectively with the foreign powers.

All these events were keenly observed and stirringly discussed by another in the line of great prophets, Isaiah of Jerusalem. He, too, believed himself commissioned to both of the Israelite kingdoms, whose faults he castigated with impartial severity. He restated and developed more fully the ideas of Amos and Hosea, with a sublimity all his own; his poetry is perhaps the high water mark of Hebrew literature. Isaiah is haunted by the thought of God's holiness—that is to say, His loftiness and perfection. But this flawless sublimity is not remote from the world: God's presence in history is Isaiah's constant theme.

It was indeed a time of crucial events. Egypt and Assyria, the two great rivals for supremacy, were coming to grips in a death struggle. Isaiah foresaw the Assyrian triumph; Israel and Judah would be crushed by the conqueror, in punishment for sins against God and man. The Assyrian is "the rod of Mine anger," the unwitting instrument of God's wrath, doing His will by destroying the nations that have violated the moral law. But the conqueror is likewise blind to the divine intent, arrogant, greedy and ruthless.

"Should the axe boast itself against him that heweth therewith?
 Should the saw magnify itself against him that moveth it?"

In the fullness of time, the proud conqueror shall also be broken. The destruction of Israel and Judah will not be the end; "a remnant shall return, overflowing with righteousness." The survivors of the catastrophe, some of them at least, will emerge purified and enlightened by their experience. The remnant—the minority, we would say—will be reconciled to the Universal God, and through this remnant Israel will have a new birth.

Like his predecessors, Isaiah pleads for social justice, for the protection of the weak, and for the maintenance of decent moral standards. But here we meet for the first time one of the great prophets who touched on questions of national policy. For Judah was drawn more and more into the orbit of the great powers. Even before the downfall of the Northern Kingdom, King Ahaz of Judah had voluntarily become a vassal of Assyria—despite Isaiah's violent protest. Then there began, as in Israel, a conflict between Assyrian and Egyptian interests. When the tribute payments became more onerous, there was a strong disposition to revolt against the Assyrians, which Egyptian agents were constantly stirring up.

Isaiah argued against involvement in the whole quarrel. Shrewdly he exposed the duplicity of Egypt, who let her little allies do her dirty work, but failed to support them when the overwhelming forces of Assyria took the field. But to Isaiah, practical considerations were secondary. He opposed the Egyptian alliance, as he had opposed the Assyrian alliance, from a basic conviction that Israel must rely not on military assistance but on the moral power of God. "In sitting still and rest shall ye be saved, in quietness and confidence shall be your strength." And again, "If ye have not faith, verily ye shall not endure." By acting, as individuals and as a nation, in accordance with God's ethical law, Israel would be able to rely on Him to fight their battles, and would not need alliances with the bloody heathen.

But this idealistic doctrine was disregarded; and Judah too rebelled against Assyria. In 702 B.C.E. Sennacherib invaded and pillaged the land, then laid siege to Jerusalem. The end seemed in sight. Suddenly the siege was abandoned and the invaders returned eastward. Just what happened remains obscure to this day. But the effects of this unexpected and miraculous deliverance upon the mind of the people of Judah were enormous. A sense of national greatness, a conviction of a high destiny was born. Above all, the prestige of the Temple, Yhwh's dwelling place, was tremendously enhanced; obviously it was His intervention which had saved the city! That Jerusalem was unconquerable became an article of faith. Isaiah's grim warnings were drowned out in the tumult of rejoicing.

The Book of Isaiah contains a number of prophecies that set forth the expectation of a world ruled by God's law and living in harmony and peace. Some of these passages must be later than the times of Isaiah; possibly all of them are. But it seems not unlikely that it was Isaiah himself, who—seeing the forces of history deploy before his eyes—attained the vision of a time when these conflicts would culminate in the establishment of a warless world.

"The wolf shall dwell with the lamb
And the leopard shall lie down with the kid,

And the calf and the young lion and the fatling together;
And a little child shall lead them."

For peace is the logical consequence of the prophetic doctrine: God
in history. At any rate it was the prophetic spirit of Israel, whether
articulated by Isaiah or by one of his unnamed successors, that gave
the world the hope and vision of a time when war shall cease and

"The earth shall be full of the knowledge of the Lord
As the waters cover the sea."

In the following century, during which the Southern Kingdom moved
to its ultimate destruction, the prophetic movement continued. We
need not name all the figures who appeared to preach the message of
the Universal God of Righteousness and to warn the people of impending doom. Each presented in his own style the basic ideas of the
three great pioneers. But we must give a brief word to Jeremiah, the
dominant figure in the last days of Judah. What makes his book so
important and so fascinating is its deeply personal character. Here we
get an insight into the prophet's inner life. Jeremiah was a sensitive
spirit, a dreamy lyric poet by nature. In him Hosea speaks again. His
convictions drove him to a life of action. He had to announce the
impending downfall of the nation; but he could not reconcile himself
to it, he grieved over the coming tragedy. A gentle soul, he had to
make enemies by speaking the unpalatable truth; but he could not
steel himself against their hatred. And so, scattered among his public
addresses, are personal confessions, fragments—so to speak—of a spiritual diary, unexcelled in their pathetic beauty. Out of the loneliness
of his sorrowful life grew something new and wonderful: *religion as
the personal experience of communion with the Divine.* "Thou, O
Lord, knowest me, Thou seest and triest my heart toward Thee,"
cries the prophet, and he hears the reply, "I am with thee to save thee
and to deliver thee, saith the Lord." The roots of all religion are in
the experience of a social group—clan, tribe, nation. In Jeremiah we
see for the first time its loveliest flower—the discovery of God within
the soul of the individual.

Jeremiah also gives us a vivid account of the prophetic impulse.
The urge to prophesy was an irresistible compulsion. When, for his
own safety, he sought to suppress his message:

"Then there is in my heart as it were a burning fire,
Shut up in my bones,
And I weary myself to hold it in, but cannot."

But this compulsion was quite different from that of the more primitive seers, who fell into ecstatic trances, and uttered words of which they were unconscious. The great prophet was possessed of a powerful truth which he was constrained to utter; but the process was perfectly conscious and normal. The prophetic visions are thoroughly rational in content, and they are masterpieces of lucid and eloquent expression. We must regard the great prophets as men of uncompromising moral character, vivid imagination, and strong intellect, who lived in an age not given to psychological analysis. They did not doubt that the powerful ethical drive within them was the word of God. Spiritual experiences were clothed in the poetic imagery of vision. Supremely gifted and utterly free of self-consciousness, they boldly introduced their messages by "Thus saith the Lord." They express magnificently the best in a people that had ceased to be primitive and had not yet become sophisticated.

We can hardly overestimate their importance. Not alone Jewish history, all human history has been fundamentally changed by their influence. After three thousand years they still have a vital message for all humanity. And yet in their day, by their own testimony, the prophets were failures. Some of them were disregarded, some were laughed at as lunatics, and some provoked popular resentment or official ire to the point of persecution and martyrdom. They were so far ahead of their listeners that they found only rare individuals who understood, appreciated, and supported them. All the more were they concerned that their teaching should be preserved, as witness and warning for the future. "Bind up the testimony, seal the instruction among my disciples," says Isaiah; and we know especially of Jeremiah that he carefully dictated his prophecies to his follower Baruch. In this way the message of the great prophets (hence called the "literary" prophets) has been preserved to us.

One reason the prophets failed to secure a hearing from their contemporaries was that they offered no substitute for the ceremonialism they attacked. Rightly they found the essence of religion in an ethical way of life; but they did nothing to embody this approach in institutions and practices, by which religion would be made tangible and comforting to average people. They did not realize that general principles are not enough for every-day existence, that every ideal—social, political, religious—must find expression in forms, institutions, and ceremonies. As a modern Jewish thinker has remarked, "You cannot live on oxygen alone."

But there were men in those days, less creative and original, who combined an appreciation of the prophetic message with a practical insight into popular needs. How they attempted to bring the vision of the great seers into the life of the plain people will be related in the next chapter.

5.

The Beginnings of Torah

THROUGHOUT THE HISTORY OF JUDAISM, TORAH IS ONE OF THE KEY words. It will be part of our task to trace the varied meanings of this term. It has no exact English equivalent; the customary rendering, "law," is not wrong, but it is not adequate. Torah means: the direction given by God to man for the guidance of his life.

Thus in the earliest period the oracles obtained by the priest through use of the sacred lot, and by the n'viim through their ecstatic practices, were known as Torah. The great prophets also referred to their message as the Torah of Yhwh. Sometimes the revelation concerned a national emergency; in other cases, it provided a precedent for legal or ritual procedure. Decisions of the latter type were recorded, orally or in writing; and thus a body of Torah was constantly available to those who sought the priests, the guardians of the Law.

There was general agreement that the revelation of Torah began with Moses, and we cannot doubt that this is correct. But it is hard to determine how much of the law in our present Scripture goes back to the days of Moses. Most likely, he only initiated a process which later underwent great expansion. As time and tradition glorified the personality of the first prophet and lawgiver, it became customary to credit Moses with Torah that had arisen in a more advanced age. Lacking the historical sense which characterizes modern thinking, people assumed that the laws and teachings they felt to be right and true must have been given to Moses, the first and greatest of the prophets.

A very ancient tradition states that the covenant between God and Israel was based on a code of ten brief laws. Scholars have discovered in the Pentateuch several decalogs of this sort. Some of them are chiefly ceremonial in content, whereas the Ten Commandments with which we are familiar are ethical. For this reason, some scholars believe that they were composed in the days of the great prophets; but others insist that our Ten Commandments—in their short original form—are from the period of Moses.

Our records report several religious reformations under the leadership of the "earlier prophets." The chief purpose of these reformations was to cleanse the national cult of foreign pagan customs and to restore its original desert simplicity. It is likely that several short codes, which scholars find as separate units within the Pentateuch were the charters on which these reforms were based.

The writings of the great literary prophets convey a feeling of tragic loneliness. These sublime radicals were so far in advance of their time that they were bound to encounter general misunderstanding. But they must have found a few disciples and followers, though there are only scattered references to such. The very fact that the teachings of the prophets were preserved and transmitted to us is sufficient proof that some persons cared about them. Having learned to appreciate the prophetic message, these individuals sought to present it more effectively to the great mass of the people.

The largest effort of this sort was made in the seventh century B.C.E., during a time of national stress. The old enemy, Assyria, had vanished. After attaining the pinnacle of glory by conquering Egypt, the great empire had crashed into destruction. But a new menace soon appeared. Barbarous hosts of Scythians, children of the Asiatic steppes, swept down from the north, eager for loot and rapine.

As Judah trembled at the threat of invasion by these wild hordes, a young and conscientious king, Josiah by name, sat upon the throne. The Temple had been polluted by the paganism of his predecessors; he ordered it cleaned and restored. During the reconstruction, a copy of the "Law of Moses" came to light; and the king and court were thrown into consternation when it was read to them.

For this document ordained most strictly that no animal sacrifice should be offered outside the Temple in Jerusalem.* Up to this time,

---

* More exactly, the code restricts sacrifice to "the place that the Lord shall choose to cause His name to dwell there." Jerusalem is not mentioned by name.

it must be understood, there was a shrine in every town and village, served by a Levitical priest. Whenever an animal was to be slaughtered, it was brought to the altar and presented as an offering, so that eating its meat had the character of a communion sacrifice. These shrines were old Canaanite "high places," which had been taken over when Israel entered the land; no doubt they still retained something of their original paganism in spirit and ritual. Now at one stroke they were declared heathenish and illegitimate; sacrifice was permitted henceforth only at the single national sanctuary.

Such a revolutionary law necessitated many adjustments. The newly discovered code gave permission to slaughter animals for food without sacrificial ceremony—since people could not travel to Jerusalem every time they wanted fresh meat. The Levites who had served at the local shrines were promised employment at the Temple, or else guaranteed support by the population. Since the festivals were no longer to be observed at the village shrines, but by pilgrimage to Jerusalem, the cult was modified to make mass celebration practicable.

The code was accepted by Josiah and promulgated as the Torah of Moses in the year 621 B.C.E. It is to be found (with extensive expansions and supplements) in the Book of Deuteronomy. And on the basis of this Deuteronomic law, a far-reaching reformation was instituted.

But the code was far more than a proposal for the abolition of the local shrines and the centralization of sacrificial worship. It was a magnificent attempt to translate the spirit of the prophets into law and practice. The law of the single sanctuary was a visible affirmation of the principle, "Hear O Israel, the Lord our God, the Lord is One." These words of Deuteronomy were destined to become the Jewish profession of faith known from its first word as the Sh'ma. They are followed by the solemn injunction, "Thou shalt love the Lord thy God with all thy heart and with all thy soul and with all thy might."

An austere and sublime tone pervades the entire code. All pagan rites, all heathen superstitions, are clearly forbidden. The noblest standards of justice are everywhere demanded. The rights of the poor, the orphan and widow, and the foreigner are safeguarded with warmest humanity. The slave is protected against harsh treatment; it is forbidden to surrender a runaway slave to his master. There are extensive provisions to prevent cruelty to animals. Here the prophetic ideals are plainly put to work.

Deuteronomy is marked not only by its distinctive laws and its high ethical seriousness, but by a characteristic eloquent literary style. These traits are found also in the historical books of Joshua, Judges, Samuel and Kings. The ancient traditions and records found in these books have been edited with an interpretive framework, expressing the Deuteronomic viewpoint. Apparently this literary activity continued for several generations.

The reformation of Josiah must have helped greatly in impressing the prophetic teaching on the minds and lives of the plain people. Old pagan elements were eradicated from the official practice of the Israelite religion. (This was not so readily accomplished with private observance; Arab peasants to this day follow customs that were ancient when the Israelites invaded Canaan.) With the cult centered in Jerusalem, it could be more scrupulously supervised by the prophetic party and their adherents in the priesthood. Moreover, when the celebration of the festivals was removed from immediate contact with the soil and transferred to the more urban and elaborate setting of the capital, the observances lost more and more their original character of nature worship and acquired a distinctively Jewish tone.

Finally, the new system tended to enhance the sanctity of Jerusalem and the Temple to a higher degree. The defeat of Sennacherib had convinced the people that their citadel was inviolable; the Deuteronomic code gave official sanction to this opinion. The new Torah, it is true, warned the people that they would enjoy God's favor only so long as they obeyed the law in letter and in spirit; but these warnings were of small influence in comparison with the concrete institutional changes.

Where, however, did the Deuteronomic code come from? The movement of literary prophecy was a century and a half old when Josiah came to the throne. Sometime during that period, it appears, a person or group under the influence of the great prophets composed a code that reflected the prophetic aims. For a long time, however, it could gain no hearing. The rulers of Judah were under the spell of foreign paganism; Manasseh, grandfather of Josiah, cruelly persecuted the champions of the old religion. But some pious priest kept a copy of the new law in the Temple; and during the extensive renovation ordered by Josiah, the scroll came to light.

But how could the king and his adherents accept this document as the Torah of Moses? How could they suppose that the revolutionary proposal to abolish the local shrines and centralize all sacrifice in the Temple had come down from a remote past? We can only repeat that the historical sense is a peculiarly modern quality. Not only the ancient Hebrews, but most other peoples and ages have lacked it. Shakespeare's contemporaries found nothing incongruous in the spectacle of ancient Romans, barbarous Britons, mythical Greeks, and medieval Danes dressing, thinking, and behaving as Elizabethan Englishmen. Thus, if the idea of the central sanctuary was a generation or two old, its supporters took for granted that this excellent program *must have been* intended by Moses. And since ancient notions of literary ethics were entirely different from our own, it seemed quite natural to ascribe not only the idea, but its written statement, to the great lawgiver.

The results of the reformation were disappointing to the great prophets, especially to Jeremiah. For the immediately visible effects were clearly to be seen in modifications of the cult—in which the prophet had no interest. But there was little change in the inner life of the people, or in the standards of national ethics—the things which were his all-absorbing concern. Men were slow to comprehend the moral intent of the Torah. The threatened Scythian invasion did not materialize; the tension and the enthusiasm relaxed. A few years later, the new Torah was in a sense discredited. For Josiah, who had been so devout in his observance of the Law, and who in accordance with its own promises should have received good fortune and happiness, died in battle against the Egyptians. Many of the people, disheartened, concluded that their God had not ordained the Deuteronomic reforms, and tried to restore the old cults. Many more reverted to foreign paganism, which began again to sweep the land.

At the same time alien political influences began to be felt once more. Assyria's place was taken by the Chaldean Empire, established by an energetic race who had occupied the territory and adopted the culture of Mesopotamia. The Chaldean King Nebuchadrezzar, a brilliant general and administrator, embarked once more on the old adventure of conquering Egypt. It was in stopping a counter-attack of Pharaoh Necho that Josiah died. But the subjection to Egypt was brief, for the Chaldean soon won a decisive victory over the Pharaoh. Though a son of Josiah sat on the throne, Judah had again to pay tribute to the Mesopotamian conqueror. The old tragic farce of pro-Egyptian and pro-Assyrian parties began again, and its end was the end of Judah.

But to return to the Torah. It did not consist only of legislation. Israel, like all peoples, had a wealth of traditional stories, quasi-historical, legendary, mythical, about its beginnings and its past. These stories, which are found in the Bible today, are extremely ancient. Many have unquestionably an historic kernel. A few are borrowed from foreign sources. But practically all of them, as they now stand, have been retold from the standpoint of prophetic religion. As one reads the stories of Genesis, one sees that great moral and religious lessons are unmistakably implied in the narrative. Thus the story of the sacrifice of Isaac is a protest against the custom of child sacrifice, which under Phoenician influence lingered for many years in the Northern Kingdom. The tales of Joseph illustrate the prophetic theme of God's providence in history. It should be understood that the re-telling of the Israelite traditions was a slow process that probably continued for a great many years.

Thus the influence of the prophets gradually seeped into the life of the people through the Torah—in its double aspect of law and narrative—even more than through the direct preachments of the great seers. But the effects of this influence were not to be seen at once. For the Southern Kingdom had entered a period of decline, and the end, both of Judah and of Judaism, seemed to be horribly imminent.

6.

Exile

IN WRITING THE BIOGRAPHY OF A MAN, ONE MUST GIVE SOME ATTEN-
tion to his ancestry, childhood, and adolescence. In them we may be
able to trace influences of great importance for his later life. Yet, it is
only when the man reaches maturity that his career really begins.

What we have been so far considering may be described as the
childhood and youth of the Jewish religion. Judaism, as we know it,
consists of well-defined principles and practices which are recorded
in authoritative sources, cherished by a loyal people, and expressed
through recognized institutions. But in the periods we have been
studying, these things were not yet fully developed. We have seen
that there was a popular Israelite religion and an advanced prophetic
doctrine. Both had grown out of the Torah of Moses, but they had
moved in different directions; for a long time there was a deep gap,
and even a certain antagonism, between them. There were various
Torah-documents, but they had not yet been fused into a single
Torah. Nor was their authority entirely unquestioned. The loyalty of
the masses even to the popular Yhwh-cult was not unshakable. Foreign deities were frequently worshipped in Israel, especially when
foreign military and political influence was strong. Many characteristic institutions of Judaism did not yet exist: there was no synagogue,
no Yom Kippur, no Jewish education. The religion of Israel had
grown much since desert days, but it had not yet grown up.

The power that brought Judaism to full maturity—the fire that
fused its component materials into a unified whole—was national

destruction and exile. It was in the ashes of the Jewish state that the Jewish religion ripened.

Judah fell, after a period of disastrous intrigue, before the might of Chaldea. The Chaldeans, indeed, had tried to forestall the complete ruin of the country. In 597 B.C.E., they had taken a group of Judean leaders into captivity at Babylon—including the young king, members of the nobility and even many artisans (to limit the manufacture of weapons). But this precaution was ineffective. Egypt continued to tamper with the Jewish leaders, and in the end there was rebellion. After ravaging the country, the Chaldean armies laid siege to Jerusalem; and this time the confident hope that God would save His dwelling place by a miracle was dashed. After a long and dreadful siege, the city fell in 586. The Temple was burned, and a great number of the survivors were deported. Only a miserable and impoverished peasantry was left in the half depopulated little country.

Thus the downfall of the Southern Kingdom followed the same pattern as that of the Northern Kingdom. Why was the outcome so different? Why did not the exiles from Judah assimilate in the Babylonian world as the exiles from Israel had assimilated in the Assyrian Empire?

It was not because they were more numerous; the reverse was the case. It was not because the Babylonians were unfriendly or exclusive; on the contrary, the exiles soon became adjusted economically and even socially, and established themselves comfortably in their new homes. It was simply because the Judean exiles regarded themselves in a special light, and took a distinctive view of their destiny and experience. It was because the outlook of the prophets had made a deep impression upon them. In sober fact, the Jews survived because of their religion.

Ordinarily conquest had been regarded as proof that the god of the conquered was weak. Under such circumstances it was the part of prudence to adopt the cult of the conqueror. But Israel's prophets had foretold that the nation would fall in consequence of its own sins, and had insisted that the destruction would be proof of God's justice, not of His debility. And now the exiles could not but think: there must be something in what the prophets said after all! Moreover, the prophets had preached not only doom, but hope. From the days of Hosea, they had promised that redemption would follow the destruction.

In the last days of Judah, Jeremiah had stressed this thought most dramatically. All his life he had predicted tragedy. Consistently he urged submission to the Chaldeans and firm adherence to the pledges of loyalty; and when these were broken, he insisted that there was no hope of saving Jerusalem. But as the people began to realize that he was right and that their case was desperate, he began to reach out toward a more remote future. He wrote to the earlier exiles already in Babylonia, counseling them to be patient and of good cheer. He bought from a kinsman a tract of land occupied by the invading armies, and took special precautions to preserve the bill of sale—a typically Jeremiah object-lesson. And in a time of despair he constantly preached that there was still a glorious future for Israel. This future glory included the restoration of the Jewish state; but its most significant feature would be the new covenant God would make with its chastened and purified people. Unlike the covenant of the Exodus, whose terms were written on tablets of stone, the new law said Jeremiah would be written upon the very hearts of the returning exiles.

Although there was much gloom among the deportees, such words made some impression on them, and perhaps gave them more confidence in the living prophets who were trying to rouse their spirit. Moreover, the exile enabled them to understand more fully and clearly the prophetic ideas which had begun to percolate into their consciousness. They had dimly sensed that Yhwh was a God whose power was not limited to the confines of Palestine. But now, actually worshipping Him on alien soil, they dramatically demonstrated His universal sway. They had heard from the prophets that righteousness and not ritual was the way to serve Him. Now that they were without Temple or altar, they could feel that through prayer and good conduct they were doing something at least to please their God.

No doubt many of the exiles intermarried and otherwise disappeared from the Jewish group. But those that remained loyal were permeated by a new and deeper conviction than had yet been seen among the masses of Israel. They were the servants, unworthy perhaps, of a universal Deity who had punished them; but their God had the power to restore them to their land, and had promised to do so. This conviction grew out of the teaching of the great prophets which had been preserved from the catastrophe, and also out of the living prophetic word that was still heard among them.

Chief among the teachers of the exiles was the prophet Ezekiel. To the modern Bible reader he is least attractive of the prophets: yet his influence was not only great, but tremendously constructive. He is not a great poet like his predecessors. His conceptions are in many ways less advanced than those of Isaiah and Jeremiah: he represents the fusion of the old national, ceremonial cult with the ethical and universal outlook of the literary prophets. Perhaps for this reason he was the more successful. For he presented to the people a doctrine that they needed and that they could understand.

Ezekiel was one of those who had been exiled to Babylonia in 597. Forced to adjust himself to new and harsh conditions, he was in some measure prepared to withstand the shock of the final downfall. God, he taught, had destroyed the nation because of their devotion to heathen rite, they had profaned the land that was specially His. By rights He should have abandoned them; but for the sake of His name, He would not do so. For though God is the God of the whole world, He is recognized only by Israel. And His name can attain recognition in the world only if the people that worships Him is preserved and ultimately restored to greatness. (Thus Ezekiel reconciles the old nationalism and the new universalism.) To a deeply depressed Israel, whom he describes symbolically as a heap of dry bones, the prophet brings the hope and assurance of rebirth. God will put a new spirit into the people; He "will remove the stony heart from them and give them a heart of flesh." Made worthy of His favor through this act of grace, they will be restored to land and to Temple. There they will follow the double rule of ethical rectitude and ceremonial precision; and Ezekiel gave detailed plans for rebuilding the sanctuary and conducting its rituals.

He provided in particular that the priestly offices should be restricted to the priests descended from Zadok, Solomon's chief priest, whose family had always been in charge of the Temple. The other Levites (who had been promised by Deuteronomy a place in the Temple organization) had not been faithful to the pure worship of God. Ezekiel assigned them less important, yet honorable tasks in the administration of the sanctuary.

Although Ezekiel was subject to ecstatic visions and trances, he was also a systematic logical thinker—more than any personality we have yet encountered. This trait is displayed in his treatment of the problem of reward and punishment, which he presents in a new and remarkable light.

Men had generally supposed in earlier days that the nation was responsible as a unit to the Deity, and that adversity or prosperity came upon them in accordance with their deserts. The sin even of a few might be visited upon the entire community. The prophets modified this doctrine by representing God as judging the nation by the law of righteousness, and not on the basis of ritual conformity. But they too thought in terms of national retribution, and the Book of Deuteronomy describes in vivid detail the material rewards and punishments which will befall the people according as they obey or disobey the Torah.

But once the ethical note was introduced, the question was bound to arise: what about individuals? Why should the righteous suffer for the sins of the wicked? And why is it that the fortunes of men are so much at variance with their deserts? This question appears already in the confessions of Jeremiah.

In Ezekiel's day it became acute in another form. The exiles argued that while Israel had deserved punishment, the actual suffering had been inflicted on innocent parties. "The fathers have eaten sour grapes and the teeth of the children are set on edge." To this Ezekiel returned the uncompromising and unqualified answer that every individual receives reward or punishment according to his own conduct. No one suffers for the sins of another; each individual must expiate his own wrong-doings. Before Jerusalem was sacked, Ezekiel declared, a heavenly agent marked the brow of every righteous person, and none of these was killed; while each of the wicked met his death.

This remarkable viewpoint, of course, has one great defect—it does not square with the facts of experience. But the uncompromising Ezekiel was willing to deny the testimony of observation rather than admit that God is unjust. His doctrine has had a lasting influence to this day, and we shall have more to say about it later. But in one respect it marks a great advance—the growing recognition of the religious importance of the individual.

From the Book of Ezekiel we learn that the exiles assembled from time to time in the house of the prophet for instruction and inspiration. Most likely these meetings took place on the Sabbaths and holy days, and perhaps the writings of the older prophets were read aloud. It is possible that in such little meetings the synagogue had its origin.

A change of fortune was soon to come for the exiles. The successors of Nebuchadrezzar lacked his great abilities; the Persian king Cyrus was shortly to conquer the Chaldean Empire and give the Jews the chance of reconstituting their corporate life. But the hottest sun will not give vital warmth to a corpse. It was the decrees of Cyrus that afforded the opportunity to reestablish organized Jewish life in Palestine. It was the prophetic spirit, enhanced by the influences of the exile, that supplied the motive power to utilize this opportunity.

7.

Hopes and Disappointments

ONLY THE MEANEST PEASANTS WERE (SUPPOSEDLY) LEFT IN PALES-
tine by the conquerors; but among them was at least one man of unparalleled gifts and sublime vision, who watched with keen discern-
ment the events in the East. As the Persian army under Cyrus
approached the city of Babylon and the end of the Chaldean Empire
was at hand, he produced the most wonderful, perhaps, of all the
prophetic works.

We do not know this man's name, and there is hardly a personal
reference in his words. His prophecy was appended to the Book of
Isaiah, and we have no better title for him than "The Second Isaiah."
Of all the prophetic writers, he has been the best loved, both by
Jews and Christians, for his message was one of comfort and hope.
As the conquerors of Judah were about to disappear from history, he
foretold in kindling words the restoration and redemption of his
people.

But it was not in military or political terms that he spoke. For the
Second Isaiah represents the full flowering of prophetic thought. He
constantly recurs to the theme of the absolute oneness of God. More
explicitly than any of his predecessors he insists that there is no other
divine power in the universe than He, and that idols are a fraud and
illusion. God, moreover, is not only the Ruler of *history*—as all the
prophets had insisted—but He is the Ruler, as He was the Creator,
of *nature*:

"It is He that sitteth above the circle of the earth,
And the inhabitants thereof are as grasshoppers;
That stretcheth out the heavens as a curtain,
And spreadeth them out as a tent to dwell in.
To whom then will ye liken Me, that I should be equal?
Saith the Holy One.
Lift up your eyes on high
And see: who hath created these?
He that bringeth out their host by number,
He calleth them all by name."

But if He is the absolutely universal Ruler, how can He be the National Deity of Israel? To this the Second Isaiah answers boldly: He is not the God of Israel alone, but the God of all mankind. To Cyrus, the Persian conqueror, the prophet applied the term "anointed of God" (*Messiah*), a title previously reserved for Israelite kings. But Israel has a special place in the universal plan of God. Israel is His witness and His servant. Through the agency of Israel, the knowledge of His ways is to be brought to other peoples. Israel must therefore live in accordance with this high destiny, must testify by preachment and action to the unity and righteousness of God, and must endure with fortitude the suffering which this mission must inevitably entail. Launching with audacious vision into the unknown future, the prophet represents the nations as at last awaking to the salvation which Israel has brought them. Astonished, they will confess that Israel, whom they had always hated and despised, has indeed been the agent through whom they were cured of their blindness and folly.

"Surely our diseases he did bear, and our pains he carried,
Whereas we did esteem him stricken,
Smitten of God, and afflicted.
But he was wounded because of our transgressions,
He was crushed because of our iniquities.
The chastisement (that insured) our welfare was upon him,
And with his stripes we were healed."

This doctrine of the Mission of Israel—which henceforth is a part of Jewish universalism—solved two problems. One was the question how a God known only to Israel could be a universal Deity; the other was the question which Ezekiel had tried to answer in a different way, the question why the righteous sometimes suffer. Ezekiel had solved the problem by denying its existence, asserting that each man is always rewarded or punished according to his deserts; the Second Isaiah suggests that suffering may be the condition of idealistic service, voluntarily endured for the achievement of a universal ideal.

And for a time it seemed as though the radiant dreams of the prophet were destined to speedy fulfilment. Babylon fell, and Cyrus allowed the various peoples deported by the Chaldeans to return to their native lands. Among them the exiles of Judah received this opportunity; and even the Temple vessels, which Nebuchadrezzar had confiscated when the city was sacked, were returned to them. A large proportion of the exiles, now comfortably settled in their new homes, were unwilling to return to the barren uplands of Judea. They remained in Mesopotamia, which has been the seat of a Jewish community ever since: by far the oldest continuous Jewish settlement in the world. But some thousands of enthusiasts came back to Jerusalem under the joint leadership of Zerubbabel, a prince of the house of David, and Joshua, a priest of the family of Zadok.*

These returned exiles, being of the aristocracy, quickly assumed leadership in the affairs of Judah. But circumstances were bad and the early enthusiasm quickly melted away. The country was poor; some of its choicest areas had been occupied by settlers from the adjacent countries. The returned exiles had to contend with unfriendly neighbors, with the general poverty of the land, and with unlucky weather conditions producing crop failures. Gloom settled over the little group, and there were even defections to heathenism. An altar was set up at once amid the ruins of the Temple; but it took years before the two prophets, Haggai and Zechariah, were able to stir the leaders and the people to build a modest edifice in place of Solomon's.

And then another blow fell. We do not know all the details. There seems to have been a revolt under the leadership of the Davidic prince Zerubbabel. Probably he was executed or deported—in any case he disappears from history. Henceforth Joshua the High Priest and his successors were the recognized leaders of the Jews of Palestine; their official powers were enhanced by the prestige of their sacred position. Some years later a worse disaster occurred. Following a second uprising against Persia, the country was ravaged, many of the people were slain, and the city of Jerusalem was reduced again to ruins. Never,

---

* The first Davidic leader mentioned is not Zerubbabel, but Sheshbazzar: there are various explanations of the discrepancy.

perhaps, was the Jewish people so close to utter disintegration and its religion so near to complete disappearance. But at this dark juncture two strong men came forward, and Judaism as we know it reached maturity.

8.

Judaism Is Complete

JUST AS WE REACH THE CRUCIAL POINT, WHERE JUDAISM AS WE KNOW it comes to full flower, our sources of information fail us almost completely. It is the most obscure period of Jewish history. For several stretches of time, the longest about one hundred years, we have no direct information; and our sources for the intervening periods are fragmentary, uncertain, at times contradictory. Not till the year 331 B.C.E., when Alexander the Great arrived in Palestine, does the veil of darkness begin to lift.

Yet we cannot pass over the period in silence: it is too important. Without involving ourselves in the theories and debates of the historians, we shall state what seems probably to have been the course of events.

The demoralized and discouraged community of Judah, we have said, was given new life by the advent of two strong men. One was Nehemiah, who had achieved a high position at the Persian court while remaining a loyal and devoted Jew. Distressed by the reports he had received of material and spiritual desolation in the Holy Land, he persuaded his royal master to give him a leave of absence and to make him governor of Judah. Under his leadership the walls of Jerusalem were rebuilt and many social and religious abuses were corrected. Above all, the political power and manly sincerity of Nehemiah greatly facilitated the spiritual leadership of the second strong man, Ezra the Scribe.

Ezra, a skilful expounder of the Law, had come up from Babylonia bringing with him the "Torah of Moses"—of which more presently. He was appalled by the conditions he found on his arrival. Religious observance was lax, the Sabbath was constantly profaned. Intermarriage was wide-spread, and the children of the mixed unions were often ignorant both of the Hebrew language and of the ancestral traditions. The sternly pious Ezra immediately took steps to change the situation. The deep earnestness of his personality and the power of his eloquence, together with the effective backing of Nehemiah, enabled him to carry through a sweeping program of reform.

Mixed marriages were halted; those who had already taken heathen wives were persuaded to divorce them. Strict Sabbath observance was enforced. And at a public assembly on the Feast of Tabernacles, Ezra read the Torah of Moses aloud. The reading moved the people to bitter tears, as they realized their neglect of God's will, and the leaders had to remind them that mourning was improper on a festival. After the holiday season was over, a solemn fast of repentance was held, and the people ratified a formal written covenant—to which the leaders affixed their signatures—that henceforth they would obey the Torah.

What was this Torah which Ezra brought up from Babylonia? We cannot give an absolutely certain reply; but probably Ezra's scroll included a considerable part of what is now called "The Priestly Code." The Book of Leviticus and extensive parts of other Pentateuchal books are drawn from this document. Most of the Biblical genealogies, the detailed account of the construction of the Tabernacle, the laws of sacrifice, priestly privileges, ceremonial defilement and purification are part of this code. Long stretches of it have little appeal to the modern reader.

And yet, despite their fondness for detail, the priestly authors had a broad and exalted concept of religion. Their code begins with the story of creation, of a world brought into being by the simple command of a universal and almighty God. The insistence on ritual precision and ceremonial purity goes hand in hand with the loftiest standards of human conduct. "Ye shall be holy, as I the Lord your God am holy" is the theme of the priestly legislation, and its climax is the Golden Rule: "Thou shalt love thy neighbor as thyself."

It is also in the Priestly Code that we find the law of the Jubilee Year, based on the assumption that the land belongs to God, and was distributed among the tribes and families of Israel according to His will. Landed property was therefore not to be sold in perpetuity;

every fifty years there was to be a "jubilee," at which time all the land was to revert to the families which originally owned it. Thus the law attempted, in the spirit of the prophets, to prevent the concentration of wealth in a few hands, to the impoverishment of the majority. But the law as it stands is not workable, and seems never to have been actually observed.

Even the ceremonial and sacrificial sections of the Priestly Code are of great importance for the history of Judaism. The laws and customs treated must have been ancient, some of them perhaps primitive and even pagan in their original intent. In the Priestly Code they have been modified so as to bring them into harmony with monotheism, and with prophetic ethical standards. The "sin offering" and "guilt offering," for example, are said to atone only for *unintentional* violations of the law. Where there is actual moral guilt, the offender must confess the wrong he has done and make restitution to the injured party before he can bring a sacrifice.

Some historians have regarded the promulgation of this code as a defeat for the prophetic spirit. The broad ethical universalism of the seers, they lament, was replaced by the narrow nationalistic ritualism of the priests. But in fact the priestly legislation represents rather the victory of the prophetic spirit. A religion without institutions and forms is impracticable. The prophetic ideals had to be clothed in visible procedures, both legal and ceremonial.

This was accomplished by the Deuteronomic and Priestly Codes. They preserved the lofty God-idea, the universal outlook of the prophets. They championed the highest standards of ethical integrity, justice, and humanitarian conduct, and embodied these standards in specific, enforceable laws governing family relations, treatment of slaves, loans and pledges, and the relief of the poor.

At the same time they recognized the need of symbol and ceremony. The Priestly Code indeed lays great emphasis on the sacrificial system. But its importance was restricted by limiting sacrifice to the Jerusalem Temple, and by rigid controls designed to eliminate the survivals of pagan practice.

We are not sure whether the Torah that Ezra read to the people included the entire Priestly Code or only part of it; for the priestly writings were not all composed at one time, or by one author. Nor can we set an exact date for the final editing of the Torah, in which the short pre-exilic codes, the ancient narratives of the forefathers and the Exodus, the Deuteronomic laws and orations, and the priestly documents were put together. These are the elements that constitute our Torah, the Five Books of Moses or Pentateuch. If the work was not completed in Ezra's time,* it was finished not long after. Whatever the extent of the scroll in Ezra's hand to which the people swore allegiance, they were loyal in the centuries that followed to the entire Torah that we still possess.

That is why we can date the maturity of Judaism from the days of Ezra. For henceforth there was a clear-cut and universally accepted written authority—the Torah. We do not hear any more of idol worship or paganism in Israel. All Jews worshipped the Creator of the world and Father of all men, whom their ancestors had called Yhwh. (In the succeeding centuries, the use of this name was more and more restricted, until it was spoken only on special occasions in the Temple service, and its pronunciation became a holy mystery. There was general agreement that the Name was too sacred for ordinary mortals to utter; but perhaps this development was also influenced by the feeling that a proper name is superfluous for a unique and universal Deity.) To worship any other being was to put oneself completely outside the Jewish fellowship.

In the second place, Judaism now had permanent and well-established institutions. The Temple was no longer under attack by prophetic idealists and pastoral conservatives. It was the rallying point of a whole people. The Jews who lived in Palestine visited the Temple on each of the three festivals—Passover, Weeks, and Tabernacles. And those unable to do this—for the Jewish people was now spreading more and more throughout the world—sent the tax of half a shekel each year for the maintenance of the Temple and tried to visit it as pilgrims at least once during their lifetimes.

Meantime another institution was developing which was destined to eclipse and to survive the Temple—namely, the Synagogue. We do not know when, where, and how it arose: perhaps it began in the assemblies held during the Exile. It certainly grew and spread after the restoration, and during the period of the Second Temple.

Let us understand: the Synagogue was something entirely, sensationally new. All earlier shrines, Jewish and non-Jewish, had been centered about an altar for sacrifice. They were regarded as in some special sense the dwelling place of deity; their basic ritual was usually performed by priests. The Synagogue (the word is the Greek equiv-

---

* A generally accepted date for Ezra's mission is 444 B.C.E.

alent of the Hebrew *k'neses,* assembly) was a gathering of the people to advance their communal and spiritual interests. Such an assembly might be held in any convenient place. It had no sacrificial procedures. Any person, regardless of birth, who was qualified to instruct the group or to lead them in prayer, might do so.

The Synagogue was the pioneer institution of spiritual worship. It was the embodiment of religious democracy, for it eliminated the need of priestly intermediaries. Its democratic character was enormously enhanced by the element of popular education, which from the start was a basic function of the Synagogue. A passage of the Torah was read and explained to the people when they gathered on Sabbaths and festivals.

But since farmers who lived at some distance from villages or towns could not travel on the Sabbath, portions of the Torah were also read on the market days—Monday and Thursday—when the country people could be present. This custom still persists in Orthodox synagogues.

It must have been a good many years before these gatherings were formally organized and special buildings were established to house them. But shortly after the time of Ezra (at the latest), the custom of regular meetings was firmly entrenched, and the beginnings of a ritual for non-sacrificial worship were formulated. These included the recitation of the Sh'ma and other Biblical passages, as well as some entirely new prayers.

The Jewish calendar also begins to resemble the one we know. The New Year, which had previously followed the fall harvest festival, was now placed two weeks earlier, at the New Moon of the seventh month; and a new holy day appears, which is not mentioned before the Exile. It is the Day of Atonement (*Yom Kippur*)—destined to become the most sacred day in the Jewish religious year. At the start it lacked its present sublime quality. The service was a complicated ritual of purification performed by the High Priest. These rites acquired a tremendous hold on the consciousness of the people, perhaps too great a hold. It was not long before the old prophetic spirit flared up again, and an unknown seer delivered the greatest Yom Kippur sermon ever preached:

"Is such the fast that I have chosen?
    The day for a man to afflict his soul?
    Is it to bow down his head as a bulrush,
    And to spread sackcloth and ashes under him?

Wilt thou call this a fast,
And an acceptable day to the Lord?
Is not this the fast that I have chosen?
To loose the fetters of wickedness,
To undo the bands of the yoke,
And to let the oppressed go free,
And that ye break every yoke?
Is it not to deal thy bread to the hungry,
And that thou bring the poor that are cast out to thy house,
When thou seest the naked, that thou cover him,
And that thou hide not thyself from thine own flesh?"

But this prophecy (still read in all synagogues on the Atonement Day) was almost the last flowering of the old visionary genius. A number of short prophetic works date from this period, but most of them are inferior both in content and expression. The movement was nearing its end. The work of the prophets had been done, and in a sense they were no longer needed. A process of education, less exciting, but far more thorough and effective, was under way. Daily and weekly, the people assembled to be instructed in the Torah, which presented the prophetic ideals in vivid concrete terms. The "Scribes"—teachers originally of priestly stock, later including many non-priests—may not have been creative personalities; but they were qualified to give the people the accumulated inspiration of the centuries. They produced a whole nation saturated with the prophetic outlook.

9.

Particularism and Universalism

THE GREATNESS OF EZRA IS NOT IMMEDIATELY APPARENT FROM THE
meager records we possess of his life. Yet it seems unquestionable that
Judaism was on the verge of disintegration when he appeared on the
scene; and by the time his work was finished, its future was assured.
Later Jewish tradition ranked him second to Moses; Ezra restored the
Torah which Moses had first taught. His stringency was justified by
the results—the preservation and steady development of the Jewish
religious community.

Ezra has been much criticized for insisting on the dismissal of foreign wives; and indeed his policy seems harsh. Apparently the situation was so critical and the fate of Judaism so uncertain that Ezra felt
he must preserve the integrity of the Jewish group at any cost. The
incident was a single and unique one, and did not serve as a pattern
for future actions. Jewish universalism was not slain by Ezra.

It may be that the Book of Ruth was written by an opponent of
Ezra's policies. This short and beautiful narrative has as its heroine
a Moabite maiden married to a Judean. Her husband dies, but she
remains faithful to her impoverished mother-in-law, returns with her
to Bethlehem, and eventually is rewarded by marrying Boaz, a distinguished member of her first husband's family. King David, we are
told, was a descendant of Boaz and Ruth. Thus by a simple tale it is
suggested that one of non-Jewish birth may enter fully and devotedly
into the life—including the religious life—of Israel.

And in these centuries (we cannot fix the date exactly) the institution of conversion became an established feature of Judaism. Of course, from time immemorial it had been customary for one who moved to a new home to worship the gods of the place, in addition to those he brought from his former neighborhood. But this was something altogether different. The Jews who left Palestine, unless they abandoned the God of their fathers altogether, worshipped Him alone. Those Gentiles who wished to marry into Jewish families were required to renounce all their former deities, and give their loyalty to the one God—this too, not only in the land where His temple stood, but in foreign countries as well. In addition, many individuals became converts, not because they wanted to marry Jews, but out of positive religious conviction, inspired by the unique spiritual faith and the high ethical standards set forth in the Torah.

> "Also the aliens (says a post-exilic prophet) that join
>   themselves to the Lord,
> To minister unto Him,
> To love the name of the Lord,
> To be His servants,
> Everyone that keepeth the Sabbath from profaning it
> And holdest fast by My covenant:
> Even them will I bring to My holy mountain,
> And make them joyful in My house of prayer;
> Their burnt offerings and their sacrifices
> Shall be acceptable upon Mine altar;
> For My house shall be called
> A house of prayer for all peoples."

Another great monument of the prophetic universalism, which may have been a kind of retort to Ezra, is the Book of Jonah, composed some time in the same period. The remarkable adventures of Jonah, says a modern preacher, "have amused the skeptic, alarmed the faithful, and confounded the theologian." But the grotesque episode of the "great fish" should not be allowed to obscure the sublime message of the book.

Jonah was an actual prophet who lived in the Northern Kingdom at the same time as Amos; but we know little about him. Our Book of Jonah is a brilliant short story, written with a purpose. Jonah is commanded to prophesy to the people of Nineveh, the capital of Assyria. He does not want to go, and in the effort to flee from God, takes a ship bound for Spain. But a storm threatens to sink the little craft; Jonah tells the sailors this misfortune has come upon them on his account, and bids them throw him into the sea. He is swallowed by the great fish, which eventually spews him out upon dry land. The expression is fantastic, the point is clear—God is a universal Lord, His power extends over the entire world, land, sea, and air.

Again Jonah is ordered to Nineveh, and this time he obeys, preaching doom upon the wicked city. His words have an enormous impact. The people of Nineveh from the king down confess and forsake their sins; God pardons them and does not destroy the city. But Jonah is angry. That is why he did not want to go to Nineveh in the first place. Why should he be instrumental in reforming and therefore saving the arch-enemies of his own people? Better that they should remain sinful and perish! At the end, God shows Jonah, by a striking object lesson, how narrow and inhuman he has been. "Should I not have pity on Nineveh that great city, which contains thousands of little children who do not yet know their right hand from their left?" Not only God's power, but His love and mercy extend over all His creatures. . . . This booklet has for centuries been the prophetic reading for the afternoon of the Day of Atonement.

There was, however, one breach which Jewish universalism could not heal—between the Judeans and the Samaritans. The latter (as we saw) were descended from settlers established in the Northern Kingdom by the Assyrian conquerors. They had no doubt intermarried with the Israelite peasants, and had adopted the religion of their new land more or less completely. When the returned exiles began to rebuild the Temple, the Samaritans approached them with offers to share in the work. But they were rebuffed as outsiders; and in consequence became intensely hostile. They denounced the Jews to the government as rebellious, and asserted that the Temple was being rebuilt as a fortress rather than a shrine.

They likewise used every resource of policy and guile to prevent Nehemiah from rebuilding the walls of Jerusalem. Moreover, they had allies and supporters within the Judean community. Even one of the priestly families had intermarried with the Samaritan aristocracy. The offending priests were banished by Nehemiah's orders, and of course went over to the other side.

Eventually, the division between Jews and Samaritans became complete. The Samaritans (probably in the fourth century) built a temple of their own on Mount Gerizim in central Palestine—it is mentioned as a sacred spot in Deuteronomy. They insisted that this was the one legitimate temple, and that the shrine in Jerusalem was not ordained of God. Thus they became the first dissenting sect in the history of Judaism.

Of the sacred books of Israel they accepted only the Pentateuch; their traditions gradually diverged widely from those of official Judaism. Yet they clung with steadfast fidelity to their own version of the religion. Through two thousand years, this little sect has persisted, despite poverty, persecution, and cultural stagnation. In recent times they have dwindled to no more than a few hundred souls, most of them living in Nablus (Shechem), near their holy mountain. The age-old rift with the Jews seems to be almost healed; though since the establishment of the State of Israel communication has been difficult, for Nablus is within the territory of the Kingdom of Jordan. It appears that within a few years, the remaining survivors will be reabsorbed by the main body of Israel.

10.

Did the Jews Borrow Their Religion?

NOW THAT WE HAVE STUDIED THE ORIGINS OF THE JEWISH RELIGION, we may pause to consider the question: To what extent was Judaism derived from foreign sources? From time to time it has been argued that the people of Israel did not originate much of the doctrine they proclaimed. The true sources of the Biblical faith are to be found, some say in Babylonia, some say in Egypt.

It was natural, when the monuments and literature of these great empires were unearthed in modern times, that scholars should have been enthusiastic about their new discoveries, and should have been tempted to exaggerate the importance of what they had found. And at least some of those who claimed that the Jews merely peddled the ideas of other nations were motivated by anti-Semitism.

Actually, the Jewish religion would be no less valid and magnificent even though many of its elements were drawn from non-Israelite sources. Truth is truth, wherever it comes from. If the Jews had only given classic expression to certain religious ideas and transmitted them to posterity, this in itself would have been a noble service to mankind. But the soberest and most objective scholarship has shown that the extent of Israelite borrowing had been greatly exaggerated, and that the Jewish religion was essentially a unique and native development.

Much, for example, has been made of the resemblances between the laws of the Pentateuch and the ancient Babylonian code of King Hammurabi. But these resemblances are not surprising. In every

52

society worthy of the name there are laws for the protection of life and property, and for the compensation of injured persons by those who have committed the injury. Especially in view of the common Semitic background, Jewish and Babylonian laws would be expected to have a certain family resemblance. But the differences are far more significant. The code of Hammurabi is frankly class legislation, guaranteeing special privileges to the landowner and stripping the slave of all human rights. The Torah insists on the equality of all persons, including foreigners, before the law. Whereas Hammurabi insisted that a runaway slave must be returned to his master, the law of Deuteronomy commands the exact opposite—the runaway is to be granted asylum. Only a biased mind could regard the crude myths and harsh laws of Babylon as the source of the soaring, humane, universal religion of Israel.

This is not to say that there were no cultural borrowings by the Jews. The Biblical story of the Flood is no doubt derived from the Babylonians, who in turn had learned it from the Sumerians, their predecessors in the valley of the Euphrates. The connection between the Biblical and the Babylonian flood story is attested by the fact that the two accounts agree in several minor details. But the Biblical authors completely transformed what they borrowed. A crude tale of warring gods and goddesses, quick to revenge an insult and dependent on sacrifice to allay their hunger, was fundamentally reworked so as to teach the universal sway and justice of the only God. The basic difference between the religion of Israel and that of Mesopotamia is nowhere clearer than in the case where a connection is plainest.

The theory that Moses derived his doctrine and laws from his Egyptian instructors is not a new one, but it has been given new plausibility by certain recent discoveries. In the fourteenth century B.C.E.—we have learned—the Pharaoh Amenhotep IV became the apostle and champion of a new cult. He declared that the sun, called Aton, was the only god, and forcibly suppressed all other cults and temples. Changing his name to Ikhnaton, he became the prophet of a kind of monotheism, which had moreover ethical elements. Scholars have found resemblances between lines in Ikhnaton's Hymn to the Sun and Psalm 104. What more natural, then, than to argue that the monotheism of Moses was derived from that of this radical Pharaoh? In a particularly fantastic form, this theory was adopted by the famous psychoanalyst Sigmund Freud.

A more careful examination of the facts, however, shows the weakness of the theory. Aton was the only god for the Pharaoh and the royal family; but according to the Egyptian sources, Ikhnaton himself was the earthly embodiment and representative of Aton to all his subjects. *They* could serve Aton only by worshipping the king. This is not monotheism as Judaism understood it.

Moreover, the revolution of Ikhnaton ended with his death. Immediately thereafter the old gods, their temples, and priests were restored, and Ikhnaton's name and memory were blotted out. It is questionable whether the Hebrews ever heard of him and his doctrine. His existence and his religious ideas were rediscovered only in recent times. The resemblances between his hymn and Psalm 104 have been exaggerated (by translating the former in Biblical phrases), and are readily explained as coincidence.

Had Egyptian influence on Jewish religious development been really considerable, we should be at a loss to explain the complete absence in Judaism of the two most noteworthy features of Egyptian religion. One is the veneration of animals, which were thought to be embodiments of the divine spirit. The bull, the cat, and the ibis were sacred in Egypt. The other is the overwhelming emphasis on life after death. This led to elaborate provision for the embalming and preservation of the bodies of the dead, and the construction of magnificent tombs, including the great pyramids. Of such tendencies there is no evidence whatever in Israel. During the period we have been studying, Jewish sources make almost no mention of life after death.

Again, we do not assert that the Jews borrowed nothing from Egypt. One short section of the Book of Proverbs appears to be a free translation of an earlier Egyptian document. It contains various maxims of practical conduct, similar to other writings on "wisdom" found throughout the ancient East. No doubt there are other limited borrowings. But the notion that the essential elements of Judaism came from Egypt cannot be seriously entertained.

More recent scholarship, sobered by the failure of these sensational theories, has dealt more responsibly with the newer discoveries. Among the most significant of these are a group of Canaanite texts unearthed at Ras Shamra, in what is now Syria. These very early documents include mythological poems and ritual pieces. The language (though not the writing) is very similar to Biblical Hebrew. From the Ras Shamra documents we learn that many of the *forms* of Israelite observance were similar to, and perhaps borrowed from, the Canaanites. Not a few allusions in the Bible find their explanation in these

Canaanite texts; and there are even a few phrases in them that occur word for word in Biblical literature.

Nevertheless, scholars agree that these ancient Canaanite documents are not to be regarded as a *source* for the Bible. The Biblical writers occasionally utilized a mythological phrase or allusion, just as English writers (much more frequently) refer to Greek and Roman myths without in the least believing in Zeus or Venus.

Near Eastern archeological research has helped us in many ways to understand the Bible better. The buildings, roads, and manufactured objects that have come to light teach us much about daily life in Bible times. The monuments and written documents supplement Biblical data and sometimes directly confirm the correctness of the Hebrew narratives. In certain cases, archeological findings seem to contradict statements in the Bible, and thus raise new problems for students. But in general, the discoveries have strengthened our confidence in the reliability of the Biblical historians.

The new information must be used honestly and objectively. Through such use, two facts are brought into clear focus. The material culture of ancient Israel was not distinguished: in engineering, architecture, manufacturing, agriculture, commerce, and the arts, the Israelites contributed little that was original, and for the most part copied the methods of their neighbors. But their religion and its magnificent literary expression are without equal and without parallel.

Beside the "comparative" method, modern historians have also made much use of another procedure: the explanation of intellectual, cultural, and religious trends in terms of economic and social conditions. In this book we have alluded to such backgrounds, and will continue to do so. But this method too must be utilized with judicious restraint. Only the pious Marxist will aver that economic circumstances alone determine the spiritual progress of man. A more sober approach will recognize that both material and spiritual factors are basic, and that they constantly react one upon the other. Knowledge of the economic and political history of ancient Israel will help us to understand *how* the new religious and moral ideas emerged, but not *why* they emerged. For other peoples have passed through a similar process of social evolution without producing an Amos or Jeremiah.

The facts remain—unique, sublime, mysterious. That is why many Jews who no longer hold to the orthodox teaching of "Torah from Heaven" still see in the history we have studied thus far the revelation of God to man through Israel.

Did the Jews Borrow Their Religion? 55

Part 2.
The Second Temple

11.

Under the Law

FROM THE DAYS OF DAVID TO THE PRESENT, THERE IS NO PERIOD IN Jewish history so obscure as that which followed the reforms of Ezra. For over a hundred years, there are practically no historical facts. But the literary productions of the time give us some information as to trends, though not as to events.

The dominant force in this period is the Torah, now complete, unchallenged—and loved. The notion that the Law was a depressing burden, observed doggedly in a spirit of gloomy resignation, was invented by outsiders unfamiliar with the Jewish spirit. "Thy word is a lamp unto my feet and a light unto my path." "Thy word is tried to the uttermost, and Thy servant loveth it." "The precepts of the Lord are right, rejoicing the heart." So spoke those who lived under the regime of the Torah. The daily discipline of religious duty, with its scrupulous attention to minute detail, served to develop character and to create an atmosphere of holiness. To sense the spiritual depth and spontaneity of the period, we need only open the Book of Psalms.

These lyrics were not all written in a single epoch. Some were composed before or during the Exile; but many of them date from the Persian period. They were intended chiefly for use in the Temple service, which included choral song with instrumental accompaniment.

But the Psalter is more than a hymnal for public worship. Its choicest songs breathe an intensely personal faith. It is a far cry from the days when religion was a ceremonial relationship between the tribe

59

and its deity to these outpourings of abiding love between the individual and the Master of the Universe. The faith of the Psalms is both sublime and intimate. Hope, doubt, repentance, bitterness, resignation, thanksgiving, trust—the whole range of human emotion is reflected in these most wonderful of religious poems. Even the prayers of the nation are frequently cast in the first person singular, so completely does the author identify the needs of Israel with his own personal concerns.

The Book of Psalms has become the chief devotional work of mankind. Jew and Christian have found in its pages the expression of their own deepest yearnings, their loftiest aspirations. It has influenced the hearts of men more than any other part of the Bible, perhaps more than any other work ever written. This treasury of spiritual religion was produced by men who practiced and—as the psalm verses quoted above testify—loved the Torah.

It seems probable that many psalms were composed by Levites, since it was from this group that the Temple singers and musicians were drawn. The teachers of the Torah, however, were generally of the priestly class, like Ezra; and like him, they bore the title of Scribes (*Soferim*). In addition to expounding the sacred law, they were probably active in compiling and disseminating books of "Wisdom."

The Biblical books of this character probably date from the centuries after the Exile. But they represent, in subject matter and style, something very old and not uniquely Jewish. The wisdom in question deals with practical questions of conduct; it is predominantly secular and prudent, rather than religious and aspiring. Such wisdom was widely studied throughout the ancient East. The maxims of Confucius are a notable example; *Aesop's Fables*, though preserved in Greek verse, originated in India. We have noted that one section of the Biblical Book of Proverbs was probably adapted from an Egyptian source.

There was an old tradition of such wisdom in Israel, centered especially around the figure of King Solomon—the wisest of mankind, according to the admiring reports in the Book of Kings. The Book of Proverbs was attributed to him, and it is entirely possible that he originated some of the sayings in the collection.

The tone of this work is predominantly conservative and sometimes worldly wise. It commends industry and thrift, contentment and tranquillity, honesty and fair dealing, respect for the authority of parents and rulers. It warns against frivolous and expensive pleasure-seeking, gossip and talebearing, and going surety for other peoples' debts. On the other hand it extols the virtue of generous charity, glorifies the ruler who seeks the welfare of his people, and roundly condemns those who would profit by human misery.

Above all, the book exhorts its readers to strive wholeheartedly for wisdom itself:

"Happy is the man that findeth wisdom
And the man that obtaineth understanding.
For the merchandise of it is better than the merchandise of silver,
And the gain thereof than fine gold. . . .
Her ways are ways of pleasantness,
And all her paths are peace.
She is a tree of life to them that lay hold upon her,
And happy is every one that holdeth her fast."

And while the emphasis is largely on standards of conduct that will keep a man out of trouble and lead to prosperity and contentment, a nobler religious note is not infrequently struck.

"The sacrifice of the wicked is an abomination to the Lord
But the prayer of the upright is his delight."

Indeed, the book begins with the declaration that "the fear of the Lord is the beginning of knowledge."

It is interesting to note that Proverbs (like most ancient wisdom books) deals with man in general, and makes no reference to Israel, or to any of the characteristic laws and observances of the Jewish religion. But it takes the belief in one God for granted, and frequently refers to Him by the name Yhwh.

Not all the students of wisdom were satisfied with the exposition of conventional morality. Others were attracted to more profound questions. Towering above them was a genius, whose name we do not know, who had explored not only the books of wisdom but the sublime writings of the prophets. In the Book of Job, which reflects intense personal experience even more than wide reading, he wrestled with the tragic riddle of human suffering.

Job, a man of blameless character and unswerving faith, is suddenly overwhelmed by a series of disasters. He is visited by his friends, the champions of orthodoxy. They hold the doctrine, taught by Ezekiel, that men are rewarded or punished according to their exact deserts. But if we accept this theory, logic forces us to accuse the afflicted of prior sinfulness. Thus Job's friends call upon him to repent, and assure him that if he mends his ways, God will restore his fortunes. To their horror, he insists on his innocence. While pleading his own cause with stormy eloquence, he points out that it is not unique. Often the innocent are crushed by suffering, while rascals live in prosperity and ease.

But the book is not a disillusioned essay in skepticism, nor is it a cynical sneer at human life. Job will not abandon his faith in the righteousness of God. But he will not abandon his own innocence either. It is the contradiction that make his suffering so tragic.

At length God appears in a whirlwind. He shows Job how small human knowledge is. All life is a mystery, the good no less than the evil. Since we cannot understand life as a whole, we cannot pass judgment on one phase of it. We must be humble in the presence of the myriad riddles we cannot solve. Yet Job is vindicated as against his friends. He has at least spoken honestly; they twisted the evidence in their effort to justify God. We need not distort the truth in His behalf.

This answer to the problem of suffering was too radical for its time. The Book of Job as we have it contains a number of changes and additions intended to tone down its heresy. The theory of retributive justice remained standard, until, a few centuries later, a new approach to the whole matter was introduced.

A third wisdom book, composed somewhat later, is of still different character. It is called Koheleth,* and has kept its place in the Bible chiefly because it too was ascribed to King Solomon. For this is a cynical and basically irreligious book. Its author is disillusioned; to him all human striving is futile. The most one can hope for is a modest (and probably temporary) measure of physical enjoyment and contentment. "Wisdom" is of value, indeed, but should not be pursued too strenuously. The author speaks indeed of God (never of Yhwh), but his God is not the object of a warm and loyal devotion; He is an inscrutable Power who does not seem to be concerned with human needs or human behavior.

Some students have thought that Koheleth reflects the negative and skeptical views of certain Greek philosophers. But there is also a pes-

---

* The meaning of the name is uncertain. The Greek translators rendered it Ecclesiastes, i.e., the speaker in an assembly; and this name is retained in our English Bibles.

simistic strain in the old oriental wisdom, and this may have supplied the author with hints which his own gloomy temperament developed. Later Jewish teachers were hard put to reconcile his cynical and often self-contradictory statements * with the accepted teachings of the religion. His book, however, is one of the most interesting that has come down to us from the Jewish past.

Meantime prophetic activity, though dwindling, had not entirely ceased. Seers still beheld visions of a future when the Jewish people and their faith should enjoy a universal triumph, and God's kingdom of peace should be established over the earth. During this period the writings of the prophets were edited and gradually compiled into a collection which was to be the second great part of the Hebrew Scriptures.

The Book of Esther is set in this Persian period. It tells how the Jewish consort of the "Great King," inspired by her cousin Mordecai, defeated the malicious Haman who had plotted to massacre all the Jews of the Empire. The romantic tale does not seem to be historical; it serves to explain the gay Festival of Purim. This carnival-like holiday, obscure in origin, has been dear to Jewish hearts through the ages. A people that suffered so often from baseless slander and murderous hostility was glad to recall the downfall of Haman, the typical Jew-hater, and gloried in the triumph of the loyal Esther.

* * *

What influence did Persian culture exert on Judaism?

This was the first time that the Jewish people had been in contact with a religion that was in any way comparable to their own. The heathen cults of their earlier conquerors could awaken only contempt and disgust in those who understood the lofty spirit of the prophetic teaching. But here was a different case. The Persian religion, as taught by Zoroaster (Zarathustra), was nobly ethical in character. It represented all existence as a struggle between two opposing principles or deities, one of light and goodness, the other of darkness and

---

* The contradictions in the book have been explained variously: (1) The original book was consistently skeptical; but an orthodox reader has added a number of corrective statements. (2) The book is a dialogue between a skeptic and a believer. (3) The author quotes many sayings in order to comment on them.

evil. All physical and moral excellences are ascribed to Ahura Mazda, all evil of whatever sort to Ahriman. Man's destiny is to take part in the struggle, to conquer the evil nature within him and range himself on the side of light. The struggle will continue through many ages, but at last Ahura Mazda will triumph. All those who have ever lived will be judged for their conduct; the wicked will be destroyed, and the righteous, made immortal through heavenly food, will live in endless bliss.

Even this sketchy outline makes plain that Judaism and Christianity have been deeply affected by Persian religion. But strangely, there is little evidence of this influence in the writings produced while Judea was politically subject to Persia. The Second Isaiah, it seems, found it necessary to defend monotheism against Persian dualism. Speaking in the name of God, he declares:

> "I am the Lord and there is none else;
> I form the light and create darkness,
> I make peace, and create evil;
> I am the Lord that doeth all these things."

This, of course, represents not Persian influence on the Jewish religion, but an instance of reaction against such influence. Nevertheless, Persian ideas must have gradually seeped into the minds of the people, for later on we shall find them widely accepted and highly important in Jewish thought. But these influences did not find clear expression until Judaism had come into contact and conflict with another and greater culture—that of Hellas.

12.

Judah and Hellas: Palestine

IN 331 B.C.E. ALEXANDER THE GREAT ENTERED PALESTINE; A FEW
months later, the Persian Empire had crumbled. The Jews welcomed
the change; the Persian yoke had been growing heavy, and Alexander
was very friendly. He remained a glamorous figure in Jewish legendary lore. The new seaport he created at the mouth of the Nile and
named Alexandria after himself was shortly to become an outstanding
center of Jewish life.

The whirlwind conqueror did not regard his exploits merely as a
quest for personal glory. He was fulfilling a mission—to bring the
superior culture of Greece to the supposedly backward Orient. This
mission had remarkable success, for the eastern world received eagerly
much that the Greeks had to offer. The language—though not in its
most classic form—the emphasis on sport and spectacles, the gymnasium and the theater became widely popular. Alexander, however,
was not a true Hellene, but a Macedonian; and the culture spread
through his agency was much adulterated with foreign elements.
Greek culture was already on the decline. The last of the giants was
Aristotle, who had been Alexander's tutor. The age of the great thinkers, poets, and artists was past. We must distinguish the genuine
Hellenic culture from the pseudo-Greek or Hellenistic culture that
spread after the conquests of Alexander.

The conqueror died suddenly in the midst of his glory, and his
empire fell to pieces. One of his generals, Ptolemy, established himself as ruler over Egypt; another, Seleucus, founded a dynasty in

Syria. These two families continued to rule for several centuries, and frequently their ambitions came into conflict. As in earlier days, the rulers of Egypt and western Asia struggled for supremacy; and again Palestine, the bridge between the empires, became a bone of contention. At first the Jews were ruled by Egypt; later they passed under the control of Syria. Apparently they did not much care to which king they paid their taxes, so long as they were not disturbed. The High Priest remained in authority, directing internal affairs with the assistance of a council of elders. Though there were periods of disturbance and bloodshed, the lot of the people was generally peaceful.

Meantime the influence of Hellenism was entering Jewish life and corroding it. The best in Greek thought and culture hardly reached Palestine; only a superficial and frivolous Hellenism was regularly imported. The Greek ways were sophisticated and fashionable. Sports were exciting, even though the athletic meets were dedicated to the various gods of Olympus. The gymnasium was attractive, despite the traditional Jewish objection to nakedness. Theaters were appealing, especially as the comedies presented were spicy. All this was justified by what called itself philosophy, but which had little in common with the spirit of the great Greek thinkers. We sometimes meet a callow youth with just enough scientific knowledge to tune a television set. He informs us glibly that "science has discredited religion." The Greek "philosophy" that reached Palestine was of this stamp, both as regards profundity and impudence!

But however flimsy its intellectual bases, Hellenism made a wide appeal. It was most popular, as we might expect, in the wealthier and more aristocratic classes. Being thrown into frequent contact with foreign officials, they were eager to appear cosmopolitan and modish. Not only did they avidly adopt the new ways, they often went to extremes in concealing their old-fashioned Jewish background. But the Jewish aristocracy consisted largely of priestly families. Thus we have the strange spectacle of men busily engaged in undermining Judaism, who had been dedicated from birth to its service.

A series of intrigues, too complicated to relate here, degraded the high-priestly office to a political plum. The Syrian rulers, swayed by bribery, made and unmade high priests at will. One of these priestly scoundrels even sent Temple funds as an offering to the games held at Tyre in honor of Hercules.

This sort of scandal was bound to provoke reaction. A vigorous anti-Greek party grew up, especially among the lower classes, demanding strict fidelity to Jewish tradition and the elimination of everything foreign. But these *Chasidim* (pious ones, as they called themselves) seemed to be fighting a losing battle; Hellenism was boring more and more into the life of the people. Then unexpected aid came to the faithful in the person of a crazy Syrian tyrant.

Antiochus the Fourth was an erratic individual, fantastically ambitious, and violently enthusiastic for the bastard culture he supposed to be Greek. He was much pleased at a suggestion from one of the political high priests, that only a little pressure was needed to convert the Jewish peasants to Hellenic modernism. The suggestion took shape when Antiochus was in a black mood. Rome had blocked his plans to invade Egypt in 168 B.C.E. Wild with wounded pride, Antiochus attacked and partly looted the city of Jerusalem. Then he had an altar to Zeus set up in the Temple, and a pig was sacrificed upon it. Decrees went forth, forbidding the Jews to observe their ancestral faith and requiring their homage to the Olympian gods.

These violent measures must have opened the eyes of many moderate Hellenizers, who liked to dabble in the new fashions, but remained Jews at heart. Lines were now sharply drawn between loyal Jews and traitors. Something new in world history appears: religious persecution, and with it religious martyrdom. The decrees of Antiochus were remorselessly executed; many, no doubt, compromised with their consciences, but hundreds of men and women, plain folk of the farms and cities, died at the hands of the Syrian soldiery rather than betray their God.

And something else new appears: a war for religious freedom. At the start it could not be called a war. Bands of Chasidim, forbidden to practice Judaism at home, fled to the hills, and made guerrilla attacks on the Syrian posts. Mattathias, an old priest of a provincial town was the first leader; his sons, the Maccabees or Hasmoneans,* became the military heroes of the age. The rebels were aided by internal confusion, corruption, and intrigue in the Syrian court. Gradually Judah Maccabee (who succeeded to leadership upon his father's death) built up a real army, poorly equipped, but hardened by experience, and dauntlessly brave. A pitched battle was fought at Emmaus in 165, and Judah won so complete a victory that he was able

---

* Properly speaking, Maccabee was the nickname of Judah—and we do not know what it meant. The entire family of Mattathias were called the Hasmoneans.

to occupy Jerusalem shortly thereafter. The Temple was rededicated amid scenes of delirious joy. The Jewish people was roused to new fervor, Judaism was rejuvenated.

* * *

Thus a new festival was added to the Jewish calendar, that of Chanuko, or Dedication. The Maccabees had set the dedication of the Temple at the winter solstice, a time when many peoples celebrated the return of the sun by kindling fires or lamps. The ancient custom of kindling lights was given a new interpretation, and added to the observance of the great victory.

Naturally, the astounding victory of tiny Judah over the great Syrian Empire fired the Jewish people with pride and enthusiasm. One of the most remarkable results was the rise of a Jewish missionary movement. We learn from the Bible itself of early attempts to bring the Jewish message to the heathen; the spirit of the Second Isaiah never died out. But after the Maccabean successes the Jews became filled with the sense of a great destiny, and their missionary efforts became more aggressive and systematic. Both in Palestine and elsewhere, great numbers of the heathen were converted to the Jewish faith. The world was ripe for the message of Judaism. The old pagan cults had decayed; intelligent people no longer took them seriously. But philosophy was too cold and abstract to fill the hearts of most people; and a real hunger for an adequate religion was keenly felt. People were experimenting with all sorts of oriental cults; various "mystery religions" had become fashionable. Judaism was a simple, rational belief; its ethical standard was high and inspiring; its message was comforting. It met the need of the time admirably. In addition to the great numbers who formally entered Judaism, many Gentiles attached themselves unofficially to the synagogue and were known as "the God-fearing."

The battle at Emmaus did not end the struggle with Syria. It went on with varying fortunes; Judah and three of his brothers met violent deaths. Ultimately the Syrian rulers, forced to play politics because of internal conflicts, recognized the national independence of Judea. In 142 Simon, the last of the Hasmonean brothers, was acclaimed as ruler of a sovereign nation.

But the people were not overenthusiastic about political independence. The Chasidim, the backbone of the Maccabean army, were satisfied when the persecution was ended and the Temple purified. The Hasmoneans had come into power through the support of the masses; but gradually, the rulers and the people drew apart. John Hyrkan, the son of Simon, was something of a conqueror, who greatly enlarged the boundaries of Judea; yet he was not entirely popular. His successor, Alexander Jannai, was so hated that he had to rely on foreign mercenaries, whom he turned loose on occasion against his own people. A few years later dynastic quarrels broke out, leading to civil war. So little did national freedom mean to the majority of the people, so much on the other hand did they desire peace and order, that their representatives turned to Pompey, the Roman conqueror, and asked him to intervene.

But of all the consequences of the Hasmonean victory, none were more significant than the new religious ideas that now came to the fore. These, however, require a separate chapter.

13.

The End of the World

WE STILL SEE AND HEAR WARNINGS THAT, IN ACCORDANCE WITH BIBLE prophecies, the end of the world is at hand. "Millions living will never die." God's final judgment on mankind will soon be pronounced: all who would be saved from condemnation must prepare themselves at once to enter the new world that will rise on the ashes of the old!

All cults and sects that preach such doctrines are survivals of a Jewish movement that began in pre-Maccabean days. The record of this movement is found in a series of strange writings called apocalypses —that is, revelations of hidden lore. And this secret lore concerned chiefly the end of the world. The adherents of the movement turned despairingly from an existence they found unbearable to visions of a better world they were sure would come soon.

This sort of thing was not entirely new. The great prophets had taught that God's will is fulfilled in history; that after a period of suffering and exile, the purified Israel will be redeemed; and that ultimately all men will be unified under God's leadership in a fellowship of brotherhood and peace. The prophets do not, however, make clear just how this great victory of the spirit will be achieved. Apparently, they expected it to result from the moral education of mankind. The Second Isaiah stresses especially the influence of Israel, the suffering servant of God. Other prophets attached greater importance to a divinely chosen personal leader, that is to say, the Messiah.

Originally this word was no more than a royal title. Israelite kings were inaugurated, not by donning a crown, but by the pouring of oil upon their heads. Thereafter they were known as the "anointed of the Lord" (*M'shiach Adonoi*). When the Kingdom of Judah fell, the people naturally hoped they would regain their independence and be ruled once more by their own king, of the family of David. Thus the expectation of the Messiah was basically political—the hope of national independence under a native ruler.

Yet the messianic dream included more than this. Even during the existence of the monarchy, the prophets had hoped for a ruler radically different from the morally feeble and even idolatrous kings who so often occupied the throne. They had drawn the picture of an ideal ruler on whom God's spirit would rest,

> "The spirit of wisdom and understanding,
> The spirit of counsel and might,
> The spirit of knowledge and the fear of the Lord."

During the post-exilic period, these ideal qualities were consistently ascribed to the hoped-for Messiah. Not alone would he emancipate Israel; he would establish a realm of righteousness on earth.

In its final stages, prophecy displayed certain new qualities. The simple, sublime poems of Amos, Isaiah, and Jeremiah were succeeded by visions fantastic in form and hard to understand. Instead of directing their message to the specific situations of their own day, the latest prophets dealt more and more with the remote future. They anticipated a change, not so much through the moral rehabilitation of the people as through the miraculous intervention of God. They pictured a catastrophic judgment upon the heathen nations, to prepare the way for the new triumph of the Jews. Such prophecies are a sort of bridge to the new apocalyptic literature.

But the apocalypses contain much that is new to Judaism and was derived chiefly from Persia. The ideas of Zoroaster must have gradually spread among the people. The Syrian persecutions brought these ideas powerfully to the surface.

This was the first great crisis in the life of Israel when no prophet was found to speak to them in the name of God. They sought desperately for firm guidance and for comfort and hope in a tragic time.

When they turned to the sacred literature which had taken the place of the living prophetic word, they encountered new distress. For the prophets had promised that the Babylonian exile would be followed by a glowing future. These promises had not been fulfilled. Why had God not made good the assurances of His own messengers?

And how were they to understand the words of the Torah? Did it not promise abundant reward to those who obeyed its precepts? Ezekiel had explained, moreover, that rewards and punishments are apportioned individually, according to each man's deserts. But these theories were absolutely contradicted by the facts of the Syrian terror. Precisely those who were most loyal to the Torah and most strict in its observance had fallen beneath the sword of the oppressor, while the traitors and cynics prospered. The people cried out in agony of spirit: Why does God let his most faithful servants come to so dreadful an end?

The new doctrine gave a clear-cut and encouraging answer to all these questions. It presented world history as a vast cosmic drama, planned in advance by God. This history moves in a logical and inevitable pattern from the opening scene of creation to the final act, the universal judgment. The drama is now rapidly approaching its conclusion. The promises made to the prophets have not failed. Earlier ages misunderstood their meaning; a more exact interpretation shows that the happy consummation will soon take place.* But before the happy ending can take place, the righteous must pass through a period of intense suffering. Things must get worse before they can get better. Good people will be strongly tempted to do wrong and to desert God. Let them not lose heart or violate their conscience! Suddenly, miraculously, God will intervene—directly or according to some accounts, through the agency of the Messiah. The wicked will be annihilated. Israel will be free and triumphant. The pious will be vindicated and glorified. A new world will arise, in which goodness, untarnished by sin, will endure forever.

But what of the martyrs, who died before they could see the triumph of God's righteousness? They have not been forgotten. "Many that sleep in the dust shall awaken." The dead will be resurrected, restored to the bodies they possessed before their death; and they will appear in God's presence for judgment. Each will receive the reward or punishment he deserves for his deeds in this life; and the injustices of earthly existence will be finally and perfectly rectified.

To express these new ideas, a new literary form was devised—the

---

* For example, Jeremiah had predicted that the nation would be restored after 70 years of exile. The Book of Daniel explains that this really means 70 *weeks* of years, i.e., 490 years. Hence the author of Daniel, writing about the year 167 B.C.E., expects the final deliverance in the near future.

apocalypse or revelation. We possess a number of such writings, dating from the last centuries before the Christian era. Each is ascribed to some ancient worthy—Enoch, Moses, Daniel, Ezra. In an age when there were no longer prophets who spoke in their own right, the apocalyptic author remained obscure and unknown, but gave his message authority through the name of an earlier seer.

The visions received by the hero of the apocalypses are set forth in cryptic, often baffling style, using fantastic symbolism. (For instance, different nations are represented by various monstrous beasts.) The visions generally review the history of mankind, leading up to the particular crisis in Jewish life which called forth the apocalypse, and which is hinted at in guarded terms. (Perhaps the mysterious style was intended to mislead foreign officials, who might regard these documents as subversive; or perhaps the revelations were considered too sacred for the general uninitiated public.) The reference to the miserable present is soon followed by visions of the coming redemption, which is painted in glowing colors.

Only one apocalypse has been included in the Hebrew Bible: the Book of Daniel. Composed during the Maccabean revolt, it must have done much to strengthen the morale of the pious. It begins with well-loved stories (laid in the Babylonian and Persian periods) of Jewish heroes loyal to their faith, and of tyrants overthrown. The apocalypse proper refers in cautious but unmistakable terms to the Syrian persecution; it predicts the death of Antiochus and the ultimate triumph of Israel.

But the Maccabean victories, as we have seen, were neither complete nor durable. As the people suffered from the tyranny of the later Hasmoneans, from the barbarities of civil war, and then from the increasing intervention of Rome in their life, many new occasions arose for the composition of apocalyptic visions. Just as the older apocalypses reinterpreted the writings of the prophets, so the later books of revelation had to reinterpret the earlier ones. When the date set for the final redemption passed without the overthrow of the heathen or the appearance of the Messiah, the computations were revised and the end of this world set a little further ahead.

Many of the Biblical writers had described God as a King surrounded by numberless attendants, and they had pictured Him as carrying out His purposes through His messengers. Gradually the word for messenger (Hebrew *mal'och*, Greek *angelos*) came to have the special meaning of one of God's supernatural agents, a being less than

divine but more than human—in short, an angel. In apocalyptic literature, the doctrine of angels was greatly elaborated, no doubt under
Persian influence. Angels were now represented as belonging to
various grades and ranks, each with its special duties. An angelic
patron was assigned to every nation of the world. And the most distinguished angels began to bear proper names, Michael and Gabriel
being the most often mentioned.

The apocalyptic writers gave a new explanation for the existence of
evil in the world. Basing themselves on certain remarks in the Book of
Genesis, they declared that a group of angels had once fallen from
grace and rebelled against God. From this primal tragedy all physical
and moral evil resulted.

The leader of the rebel angels is often called Satan. The Bible usually
speaks of *the* Satan, that is the opponent; this title designates one of
God's messengers whose duty it is to detect human sins and accuse
the sinners before God's court. The Biblical Adversary is a kind of
celestial prosecutor. Later, however, Satan was used as a proper name,
and sometimes at least, he acquired the traits of Ahriman, the evil
deity of the Persians. In certain apocalypses, Satan is a real devil, a
rebel against God and the enemy of man.

This view of the matter was later adopted by Christianity. But with
rare exceptions, the teachers of Judaism rejected the idea. There is
much about Satan in later Jewish literature, but it belongs to folklore
rather than to theology. Moreover, in these writings Satan appears
in his original role as prosecutor and sometimes executioner. He is an
agent of God, not His enemy.

Except for the Book of Daniel, the apocalypses were not included in
the Bible; and we must thank the Christian churches for having preserved a number of them. We can only surmise the reason why the
responsible leaders of the Jewish community rejected them. It was
not out of opposition to the ideas contained in these writings; for there
is little (except the stories of the fallen angels) taught in the apocalypses which is not also mentioned in the Talmud—the "official literature" of Judaism.

There may have been some objection to the apocalypses on the
ground that they imitated the Biblical style (as a rule not very well),
and yet were known to be of recent origin and so unworthy to be
regarded as sacred Scripture. But probably the opposition to these
writings was due chiefly to their general tone. For they are permeated
by an utter despair of the present world, and so encourage an "escapist"

concentration on the visionary future. Such dreaming must have weakened interest in present tasks and duties. Moreover, the Jewish teachers recognized the great dangers in attempting to calculate the exact moment of the messianic advent. As the expected day approached, excitement would mount sometimes to the pitch of violence; and when the reckoning proved false, a terrible disillusionment and discouragement would follow.

Thus the most responsible leaders tended to stress other aspects of religion; but they did not challenge—indeed they fully accepted—the main ideas of the apocalyptic teachers. It would have hardly been possible for Judaism to survive without a powerful hope of a better future. And the doctrine of the resurrection of the dead—however strange it may seem to us—was destined to be for centuries an official doctrine of Judaism. But the history of this belief is part of the story of the great Jewish sects—the Pharisees and Sadducees—to which we now turn.

14.

The Struggle for Religious Democracy

FEW ENGLISH WORDS HAVE MORE UNPLEASANT ASSOCIATIONS THAN *Pharisee*. It has come to mean a narrow, self-righteous formalist with more than a touch of hypocrisy. Some modern Jews may be startled to learn that they are the spiritual heirs of the Pharisees. Yet it is a fact that our Judaism is rooted in the Pharisaic tradition. Still more remarkable, Christianity—through which the Pharisees got their bad name—itself grew directly out of the Judaism of the Pharisees. Who then, were these men, and what did they stand for? Before we answer these questions, we must sketch the events of the last pre-Christian century.

John Hyrkan, the son of Simon the Maccabee, had conquered Idumea, south of Palestine and forced its people to adopt the Jewish religion. This episode was not part of the great Jewish missionary movement, but resulted rather from political considerations. Just as Antiochus had tried to compel the Jews to adopt the Greek religion, in order to increase the solidarity of his empire, John Hyrkan had employed Judaism to further *his* imperial aims. The results were tragic. For a certain Idumean, Antipater by name, was able to rise to the highest power in Judea during the dynastic quarrel between the last members of the Hasmonean family. A little later, his son Herod secured the backing of the Roman leaders and made himself king of the Jews under their sponsorship. Herod—brilliant, capricious, unscrupulous, and abominably cruel—reigned for many years (37 B.C.E.– 4 C.E.) with Roman military support. But even though he rebuilt the Temple with great magnificence, the people hated him for his alien origin, his lack of real Jewish loyalty—for he also patronized heathen temples—and his cruelty. A few years after his death, Judea was formally incorporated into the Empire and ruled by a Roman governor.

The whole period of the Second Temple was one of intense and vital interest in religion, and also of rapid political, economic, and cultural change. Under such circumstances, wide differences in religious thinking were bound to develop, and some of these differences gave rise to religious parties and sects.

Originally, we saw, the Torah was in the hands of priestly teachers, who carried on the tradition of Ezra by instructing the people in the Law. But the priests were a hereditary class; their number was bound to include a good many whose only right to the priesthood was that of birth, but who had no qualifications for its tasks. Meantime, knowledge of the Torah spread among men who were not of priestly descent. Soon these pious and learned laymen came to be regarded as authorities in their own right. Their prestige grew as tl.at of the priesthood sank, due to the defection of many priests to Hellenism and the venal corruption of others. When the Maccabean struggle broke out, the Chasidim—a lay group—were the backbone of the revolt, though a priestly family supplied the leaders. This alliance, however, hardly outlasted the revolt. For the Maccabean rulers assumed the title both of king and High Priest, though theirs was not a high-priestly family. When, moreover, they began to immerse themselves in worldly pursuits to the neglect of learning and holiness, the gap between the later Hasmoneans and the popular party widened until it was unbridgeable.

But there was another reason for the growing rift between priests and laymen. Vested authority is usually conservative, indifferent and even hostile to the changes that life itself produces. The priests tended to regard the Torah as rigid and unalterable—an attitude which would have made the Torah more and more a venerable but ineffective antique. The lay teachers, however, sought to keep the Torah co-extensive with the life of the people, a constant force for righteousness and holiness in every-day affairs. They therefore tried to make the Torah more flexible, modifying it by interpretation to meet new conditions. Thus the democratic party was the party of progress.

From time to time, problems of religious or legal procedure would arise for which no clear Biblical ruling could be found. The lay teachers met these contingencies by construing broadly such passages in the Law as might offer some suggestion—even a remote one—for dealing with the present case. Thus they came to adopt rather free methods of interpreting the Bible, even to the point of reading into the text the ideas of their own age. To all this the priests objected stoutly. They would not extend the provisions of the Torah beyond its explicit statements. When new cases arose, they claimed the right to legislate in accordance with their own judgment and the priestly traditions.

There were also many customs, some of them ancient, which the people held sacred and practiced faithfully, though they are not mentioned in the Written Law. One such was the pouring out of a libation of water in the Temple during the Sukos festival. The lay scholars treated such customs as obligatory; but the priests, holding to the strict letter of the Law, refused to admit the binding power of these popular traditions, and even ridiculed some of them.

These divisions between priest and layman, aristocrat and democrat, conservative and progressive, strict and broad constructionist, no doubt have roots that go far back into our history. But the sharp division into sects appears only in the days of the later Maccabean rulers. The priestly caste began to be called Sadducees (the name comes from Zadok, the first priest of Solomon's Temple); the lay party was known as Pharisees. This name means "those who are set apart." It refers not only to their separation from the priestly group, but also their avoidance of the peasantry (am ha-arez) whom they suspected of laxity in observance of the Law. For the Pharisees were rigorists. They demanded meticulous obedience to the Torah as they understood it. They laid particular stress on the payment of tithes—even though these taxes on produce provided a large income for their priestly opponents.

In their effort to set up a leadership based on learning and character rather than on birth, the Pharisees undertook to make the priestly law of purity operative in ordinary life. The family table was to be an altar. Hence, the law that the priest must wash his hands before approaching the altar was transferred to the home; and the ceremonial washing of the hands before meals—a law of obvious hygienic benefit—became standard in Judaism.

The masses could not afford the time and trouble to observe all the refinements of ritual which the Pharisees recommended; and certain scholars may have taken a supercilious attitude which the plain folk resented. Nevertheless, popular Judaism was overwhelmingly Pharisaic in tone, and the lay leaders were generally revered. This was especially true of Hillel the Elder, the outstanding Pharisee in the days of King Herod. A native of Babylonia, he had come to Jerusalem in his youth, and was soon recognized as the greatest legalist and the best loved personality of the time. In his zeal to make the Torah a vital force, Hillel went to daring lengths. Of his innovations, the following is the most remarkable.

The Torah provides for a general cancellation of debts every seven years. This law was workable in a simple agricultural civilization, where a loan was usually a favor extended to someone who had a crop failure. But as commerce developed, the law worked severe hardships. In the sixth year of each cycle, credit froze, and the original purpose of the law was altogether frustrated. Hillel therefore introduced a legal device called the *prosbol*. By filing this document with the court at the time of a loan, the lender retained the power to collect his debt even in the Sabbatical year. To all intents and purposes, Hillel repealed a Biblical law!

This indicates how little truth there is in the charge that the Pharisees were blind, mechanical literalists. As for the spirit of Pharisaic Judaism, two familiar sayings of Hillel are sufficient illustration. The first runs: "Be of the disciples of Aaron, loving peace, and pursuing peace; loving all creatures, and bringing them near unto the Torah." The second is his summary of Judaism, addressed to a prospective convert: "What is hateful to thee, do not to thy neighbor. That is the whole Torah, the rest is commentary. Go learn!"

The differences between Pharisees and Sadducees were not limited to points of law. One theological matter became a serious bone of contention. The Pharisees, heirs of the Chasidic martyrs, upheld the doctrine of the resurrection. The Sadducees, finding no warrant for this belief in the Torah, rejected it. So sharp did this controversy become that the Pharisaic teachers ultimately made it a test of orthodoxy. Ordinarily, doctrinal matters were left to the conscience of the individual, and no attempt was made to draw up a uniform creed. But on this point the Pharisees took an uncompromising stand. Anyone, they asserted, who denied the resurrection would have no share in the world to come.

The exact position of the Sadducees on this and other questions is not entirely certain; for all our information about them comes from Pharisaic, and consequently partisan, sources. But we are not to suppose that all priests were Sadducees and all Sadducees priests. Many conscientious lay students must have recognized that the Pharisees were reading more into Scripture than was really to be found there, and that the Sadducean interpretations were closer to the plain meaning of the Bible text. On the other hand, many priests were attracted by the progressive spirit and the deep piety and wisdom of the lay teachers. The authority of the latter grew constantly. Originally the Sanhedrin, the high court of Judea, was probably a council of priests; in time it became predominantly Pharisaic. At the beginning, the High Priest was the presiding officer. Later this dignity passed into the hands of a layman, known as the *Nasi,* president. Hillel gave this office its highest prestige; and thereafter (save for two brief and exceptional periods) it became hereditary in his family.*

In the last years of the Temple, the Pharisees had such complete popular support that they could even regulate the Temple service according to their notions; and the priests had to submit to their supervision with what grace they could muster.†

The Pharisees had an institution ready to hand which they could use as the center of their activities: the Synagogue. Its ritual and procedures had taken shape a century or more before the Christian era, though everything was still informal. The Synagogue was one of the regular institutions of the community, and the elders of the village or city governed its affairs. Each synagogue had further a presiding officer (*rosh ha-k'nesses*) and a caretaker (*chazan*). The latter had charge of the synagogue building and the scrolls of the Torah. The ruling elder might designate any competent person to lead the recital of the prayers and to read the Biblical selections; and anyone capable of teaching was given an opportunity of presenting his message. The preacher remained seated while he delivered his address; in time it became customary to have a spokesman (*Turg'mon*) selected

---

* We cannot enter here upon the complex and difficult history of the Sanhedrin. Some scholars think that there were two national Sanhedrin—besides local courts—one dealing with political, criminal, and similar matters, the latter with religious law. The first was gradually stripped of its power by the Romans, and came to an end with the fall of the state. The latter continued at Jabneh and elsewhere. See Chapter 17.

† Recently an attempt has been made to interpret these sectarian divisions in social and economic terms. The Pharisees are regarded as representatives of the growing urban proletariat, the Sadducees reflect the viewpoint of the country dwellers. This rural outlook was maintained by the landed gentry, even after the majority of the poorer peasants accepted the Pharisaic leadership.

for his resonant voice and fluent diction to stand beside the scholar and repeat in a clear tone the thoughts which the latter whispered to him.

It is customary to speak of three sects in this period: Pharisees, Sadducees, and Essenes. The Essenes, however, were not a religious party, but rather an organized fellowship, comparable to the monastic orders of the Christian church. Their numbers were relatively small. They lived in segregated communities, some of them celibate, while others permitted marriage. In many respects, their outlook was Pharisaic; but unlike the other Pharisees, they shielded themselves from contact with the outside world, devoting themselves to a regimen of special piety, which included much fasting and self-denial, frequent baths of purification, and secret studies. The Essenes were vegetarians, and were apparently unwilling even to give animal sacrifices to the Temple. They refused to deal in weapons. They admitted persons to their fellowship only after a lengthy probation, and maintained a severe and inflexible community discipline.

Recent explorations in the desert country near the Dead Sea have brought to light the buildings and cemetery of what was probably a large Essene colony. Caves in the same neighborhood have yielded the famous "Dead Sea Scrolls," which are still the subject of scholarly investigation and debate. There is good reason to believe that the documents record the ideas and practices of the Essenes, or of a group much like them.

As the Roman governors became more and more oppressive, the populace grew ever more sullen and hostile. This in turn made the Romans bitter and more cruel. Both the priestly and the Pharisaic leaders tried to cooperate with the ruling officials, and used their influence to allay the growing resentment of the masses. But this task became steadily harder. A sizable group emerged which was dedicated to rebellion. Some of these people were simple desperadoes, eager for violence and loot, in revolt against any authority. But many were sincere though fanatical patriots, who believed that it was sinful to recognize any ruler but God, and that honest religious conviction required them to throw off the Roman yoke. They are referred to in the sources as the Fourth Philosophy, the Sicarii (dagger men), and the Zealots. These names may designate different groups and parties; but they were alike in their commitment to open rebellion. They were willing to employ terrorism not only against the foreign rulers but also against fellow Jews who opposed their desperate measures. But except

The Struggle for Religious Democracy 81

on the question of armed resistance, the Fourth Philosophy did not differ from Pharisaism.

The Pharisees led a revolution, bloodless and gradual, but complete. It marks the final break of Judaism with any absolute ecclesiastical authority, and the triumph of the democratic principle. By recognizing learning as the test of leadership, and by adopting the principle of oral tradition as the supplement and interpretation of the Written Law, the Pharisees freed the Torah from confining fetters, and opened the way for a fruitful development. Their methods and institutions enabled Judaism to survive the catastrophe that was now rapidly approaching. The Pharisees have been the most slandered of all religious groups. Like all such, they had their unworthy representatives. But as a body they stood for everything that is precious in the spiritual life of humanity. They were the heirs of the prophets; and all Jews, Christians, and Moslems are the heirs (witting or not) of the Pharisees.

15.

Judah and Hellas: Alexandria

1. *The Diaspora*

MEN AND PEOPLES HAVE ALWAYS WANDERED. SOME ARE DRIVEN FROM their homes by famine, disaster, or human enemies. Some are attracted to new lands by the hope of better opportunities or pleasanter surroundings. Some seem to feel an inner need to keep moving. The Jews in particular have been a wandering people; and their mobility must be kept in mind if we are to understand the history of Judaism.

When relatively small groups of immigrants have settled in new homes, they have usually mingled quickly with the older inhabitants, adopted the language, culture, and gods of the land, and been rather fully assimilated—though sometimes on a lower social level. When the newcomers arrived in somewhat greater force, they have often established colonies that preserved the language, customs, and religion of the old home, while the previous inhabitants were displaced or reduced to an inferior status.

But when the Jews dispersed through the ancient world, they did not follow either of these patterns. Rarely if ever did they establish independent colonies. They were subject to the rulers of the lands where they settled; they adopted the language and many of the customs of their neighbors. Yet their religion kept them a separate group, distinguished by their refusal to participate in the national or local cults, by their special beliefs and practices, and by their dietary restrictions.

83

Moreover, though they had severed their political ties with Palestine, they still regarded it as their spiritual homeland. Every Jew sent his annual tax of half a shekel for the maintenance of the Temple, and endeavored at least once in his life to visit that sacred shrine. The religious leaders of Palestine carried on a regular correspondence with Jewish communities in many lands, and their authority was generally recognized. The fact that the Jews in so many countries were a minority, compact, distinctive, and not assimilable, was bound to have far-reaching consequences.

The Jewish Diaspora (dispersion) began no later than 597 B.C.E., when the first exiles were removed to Babylonia. After the fall of the state, some of the survivors in Judah made an unsuccessful attempt at revolt; then fearful of punishment, they fled to Egypt, forcing the aged Jeremiah to go with them. Jewish settlement in Egypt continued thenceforth. We have interesting records from the fifth century of a Jewish military colony which the Persians established to garrison an island in the Nile. These Jews for a time had a temple of their own, which the Egyptians destroyed. Much later, during the intrigues that preceded the Maccabean revolt, a High Priest named Onias was forced to leave Jerusalem and was replaced by a favorite of King Antiochus. Onias fled to Egypt and established a temple in the city of Leontopolis, where he and his descendants officiated for several centuries.

Meanwhile, during the entire period of the Second Temple, Jews left the homeland, chiefly for economic reasons, and settled throughout the ancient world. Eastward into Persia (which had again become independent in 250 B.C.E. under the Parthians), northward into Syria and Asia Minor as far as the Black Sea, westward to the Mediterranean shores of Africa and Europe, Jewish traders and settlers made their way. By the beginning of the Christian Era, they were found in almost every land and city. Rome in particular had a large Jewish population; such writers as Cicero and Horace repeatedly mention the Jews, generally in hostile tones.

But the ancient Jewish Diaspora can be studied best in the great seaport at the mouth of the Nile which Alexander had founded and named for himself.

2. Alexandria

Ancient Alexandria reminds one strikingly of modern New York. It was big, busy, and cosmopolitan, without much national background.

Its language and culture were Hellenistic, Egyptians being second-class citizens. Alexandria was the center for the sophisticates both of art and of pleasure. Here were the great library, the philosophic academies, the Bohemian colonies, the refinements of vice, the head-quarters of every odd religious cult, the sporty crowd, the artists and would-be artists, the serious proponents of new ideas.

And here, as in New York today, was a huge Jewish population, which occupied several quarters of the city. So tremendous was the synagogue of Alexandria that the voice of the prayer-leader was lost in its vastness, and it was necessary to signal by waving a flag when the congregation was to respond. Though they did not have equal rights of citizenship with the Greeks, the Jews had achieved a position of considerable dignity and prestige and many of them occupied important posts.

In outward matters, they were completely assimilated. Greek was their mother tongue; most of them knew little Hebrew or Aramaic.

As early as the third pre-Christian century, need was felt for a Greek version of the Torah; and thereafter all the sacred writings were translated into Greek. This translation, known as the Septuagint, was so highly revered by the Alexandrian Jews that few of them troubled to study the original. It is still of great interest today, for it shows us how the Bible was understood and interpreted more than two thousand years ago. It marks the first step in that process of translation by which the Hebrew Bible has become the possession of all peoples.

The constant and intimate contact between Jew and Greek in Alexandria led naturally to a cultural interchange. In Alexandria as in Palestine, there were some Jews who left the Jewish fold altogether under the spell of Hellenism—in its nobler or its baser forms. But in Alexandria, the impact of Jewish life and thought was felt in the Greek world; and on the other hand, loyal and devoted Jews, who defended and championed their own faith, did not hesitate to borrow valuable elements from their Hellenistic environment. An interesting example is the poet Ezekielos, who retold some of the Bible stories in Greek verse. We still possess a few lines of his drama, "The Exodus."

Such a subject might seem an unpopular choice for presentation in Egypt, since it depicts the Egyptians and their king as wicked. Apparently many Egyptians were familiar with the Biblical history, and resented it. This may have been one of the reasons for the bitter anti-Jewish feeling which flared up from time to time in Alexandria.

But the "anti-Semitism" of this period seems to have been rooted in the general position of the Jews as we have described it. They were active and even prominent members of the Alexandrian community, yet their religion set them apart. Though all the inhabitants of the Roman Empire were required to pay divine honors to the statues of the emperors, the Jews were by law exempted from this requirement. This made it easy for men of ill will to question their patriotism. Their refusal to eat at the tables of non-Jews must likewise have been a source of irritation.

An Egyptian named Apion who wrote in Greek accused the Jews of hating all mankind, especially the Greeks. The inner shrine of their Temple in Jerusalem, he declared, contained the image of an ass' head, to which they annually sacrificed a Gentile victim. He also peddled a tale that the ancestors of Jews had not left Egypt in triumph, but had been expelled by Pharaoh because they were infected with leprosy!

As today Jews find it necessary to counteract anti-Semitic ideas, so it was then We know of Apion, in fact, only from a reply written by Josephus, the Jewish historian. Josephus was a Palestinian; but he wrote in Greek, and probably drew on Alexandrian materials for his defense of the Jews. He answered the foolish charges of Apion, heaping ridicule and abuse on his opponent; and then presented a noble statement of the truth and glory of his religion. And he pointed out— what perhaps was one reason for the hostility of Alexandrian and Roman writers—that the Jewish religion, with its doctrine of the one invisible God and its lofty ethics, as well as the Sabbath and other observances, had been widely adopted by the Gentile world.

Converts to Judaism were in fact very numerous, and the Jews carried on a deliberate propaganda to win them. The ancient world possessed several collections of cryptic verse in Greek, ascribed to heathen prophetesses called Sybils, which allegedly foretold the future of Rome and were consulted in times of crises. Some Jewish writers composed new books of Sybilline oracles, in which the ancient pagan seeress proclaimed the unity of God, denied the reality of the heathen deities, and summoned the Gentiles to repent and convert before the coming of the last judgment.

Thus the contact between Judaism and Hellenism, which provoked antagonism toward the Jews on the part of some pagans, attracted others to the Jewish faith. But this same contact produced remarkable effects on the minds of many earnest Jewish thinkers—effects which were to have far-reaching consequences for the history of all human thought. We must now examine the first attempts to combine Jewish religion with Greek philosophy.

3. *Alexandrian Philosophy*

Repeatedly, Judaism has had to encounter the challenge of philosophic thinking. Some Jews, charmed by the new doctrines, have abandoned Judaism for another, more fashionable "ism." Others, sensing a possible danger to faith, have refused to know anything about philosophy. But some of the greatest Jewish teachers, in different ages, have seen in new philosophies a means of enriching Judaism, or at least of displaying the contemporary relevance of their religion; and these teachers have attempted to harmonize their Jewish beliefs with the prevailing philosophy of the age. The first instance of this sort occurred in the city of Alexandria.

Philosophy is no trifling subject to master. While our presentation will seem superficial to those well grounded in general philosophy, it may impose some strain on the reader without previous training in the field. Without attempting a full exposition, we shall try at least to indicate the problems with which men struggled in various generations.

By philosophy we mean a study of the basic questions of existence (including human existence and conduct) in a broad inclusive manner, and by the systematic application of reason. On the one hand, philosophy is analytical, examining, testing, and criticizing the evidence and ideas under discussion. On the other hand, it attempts to organize ideas and facts into a logical and consistent pattern. Philosophy in this sense was the creation of the Greeks. The ancient Orient had produced a great literature of "wisdom," but that consisted largely of shrewd observations on individual points of conduct. The prophets and seers of Israel had discovered profound and indeed decisive truths of ethics and religion; but they had arrived at these discoveries by intuition and inspiration. They did not prove them by logic, but rather proclaimed them with burning enthusiasm. The philosophic method was introduced by the great thinkers of Hellas.

The great problem of Greek philosophy was to attain a unified view of life. The world appears to us as a confusion of numberless disconnected things and occurrences; and all this variety and conflict trouble our minds. How can we find a simple explanation which will bring order and unity into this confusion?

The earliest Greek thinkers tried to find a single physical substance, of which all existing things are but modifications. Later, they sought a governing and unifying *principle* in the universe, which they called by such terms as mind (*nous*) or word (*logos*). Thus they moved gradually toward monotheism—not as an ethical-religious faith, but rather as a scientific hypothesis.

For our present purpose, the most important of the philosophers was the great Athenian sage, Plato (about 427–347 B.C.E.). He first made an adequate and clear-cut distinction between matter and spirit. The physical universe, he declared, is an imperfect replica of the world of ideas, which is perfect and eternal. Any material object— say, a tree—is a partial, incomplete, and temporary embodiment of the *idea* of a tree. Unlike the material tree, the idea of the tree is universal and all-inclusive; it is not subject to destruction or decay; it is perfect and eternal. Thus for Plato, the genuine and permanent realities are intellectual—mathematical relationships, for instance, and such general ideas as truth, justice, and beauty. The visible universe is secondary and derivative. But when Plato tries to explain how the physical world came into existence from the world of ideas, his language is so figurative and mythological that we are not certain just what he meant.

But Plato's distinction between mind and matter opened the way to a new conception of the nature of man. Virtually all ancient peoples agreed that man consists of a body and a soul; but they thought of the soul as a material substance, somewhat less solid than the body. It was often identified with the breath or the blood. Plato, however, taught that the soul is absolutely immaterial. It is therefore not subject to destruction or disintegration (for they affect only physical things) and is truly immortal. Insofar as immortality is achieved, it is won by dedicating the soul to ideal values while it is still within the "prison house" of the body; it has nothing to do with embalming or elaborately provisioned tombs, which primitive peoples relied on.*

Thus it happened that while in Palestine, people thought of immortality in terms of bodily resurrection; an Alexandrian Jew could write:

---

* Plato's own argument for immortality is more complicated; but it is based ultimately on the premise we have stated.

"The souls of the righteous are in the hand of God
And no torment shall touch them.
In the eyes of the foolish they seemed to have died,
And their departure was accounted to be their hurt,
And their journeying away from us to be their ruin:
But they are in peace.
For even if in the sight of men they are punished,
Their hope is full of immortality."

These beautiful lines are from a book called *The Wisdom of Solomon*, which reflects the influence of Greek ideas—sometimes by adopting them, sometimes by reaction against them.

The Alexandrian schools of philosophy flourished at the beginning of the Christian Era and for several hundred years thereafter—some centuries later than Plato. To thinkers of this period, the basic problem of "the one and the many" appeared in a new form. The earlier Greeks sought to find unity in a complicated world; the Jewish and also the non-Jewish philosophers of Alexandria tried to understand how so complex a world could issue from the Primal Unity. Under the discipline of Greek logic, the one-ness of God was taught in the strictest terms:

God is one—therefore He cannot be material. For matter is divisible, and therefore not a perfect unity.

God is infinite. For if He were finite, He would not be perfect.

God is perfect—therefore He cannot change. For any change would be either for the better or the worse. If God could change for the better, He would not be perfect; if He were to change for the worse, He would cease to be perfect.

But how could an immaterial God produce a material universe? How could an infinite God produce a finite world? How could a changeless God create something that is constantly changing?

The Alexandrian thinkers all gave the same general answer to this problem, though the tone and emphasis of the answer varied greatly. The Jewish version is found at its best in the writings of Philo, an outstanding figure of the first century c.e. By temperament, tradition, and faith, an enthusiastic Jew, Philo was widely read in Greek philosophy and poetry. He drew on the thought of many philosophic schools, but his greatest debt was to Plato. His object was not to win fame as an original thinker, but to bring men to God and to His law. His writings are therefore chiefly expositions of various sections of the

Torah. The simpler treatises seem to be addressed to Gentiles: they display the sublimity, ethical excellence, and human kindliness of Judaism. For Jews who like himself were saturated with Greek culture, Philo composed more elaborate works, which attempt to prove that whatever is true in Greek philosophy had already been taught by Moses.

But this method raised a new problem—the unphilosophic language of the Bible. The Torah speaks of God's hands and eyes; it reports that God became angry, or sad, or changed His mind; it pictures Him as descending from heaven to earth. Does this not contradict our logical conclusions that God is incorporeal, changeless, and infinite? Philo's answer was to become standard for centuries: the Biblical expressions are not to be taken literally. They are figures of speech, allegories. When the Torah speaks of God's eyes, it means not that He possesses physical organs of vision, but that He knows all that happens; and so for all the other difficult phrases.

In some cases, such explanations are doubtless correct; yet Philo and his successors "explained away" many a Biblical passage by sophisticated interpretations which would have puzzled the original author. Moreover, once you embark on the allegorical method, there is no end to it. For Philo, the deep, inner meaning of whole chapters is symbolic. The story of Cain and Abel, for example, depicts a struggle that goes on in every soul—between the acquisitive instinct that ascribes all power to self, and the piety that ascribes all inner and outer possessions to God.

By means of allegory, Philo was able to attach his philosophic views to the Torah. What were these views? First, Philo is overwhelmed by the reality of God, the only true, perfect, and fully existent Reality. Second, this imperfect and changing universe was brought into existence and is governed by means of the logos.

Now logos, which means *word* or *reason*, was the term used by some Greek thinkers for a governing principle in the universe. Philo often identifies the logos with Plato's world of ideas. God first created the ideal world, and this served as a blue-print for the visible world. This theory fitted in well with the passages of Scripture which represent God as creating the world by a command—that is, a word, or logos.

But Philo employs this term in a variety of meanings. Sometimes the logos is an idea in the mind of God. Sometimes it seems to be an actual being (Philo even speaks of the logos as the "first born son of God!") endowed with great authority in the government of the world.

Often the logos is no more than a figurative expression for God's influence on human life. For while as a philosopher Philo sought to keep God far from this material, changeable, corruptible world, as a devout Jew he would not and could not separate God from relationship to man. Philo constantly asserts that in all our experiences we must recognize God's rulership and His goodness. This apparent contradiction finds its solution in Philo's mysticism.

4. *The Mystic Vision*

Mysticism means a direct, immediate sense of God's Presence. It is the summit and essence of personal religious living. It was the experience of the great prophets, and finds utterance in many of the Psalms:

> "I am continually with Thee,
> Thou holdest my right hand . . .
> Whom have I in heaven but Thee?
> And beside Thee I desire none upon earth . . .
> Whither shall I go from Thy spirit?
> Or whither shall I flee from Thy presence?"

It is akin to that surge of exaltation and peace which the average person may feel as he looks at the stars on a clear night.

But the more determined mystics—and they are found in all the advanced religions—do not content themselves with such occasional moments of inspiration. They seek by consistent self-discipline and self-purification, and by various practices of meditation and prayer to attain a more constant and intense union with God.

The mystic experience, for one who has known it, is its own justification. The mystic does not argue about God; he has possessed Him. On the other hand, the mystic vision cannot be communicated adequately; it is as indescribable as a flavor. For this reason, some mystics have tried to avoid speaking of their experience. Others have described their quest and its fulfilment in symbols that are difficult to understand. In the course of our study, we shall meet whole groups of mystics, and a number of popular mystical movements. The religion and philosophy of Alexandria was, in fact, strongly tinged with mysticism.

Philo often refers to moments of vision when the soul (as he puts it) seems not only to leave the body, but to flee from its very self, drawn upward in ecstasy toward God. I have heard, he declares, "a voice in my own soul, which oft-times is God-possessed, and divines where it does not know." Such inner experience, not only strengthened the noble character and ardent piety of Philo, but also provided a unifying factor in his thought. God is indeed remote from matter. But Philo insists that in every man there is a spark of divinity, that reaches out to its Fount and Origin. By rising above material desires, by disciplining the mind and purifying the heart, man can come into direct contact with the Eternal. Thus, the changeless and unknowable God is also the vital and inescapable Power in our lives.

5. The Decline of Alexandrian Jewry

After the first century of the Christian Era, the Jewish community of Alexandria fell upon evil days. Its numbers dwindled and its importance shrank. The original ideas and methods of Alexandrian Judaism had almost no influence on the development of the Jewish religion in subsequent centuries. The inspiring *Wisdom of Solomon,* the prophecies of the Jewish "Sybil," the works of the wise and noble Philo, even the old Greek translation of the Bible were preserved only by the Christian church. The very name of Philo did not appear in any Hebrew book until the sixteenth century.

How shall we explain the fact that this new interpretation of Judaism, which had so many merits, was lost or ignored by the main body of Jewry? Was it because it detached itself from the Hebrew language (or its near relative, Aramaic) that the Jews of Palestine and Babylonia regarded it as basically foreign? The fact that the rising Christian church was for a long time a Greek-speaking body, in which the Septuagint altogether replaced the Hebrew Bible, may have had something to do with this.

Or was there objection to the basic character of Hellenistic Jewish thought? The official Judaism of Palestine, as we shall see, was generally opposed to allegorical explanation of the Torah. Such a method makes it possible to read anything into any Bible passage. It is especially risky when applied to laws.

Philo, indeed, insisted that though it is important to know the inner symbolic meaning of the commandments, it is equally important to obey them literally. But others, it appears, were less conscientious. Expounding the dietary laws, they seem to have argued that such laws really teach us that we must control our animal appetites; but once this is understood, one may eat in moderation of whatever food he desires. Judaism, however, survived largely through its pattern of consistent observances. Was it because of their indifference to these things that Alexandrian Jewry ceased to influence Jewish life?

Or was the decline simply due to economic and political disaster, and to persecution by Christian rulers? Or was there a combination of causes?

It is difficult to answer these questions. But the fact remains that, despite its intellectual vitality, its cosmopolitan breadth, and its cultured tolerance, Hellenistic Judaism is but a bypath in this history. The main road of Judaism took a very different direction.

Only a thousand years later did Alexandrian ideas, by a very indirect route, arrive at a junction with the central developments of the Jewish religion.

16.

Birth of a New Religion

PERHAPS THERE WILL NEVER BE AN ENTIRELY UNPREJUDICED WORD written about Jesus of Nazareth. So glamorous is his personality, that even those Christians who have ceased to regard him as divine are still under his spell and usually see in him something different and better than the rest of humankind. Jews, having suffered so long and so much in his name, are likely to approach him with a certain prejudice, or else, in the effort to avoid this, to go to the opposite extreme. There is especially broad room for these subjective reactions because the facts about the man are so uncertain.

All our information about him comes from the New Testament, and chiefly from the first three Gospels, known as the Synoptic Gospels. But these writings are full of miracle stories; they contain some statements that contradict known historic facts, and other episodes that are psychologically unconvincing. In addition, they frequently contradict themselves and one another. In the absence of any solid external evidence, some scholars have even declared that no such person as Jesus ever lived; and we cannot give absolute proof that he did exist.

But all the probabilities are that Jesus was a historical figure. Assuming this, and assuming that the Gospels contain some true information about him, however overlaid with legend and propaganda, what are the probable facts of his life? These briefly: that he was born in Galilee (not Bethlehem), had a modest education in the Judaism of the Pharisees, and when he was in his late twenties became a wandering teacher and preacher. This change came about under the influence of one John the Baptist, a man of Essene tendencies, who was teaching that the end of the world, "the Kingdom of God," was at hand.

Jesus acquired a small following and went about the country for several years. His influence and reputation must have been limited; the country was full of wandering religious men, some emphasizing orthodox principles, others expounding new and strange doctrines. They did not create a great stir except within the circle of their own adherents.

Then the notion arose that this Jesus was the long awaited Messiah. How this happened we cannot be sure. Perhaps Jesus got the idea and announced it to his disciples; perhaps in their enthusiasm for him they hailed him as the deliverer and convinced him that he must be the chosen one. At any rate he and his disciples went up to Jerusalem for the Passover in the year 30. Passover was always a time of considerable tension. Great masses of Jews from all over the world assembled at the Temple for the festival; national feeling was bound to run high. The sight of Roman soldiers keeping order in the Holy City was a natural irritant. The Zealots were constantly trying to whip up the people to revolt. When, therefore, messianic honors were paid to Jesus, a situation was created which might have led to a serious outbreak against Rome. Jesus was arrested and executed as a rebel, by order of the Roman governor, Pontius Pilate.

He was probably not the first, and certainly not the last, to meet such a fate. One Theudas, who claimed to be a prophet and miracle worker and apparently planned a revolt against Rome, was similarly executed a few years later. The Gospels assert that Jesus was denounced to the Roman governor by Jewish officials. This may well have happened. The collaborationists whom the Romans had given authority over the Temple and city must have been desperately anxious to curry favor with their masters by restraining the angry people and forestalling an open outbreak. Such men may have deemed it prudent to get rid of a dangerous "fanatic." But the people as a whole never demanded the death of Jesus. Few of them had so much as heard his name.

So great was the impression he had made on the little group of his followers that they could not give him up even after his death. They had visions in which he appeared to them, assuring them that he had risen from the dead, and that he would soon return to them. They had no intention of establishing a new religion. They were loyal and observant Jews who believed that Jesus was the Messiah. In accordance with God's mysterious will he had suffered death; but he had been resurrected and taken up into heaven. At any moment they expected his return, when he would reveal himself in full messianic splendor and establish the kingdom of God.

They organized themselves into a closely knit community, sharing all their possessions, zealously spreading their doctrine. Their enthusiasm won them a number of adherents, Gentiles as well as Jews; but they also roused resentment, and were the objects of persecution. The attacks on the new sect, however, were not approved by Rabban Gamaliel the Elder, Hillel's grandson, who was the leader of the Pharisees. Both in Jewish and Christian writings Gamaliel appears as a man of unusual wisdom and broad tolerance.

The teaching of the new sect did not mean the same thing to Gentile converts that it meant to native Jews. The latter were familiar with the word Messiah; but when Gentiles heard that Jesus was the Christ (the Greek for "anointed"), the term appeared to them rather as a proper name. Moreover, the story of the crucifixion and resurrection must have had a familiar ring, for the myth and ritual of many pagan cults centered around a god who died, or was killed, and then was restored to life.

Yet the transformation of the Christian sect into an independent church was due chiefly to a Jew—Saul of Tarsus. A native of Asia Minor, Saul was well versed in Greek literature and ideas. He had come to Palestine and studied under Rabban Gamaliel; but though he prided himself on being a devoted Pharisee, it is doubtful if he ever understood the inner spirit of Pharisaism. For a time, he was a bitter enemy of the Christians and tried to stir up hatred against them. Suddenly, as the result of a vision, Saul became a convert to the new sect. Calling himself Paul (the "little man"), he devoted his tremendous energy and extraordinary gifts to his new faith.

Paul had never known the living Jesus. He interpreted his overwhelming personal experience in the light of his own background, which was more Greek than Jewish. His chief concern was not with the earthly career and teaching of Jesus, but with his death and resurrection as a redemptive sacrifice for mankind.

According to Paul, the offense of Adam and Eve produced a sinfulness which was transmitted to all their descendants. This is the doctrine of "original sin," which regards sin not as an act but as a sort of chronic disability. The giving of the Torah did not correct the situation, but made it worse. For though the Torah is holy, no man can obey it adequately. God gave it, in fact, to make us aware of our desperate plight. To Paul, Jesus was no mere religious teacher, prophet, or national deliverer, but a divine being, sinless and perfect, who donned the garment of mortal flesh for the sake of sinful man. By his voluntary suffering and death he redeemed man from the heritage of Adam's sin and from bondage to the Law. By faith in him, by accepting him as savior—and thus alone—can men be made worthy of the resurrection and of eternal life. These ideas, which Paul propagated with enormous persistence and persuasiveness, made Christianity a different religion, and indeed a different *kind* of religion, from Judaism. For Judaism is a religious discipline of acts and duties; Pauline Christianity is a scheme of salvation achieved through faith. Moreover, Judaism is centered around a divine command, Christianity around a divine person.

Paul's view that the Torah has been superseded by the sacrifice of Jesus opened the way for a revolutionary proposal. Let us become missionaries to the Gentiles, he urged, bringing them good tidings of salvation which they may accept without assuming the burden of the ceremonial law! The proposal was not adopted at once. The older Christians were loyal Jews who, like Jesus himself, had always obeyed the Torah; they were inclined to accept only such Gentile converts as conformed to the usual requirements for a convert to Judaism. But after a short struggle Paul's influence prevailed. A world-wide missionary movement was launched. The results were phenomenal. The Gentile group soon outnumbered the Jewish Christians; and instead of being a Jewish sect, Christianity became an independent religion. The doctrinal departures which Paul had made were carried still further. The author of the Fourth Gospel took up the idea of the logos, which Philo had taught. This divine spirit, which had existed eternally with God, was made flesh in the person of Jesus. Eventually, the Church evolved the doctrine of the trinity, and Jesus was worshipped as God.

Gentile Christianity became not only un-Jewish but anti-Jewish. The story of Jesus was modified by bitter interpolations. Pontius Pilate—according to the Roman historians, a brute and a bully, who hated the Jews he had to govern and abused them on every occasion —was represented as a kindly soul who did not want to crucify Jesus. He wished to spare him in accordance with a custom (known only to the Gospel writer) of releasing a condemned criminal in honor of the Passover. The Jews however (as if all the Jews in the world were in front of Pilate's house!) unanimously demanded that another criminal be released instead, and formally took upon themselves and their posterity forever the responsibility for the blood of Jesus. Moreover, Jesus was made to appear as the uncompromising foe of the Pharisees; hence the distorted notion of them now possessed by the world. In the Fourth Gospel, Jesus is depicted as coldly hostile to the Jews, and reserves his friendly interest for Gentiles only.

The absolute division between Judaism and the Jewish branch of Christianity did not occur until about a century after the death of Jesus. By that time the two religions were not only completely apart but mutually hostile. But before we speak of these things, let us return to Jesus and see what he taught. This is the more important because many liberal Christians of today, abandoning the doctrines of Paul, rejecting the belief in the trinity and the divinity of Jesus, insist that his own teachings are of paramount worth. Not a religion *about* Jesus, but the religion *of* Jesus, they assert, is the pinnacle of human faith. What then was the religion of Jesus?

So far as we can judge, it was 90 per cent the Judaism of the Pharisees. "Not one jot or tittle of the Law," he declared, "shall pass away." True, he was indifferent to some Pharisaic refinements which the common people found burdensome and for which there was no scriptural warrant; but his attitudes were generally Pharisaic (like those of most Jews in his time) and his teachings were drawn largely from the common stock of Pharisaic lore. Most of the sayings and parables of Jesus have close parallels either in the Hebrew Bible or the Talmudic literature. In his emphasis on the ethical and devotional aspects of Judaism rather than on the legalistic ones, he did not differ from many of the Pharisaic teachers. Some of the latter were specialists in *halakah*—law—others were devotees of the *aggadah*—the non-legal teachings. The chief contribution that Jesus made in this respect was one of personal charm; his sayings and parables as recorded in the Gospels are particularly beautiful.

In two respects, however, Jesus diverged from the main body of Pharisaic thought. One was his heavy emphasis on the coming end of the world. "The Kingdom of God is among you," he declared, that is, it is "just around the corner." This explains the extreme form of many of Jesus' teachings: his insistence on making no provision for his material needs and his advice to his followers to get rid of all their possessions. With the end of the world at hand, the only thing to do is to concentrate on preparing oneself spiritually—all external concerns and responsibilities are a snare.

This may also explain Jesus' predilection for "sinners," in contrast to his decided impatience with the smugly respectable. The latter may be socially useful, may be good citizens, but their very respectability prevents them from turning humbly and penitently to God. Those who have been moral failures—the criminal and the prostitute —are better prospects for the revivalist, seeking completely to transform men in anticipation of the end of the present world.

This was a difference in emphasis, but not in substance; for the Pharisees also expected the end of days. But altogether new with Jesus, so far as we can judge, was his radical doctrine of non-resistance. "Love your enemies," he preached; "resist not evil; but whosoever smiteth thee on thy right cheek, turn to him the other also." This is indeed sublime, though perhaps beyond the power of human beings to accept. It has but rarely been followed by the adherents of Jesus; indeed, he did not always follow it himself. Judaism has advocated meekness, forgiveness, and even the acceptance of insult without retaliation; but it has not counseled passive submission to violence and injustice.

It is necessary, however, to set definite limits to the originality of Jesus. He did not—as Christian writers frequently assert—add anything to the concept of God and His relation to man. To say that Jesus originated the idea of the God of Love, or of God as Father, is to disregard plain statements of the Hebrew Bible. Nor was Jesus a teacher of social righteousness, as were Amos and Isaiah. Despite his warm human sympathies, he was hardly interested in social problems as such, because he was preoccupied with the imminent world judgment. He taught (by precept and example) the disregard of family responsibilities and of communal duties; he advocated withdrawal from the problems of social life rather than their solution. When he urged the rich young ruler to sell all his possessions and give the proceeds to the poor, he was concerned primarily not with the material benefit to the poor but with the spiritual benefit which would accrue to the young ruler when he had no more financial cares and could live the spiritually carefree life of a beggar.

The chief significance of Jesus in history is not what he taught, but what was believed about him. As regards his own doctrine, he has chiefly the glory of proclaiming the enchanting, if not entirely practicable, doctrine of non-resistance to evil. For the rest, his sayings are a particularly beautiful formulation of sound rabbinic doctrine. It appears however impossible for Judaism ever completely to recapture Jesus for its own. First, his teachings are preserved in a work which mixes with his noble sayings many theological ideas—a God-man, vicarious atonement, and the like—that are not compatible with Judaism. It also contains bitterly hostile and even slanderous attacks on the Jews and Judaism. And then, the religion which deified Jesus began a systematic oppression of the people from which he sprang.

For three centuries, Christianity made rapid progress, despite ridicule and persecution. Its spokesmen spread their doctrine with magnificent zeal; many died heroically as martyrs. The Emperor Constantine 1 (died 337) became a convert to the advancing faith and made it the official religion of the Roman Empire. Before long paganism was outlawed, Christianity was recognized as the sole legitimate religion, and the leaders of the Church and the Empire worked together closely. The culture of the Roman world was greatly modified by Christian influences; but the outlook and the spirit of the Church was also greatly changed by the acquisition of power and the realities of imperial politics and administration.

The Jews and Judaism constituted, as we shall see, a problem for all Christian states. Judaism could not be outlawed as paganism had been; for it was, after all, a religion revealed by the same God whom the Church proclaimed. On the other hand, the refusal of the Jews to acknowledge the divinity of Jesus and the story of their alleged responsibility for his death made them the targets of popular hatred and of ecclesiastical oppression. The triumph of Christianity in the Roman Empire marked the beginning of a movement to degrade, oppress, and persecute the people of Jesus and the religion in which he had grown up.

17.

Judah and Rome

WE HAVE SEEN THAT ROME GRADUALLY BECAME THE DIRECT RULER OF
Judea. She had long since been the mistress of thousands of Jews
living in the Diaspora, many of whom had acquired Roman citizenship. Early in her relations with the Jewish people, the Mistress of
the World recognized that she had to deal with a unique group. The
Jews in Palestine and elsewhere were granted special privileges. Chief
of these was their right to abstain from the worship of the emperor.
This cult was in truth more political than religious; it was deemed a
good policy to place the statues of the dead Caesars in all the temples
of the empire and to exact divine honors for them. But the Jews
would never have consented to such a requirement, and in the interests of tranquillity they were officially excused from it. Even the
Roman soldiery that patrolled the city of Jerusalem could not bring its
eagle-topped standards into the city; the people would not tolerate
graven images within its holy precincts.

But despite such concessions, the Jews of Palestine grew more and
more restive. A series of Roman governors, one more oppressive than
the other, ruled Palestine. Such posts were regarded in Rome as opportunities for making a fortune by graft and by systematically robbing the populace under pretext of taxation. Not a rich country to
start with, Judea groaned under the burdens.

But though other subject peoples submitted in silence to Rome's
overwhelming might, the Jews were not cowed. "You are the only
people," one of their leaders remarked, "who think it a disgrace to be

servants to those to whom the whole world has submitted." For the Jews were conscious of their own spiritual superiority. The Romans were unredeemed heathens, idolatrous, immoral, and brutal. They did not even have the intellectual and artistic polish of the Greeks. Many of their best spirits were converts to Judaism. The day must soon come when Israel's vassalage, a punishment for past sins, would be over; and the Messiah, overthrowing the might of Rome, would set up the Kingdom of God with its capital in Jerusalem.

This attitude was intensified by the tax-gouging and oppressive laws of the Roman governors. The latter were fully aware that the Jews not only hated them, but held them in contempt—and of course this made the Roman rulers the more hostile, so that the situation steadily grew worse. But for a long time, the Jews were divided as to policy. The hot-heads of the Zealot party, whether fanatics or mere desperadoes, constantly urged revolt. The aristocrats, including the priestly Sadducees, sought to collaborate with the Roman authorities. Most of the Pharisees as well sought to keep the peace. As practical men, they realized that revolt would lead to disaster; but they also believed that religion required them not to force the hand of destiny. Only when the Messiah arrived and clearly manifested himself as the legitimate king of Israel would it be possible to throw off the Roman yoke.

Gradually the masses lost patience and rejected the leadership of the moderates. In 66 c.e. an "incident" occurred which led to open rebellion. The war that followed lasted four terrible years. Despite some early successes, the cause of the Jews was clearly hopeless; but the people fought every inch of the way with a heroism born perhaps of despair.

Only one leader showed weakness, Joseph ben Mattithiah, who was to attain dubious fame under the name of Flavius Josephus. Joseph was of priestly family, but he had studied the lore of the Pharisees and had lived for a time among the Essenes. He was also a man of the world, who was at home in Alexandria and Rome. He was made a general of the Jewish armies in Galilee; after a crushing defeat, he surrendered (though none of his army followed his example) to the Roman general, Vespasian. In time, he won the favor of his captors. His later years were spent in Rome, where he wrote extended histories of the Jewish people, treating both ancient times and the events of his own day, Josephus naturally sought to justify his own shady conduct, and to flatter his imperial patrons. But he sought also to present the history and religion of Israel in such a way as to win respect for his people and faith. His voluminous writings (some were composed in Greek, the others were translated into that language from his Aramaic original) served the cause of "public relations" in his own time, and have remained a valuable source for Jewish history up to the present.

The other leaders, not so clever and worldly, were braver and more determined; but they were no more successful. The Jewish armies were shattered, and the siege of Jerusalem began. After months of desperate fighting, the capital fell. Against the orders of Titus (who had succeeded his father Vespasian as the Roman commander in Palestine) the Temple was burned. Thousands died in the fighting or because of the rigors of war; thousands more were sold into slavery. The Jewish nation had all but ceased to exist.

Once more the end of Judaism seemed imminent. The material bases of Jewish life—human resources, property, national polity—were largely destroyed. The central institution of Israel, the Temple, the rallying point of world-Jewry, was gone. The prestige of Israel's God had been—presumably—impaired by His failure to protect His earthly abode. The messianic dream had led to utter disillusionment.

But amazing inner resources were left. An ancient writer reports that a number of Roman soldiers deserted to the Jewish side during the siege of Jerusalem, convinced by the heroism of its defenders that theirs was indeed a living God. Be this as it may, it is certain that during the century after the fall of the Temple, a number of converts to Judaism were made among the most aristocratic families of Rome—a striking testimony that the soul of Israel was still unconquered. Pharisaic Judaism had already provided adequate substitutes for Temple and priesthood in the Synagogue, a living Torah, and something like universal education. And it also provided leadership. "There were giants in the earth in those days."

The crisis was intensely dramatic; yet seemingly, nothing much came of it. The last of Hillel's pupils, Johanan ben Zakkai, was now a very old man. Before the final catastrophe, he managed to escape from the city, and to get an audience with Vespasian just before the latter was proclaimed emperor. All that he obtained—and apparently all he asked—was the right to establish a school in the village of Jabneh which should be protected against molestation. This seemingly trivial concession was as much as the aged teacher required. While the physical forces of Judea were going down into the dust, he was already engaged in building a new social and religious structure that was to endure and flourish long after imperial Rome was a faded memory.

Through the synagogue and the school, Johanan ben Zakkai sought to rehabilitate Jewish life. Presiding as Nasi over the Sanhedrin of scholars, he promulgated numerous decrees, modifying Jewish practice in accordance with the changed conditions. After his death the presidency reverted to the family of Hillel, in the person of a second Gamaliel. The new Nasi devoted all his great energies to standardizing Jewish religious procedure. Around the banner of a Torah universally studied and systematically observed, the ranks of Israel regrouped, and a new period of great productiveness began.

The work of the school of Jabneh began about the year 70, just before the fall of the Temple. Less than sixty-five years later another rebellion against Rome broke out. We know little about this second war. It was headed by a man called Bar Kochba ("Son of the Star") who was hailed even by the great Rabbi Akiba as the Messiah. Under his bold leadership, the Jews fought the professional soldiers of Rome with such success that the emperor called his ablest general from Britain to put down the revolt. Only after three years of heroic resistance was the last Jewish stronghold captured. Then followed a long period of relentless persecution. People were put to death for teaching the Torah, and for observing such cardinal practices as circumcision and Sabbath rest. And yet the survival of Judaism was never really in doubt. In a little more than half a century, Johanan ben Zakkai and his colleagues had given Judaism a coherence and a driving power that enabled it to continue and to advance toward larger possibilities. The character, methods, and ideals of this Rabbinic Judaism must now be considered.

Part 3.

The Study of Torah

18.

The World of the Rabbis

IN THE DAYS OF JESUS, THE TERM RABBI—MY MASTER—WAS STILL only an expression of respect used in addressing an older or more learned person, the equivalent of our "sir." But a half-century later it became a title, indicating that its bearer had been duly recognized by the authorities—the heads of the Sanhedrin—as a competent authority on Jewish law. The disciples of Johanan ben Zakkai were the first to bear the title of Rabbi, while Johanan and his successors in the office of Nasi bore the special style of Rabban—*our* master. From this point on we speak of Rabbinic Judaism instead of Pharisaic Judaism. The change is all the more appropriate since, with the fall of the Temple, the power of the priests, and hence the Sadducean party, practically disappeared. Pharisaism was no longer a sect but the Judaism of the overwhelming majority, and the Rabbis were its spokesmen and interpreters.*

The Judaism of the Rabbis is also called "Talmudic" because the Talmud is the creation of this period and the chief source of our information about it. We shall deal with this epoch in considerable fullness, and this for several reasons. First, Talmudic Judaism possesses in itself great interest and merit, which have too often been obscured by ignorance and misrepresentation. Second, traditional Judaism, especially on the side of observance, remains to this day very much as

---

* The custom of ordination was unquestionably older than this—tradition traced it to Moses!—but the *title* of Rabbi dates from this time.

the Rabbis of the Talmud left it. Third, the Talmud has been the chief authority in Jewish life. True, the Bible was theoretically the ultimate authority, but the Bible was understood as the Talmud interpreted it. On the other hand, later codes were accepted only insofar as their decisions were in accord with the Talmud.

These chapters will not tell, except incidentally, the fascinating story of the Talmud as a literary work—they will attempt to recreate the life and attitudes which that great work mirrors.

From the time when the written Torah was accepted as the norm of Jewish life, and people began to study it and to try to practice it, problems of interpretation began to arise. This is the case with any written legal document or constitution, but it was especially true of a sacred document which could not be directly amended. Thus, there grew up a substantial body of "oral Torah," parallel and supplementary to the written Torah.

The Oral Law included the following elements:

1. Clarification of the Written Law. For instance, the Torah forbids work on the Sabbath, but the only task specifically prohibited is the kindling of fire. What other activities are to be defined as work? Is it work to write? to study? to carry one's overcoat? And so on. The Torah contains three times the cryptic command: "Thou shalt not seethe a kid in its mother's milk." What does this mean?

2. Extension of the law to cases not specifically mentioned in the Torah. Thus the law forbids plowing with an ox and ass yoked together. The oral Torah, concerned to prevent cruelty, extends this to any case of animals of different species and unequal size. Such extensions and applications of the Torah were the result both of searching study and of new cases constantly arising in practice, for which the Torah did not provide.

3. Popular customs and traditions which are not mentioned in the Torah. Such are the customs connected with burial and mourning, many of them so ancient that they antedate not only Judaism but even the ancient Semitic religions. Yet there is hardly a word about them in the Written Law.

4. Legislation on matters not covered in the Torah—in which legal practices traditional in Israel or among the Semites in general were molded by the scholars. For instance, the Biblical law, while very full on the subjects of damages and bailments, has little or nothing to say regarding the transfer and division of real estate. Concerning divorce, it provides that the husband must give the wife a bill of divorcement;

further, that a divorcee who has remarried can never under any circumstances be married again to her first husband. But it does not state plainly what grounds justify divorce, or on what terms it is to be arranged.

5. Modifications of Biblical laws in accordance with changing standards of ethics and culture. The most famous instance is the law "An eye for an eye, a tooth for a tooth." There were some who took the phrase literally: one who injured another physically must have the same injury inflicted on him. But such a procedure seemed barbaric to most of the Pharisees. And since the Torah, given of God, could not possibly have commanded a barbaric practice, therefore the phrase *must* mean something else. They explained that it required the payment of money damages for injury inflicted.*

6. We have already seen that when necessity demanded, Hillel went so far as to abrogate a Biblical law. Such drastic action was rare, but not unparalleled. Thus, the Torah provides that a man who suspects his wife of infidelity may subject her to a humiliating ordeal. Rabban Johanan ben Zakkai abolished this objectionable custom. To justify his radicalism, he invoked a verse from Hosea, which suggests that women will not be held accountable when men are unfaithful; and in his particular generation, he declared, men were not perfectly virtuous!

7. Innovations and decrees advanced by the Rabbis on their own authority on specific occasions. Such ordinances (*takonos*) were not given any Biblical warrant, but represented the purely legislative activity of the teachers. We shall have to speak of a number of these; we may mention for the moment the institution of the marriage contract, and the numerous changes introduced by Rabban Johanan ben Zakkai after the fall of the Temple.

It will thus be seen that the Oral Law was not merely a commentary on the written Torah, but contained creative elements of its own. It reflected the popular conscience as transmitted through the most enlightened spirits among the leaders. It was the means by which Torah and life were made co-extensive. No phase of human existence was left outside the direction of religious law; and where the old law cramped and distorted life instead of enriching it, some way was usually found to modify it by interpretation.

---

* Actually, the entire passage in Exodus 21:22 ff. can without violence to the plain sense be interpreted as a provision for financial compensation.

As we have seen, the Sadducees opposed the whole idea of the oral Torah, which they attacked as unscriptural and consequently invalid. The Rabbis were thus at pains to find as far as possible a Biblical basis for the oral teachings. The latter had indeed begun as a commentary on the sacred text, and were in many cases only its explanation. But for many laws, no clear warrant could be found. Thus there developed the technique known as *Midrash*—searching—by which unsuspected meanings could be derived from Scripture. In theory, Midrash was the discovery of the underlying implications of a passage. In practice, it was often the reading into a Biblical verse of an idea manifestly not there.

To give a simple example, Jewish custom required a quorum of ten men for public worship. A Biblical support for this rule was found in the following: The spies returned to the Israelites in the wilderness, after their survey of the Promised Land, and terrified the people by their accounts of the fierceness of the inhabitants. Whereupon God said to Moses, "How long shall I bear with this evil congregation?" The Rabbis suppose that He refers here not to the people of Israel, but to the spies. Now there were twelve spies, but Joshua and Caleb, who gave an encouraging report, were not included. Therefore the minimum number to constitute a congregation must be ten.

An interesting specimen of non-legal Midrash is reported in the New Testament. Jesus, who shared the Pharisaic belief in resurrection, was asked by some Sadducees to adduce scriptural evidence for this belief. He replied, the Torah calls God "the God of Abraham, Isaac and Jacob." He is not the God of the dead, but of the living. Therefore the patriarchs are still alive.

Obviously, the Midrash method was in many cases only a pretext, whereby a rabbinic principle (which had its own good justification) was attached to a Biblical text—partly to answer criticism, partly to facilitate memorizing. But it must be remembered that, to the Rabbis, the Torah was a document of supernatural perfection, and they naturally expected that all good ideas would be found there—at least by way of suggestion. A system of interpretation drawn up by Hillel and enlarged by R. Ishmael in the second century, treated the Torah as a document speaking in human terms, whose implications are to be derived by logical reasoning. But another viewpoint, upheld by Ishmael's great opponent Akiba, insisted that there was not a superfluous letter in the text, and read special meanings into every "if," "but," and "and."

According to the rabbinic theory, the oral Torah was given to Moses at Sinai along with the written Torah; all interpretations, even those which have yet to be discovered, are of Sinaitic origin. This theory has a certain element of truth—as long as there was a written law there must have been a tradition of interpretation. But the Pharisees and the Rabbis, whose historical knowledge was far from accurate, overstated their case. They regarded themselves as the custodians of the original Judaism and the Sadducees as sectarian; actually the Sadducees were the conservatives and the Pharisees were the innovators.

The oral Torah was first taught in conjunction with the written text. But certain reasons prompted a change, and the teachers began to transmit the oral teachings in detached rules—*halakos*—which were phrased succinctly and memorized. There was a distinct objection to publishing these rules in written form. Probably the reason for detaching the oral laws from the Bible was the recognition that the Biblical basis adduced for many of them was not convincing. To present such flimsy proofs to young students might unsettle their minds. It was deemed wiser to instruct them first in the *conclusions* of the Oral Law, the study of Midrash being reserved for advanced students.

Gradually, the body of short memorized legal rules grew enormously, and various methods of grouping them were adopted to facilitate memorizing. By the time of Rabbi Akiba (about 100 C.E.), the material had become so bulky that greater system became imperative. He therefore perfected an arrangement already in vogue, whereby all the traditional materials were grouped under about sixty headings, which in turn came under six main topics. That so elaborate a system and so voluminous a subject matter should have been transmitted by word of mouth through several centuries may seem amazing; but when we consider that the students of that day did not have to burden their memories with telephone numbers, state capitals, the names of movie stars, baseball batting averages, and the thousand and one things that clutter up our minds, it is not surprising that they should have been able to commit to memory the equivalent of a few solid volumes.

The classic period of Rabbinism is the half-century between the fall of the Temple and the outbreak of the Bar Kochba rebellion (70–132 C.E.). A series of men outstanding both as to character and intellect led the school of Jabneh. Their chief purpose was to sift and clarify the oral teachings, and to resolve the many differences of opinion which they recorded. Rabban Gamaliel the Younger was especially concerned to eliminate controversy, and insisted that the decision of the majority should determine the Law.

Though some conservatives objected that this was no way to establish divine truth, and that the correct tradition in the possession of one man should outweigh the mistaken inference of a hundred, this democratic procedure was adopted.

Indeed, the democracy of the Jabneh academy was remarkable. Though the aristocratic Gamaliel presided, the dominant figure was R. Joshua ben Hananiah, a needle maker who lived in abject poverty. (The "Rabbis" of this period and for many centuries thereafter were not professional teachers, but business men or workers who devoted their leisure to scholarship.) In the course of events, the two came into conflict, and in asserting his authority, Gamaliel humiliated Joshua several times. At length, the scholars rebelled, and removed Gamaliel from the presidency. But to install Joshua in his place would, they felt, be a breach of propriety. A young man, Elazar ben Azariah, of modest attainments but distinguished family, was made Nasi. During this period, when many of his cherished policies were reversed, Gamaliel remained a member of the body and took an active part in its discussions. Finally he went to Joshua, apologized for his discourtesies, and at the request of the latter, was reinstated as Nasi. Henceforward, he and Elazar ben Azariah presided alternately, in amiable accord. The outstanding disciple of the scholars just mentioned was Akiba ben Joseph, the greatest figure perhaps in the entire rabbinic period, a peasant of the poorest class, illiterate until after he was the father of a family. Under his wife's influence he began to study and become first the darling of his contemporaries and then their titanic leader.

Few of the innumerable legal controversies generated personal ill will; a striking contrast to the acrimony that marked the contemporary debates of the church councils. Minority opinions were recorded even when the decision against them had been finally made: by this means succeeding generations were assured that such alternative possibilities had not been overlooked.

How was the work of the academy transmitted to the people? Chiefly, it seems through lectures in the synagogue and through the elementary schools. The Nasi had some worldly authority. He was recognized as the official spokesman of the Jews by the Roman government. But his political power was slight, and the institution of the Patriarchate (the Romans called the Nasi "Patriarch") was not very popular. Even Gamaliel, we have seen, was roughly handled, and his son, Simeon, was subjected to hazing by some of those who considered themselves his intellectual superiors. The influence of the scholars upon the people was almost entirely a moral one, with little support from external authority. The fact, moreover, that the Rabbis were recruited from all classes, and that some of the greatest were of plebeian stock must have made them the more acceptable. In their forlorn and broken condition, after the downfall of the year 70, the people were groping for guidance and comfort, and the rabbinic sages gave both. Their preachments combined instruction in the law with glowing words of encouragement and hope.

The Rabbis had indeed one means of enforcing their authority: the ban. A person who disobeyed their decisions could be officially suspended from participation in Jewish life. If he persisted in his defiance, his excommunication was made permanent. This mode of discipline had no theological implications: the excommunicated person was not given over to perdition like one excommunicated from the church; he was simply the object of complete social ostracism. So severe was the punishment that most offenders were completely humbled by the temporary ban. This form of discipline, however, depended for its effectiveness on the cooperation of the entire community. Only insofar as they obtained the respect and loyalty of the masses could the scholars make their will effective.

We may pause here to see how the synagogue had developed. The service had taken definite shape. The prayers that had grown up into a traditional pattern were revised in the light of the situation after the downfall of the Temple, and were cast into set form under the direction of Gamaliel the Younger. In addition to the Sh'ma (the Biblical sections proclaiming God's unity), preceded and followed by appropriate benedictions, there was now a complete t'filo (prayer), consisting of praise and petition, with special passages to be used on the Sabbath and the various holy days. These two elements are the kernel of all Jewish prayer books up to the present. Following the morning t'filo on the Sabbath there was a reading of the Torah. (There were also brief readings at the morning service on Monday and Thursday.) The Law was divided into portions in such a way that the entire work was read completely in three years. The Sabbath service concluded with a reading from a prophetic work. This selection was related in some way to the Torah portion, and concluded wherever possible on a note of comfort. With the Torah portion was read a translation (*Targum*) in Aramaic, so that all might understand its contents.

The translation sometimes expanded from a literal rendering of the Hebrew text into an explanation of its content. This development led to the institution of preaching, which generally took place on the Sabbath. The early sermon was not a logically ordered discourse (such as the Greek orators produced) but a series of comments on a general topic, based upon scriptural passages and their midrashic explanation. The Jewish preachers were skilled in the use of proverbs and stories to illustrate their lessons.

At the conclusion of the sermon (which was of course in Aramaic) the preacher recited a prayer, praising God, appealing for the speedy arrival of His kingdom and invoking peace upon all Israel. This prayer was destined to be detached from the sermon and to become a cardinal element of Jewish worship under the name of the *Kaddish*. The so-called "Lord's Prayer" is closely related to it in thought and language.

The scholars exerted their authority even outside of Palestine. They continued the practice of regulating the calendar, which had always been the prerogative of the Sanhedrin. At this time the calendar was still fixed by direct observation. A month began when the new moon was seen by two witnesses and testimony to the effect given before the high court. A year of twelve lunar months amounts only to about 354 days, so that it falls behind the solar year very rapidly. When the scholars saw that Passover was scheduled to fall too early—before the first grain would be ripe—they would add an additional month to the year.

The fixing of the calendar was not merely a matter of practical convenience, but of prime religious importance. The Torah is specific as to the dates of the holidays; and to obey the Law exactly, one had to be sure when those days fell. After the court in Jerusalem ceased to exist, the Jews in Palestine and outside the land looked to its successor in Jabneh for guidance in this and other matters. Gradually the rabbinic interpretations of the Law became current in all save a very few remote backwaters of Jewish life.

The Bar Kochba rebellion and its tragic aftermath constitute a dreadful though heroic chapter in the history of the Jewish people. For a time it seemed that the survival of Judaism was again in doubt. But these terrible events, while a *national* calamity of the first order, proved to be only an episode in the history of the *religion*. For after the persecution was over, the work of the Rabbis was resumed, and Jews who had been driven to practice their religion in secret returned promptly to its public observance. Five brilliant pupils of the aged Akiba were ordained by a certain Rabbi Judah ben Baba (who was killed for this act by the Romans), and by this means the chain of authority remained unbroken. Akiba himself died as a martyr for refusing to discontinue his teaching of the Law. A notable decision, promulgated by the scholars at the outbreak of the Hadrianic terror, permitted a Jew to disobey any command of the Torah to escape death—with the exception of the prohibitions against murder, sexual immorality, and idolatry.

After the period of persecution was ended and some measure of tranquillity was restored, a new and impressive leader came to the fore, Rabbi Judah the Nasi—the grandson of the younger Gamaliel. The prestige due him because of his office and distinguished descent was reinforced by his outstanding gifts of scholarship and personality. Rabbi Judah devoted himself to the further sifting and arranging of the oral traditions, the process to which Akiba had given such great impetus and which Rabbi Meir, the latter's most gifted pupil, had carried still further. The official collection of the most generally approved and authentic traditions was already known as the *Mishnah* (meaning study) before Rabbi Judah gave it a more or less final form. The original intent was to make of the Mishnah no more than a reliable compilation for the use of students. But it soon came to be regarded as an authoritative code. Henceforth the schools devoted themselves chiefly to the study of the Mishnah. Other traditions, preserved singly or in collections, were likewise utilized, but chiefly to elucidate or supplement the official corpus.

Shortly before the rebellion against Hadrian, the canon of the Scriptures was definitely settled. Several books were finally included after considerable hesitation—Proverbs, Song of Songs, and Ecclesiastes among them. Others, excluded by the Rabbis, were preserved by the church and are known as the Apocrypha, that is writings that were hidden away. The Apocrypha include the Books of the Maccabees, the Wisdom of Solomon, and other interesting works.

With the completion of the Mishnah, the first era of Talmudic Judaism comes to a close. Those teachers whose names appear in the Mishnah are known as Tannaim (teachers, repeaters); their succes-

19.

The Way of the Law

WE HAVE SEEN THAT THE CHIEF CONCERN OF THE RABBIS WAS THE fixing of the law—*halakah* they called it, meaning: the way in which one should go. This is the backbone of the Talmud, as it is the backbone of traditional Judaism. Halakah includes both law in our customary use of the term—civil and criminal matters—and the regulation of ceremony and ritual. It attempts to formulate man's duties, personal and social, in exact and clear-cut rules.

The spirit of the halakah has been misunderstood by some of its critics. It did not destroy spontaneity and enthusiasm in ethical and religious conduct. People were urged by their teachers (and frequently followed the advice) to do more than the strict letter of the law demanded of them; but the halakah set minimum standards of conduct, below which no one might fall. Moreover, the detailed character of the law was regarded not as a burden, but as blessed guidance. "The Holy One, blessed be He!"says the Mishnah, "wanted to make Israel meritorious: to this end He conferred upon them a law and commandments of great volume." * Through the multitude of regulations, religious purposes and sanctions were woven into the texture of every-day life; vague ideals were translated into rules of conduct; no phase of human activity was left untouched by the spirit of holiness. Thus the Jewish legalists, despite their emphasis on ritual-

---

* This statement is perhaps directed against Paul's view that the law is a curse because it "convicts" man of sinfulness.

117

ism, were the spiritual heirs of the great prophets, since they transformed the ethical generalizations of the seers into a way of life adopted by a whole people. We shall illustrate this by presenting some of the provisions of the Talmudic halakah.

The spirit and meaning of the Sabbath underwent considerable development in the Biblical period. The Deuteronomic law regards the Sabbath as a memorial of the Exodus, and stresses the importance of allowing slaves and animals to enjoy the rest of the holy day. The priestly writings declare that the Sabbath was instituted by God at the creation of the world, and that it is the sign of a perpetual covenant between God and Israel. One of the later prophets goes further and insists that the Sabbath must be a delight. But while the Sabbath had thus acquired profound ethical and religious meanings, the Biblical *law* on the subject is almost entirely negative—you must not work. Under Sadducean influence the observance of the day tended to be one of gloomy inaction: some sects were so extreme that their members remained seated and motionless from the beginning to the end of the Sabbath.

The Pharisaic law stresses rather the positive aspects of Sabbath observance. Even the minute and technical analysis of the different types of labor was intended to reassure the people, making clear to them what they *might* do as well as what was forbidden. Certain legal devices were contrived to permit greater freedom of movement. To drive away dreariness on the Sabbath eve, the scholars insisted that extra lamps must be kindled on Friday just before sundown. This duty of providing light and cheer for the Sabbath was imposed upon the woman of the household, and is the origin of the later ceremonial of kindling the Sabbath light.

The Rabbis also ordained that one must wear his best clothes on the Sabbath: If he cannot afford two suits, he should at least change the manner of wearing his garments. To eat three Sabbath meals, one of which must include meat and wine, was regarded as a religious obligation. By such means the Sabbath was made joyous and lovable. Supplemented by the more elaborate synagogue service and the exposition of the Torah, it became one of the chief vehicles of inspiration in the life of the Jew.

The rabbinic laws concerning charity expand magnificently a noble Biblical tradition. The written Torah deals chiefly with agricultural dues—the right of the poor to glean harvested fields, and the obligation to leave the corners of the field uncut for their benefit.

Rabbinic law makes these matters more exact, but also deals with the support of the urban poor. Provision was made for assistance both in food and in money. To contribute to the charity funds was not only a moral but a legal obligation: if a citizen failed to give his just share, the collectors—who had to be men of the highest reputation—were empowered to attach his property. In the disbursement of charity great emphasis was laid on procedures which would spare the feelings of the recipient; assistance had to be rendered with all possible privacy. It was also recognized that the needs of all people are not the same. The basic requirements of every needy person must be met, but individual cases may require special treatment.

It is interesting to note—in these days especially, when the use of funds derived from taxation for social purposes has been held to weaken the charitable impulse—that by and large Jews have given far more than the minimum required. There was even a law that a man must not give away more than 20 per cent of his capital during his life, lest he himself become a charge on the community.

Nowhere is the progressive character of the rabbinic law more apparent than in its provisions regarding marriage and the status of woman.

During the greater part of the Biblical period, a marriage system prevailed in which the wife was the virtual chattel of her husband. (In the early days he paid a purchase price to her father, although as time went on the institution of a dowry given by the father to the husband became usual.) The woman was subservient to her husband in all legal respects; she was not an heir of his estate, though all her property and earnings belonged to him. He could divorce her at will, but she had no corresponding right.

The Bible recognizes polygamy as legitimate. After the patriarchal period, however, the only polygamous households mentioned are those of pre-exilic royalty. Throughout most of the Hebrew Bible, monogamy is taken for granted as normal. Cases of polygamy in the Talmudic era are extremely rare. As a matter of fact, monogamy is determined—aside from everything else—by economic factors. Few Moslems can afford more than one wife, even though their law permits them to have four.

In protecting and enlarging the rights of women, the Rabbis made notable advances. The most important of these was the marriage contract (k'subo). This instrument has a complicated history; the earliest known example is from the fifth pre-Christian century. In the form we know best, it requires the husband to set aside a sum, the minimum amount being fixed by law, as his wife's marriage portion. This portion constitutes the first claim on his estate should he die, and is to be paid to the wife if she is divorced without misconduct on her part. Thus a widow—who, as we have seen, is not an heir in Jewish law—is not at the mercy of the heirs, who might be ungenerous if they were the children of a previous wife. If she prefers, the widow may receive support from the estate in lieu of the fixed sum.

The marriage contract was a strong deterrent to divorce. A tyrannical husband could not so readily threaten his wife with immediate divorce if she displeased him, for now he would have to pay her the amount specified in the k'subo. Thus the woman acquired a more independent and dignified status. The contract provided, moreover, that as long as the marriage lasted, the husband received the income from the marriage portion. The delay involved in liquidating such an investment doubtless prevented many divorces by giving tempers a chance to cool.

Yet divorce was legally a very easy matter. It was always obtainable by mutual consent, in which case all that was necessary was for the husband to pay his wife's claim and hand her a properly witnessed bill of divorce. Where mutual consent was lacking, the school of Shammai (followed in this respect by Jesus) restricted the grounds for divorce to infidelity; but the other authorities permitted it in almost any case of incompatibility. Where adultery had occurred, divorce was mandatory whether the parties desired it or not.

Since the Bible specifically provides that the man must give the bill of divorce to the wife, it was impossible for a woman to divorce her husband. But the Rabbis gave her the right to sue for divorce, in which case they would compel the husband to give her the bill. Generally speaking, the person at fault had to pay the marriage portion. If the wife had given her husband grounds for divorce, or if she sought the separation for a trivial reason, she received nothing from him. If he was the guilty party or divorced her without adequate reason, he had to pay.

This procedure, unfortunately, worked well only when the husband was available. Should a woman desert her husband, he might write a bill of divorce and deposit it with the court as his agents, to give it to her if she reappeared. But if a man disappeared, by intent or accident, the wife's position was truly deplorable. She could neither obtain a divorce nor have her husband declared legally dead—a concept unknown to Jewish law. Unless proper proof of his demise could be obtained, she must remain an *agunah*, "neither maid, wife, nor widow." This flaw in the Jewish marriage law has remained unremedied up to the present, and has been a source of extreme hardship, especially because of the recurring crises of Jewish life. It is the one glaring defect in a system otherwise far more civilized than that prevailing in many modern countries.

But the Rabbis went as far as they dared to mitigate this difficulty. Biblical law requires all legal evidence to be established by two witnesses; the halakah makes the further proviso that such witnesses must be known to be disinterested. But Rabban Gamaliel the Elder ordained that the word of a single witness, or even hearsay evidence, might be accepted to establish the death of a husband and permit his wife to remarry. If the husband died while he and his wife were living abroad, the latter herself was allowed to testify that she was a widow.

In rabbinic law, woman did not attain equality with man, but she had a dignified status and a large measure of protection. Her degree of independence was far greater than that possessed by American women up to a few generations ago.

While Christianity glorified the celibate life and regarded marriage as a concession to mortal weakness, Rabbinic Judaism views marriage as a positive duty. One who fails to marry and to raise a family is considered a sinner; moreover, "he who has no wife is not a complete man." In particular, a bachelor was considered unfit for any post of communal or religious responsibility.

The civil law of the Rabbis is quite comparable to the systems of Rome and England. It is probable, in fact, that Roman and Jewish law influenced each other. The Talmud deals in great detail with such matters as purchase and sale, damages, the transfer of real property, deposits, loans, evidence, and so forth. But throughout, the severely legal tone is relieved and beautified by the idealistic spirit of Judaism.

A remarkable provision concerns the application of the interest laws. The Bible forbids the taking of any interest—no matter how low the rate—from a fellow Jew. The Rabbis extended this to prohibit trading in futures. The possible enhancement of the value of a commodity between purchase and delivery was considered a usurious

The Way of the Law 121

gain. Our modern commodity exchanges would not have met with rabbinic favor.

The law also contains interesting rules concerning fair trade practice. A storekeeper should not give nuts or parched grain to children to attract them to his establishment. On the other hand, customers are forbidden to "shop" when they have no intention of buying.

The rights of labor are carefully guarded by provisions which spell out in detail the humanitarian rules of the written Torah. The law is concerned also with the responsibilities of the worker to his employer, but it recognizes the special need of protecting the former. One who hires a workman for a stipulated time must pay the full wage even if he decides to suspend operations before the end of this period; but the workman who quits before finishing his stint is entitled to pay for the time he spent on the job.

Not all of the halakah was in force during the Talmudic period. Criminal cases had long since been removed from the jurisdiction of the rabbinic courts and were handled exclusively by the Roman power. Nevertheless, the Rabbis continued to discuss the sections of the Torah concerned with criminal offenses, and they did so in a remarkably idealistic spirit. The Bible provides only two forms of punishment for crime; minor offenses are punished by flogging, the more serious ones by death. The Rabbis, however, felt that human life is too sacred to be terminated by human agency. They therefore devised an elaborate series of technicalities which, if permitted in practice, would have rendered a death sentence impossible. Thus, according to the halakah, a man might not be executed for a capital offense unless two witnesses had previously warned him that such an act was punishable by death, specifically naming the form of execution (stoning, strangulation, etc.) prescribed for that crime. The Rabbis did not conceal their motives. Had I, said R. Akiba, sat in the old Sanhedrin, I would never have permitted anyone to be put to death.

Another topic of purely theoretical interest was the sacrificial law. It was confidently hoped and expected that the Temple would be restored and the cult reinstituted; meantime one who studied about the sacrifices had just as much merit as if he had actually offered them.

We shall mention only one other type of law discussed by the Talmudic Rabbis—the dietary regulations. The Biblical laws on this subject do not, despite opinions often heard, inculcate hygienic principles. They proved to be hygienic in effect; they were not so in intention. The prohibition of certain foods is rooted in ancient custom, the reasons for which are difficult to determine. (One is at a loss to explain rationally why Americans are so horrified at the thought of eating horse meat.)

But the additional regulations introduced by the Rabbis have, for the most part, a clearly defined and enlightened motive. The method of slaughtering which they prescribed was designed to make the death of the animal instantaneous and painless. The windpipe and the jugular vein of the animal must be severed with a single, uninterrupted movement of the knife; if there should be any hesitation or tearing, or if the knife should contain the slightest nick, the animal is not permitted for food.

The Bible had prohibited the eating of an animal killed or injured in the field or dying a natural death. The Rabbis implemented this rule by requiring a minute examination of the carcass. If it appeared that the animal had been diseased, and that it might eventually have died from this disease had it not been slaughtered, it was pronounced t'refo—unfit for food. These provisions exemplify the humanity and scientific knowledge of the Rabbis, who set forth in considerable detail the appearance of healthy and diseased organs in cattle and fowl.

We have selected merely a few bits of the halakah which are of particular interest to the modern readers, to give an idea of its content. Its value was twofold. First, by providing a network of law and ceremonial over the whole of life, it was a tremendous force for the preservation of the Jewish group. Even more important, it was a means of constantly driving home religious and ethical attitudes. The halakah illustrates the thesis that the way to be a successful idealist is through the self-discipline of *good habits*.

20.

The Ideals of Rabbinic Judaism

LAW IS THE BACKBONE OF RABBINIC JUDAISM, BUT BY NO MEANS ITS sole component. The halakic discussions which are central in the Talmud are interspersed with material of a non-legal character, consisting chiefly of ethical and religious utterances, elaborations of the Biblical stories and the like. The non-legal materials are known as *haggadah* or *aggadah*, which may be somewhat sketchily rendered as "narrative." There are also special works, including an entire treatise of the Mishnah (well known in Jewish life as *Pirke Aboth*, the "Sayings of the Fathers"), devoted entirely to the aggadah. Many of the Palestinian Rabbis, though they had an adequate legal knowledge, preferred to specialize in this field, becoming popular preachers rather than legal authorities. The aggadah discusses every subject imaginable; but it is devoted chiefly to religious and ethical topics. It contains many folk-elements: legends, proverbs, bits of lore that come directly from the life of the people. These popular materials were adapted by the preachers for their own purposes and combined with the results of their scriptural study and with their own creative thought. In the aggadah—that gayly colored flower garden, as Heine describes it—the Rabbis made explicit the ideals and beliefs that helped to mold the halakah. The aggadah affords us a more general picture of rabbinic religion.

The first characteristic that strikes us is the lack of any systematic theology. The Rabbis thought seriously—and in many cases profoundly—about questions of belief, but they never tried to fuse their concepts into a philosophic scheme or a fixed creed. The halakic principles—specific rules of behavior—were analyzed in minutest detail and their implications followed to the ultimate conclusion. But theological utterances were not so relentlessly scrutinized. Conflicting views were tolerated, or were harmonized by superficial explanations. In particular, difficulties of a purely philosophic character were glossed over. The Rabbis were not troubled, like the Alexandrian thinkers, over the impropriety of applying human concepts—such as anger or regret—to God. Yet their monotheism, if not so philosophically precise, was at least as genuine. It was expressed, for example, in the prohibition against praying to angels or other agents of God. At the same time, the Rabbis emphasized God's close and tender concern with the lives of all His creatures.

The second quality of rabbinic thinking is allied to the first. It is tolerance. There were but three basic principles on which the Rabbis would not give ground: The unity of God—in its practical implications, as just explained—the divine origin of the written and oral Torah and the consequent validity of the halakah, and resurrection with its implications of reward and punishment. But the greatest latitude was allowed in the interpretation even of these fundamentals, and in all other matters. Of disputes among the scholars, the principle was adopted: "Both opinions are the words of the living God." In an age when church councils were torn by controversy over minute credal details, one Rabbi Hillel advanced the notion that there would be no personal Messiah, the messianic prophecies of the Bible having been fulfilled in King Hezekiah. For this audacity in challenging a fundamental Jewish belief he was neither excommunicated nor executed; someone pointed out calmly that his Biblical interpretation was wrong.

The tolerance of Rabbinic Judaism is not limited in its scope to Jews. One of the strange injustices of history has been the venomous attack of some Gentile scholars and would-be scholars upon the "narrow misanthropic intolerance" of the Talmud. The best commentary on this phenomenon is furnished by the Rabbis themselves: "We often impute to others the shortcomings of which we are guilty." It is not surprising that the victims of persecution both by pagan and Christian emperors should have occasionally spoken bitterly about the Gentiles. The wonder is that such expressions are so few in the Talmudic literature, and that the echoes of prophetic universalism are so many. Following Rabbi Joshua ben Hananya, Rabbinic Juda-

The Ideals of Rabbinic Judaism 125

ism upheld the principle: "The pious of all peoples have a share in the world to come."

Still a third quality of Rabbinic Judaism is its sanity. This is little short of miraculous considering the catastrophic events of the age. The Rabbis were not withdrawn from the world of practical affairs. Yet the wars, persecutions, crises of all sorts, did not make them hysterical, one-sided, or fanatical. A wonderful spirit of wholesome tranquillity breathes from the pages of the Talmud. Thus the Rabbis gave only a limited place to apocalyptic computations, for they recognized the dangers of poring too much over prophecies of the future. Though some of the most eminent—notably R. Akiba—were devoted to mystic speculations concerning the "Chariot of God" and the "Work of Creation," they were forbidden to discuss such matters in public. The preachers spoke freely enough about angels and demons, heaven and hell—but these things never became major issues of religion. Self-control was constantly preached, but the ideal was always to stop short of asceticism. The association of the world and the flesh with the devil, which was producing great monastic movements in Christianity, was rejected by the vast majority of the Rabbis.

Their sane and tolerant outlook enabled the Rabbis to solve in their own way the contradiction between God's demands and human performance. No mortal man can fulfill completely and perfectly all the commandments of the Torah. This realization had plunged Paul into despair, until he concluded that the whole purpose of the Torah was to reveal to man his hopeless plight and so rouse him to seek salvation through divine grace.

The Rabbis meet the difficulty through their teaching of repentance, or to use their own word, return (t'shuvo). Both the idea and the word are Biblical, but are more fully developed in rabbinic thought. God expects us to obey His law; but when we fail—as fail we must sometimes—we should recognize our shortcomings, confess them with honest regret, and return to God and His Torah. Sincere repentance will not be rejected by God, the loving Father of mankind. If the sinner has even the smallest impulse to do better, God's grace will strengthen that weak effort at improvement.

A young prince, we read in the Midrash, left his father's house, and wandered through the world till he found himself in a distant land. One day messengers arrived from his father, urging him to come home. The king's son replied, "I would like to return, but I fear the journey is too long for me." The messengers responded, "Thus said your father: come back as far as you can, I will go to meet you the rest of the way." This, say the Rabbis, is the meaning of the prophetic summons: "Return unto Me, and I will return unto you, saith the Lord of Hosts."

The Day of Atonement is the fullest expression of this idea of return; but repentance should not be confined to one occasion. The Rabbis urge man to return constantly, and a short prayer of repentance is included in the daily service. Nor does Yom Kippur possess any magical efficacy to clear the sinner of guilt. The Mishnah makes plain that one who commits a sin with the intention of repenting later, or in the expectation that it will be forgiven on Yom Kippur, will not be pardoned. Moreover, repentance on the Day of Atonement can only cancel out sins "between man and God." If we have wronged a fellow man, we must first seek his forgiveness by making amends; only then can we look for divine pardon.

* * *

The primary element in the rabbinic program is Talmud Torah—study of the Law. This is the basic commandment and the highest virtue—a viewpoint found in no other religion. The Rabbis insist that learning without piety and righteous conduct is futile, but they stress the value of study *for its own sake,* as a means for the self-fulfilment of man and an activity pleasing to God. This emphasis on mental effort was perhaps the reason that Judaism remained sane through succeeding centuries of darkness and horror.

We have just mentioned the stress on study *for its own sake.* This ideal of disinterestedness was applied to the entire religious life. Though they taught the doctrine of future rewards and punishments, the Rabbis minimized its importance as a motive for good conduct. Judaism is not a scheme of salvation but a way of life ordained by a loving God. We should therefore avoid all ulterior considerations, and do good for its own sake (*lishmo*), for the sake of God (*l'shem shomayim*), out of simple love (*meahavo*). Rewards and punishments are really but pedagogical means—the sweetmeats given to the child for obedience till he learns to find his satisfaction in pleasing his father.

A further motive for righteousness is found in the concept of *Kiddush haShem*—Sanctification of the Name of God. (The familiar phrase "Hallowed be Thy name" echoes the idea.) This means that

The Ideals of Rabbinic Judaism 127

God's reputation among men is affected by the conduct of His professed worshippers. Any action that tends to bring discredit upon the Jewish group is a profanation of the divine name (*Chilul haShem*); conduct that reflects honor on Judaism is a sanctification of God's name. But Kiddush haShem does not mean the courting of popular favor. It is achieved not by receiving approval but by meriting it. The supreme act of Kiddush haShem is to suffer martyrdom for one's faith.

It is not necessary to review in detail the ethical lessons of the Rabbis, their high standards of family life, of integrity in business dealings, of kindness to those in need, and of courtesy to the stranger: in these matters the ideals of the Bible were reemphasized and applied to the situations of daily life. The Talmudic teachers were also concerned with what they called *Derech Eretz* (literally, the way of earth)—a term that includes both formal etiquette and the niceties of good taste and gentlemanly behavior. On such questions, their motto was "Avoid what is ugly, and what borders on ugliness."

Two other points may be mentioned because they were a marked departure from the general standards of the age. One was the rabbinic emphasis on the value of work. "Excellent is the study of the Torah combined with a worldly occupation; the effort involved in both makes sin to be forgotten." This is in direct contrast to the view current among the Greeks and their cultural heirs that labor is degrading, fit only for slaves, and a disgrace to the freeman. Second, we should note the strong rabbinic emphasis on kindness to animals (an attitude derived from the Bible) in an age which found its chief amusement in circuses where wild beasts were slaughtered.

Rabbinic idealism finds its culmination in the hope of the "Kingdom of God" (kingdom of heaven). God is of course the Ruler of all men; but His rulership will not be perfected until it is completely and fully recognized, both in belief and conduct. Each time that a Jew recites the Sh'ma, he takes upon himself "the yoke of the kingdom of heaven." But God's purposes will be fulfilled only when all men do the same.

In the apocalyptic writings, as in the words of Jesus, the expectation is voiced that the Kingdom of God will come about speedily through the miraculous intervention of God in human affairs. Men cannot do much to hasten the advent of the new day; they can only prepare themselves so that when it arrives they may be among the saved. The Rabbis, too, agree that salvation is of God's making. But they usually prefer to emphasize the ethical aspects of the idea. We must *merit* the Kingdom of God before it can arrive. "Were Israel to observe one Sabbath properly, the son of David would appear."

The line between the two interpretations is never drawn sharply, but in rabbinic literature the ethical aspect tends to prevail. It is this which appears gloriously in the prayer book—the most nearly official formulation of rabbinic beliefs. Especially in the New Year prayers does the prophetic spirit manifest itself: "Our God and God of our fathers, reign over the whole universe in Thy glory and in Thy splendor be exalted over all the earth. Shine forth in the majesty of Thy triumphant strength over all the inhabitants of Thy world, that every form may know that Thou hast formed it and every creature understand that Thou hast created it, and that all that hath breath in its nostrils may say: The Lord the God of Israel is King and His dominion ruleth over all."

21.

The Torah Returns to Babylon

THE COURSE OF PALESTINIAN LIFE CONTINUED WITH LITTLE CHANGE
after the completion of the Mishnah. Other collections of Tannaitic
material were made, and the entire body of tradition was subjected to
scholarly examination. The discussions on the Mishnah, known as
Gemara (also meaning "study"), were in their turn memorized and
transmitted. A new body of rabbinic material was gradually taking
shape. Within a century the Gemara had grown to such proportions
that it seemed necessary to systematize and edit it. The beginning of
this task was made by Rabbi Johanan ben Napaha, the outstanding
Jewish leader during the third century.

But the great man had no successor of the same caliber. Before
very long, Christianity in the saddle had begun the systematic persecution of the Jews. In addition to the political complications, a period
of economic decline set in. Henceforth, there were no great halakists
in Palestine, though for several generations there were preachers of
marked talent and productivity. One of them summed up the matter
thus: "When conditions were happier and people could find a penny
in their pockets, they liked to hear a word of Mishnah and halakah.
Now, in their poverty and misery they prefer to hear comforting
words of Scripture and aggadah."

But still, before the decline had gone too far, the scholars sought
to preserve the learning of the Palestinian schools: and a Gemara was
edited and reduced to writing. Together with the Mishnah to which
it is attached, it constitutes the Palestinian Talmud. Most of it has

survived to the present; but it was never very widely studied, and its obscurities often baffle the most learned Talmudists. The full flowering of Rabbinic Judaism is to be found in the Talmud of Babylon.

The Jewish community in Mesopotamia, founded by Judean exiles even before the First Temple fell, had maintained a continuous (and for the most part, tranquil) existence. The Parthian and Neo-Persian (Sassanid) kings who ruled the land in the first centuries of the Christian era were generally tolerant; there were only a few episodes of persecution. The Babylonian Jews were numerous, comfortable and respected, and they had won many converts. They possessed a semi-independent status through the institution of the Exilarch, or Prince of the Exile. The exilarchate was a hereditary office, and its holders claimed to be descendants of King David. They bore themselves in royal style, and were recognized by the government as the official representatives of the Jewish communities and as the agents for the collection of taxes from the Jews. Though the essentially democratic spirit of Judaism evoked occasional challenges to the power of the Exilarch, he dominated Babylonian Jewry for hundreds of years.

We do not know a great deal about the internal life of the Babylonian community before the second Christian century. Hillel came from there, and at one time a disciple of Akiba had an academy at Nisibis on the Euphrates. But it is not till the end of the Mishnaic period that Babylonian Jewish life begins to loom great. Two young men had gone up to Palestine to study with Rabbi Judah the Nasi. After the Mishnah was completed, they returned to their native country and opened academies for the promulgation and study of the new code. One of these men was named Abba Areka, but is best known as Rab. The other never received ordination, and was simply called Samuel. Their schools at Sura and Nehardea, and another academy shortly thereafter established at Pumbeditha, were destined to become new and glorious centers of Jewish learning.

For a time they continued to look to Palestine for guidance. Young scholars were attracted to the schools of the Holy Land, especially by the great personality of Rabbi Johanan. But not long after his death, persecutions broke out, and they returned to their old home. Thenceforth, Babylonia was the true center of Jewish legal authority. This, despite the fact that the Babylonian teachers were never given complete ordination and bore only the style of Rab (master) instead of Rabbi (my master).

By the fourth century, the Palestinian leaders themselves must have recognized how uncertain was the future of their institutions. Under the direction of a Nasi bearing the honorable name of Hillel, a system was drawn up for computing the calendar mathematically. Previously it had been fixed by direct observation of the moon, as reported to the Palestinian high court. Now the foreign communities were no longer dependent on the Holy Land for the fixing of the calendar. The reckoning made at this time was amazingly accurate in its harmonization of the lunar and solar years. It has remained in use to the present.

This new departure rendered unnecessary a custom that had become general outside of Palestine. The Diaspora Jews, unable to get prompt word of the announcement of the New Moon, had been uncertain as to the beginning of the months. To allow for a possible error of one day, they observed all the holy days (except the fast of Yom Kippur) for forty-eight hours. With the promulgation of an exact calendar, this became superfluous. But such is the force of inertia that the celebration of the extra day has continued in traditional Judaism up to the present!

The premonitions of Rabbi Hillel were fully justified. In the year 425, the Romans abolished the office of the Patriarch. The Sanhedrin and ordination, the last vestiges of an official authority for world Judaism, had come to an end.

The Babylonian Jews diverged in a number of matters from the customs and observances current in Palestine. One of the most important was their habit of reading the entire Torah in an annual cycle, whereas the Palestinians spread out the reading over three years. The completion of the annual reading on the additional day of the Sukos festival, and the festivity attendant upon the "Rejoicing of the Law" (*Simchas Torah*) is a distinctive Babylonian contribution to the Jewish religious calendar.

The Babylonian authorities were masters of halakah. They pursued this subject with a keenness and subtlety that had perhaps never been attained in the palmiest days of the Tannaim. In their love of dialectic sport, the Babylonian teachers frequently indulged in hair-splitting of no practical value, "pulling camels through needles' eyes to sharpen the wits of the students." In the field of aggadah they were not so successful. For the most part they contented themselves with preserving and repeating the beautiful homilies of the gifted and poetic Palestinians; their own aggadic creations are of lesser merit and were sometimes marred by superstitious notions.

The Babylonians developed a remarkable instrument of popular education, known as the *kallah* (the word is of uncertain origin). Twice a year, preceding Passover and the fall holy days, the people from miles around traveled to the cities where the academies stood. There vast assemblies heard the scholars expound the results of their preceding six months of study. Two treatises of the Mishnah were discussed each year; and at the kallah the people received the benefit of this intensive research.

Babylonian life, too, had its ups and downs. The rise of a fanatical Magian movement in the fifth century was a cause of considerable suffering to the Jewish group. The academies had to struggle for existence, and it was feared that the vast Gemara which had grown up around the Mishnah in Babylon might be lost. Two scholars, Rab Ashi and his pupil Rabina, devoted their lives to compiling and editing this material. The Mishnah and Babylonian Gemara together are the work which is known as *the* Talmud, without any qualification. It has been the subject of constant study from the time that it was reduced to writing, and it has been a vital factor in the molding of the Jewish mind and the direction of the Jewish destiny.

This is not a literary history; but the Talmud is not exactly a literary work. It has neither structure nor style, in any ordinary sense. Its rambling, unsystematic form and its contrastingly tight, logical texture have had a great effect on Jewish thinking, which is typically quick and analytical. The Babylonian preoccupation with legal questions and the fondness for hair-splitting have left their impression on the Jewish consciousness to this day. But it was fortunate that in succeeding centuries the Jewish people attached so much importance to knowledge of a work that demanded keen logical reasoning. The influence of the Talmud, so constantly studied, kept the mind of the Jew alert, objective, and balanced in centuries when an environment of illiteracy and an atmosphere of persecution were all too common. The mental discipline of the halakah was a prophylactic against credulity, hysteria, and fanaticism.

The Talmud itself has had an extraordinary history. It has been the victim of a long and strange persecution. In the Middle Ages, during the Renaissance, and again in Nazi Germany, it has been assailed as the source of pestilent ideas, a treasury of evil doctrine, teaching hatred, dishonesty, and cruelty. That these charges have nothing to do with the Talmud, that they are in no way sustained by an examination of its contents, that they are based on ignorance or on the wilful distortion of Talmudic passages, made no difference. The charges have been repeated from generation to generation, and to this day the Talmud is regarded with horror by thousands who have not the faintest notion what it is.

The Talmud can never have the same kind of appeal that attached to the words of Amos and the Second Isaiah. It is hard to understand and lacks literary beauty. But in the Talmudic record we see how the Jewish people put the ideals of prophecy to work!

22.

New Paths

1. The Palestinian Center

THE FLOWERING OF BABYLONIAN JEWRY DID NOT MEAN THE END OF the Palestinian community. Burdened by poverty and persecution, the Jews of the Holy Land saw the leadership in matters of religious law pass to the heads of the Babylonian academies; but even in decline, Palestinian Judaism showed spiritual vitality. The ruins of synagogues in Galilee, built during the sixth and seventh centuries, testify to the generosity and taste of the Palestinian Jews. During the same period, the Midrashim were edited. They are compilations of the sermons, sayings, and parables of the Talmudic teachers, in the form of rambling commentaries on various Biblical books. In content the Midrashim are closely related to the aggadic material in the Talmuds.

This age also saw a new kind of Biblical study—the fixing and transmission of an accurate Bible text. Ancient books, written by hand, were constantly subject to error. The scribes often made careless mistakes, which were transmitted from copy to copy. Those who tried to "correct" the manuscripts often made them worse. If a scribe omitted a paragraph and later discovered his error, he might copy it in wherever he had a blank space, and later scribes would leave it in the wrong position. Marginal notes were often incorporated in the text. Such accidents occurred to the books of the Hebrew Bible in an earlier day. The Greek translation, for example, was made from a Hebrew text somewhat different from the one we possess.

Early in the Christian era, however, the Palestinian scholars had largely standardized their Bible copies. This work was elaborated and completed in post-Talmudic days by a group of scholars known as Massoretes. All the available Bible manuscripts were examined in minutest detail. Those that departed from the standard version were corrected or destroyed. As a result, Hebrew Bible manuscripts are almost completely uniform. This is not true of any other ancient book of which we have many hand-written copies.

Up to this time, moreover, Hebrew was written with consonants alone, the vowels (with certain exceptions) being supplied by the reader. A change in vowels can completely change the meaning of a word. (For example, *dovor* means word or thing; *dever* means pestilence.) The Massoretes invented several systems of indicating the vowels, of which one became standard. These little dots and flourishes, placed above and below the letters, provide correct readings for the entire Bible. The Massoretes also devised an elaborate system of accents, which serve as punctuation marks and likewise indicate the traditional chant to which each book was sung.

No doubt it was this constant study of the Bible (by both the Midrashic and the Massoretic methods) which inspired Palestinians in the early Middle Ages to write in the language of the Bible. Once again, religious poetry was composed in Hebrew. The first attempts were clumsy; gradually the poets acquired more assurance and skill.

The most famous of these poets was the mysterious Eleazar Kalir. We do not know just when he lived, and are not even certain that he was a Palestinian. His hymns are complicated and difficult; they include many new words which he himself seems to have coined, and contain obscure references to the Midrashim. But they have a certain austere grandeur, and many of them have been included in the prayer books, especially for the High Holy Days.

Other poets adopted a simpler style, closer to the pattern of the Psalms. Outstanding is a hymn for New Year, which has been called "the Marseillaise of Judaism":

> "All the world shall come to serve Thee
> And bless Thy glorious name,
> And Thy majesty triumphant
> The Islands shall acclaim. . . .
> And all their congregations
> So loud Thy praise shall sing,

That the uttermost peoples, hearing,
Shall hail Thee crowned King."

2. The Work of the Geonim

Despite continued activity in the Palestinian center, the spiritual capital of world Jewry was now in the East. After the Romans abolished the Patriarchate, the Jews had no official authority in Palestine, but under the Persian kings and their Arab successors the exilarchs still held sway. As incumbents of a truly ancient office and as reputed descendants of King David, these Princes of the Exile had great prestige; to this was added a substantial grant of power from the rulers of the land. The exilarchs appointed judges for the local Jewish communities: it was out of this judicial office that the rabbinic profession of later centuries developed.

But the chief glory of the Babylonian Jews was not in the court of the exilarch, but in the ancient academies of Sura and Pumbeditha. (The Pumbeditha school was later transferred to Bagdad.) The Talmud had been completed during a time of oppression and danger, but the crisis passed and the scholars could continue their work in tranquillity. They made only a few additions to the text of the Talmud but devoted themselves wholeheartedly to mastering its contents. Through the Babylonian schools and their successors, we have a continuous living tradition of the interpretation of this difficult and often cryptic work—a tradition that goes back to the time when it was first written down.

In the post-Talmudic period, the presidents of the two academies bore the title of *Gaon*—Excellency. The centuries from 600 to 1000 are often called the gaonic period of Jewish history, for the *Geonim* were without question the chief spiritual authorities of world Jewry. Though the gaon had to be confirmed in his office by the exilarch and was thus technically subordinate to the latter, the area of his influence was far wider. The communities of North Africa and of Europe, which were in no way subject to the political control of the exilarch, voluntarily submitted their religious problems for decision by the geonim.

For again it became evident that no legal system, however elaborate, is ever complete. The changing conditions of life raised issues for which no ready answer could be found even in the lengthy discussions of the Talmud. Messengers came to Babylonia from every part of the Jewish world, bearing letters of inquiry together with gifts for the maintenance of the schools.

Sometimes the question addressed to the gaon was simply for information: what was the meaning of a difficult term or knotty passage in the Talmud or some other rabbinic text? More often, the gaon was asked to rule on a practical matter. A question of law had arisen on which the Talmudic halakah is not clear, or on which it reports conflicting opinions without giving a final decision, or—most frequently— the problem was a new one which earlier authorities had not considered. To each question submitted, the gaon provided a t'shuvo or responsum; no doubt he often consulted his colleagues in the academy before delivering his opinion.

The responsa of the geonim were later collected and published; they inaugurated a new era in the literature of the halakah. (The questions and answers of the earlier scholars had been incorporated into the Mishnah and Talmud.) The custom of submitting problems to outstanding authorities for answer in writing did not come to an end with the Babylonian schools, and rabbis have continued to produce responsa up to the present day.

Most of the gaonic responsa are brief decisions on points of law. But some of the questions required more extended answers. The first complete Jewish prayer book was compiled by Rab Amram Gaon in the ninth century, at the request of communities in Spain. When scholars in the North African city of Kairawan sought to learn more about the origin and history of the Mishnah and Talmud, the great Gaon, Sherira, supplied an account of the subject which is still of value to students. For help in philosophic and theological difficulties, too, men turned to the sages of Babylonia.

The community of Kairawan was greatly puzzled during the ninth century by a visit from a strange character who called himself Eldad the Danite. He claimed to be a representative of the "Ten Lost Tribes" and told fantastic tales of his people, dwelling beyond the River Sambatyon which does not flow on the Sabbath! The men of Kairawan thereupon wrote to Rab Zemah Gaon, giving a full account of Eldad's story, and inquiring how much credence should be given to it. Rab Zemah replied in guarded terms—from so many thousands of miles away, he wisely refrained from committing himself.

These examples date from the second half of the gaonic period, when new religious and cultural forces were affecting Jewish life, and the need was felt to reexamine the bases of Jewish tradition. Chief among these new forces was the third great monotheistic religion, which arose in Arabia.

3. *Islam*

Once again, a world-conquering religion arose out of Judaism, but this time under entirely different circumstances. Christianity grew directly out of Jewish roots. It started as a Jewish sect; it has always accepted the Hebrew Scriptures as sacred. The final separation from the mother religion occurred only after a considerable lapse of time; by then, Christian doctrine had diverged widely from the teaching of the Synagogue.

Islam, on the other hand, never had any connection with corporate Jewish life, but sprang from a seed planted in alien soil. Yet its teachings closely resemble those of Judaism.

For centuries, a considerable Jewish population had dwelt in Arabia; there were even some all-Jewish tribes which had won converts. Though they maintained their distinctive religion, these Arabian Jews were outwardly not very different from their neighbors. Christianity too was known in some sections of the peninsula. But most of the Arabs still practiced a crude paganism. Mohammed, the founder of the new faith, stemmed from this heathen majority.

The religion he taught was derived largely from what he learned in conversations with Jewish acquaintances. He talked with Christians also, and concluded that Jesus had been a great prophet. In middle life, he began to have intense visionary experiences, which convinced him that he was the chosen agent of divine revelation. The one new element in his teaching is the claim that he, Mohammed, was the last—"the seal"—of the prophetic line.

Early in his career as a prophet, Mohammed sought acceptance by his Jewish neighbors; they, however, only laughed at this unlettered Gentile. But though Mohammed was neither a scholar nor an original thinker, he proved himself a leader of enormous energy, resourcefulness, and courage. At the start, he had to face bitter antagonism among the heathen; but after a slow beginning he made steady progress. In the last ten years of his life, he headed a growing and well-disciplined army; when he died in 632, he was the ruler of all Arabia, and paganism had been outlawed from his domains and his followers were poised for world conquest.

His successors ably exploited the great energies which Mohammed had released. Hitherto, the strength of the Arabs had been dissipated in inter-tribal feuds; now united by the new religion, they went forth to create a vast empire. Western Asia, North Africa, Sicily, the Balkans, and Spain ultimately fell under their sway.

The religion taught by Mohammed is called Islam—submission, that is to say, submission to the will of God. Its cardinal doctrine is monotheism, and idolatry is condemned as the greatest of sins. To the acknowledgment of God's supremacy and unity is joined the acknowledgment that Mohammed is his prophet. The sacred scripture of Islam is called the Koran. It contains the revelations given to Mohammed (as he claimed) through the angel Gabriel, and later written down from the prophet's dictation.

The Koran displays a wide, though inaccurate, acquaintance with the stories of the Hebrew Bible as interpreted and embellished by the aggadists. Though it strongly affirms the unity of God, the Koran often describes Him in rather crudely human terms, which later on were to constitute a problem for Moslems who had studied philosophy. These thinkers also had trouble with the detailed and graphic descriptions of Hell and Paradise, which go back to Persian sources, and which Mohammed borrowed from Jewish and Christian informants. The ethical standards of the Koran are fairly high, and did much to raise the tone of moral life among the Arabs: but they do not reach the full measure of universalism and sensitive tenderness found in the best Jewish teachings. The tone of the Koran is rather austere and rigorous; it gives free play to the military spirit of Arabia.

Mohammed, untrained in systematic thinking, was sometimes inconsistent. Though he stressed the moral responsibility of the individual, he also taught the doctrine of Kismet—predestination. Allah determines the destinies of men, including their own acts, in advance. This teaching was to trouble the more disciplined thinkers of later times; perhaps also it was an ethical stumbling block, since the weak-willed might allege that their sins were foreordained.

Islam resembles Judaism not only in doctrine but in many of its forms. Like Judaism, it has a sacred book, and it soon developed a tradition comparable to the Oral Law. The mosque is the Islamic version of the synagogue, and Friday was designated a weekly day of worship. The faithful were required to recite fixed prayers five times daily (Jewish tradition knows only of three daily periods of prayer), and originally the Moslem was required to face toward Jerusalem in worship. Later, Mohammed ordained that prayers should be recited while facing Mecca—the emphasis on the sanctity of this shrine and its black stone were his only concession to the old Arab paganism.

The heathen peoples conquered by the Arab armies were offered the choice between "the Koran and the sword." The Jews, however, could not be dealt with in the same manner. Mohammed may have resented their refusal to admit his prophetic claims, but he was forced to accord them a special status. Though the Arabs, according to the Koran, were the descendants of Abraham's older son Ishmael, the Jews were also descendants of Abraham, and had preserved the faith in a somewhat garbled form. They were monotheists, they were the "People of the Book." The Christians, too, though their claim that Jesus was divine must be rejected, were after all followers of a great prophet. In the Moslem states, therefore, Jews and Christians were generally tolerated, though their status was inferior to that of Moslems, and they were subject to certain additional taxes.

The Arabs changed the face of the world in an amazingly short time, but in the process they also were changed. Tribal chieftains learned the techniques of governing an empire; and with the increase of wealth and leisure, the Arabs became ever more interested in artistic and intellectual matters. The Christian communities of Syria had preserved many scientific and philosophic masterpieces of ancient Greece, and these were now translated into Arabic. It was through Arab and Jewish channels that the cultural treasures of Greece were later brought to medieval Europe.

The structure of Jewish life was not greatly altered by the Moslem conquest. The chief outward change was the adoption of the Arabic language which rapidly displaced Aramaic as the spoken tongue of oriental Jews, and has remained so up to the present. More surprisingly, Arabic was for centuries a major language of Jewish scholarship. It is understandable that Jewish writers on grammar, science, medicine, and philosophy should have used Arabic, since it had acquired technical vocabularies for these subjects long before corresponding terms were developed in Hebrew. But many of the responsa of the geonim and works on Talmudic law were also written in Arabic—though often in Hebrew characters.

The meteoric rise of Islam greatly affected Jewish thought. Such dramatic and revolutionary events were bound to unsettle men's minds. Long accepted ideas and customs could no longer be taken for granted. Through conversation and discussion, Jews, Moslems, and

Christians alike became aware of problems not hitherto noticed. Moreover, various sects and parties arose within Islam which sometimes stimulated divisions and conflicts in the Jewish world. A writer of the tenth century enumerates no less than seventeen Jewish sects known to him. Most of them had only a brief existence. This writer himself belonged to the most important of the dissenting groups—the Karaites.

23.

New Paths

(continued)

4. *Karaism*

THE BASIC TENET OF THE KARAITE SECT WAS THAT THE WRITTEN Torah, interpreted with the strictest exactness, is the one and only authority in Jewish life. (The sect derives its name from *K'ra* or *Mikra,* that which is read.) The oral Torah, as reported in the Talmud and expounded in the academies, was flatly repudiated. Karaism was thus a return to the Sadducean viewpoint, which had apparently continued a kind of underground existence during all the centuries since the fall of the Temple.

But whereas the earlier Sadducees had been priestly aristocrats, the new Sadducees were drawn in large measure from the poor and obscure elements of the population. Many of the Karaite strongholds were in mountain villages, whose people were physically and spiritually remote from the center in Bagdad. For Rabbinic Judaism, which had begun in a democratic movement opposed to the official religious leadership of the priesthood, had now itself become official. The prestige of the geonim was derived not only from their scholarship, but from their position. They were closely associated with the exilarch, whose agents enforced the will of the Arab rulers and collected the taxes in their name.

Talmudic Judaism had introduced many laws and customs that have no Biblical basis. Often these innovations were substantial improvements, but some of them were burdensome. Altogether, they made Jewish practice rather complicated. A return to the Bible, examined without reference to tradition or to the artificial Midrashic method, seemed nothing less than a fresh revelation. Men were stirred again by the simple, severe beauty of Scripture.

It has been customary to trace the beginning of the Karaite movement to one Anan ben David, who in the middle of the eighth century sought to be appointed Exilarch. Disappointed in this ambition, he became so rebellious that he was imprisoned by the authorities. Finally he solved his problem by proclaiming himself the restorer of the true faith of Israel. The traditionalists, according to Anan, were the heretics and sectaries.

Scholars now hold that Anan did not actually found the Karaite sect, but rather gave prestige and publicity to a movement (or movements) already wide-spread. But his *Book of Precepts,* in which he attempted to define the true meaning of the Biblical laws, was probably the first written document expressing this trend. Anan did not claim absolute authority for his exposition. His motto is said to have been "Search the Scriptures and do not rely on my opinion." It was the logical outcome of this position that a leading Karaite some hundred and fifty years later characterized Anan as "the chief of the fools." For experience shows that men do not consistently agree on the meaning of a basic text. (Centuries later, the Protestant Reformation, which was likewise a return to the Bible, led to innumerable controversies and sects.) The Karaites were constantly debating as to how the commandments should be performed. Although they all had repudiated the Talmudic tradition, they were not able to escape its influence. Many of their interpretations were borrowed from the very Rabbis whose authority they had denied.

The Karaites never had vast numbers, but they did not lack in fervor and even fanaticism. Karaite law is far more stringent, severe, and uncomfortable than the Talmudic halakah. The Rabbis had made many concessions to health and safety which the Karaites would not permit. The Talmudic Sabbath law allows the enjoyment of light and fire kindled before the Sabbath, but the Karaites insisted that all fires be extinguished before nightfall on Friday, and permitted the eating of cold food only. They were in fact inclined to ascetic and gloomy habits. At an early date, they established in Jerusalem a colony of "Mourners of Zion," who devoted themselves to fasting and prayer for the restoration of the Temple.

For a century or more, the Karaites carried on an active propaganda for their views. They tried to maintain friendly relationships with the Rabbanites, and to win them over to their doctrine. The geonim, on the other hand, seem to have taken few counter measures against them, hoping perhaps that the movement would burn itself out. But in the ninth century the Gaon Saadia took an uncompromising position against them. His writings refuted their arguments in detail; in effect Saadia read the Karaites out of the Jewish fold. From then on, Karaism ceased to be an aggressive force, and its leaders were more concerned to consolidate their group than to enlarge it.

The Karaite movement helped to stimulate among all Jews a greater interest in Biblical studies, and therefore in a more systematic study of the Hebrew language. But the greatest figures in this field were Rabbanite, not Karaite scholars. Nevertheless, through the Middle Ages, the Karaites produced a number of Biblical commentators, as well as writers on law and even a few on philosophy. As late as the seventeenth century the Karaite Isaac of Troki (in Lithuania) composed a refutation of the claims of Christianity which was translated into Latin, and was enthusiastically praised by the skeptical Voltaire.

But the Karaite communities were in decline by the end of the Middle Ages. In modern times their numbers were largest (though not large) in Russia, especially in the Crimea. During the nineteenth century, when Jews were persecuted by the tsars, the Karaites deliberately emphasized the difference between themselves and other Jews in the effort to obtain milder treatment. But despite this hostility to the Jewish group, the Karaites remained impressively faithful to their own traditions, spending their Sabbaths in darkness and cold even amid the rigors of the Russian winter.

The fate of the Russian Karaites under the Soviet dictatorship is not fully known, but may be guessed. Of this once vigorous group, there remain today only small remnants in Turkey, Israel, and a few other places. The few survivors tend to reattach themselves to the main body of Judaism. Indeed, even during the Middle Ages, there were efforts on both sides for a reunion, though it has never been fully consummated.

5. Mysteries

We have noted among the Karaites a strong tendency to fast and pray for the messianic redemption. In fact, several false Messiahs had arisen in those same remote corners of the Orient where the Karaite movement found strong support. But the Rabbanite Jews were likewise animated by messianic hopes and dreams. The wars waged by the Arabs to conquer the world for Islam were hailed in many quarters as the prelude to the appearance of the Messiah. And though this hope was not fulfilled, it revived whenever a major upheaval—the Crusades, for instance—occurred in the Gentile world.

Indeed, the speculations and visions of the men who wrote the great apocalypses had never been forgotten. In the gaonic period, many new apocalypses were composed, similar in form and style to those of the Maccabean and Roman periods, but shorter and less interesting. In these booklets, the coming of the Messiah is predicted in the near future—always a little ahead of the date of the writing. When the predictions failed of fulfilment, the old data were reinterpreted.

The resemblance of these works to the ancient apocalypses is the more remarkable because (except for the Book of Daniel) the Hebrew originals of the earlier books had long since disappeared. Evidently there was a living apocalyptic tradition that persisted through the centuries.

The gaonic period also witnessed a revival of mystical religion— the systematic effort to experience the immediate presence of God. Something of this sort was also known in Talmudic times; the lore of God's chariot-throne and the mysteries of creation. But the earlier Rabbis regarded these matters as deep secrets, into which only the most soberly pious could be initiated. The mystics of later centuries were less reticent. They developed a regular technique of contemplation, and they recorded their inner experiences in documents which describe the progress of the soul through various levels ("palaces") of the spiritual world until it arrives at the very chariot of God and knows the unspeakable bliss of the Divine Presence.

From a mystical booklet (itself not widely read), the synagogue has derived one of its most familiar hymns, *En Kelohenu*—"There is none like our God." In later ages it was set to various folk melodies, and sung as a favorite part of the Sabbath morning service.

It was probably among the mystics of this period that the Kaddish prayer first received its present association with the dead. It was supposed that the soul of a departed parent might benefit from the piety of his surviving son; and the son might demonstrate his piety by responding regularly to the *Bor'chu* ("Bless ye the Lord") with which the service began, and to the Kaddish with which the preacher dismissed the congregation. Gradually the emphasis was concentrated on the recitation of the Kaddish, now detached from the sermon, as a kind of intercession for the departed soul.

Another sort of mystical teaching is found in a brief but puzzling work called the Book of Creation (*Sefer Yezirah*). This enigmatic little pamphlet, which ascribes cosmic power to the Hebrew letters, was to call forth a dozen voluminous commentaries in later centuries. It was supposed to have been written by the Patriarch Abraham, and in time became a classic of the Cabala.

6. Saadia

All the concerns and interests of Judaism during the gaonic period were interwoven in the life and work of the greatest of the geonim, Rab Saadia ben Joseph (882 or 892–942). He was not only a scholar of fabulous attainments and profound intellect, but a personality of tireless energy and of militant and aggressive instincts. Born in Egypt of obscure family, he first came into prominence during a controversy —and he was involved in battles for the rest of his life.

There had been a minor revival of the Palestinian schools, whose leaders also called themselves geonim, though their scholarship was mediocre. About 921, a Palestinian scholar named Ben Meir precipitated a storm over the fixing of the calendar. This had always been a matter of great concern in Jewish life, since it involved the correct dating of the festivals. After the abolition of the office of the Patriarch, the calendar calculations had been made for world Jewry by the Babylonian scholars. Now Ben Meir accused them of error, and proposed a revision which would have set the Passover two days earlier than the Babylonian reckoning fixed it. Clearly, Ben Meir intended not merely to correct this supposed mistake, but to restore the authority of the Palestinian schools in the world Jewish scene.

Saadia, who had spent some years in Palestine and other countries of Asia, now came to the fore. His thorough and penetrating criticisms of Ben Meir decided the contest between Palestine and Babylon in favor of the latter, and established Saadia as a scholar of the first rank.

In 928 he was made Gaon of the ancient academy of Sura, which had been in decline, and which regained its former glory under his powerful leadership. But Saadia soon came into conflict with the Exilarch, David ben Zakkai, who had appointed him to his post and who expected a deference to his views which the fiery Gaon was unwilling to render. After prolonged quarrels, Saadia was forced out of office and spent several years in retirement. But his prestige remained unimpaired; at length he and the Exilarch were reconciled, and he returned to the leadership of the academy.

Saadia was also the leader of the fight against Karaism, the claims of which he challenged in a series of sharp polemical essays. Subsequent Karaite writers always regarded him as their bitterest enemy, and blamed him for the failure of their movement to win new followers.

Another who drew the lightning of Saadia's pen was one Hivi Al-Balkhi, an early precursor of Robert Ingersoll. Hivi had attacked the Bible, pointing to flaws in its morality, and rationalizing its miracles. The crossing of the Red Sea (he declared) took place at low tide, manna was a natural substance found in the wilderness, and so on. Hivi is said to have prepared an expurgated text of the Bible, from which everything irrational or otherwise objectionable was omitted. He had no lasting influence, but is an interesting example of the spiritual unrest of the age.

Saadia's work, however, was by no means of a negative character. Though he loved a fight and never hesitated to attack by tongue and pen those whom he felt to be a menace to the true faith, he was also a productive and creative thinker and writer. He translated almost the entire Bible into Arabic (his version is still the standard one in that language), and provided it with a voluminous commentary, which treats both the language and the subject matter of Scripture. He also pioneered in the field of Hebrew grammar. In both these fields he far outshone any of the Karaites, who had made the Bible their special interest. Like all geonim, he wrote on legal and ritual questions, and furnished responsa to inquiries addressed to him. He produced a masterful edition of the prayer book with a full commentary. He also attempted to interpret the mystical Book of Creation, which he approached with much independence, pointing out that it could not have actually been written by Abraham. He was even interested in Hebrew poetry, though his hymns are more ingenious than inspiring.

Above all, Saadia was a pathfinder in Jewish philosophy, attempting to reconcile reason and revelation; but this side of his labor will be discussed in a later chapter. For his independence, courage and devotion, as well as for his enormously productive scholarship, Saadia ranks high among the immortals of Judaism.

7. The End of the Gaonate

With the death of Saadia, the school at Sura ceased to be a power, though it survived for a number of years. Babylonian Jewry, after providing the leadership of the world Jewish community for some six hundred years or more, had apparently exhausted its inner resources. Two great figures guided the school of Pumbeditha-Bagdad in a final outburst of glory—Sherira and his son Hai, who rivaled Saadia in profundity of learning, breadth of interest, and liberality of outlook. But after Hai's death in 1034, no commanding figure filled the gaonic office, and the academies eventually slipped out of existence. For a long time historians thought that Hai was the last of the geonim; more recent discoveries have brought to light the names of his successors, whose accomplishments were insufficient to give them fame.

But by the time the great period of Babylonian leadership was ended, the star of Israel had risen in the West.

Part 4.

Judaism in Medieval Europe

24.

The Golden Age

THE LAST CENTURIES OF THE GAONIC PERIOD SAW THE RISE OF A
vigorous Jewish cultural life in North Africa, centered chiefly in
Kairawan, in what is now Tunisia. This prosperous community was
spiritually a colony of Babylonia, to which its leaders turned for intellectual and practical guidance. Scholars from Bagdad settled in
Kairawan, and for a time the traditional studies were pursued there
with great distinction. Commentaries on the Bible and Talmud by
the savants of Kairawan display not only learning, but considerable
independence of judgment. But the North African center contributed
little that was really new to the development of Judaism.

The focus of Jewish life was shifting to Europe. Not, of course, that
the European Jewish community was new. In Roman times, thousands
of Jews had settled in Italy, Greece, Spain, Gaul, and southern Germany; and thousands more had been brought to these territories as
slaves after the great rebellions. Jewish centers in the valley of the
Danube and the area about the Black Sea were also ancient. But,
for many centuries these settlements produced few notable personalities, and originated little or nothing in Jewish doctrine and practice.
They were content to follow the tradition with more or less devout-
ness. On occasion, their zeal brought them converts, despite the prohibitions and penalties imposed by the Church. For guidance they
turned to the great centers of the Orient.

Naturally, variations in rite and custom developed in different countries. These in turn go back in many cases to differences between

153

Palestine and Babylonia. The Jews of Italy, and through them those of France and Germany, were in close contact with the schools of the Holy Land. The Spanish communities, being under Arab rule, had more intimate ties with the Babylonian academies.

An interesting case of divergence concerns the covering of the head. The Jews of Palestine, in common with most oriental peoples, required women to conceal their hair as a measure of modesty, but they considered it proper for men to go bareheaded even during worship. Following this custom, the Jews of France and Germany entered the synagogue with heads uncovered until late in the Middle Ages. Some Babylonian teachers, however, commended the practice of covering the head, as a mark of special piety. Gradually more emphasis was laid on the custom, until at length it was regarded as highly improper to pray bareheaded. This custom was transmitted from Babylonia to Spain. It became universal among Jews only at a later date, through the great influence of Spanish legalists. And it became a controversial issue only when Reform Jews discarded the head covering in the nineteenth century.

The differences between Palestine and Babylonia explain in part the division of European Jewry into two groups. The Jews of Spain and Portugal were called S'fardim; those of northern Europe were known as Ashk'nazim.* The two groups differ in their pronunciation of Hebrew, in many details of ritual and worship, in their traditional tunes, and to some extent in the mood and character of their scholarship and daily life. Oriental Jews are closer in tradition to the S'fardim.

European Jewish leadership first became important in Spain, where it also attained its most brilliant glory. Oppressed for centuries under the Christian Goths, the Spanish Jews began a new and happy era in the eighth century when the peninsula was conquered by the Arabs. Under a series of enlightened Moslem rulers they attained a status of security and honor such as they had not known since their own national life was destroyed. In numbers, wealth, and prestige, the Jewish community of Spain became by far the greatest in the world.

The civilization to which they belonged was the most advanced seen by Europe between the decline of Rome and the Renaissance. The Arab rulers were men of education and taste. Their architects produced such masterpieces as the Alhambra. Literature and music flourished. The scientific writings of the Greeks, especially the medical treatises

---

* Sefarad and Ashkenaz are two Biblical place names, which medieval Jews erroneously identified with Spain and Germany respectively.

of Hippocrates and Galen, were enthusiastically studied. The Arab and Jewish physicians attained a peak of skill in the eleventh century which was not to be equaled elsewhere for another seven hundred years.

Under the liberal Arab rule, the Jews entered freely into this dynamic culture. In commerce, professions, government, literature, science, philosophy, they participated on all but equal terms with the dominant group. Of course, their daily language was Arabic. Yet those Jews who shared in the secular culture of Arab Spain also displayed an intense and creative interest in things Jewish and especially in things Hebraic.

It is often supposed that Jewish loyalty is at its highest when Jews are segregated and even persecuted. Equality of opportunity in the larger world is thought to weaken Jewish ties and to result in the decline of Jewish religious and cultural activity. An astounding exception to this rule—if rule it be—is furnished by Moslem Spain. Living in an atmosphere of tolerance, sharing fully in the public affairs and the cultural movements of the day, the Jews of Spain set a standard of Jewish creativeness that was not to be equaled until modern times.

The Spanish Jews produced leaders of a type different from all earlier teachers except the Geonim Saadia, Sherira, and Hai. Their outstanding trait was the many-sidedness of their knowledge and their interests. Samuel ibn Nagdela was grand vizier of Granada, a post that he owed in the first instance to the beauty of his Arabic penmanship. As such he was not only a competent administrator, but a successful general. Yet he also wrote an introduction to the Talmud, treatises on Hebrew grammar, and the first really good Hebrew poetry composed in Spain. Judah HaLevi was a physician and a philosophic thinker of considerable originality. He was deeply versed in Arabic *belles-lettres* and the greatest Hebrew poet of the Middle Ages. The most influential leader of all, Moses ben Maimon (Maimonides), was the first physician of his day, attached for many years to the court of Saladin's vizier. (This was in Egypt; but Maimonides was of Spanish birth and training.) His medical treatises are viewed with respect by modern students of medical history; and his position demanded no less skill as a courtier than as a healer. For decades he acted as spiritual head of oriental Jewry, solving their practical communal and religious problems. He was a profound and magnificent Talmudist, and a philosopher both widely read and independent in his judgments. These men were, of course, exceptional in their attainments; but they are unusual examples of a trend that was typical. The Spanish Jewish thinkers had breadth as well as depth.

The Golden Age 155

The appearance in Spain of great Hebrew poets is significant for the history of Judaism as well as of Jewish literature. It was understandable that Hebrew poets should have arisen in Palestine, and in particular that those who wished to compose hymns should have done so in the language which was alone deemed suitable for public prayer. But that the Jews of Spain, living in comfort and security, should have felt the need to compose hymns; and that moreover they should have written secular poetry in the ancient Hebrew tongue—this is worth stopping to wonder at. The secular poems are largely in imitation of Arabic models, and suffer at times from the artificial and allusive style then in fashion. Though many are graceful and charming, they are overshadowed by the magnificent religious poetry produced by the same writers. Here Arabic influence was less marked. Nor did the Spanish poets imitate Eleazar Kalir, whose long rhymed puzzles can hardly be understood without a commentary. Though they employed meter and rhyme, they wisely took for their models the Biblical poetry, especially the Psalms.

Two brief examples in translation will give the reader some notion of the intensity and power, as well as literary elegance, achieved by the best of the Spanish Jewish poets. The first is a morning hymn by the mystical Solomon ibn Gabirol:

"I have sought Thee daily at dawn and twilight,
 I have stretched my hands to Thee, turned my face,
Now the cry of a heart athirst I will utter,
 Like the beggar who cries at my door for grace.
The infinite heights are too small to contain Thee,
 Yet perchance Thou canst niche in the clefts of me.
Shall my heart not treasure the hope to gain Thee,
 Or my yearning fail till my tongue's last plea?
Nay, surely Thy name I will worship, while breath in
 my nostrils be."

Judah HaLevi likewise wrote exalted poems for personal and congregational devotion; but perhaps his most perfect productions are those in which he poured out his romantic devotion to Zion—a devotion which led him at the age of about fifty-five to leave Spain on a pilgrimage to the Holy Land. This is his address to Jerusalem:

"Beautiful height! O joy! the whole world's gladness!
 O great King's city, mountain blest!

My soul is yearning unto thee—is yearning
From limits of the west.

"The torrents heave from depths of mine heart's passion
At memory of thine olden state,
The glory of thee borne away to exile,
Thy dwelling desolate.

"And who shall grant me, on the wings of eagles,
To rise and seek thee through the years,
Until I mingle with thy dust beloved
The waters of my tears?"

Creative expression in Hebrew was accompanied by intensive study of the language itself. The Arabs of the period compiled grammars and dictionaries of their tongue, and this may have helped to stimulate similar studies among the Jews. The Spanish Jewish grammarians were fortunate in knowing two languages cognate to Hebrew—the Aramaic of the Talmud and the Arabic of their daily speech. They made splendid use of these resources. Two scholars of the eleventh century, Judah ibn Hayyuj and Jonah ibn Janach, virtually exhausted the subject of formal Hebrew grammar. No important advance in the understanding of the language was made thereafter until modern times.

In study of the Bible the Spanish Jews made equally remarkable progress. The Midrashic habit of thought was gradually stripped off—even the Karaites had not been able to free themselves from it entirely—and more and more skill was attained in determining what the Biblical writers themselves had meant. Great daring was shown by some of these scholars. They recognized that rabbinic interpretations were often at variance with the plain sense of the Bible, and said so—though insisting that tradition must be followed in deriving halakah from the Bible. One of the most critical of these commentators, Moses ibn Gikatilla, went so far as to recognize the existence of a Second Isaiah, to suggest that David had not written all the Psalms, and even to hint that certain passages of the Torah could not have come from the pen of Moses!

Such studies might seem perilous to orthodoxy; yet such was not apparently the result. Talmudic learning continued to thrive, and great authorities appeared in the field. The influence of the Arab culture with its Greek borrowings was felt here too, in the tendency toward a more systematic arrangement of the material. During the gaonic period, a start had been made in this direction. The practical task of determining the law on a given question was often complicated by the need of examining the lengthy and involved Talmudic discussions. To simplify this task, some scholars compiled lists of the principal laws, others wrote monographs on specific legal topics, and still others attempted to abridge the most important sections of the Talmud. All these efforts were in a sense preliminary sketches for the great work of Rabbi Isaac Alfasi (1013–1103).

As his surname indicates, he lived in Fez, Morocco; but he was of Spanish origin and outlook. Alfasi produced a condensed version of the Talmud annotated for practical use. He eliminated from his work all material which applied only to Palestine and to the Temple, the lengthy and sometimes inconclusive debates, the many digressions, and the aggadic passages. Where the Talmudic discussion left a point of law unsettled, Alfasi supplied the decision—from another part of the Talmud, or from the Palestinian Gemara, or from the pronouncements of the geonim and other post-Talmudic authorities.

But even this valuable work was eclipsed by the monumental creation of Maimonides, who undertook to construct an entirely new code, systematically presenting the whole body of rabbinic law. The titanic task was accomplished in ten years, in the spare time which he could save from his medical practice. Called *The Repetition of the Torah* (and more familiarly, *The Strong Hand*), the code of Maimonides is unsurpassed for scope, accuracy, logical arrangement, and clarity of style. Each topic is introduced by definitions and general statements which enable the student to advance with assurance to the details of the subject; and the whole is presented in the most attractively simple Hebrew. In form and in expression, this work far excels any code produced before or afterwards.

The spirit of the work is noble, enlightened, and liberal. It begins with a statement of the basic Jewish beliefs, presented in a philosophic, yet popular style. Next, the author explains the ethical attitudes and ideals that underlie Jewish practice. There is even a short treatise on hygiene, which Maimonides, the physician, justifies on the ground that a sound body is needed for the observance of the commandments.

The code proper follows these introductory sections. It sets forth the law in complete detail, and likewise answers theoretical questions that may arise in connection with it. For example, in codifying the law about dealings with idolaters, Maimonides attempts to explain how paganism first arose. He also discusses such superstitious practices as telling fortunes by the stars, or by consulting the spirits of the dead. These practices are forbidden by the Bible because of their pagan character. Maimonides goes farther. One should not, he says, regard magic, astrology, and necromancy as tampering with dangerous and illicit forces. Such procedures are one and all sheer nonsense, without any effect whatever. The Torah outlaws them simply to keep the simple-minded from being led astray.

The fact is that the Talmud (closer to the life of the common folk) tolerates a number of superstitious customs; and many other such practices not mentioned in the Talmud were popular among the medieval Jews. But Maimonides would not give any of them his sanction by including them in the code.

Unlike Alfasi, he treated in his work even those laws which had long been inoperative—such as those on criminal procedure, the Temple, and the sacrifices. His concluding section deals with the institution of the monarchy, and this leads naturally to a discussion of the messianic hope. Maimonides approached this subject as a strict rationalist. He ignored the apocalyptic fantasies, and interpreted the prophetic visions as no more than poetic imagery. The Messiah, he insisted, will be simply a great political ruler who will liberate the Jewish people and restore a national life upon the soil of Palestine.

The appearance of the Messiah will be one step in the continuing process by which mankind is to be redeemed and the Kingdom of God established. To this process the rise of Christianity and Islam have contributed much; for these religions contain a substantial measure of revealed truth, and have served to liberate millions from degrading paganism. Some day the education of humanity will be complete, and "the earth will be full of the knowledge of God as the waters cover the sea."

The Strong Hand had a double influence. It marked a great advance in the crystallization of the halakah; and for centuries it was the chief source consulted by Christian scholars seeking information about Judaism. For this purpose it was ideal, both because it was easy to understand and because of its consistent breadth and elevation of tone.

Thus, the Spanish Jews maintained the traditions of Judaism they had received and created new and excellent traditions of their own. But there was one great problem that they had to face in those days: the same problem that, in a different form, we speak of today as the conflict between science and religion. This will be the theme of our next chapters.

25.

An Age of Reason

1. *The Rediscovery of Greek Thought*

IN PERIODS OF MATERIAL PROSPERITY, SOCIAL ORDER, AND TECHNICAL progress, men gain increasing confidence in their own ability to solve problems. With greater leisure for thought and discussion, they begin to scrutinize and criticize the beliefs and standards they have inherited from the past. Elaborate doubt takes the place of simple faith, and novel answers are offered to the ancient questions of human experience. The reactions of men to such a tendency differ sharply. Some blithely adopt the new viewpoints, throwing overboard all the inherited beliefs and doctrines. Others, clinging almost fearfully to what they have received from the past, denounce the new ideas as sinful, and refuse even to consider them. Still others attempt to find some middle ground, allowing a proper place to both reason and faith.

The conflict between the independent human mind and the tenets of an established faith has occurred many times in world history. We have seen one instance already in our story, when Judaism and Hellenism met in Alexandria. At that time, however, the struggle does not seem to have reached a critical point. It hardly troubled students in Palestine, the chief center of Jewish life. Moreover, the Jewish thinkers at Alexandria had to reckon chiefly with the Platonic and Stoic philosophies, which—in their ethical tone if not in their specific doctrines—had much in common with the spirit of Judaism. It appears, moreover, that the problems Philo so earnestly pondered were not much discussed outside a small group of intellectuals. Most of the Alexandrian Jews did not worry about philosophy.

But there are times when even the average man is deeply affected by theoretical developments. Millions today who have never read a line of Darwin and possess only the sketchiest notions of biology have heard about evolution ("that man is descended from monkeys") and recognize some of its implications. Something similar occurred in the later Middle Ages. It was a conflict, not between science and religion, as in the nineteenth century, but between philosophy and faith. The challenge to orthodoxy came about through the rediscovery of Greek thought, and it occupied the most brilliant intellects among Christians and Moslems, as well as Jews. But even those who had no technical training in philosophy were drawn into the conflict. They were aware of the three great faiths, all based directly or indirectly on the Hebrew Scriptures, each claiming to be the divine revelation in its purest form. They were aware also of conflicting sects and parties within each of the great religions. Thus many persons became interested in philosophic discussion, even though they did not fully understand it.

How did the philosophic revival come about? After the Roman Empire became officially Christian, the philosophic schools of Athens and Alexandria were closed, philosophy was neglected, and its classic writings disappeared from Europe. But on the eastern fringe of the Empire, Syrian Christian scholars continued to study the Greek thinkers in Syriac translation. When the Arabs conquered western Asia, Moslem teachers learned about these philosophic writings and soon translated them into Arabic. Before long they were composing treatises on the relation of philosophy to the doctrines of Islam. Then Jews took up the new ideas, first by reading the books of the Arab thinkers, and later by studying the Greek authors in Arabic translation. In turn, the Jews introduced Greek philosophy into medieval Christendom through Latin translations which they made from Arabic or Hebrew versions. Five centuries before the Greek originals of Plato and Aristotle were restored to Europe, the ideas of these thinkers became known through this roundabout series of translations.

The hitherto naive mentality of the Middle Ages was severely shaken by the impact of Greek thought, with its independent, logical method. But there was no revolt against religion as such. It simply did not occur to medieval man to question the existence of God and the authority of the Bible or Koran. It was not revealed religion, but rational thought that was on trial. Could faith and reason dwell together?

To this question, the fundamentalists replied with a vehement negative. All philosophy, they asserted, was dangerous, and besides it was unnecessary. Why should the human intellect try to prove or disprove matters on which God has already told us whatever we need to know?

The progressives of the age replied that the best teachings of philosophy, as found in Greek and later sources, are in full agreement with the doctrines of revealed religion. The study of philosophy will strengthen faith by showing that the principles of religion can be logically proved. It will also help us to understand the sacred writings properly, saving us from the naive and even blasphemous error of too literal an interpretation.

The method of the medieval philosophers is called scholasticism. Its purpose was to define, organize, and harmonize truths already known, not to foster creative thinking. The Moslem, Jewish, and Christian scholastics employed much the same methods, and therefore borrowed much from each other. The pathfinders in this movement were Arabs, and the Jewish thinkers we shall discuss owed a great deal to them. But they were not slavish imitators, and always retained their independence of judgment.

2. Saadia the Pioneer

As knowledge of Greek thought spread through the Middle East, a group of Moslem teachers attempted to restate the principles of Islam in philosophic form. Soon Jews were influenced by their ideas, and so the great Gaon Saadia found it necessary to write a major work on the relation between religion and philosophy. This book, *Beliefs and Opinions*, was composed in Arabic, not only because that language was familiar to most of Saadia's readers, but because it had acquired a philosophic vocabulary which Hebrew did not yet possess. All but two of the works we shall consider in this chapter were written in Arabic.*

---

* Since our presentation will not follow a strictly chronological order, it will be convenient to list here the chief philosophers and their writings: Saadia (9th century), *Beliefs and Opinions;* Solomon ibn Gabirol (11th century), *The Fountain of Life;* Bahya ibn Pakuda (12th century), *The Duties of the Heart;* Judah HaLevi (12th century), *The Kuzari;* Abraham ibn Daud (12th century), *The Exalted Faith;* Moses ben Maimon (Maimonides, 1135-1204), *The Guide of the Perplexed;* Levi ben Gerson (1288-1344), *The Wars of the Lord;* Hasdai ben Abraham Crescas (1340-1410), *The Light of the Lord.*

Saadia took a position of extreme rationalism: Judaism is completely in harmony with the dictates of reason. Revelation may give us some truths which we could not prove by logic alone, but it never teaches us anything repugnant to logic and good sense. And many of the basic principles of revealed religion can be demonstrated by reasoning—Saadia offers such proofs for the existence and unity of God. The great advantage of revelation is that it provides certainty—since we might make errors in the use of logical proof—and that, moreover, it makes the truth available and clear to the simple and uneducated who have not the time, talent, or maturity for philosophical study. It is precisely for the benefit of such minds that the Bible was written in concrete and vivid style.

Wherever the colorful and poetic language of the Bible seems to teach something that is repugnant to reason—for instance, that God has bodily form—we must assume that this language is not meant literally. Scripture cannot teach anything that is contrary to demonstrable truth. What seems to contradict reason must be interpreted as a symbol or allegory.

Saadia, we see, followed the same general method as Philo in explaining away the theological difficulties of certain Biblical texts. This method had long been utilized by Christian and Moslem writers, and it was adopted by all the medieval Jewish rationalists.

The Spanish philosophers who followed Saadia, more profoundly educated in Greek thought, produced works which were technically more adequate. But none exceeded him in the bold faith that religion can be fully harmonized with the most advanced and independent thought that human beings can achieve.

3. *The Aristotelian Outlook*

The development of medieval philosophy—in Christianity and Islam, as well as in Judaism—was marked by the steadily growing influence of Aristotle. Unlike his teacher Plato, whose writings include poetic and mystical elements, Aristotle was cool, rigidly logical, scientifically

---

The last two books in the list were composed in Hebrew, all the others in Arabic. Except for Saadia, the Oriental, and Levi ben Gerson who lived in southern France, all the philosophers were of Spanish birth.

detached. Study of his works would not kindle the imagination, but train the mind to precise, methodical reasoning.

Aristotle was deeply interested in the natural sciences, and conducted extensive observations and experiments. But his medieval followers did not follow this example; they simply studied science out of Aristotle, reverently repeating even his mistakes.

The universe, as he conceived it, is finite in extent, with the earth—a motionless sphere—at the center. Around it a series of crystalline spheres revolve; in them are set the moon, the sun, the planets, and in the outermost sphere, the fixed stars. These spheres are alive, composed of an unearthly matter which is not subject to change or decay. Beyond the furthest sphere is the First Cause, the Unmoved Mover, the only non-material Being. The attraction of the First Cause sets the outermost sphere in motion; this movement is transmitted to the other spheres in turn, and so ultimately the creatures on earth are stirred to activity. The universe is eternal: it has always existed and always will.

The First Cause neither moves nor changes; the heavenly bodies move in their orbits, but do not change otherwise. Only in this earthly sphere is change constant. The endless processes of growth and decay, generation and disintegration are rearrangements of matter and form.

By form, Aristotle sometimes means the physical shape of a material object, but the form is also the Platonic idea; it is the purpose and end for which a thing or person exists. Thus the soul may be regarded as the form of the body. Only Aristotle does not, like Plato, ascribe a separate and independent existence to the ideas. Aside from the Prime Mover, who is pure form, the forms exist only in conjunction with some kind of matter. All existence is a process by which matter, which is the *possibility* of true existence, becomes more truly actual by the acquisition of form, and then again of higher and more perfect form. In fact, existence is a sort of evolution.

The form—the true end—of man is his reason by which he is distinguished from all other animals. Hence, the cultivation of the intellect is man's highest good and purest happiness. In his conduct he should follow the basic principle of moderation. Virtue is always a mean between two extremes: for example, courage is a mean between foolhardiness and cowardice. By adopting this principle of the Golden Mean, man attains balance and sanity; and if he is fortunate, he may give himself over to meditation, becoming (as far as human limitations permit) like the First Cause, who is constantly thinking about thought, contemplating His own essence.

We can readily see, even from this brief sketch, how utterly different the Aristotelian philosophy is from Judaism. Aristotle presupposes the eternity of the material world, whereas the Bible opens with the statement that "God created heaven and earth." Moreover, there is little resemblance between the Unmoved Mover of Aristotle and the God of Sinai. The Prime Mover has no knowledge of men and no concern with their affairs—he has knowledge only of universal and ultimate truths. Being changeless he has no relationship to changing mortals. Whether they are good or bad, wise or foolish, does not concern him. Moreover, the intellectualism of Aristotle's ethics is foreign to the prophetic spirit of Judaism, with its intensity of outlook. That extreme type of courage which produced martyrs, and which is yet far removed from foolhardiness, is unintelligible to the Aristotelian mind.

Yet the philosophy of Aristotle, with its comprehensive scope and its logical power, dazzled the minds of men for centuries. The religions of revelation could not accept it without some reservations, but they could not refuse to reckon with it. Aristotelian concepts pervaded the thought of Judaism and Islam for many generations. And to this day, the Roman church regards St. Thomas Aquinas—the most eminent Christian Aristotelian of the thirteenth century—as the official expositor of Catholic doctrine.

4. The Jewish Aristotelians

The scholastics accepted the method and viewpoint of Aristotle, to a great extent, often identifying "reason" or "science" with Aristotelian opinions. But the Jewish thinkers did not follow "the Philosopher" blindly. They criticized some of his teachings and rejected others— notably, the doctrine that the world is eternal. But for the most part, they tried to show how Aristotle and Judaism are in agreement.

Their chief problem was to make room in the changeless Aristotelian scheme for a divine revelation, given to mankind at a specific date in history through inspired prophets. The Biblical God was identified with the absolute and abstract First Cause; but the Aristotelian deity was likewise invested with the moral qualities of the God of Sinai. Though man is frail and impermanent, God is nevertheless concerned with his welfare, and man's welfare depends on righteous conduct and knowledge of divine truth.

Similarly, the living spirits of the heavenly spheres were identified by the scholastics with the angels of Scripture. These beings were conceived as intermediaries between the Absolute Divinity and mortal man; the last in the series, the one closest to earth, was called the Active Intellect. It is through the Active Intellect that communication between God and man is effected.

The prophet is a man in whom are combined lofty character, informed intelligence, and powerful imagination. By these gifts he can rise to communion with the Active Intellect, and thus become the instrument of God's revelation. It is true, however, that the best preparation on the part of the human individual does not insure that he will become a prophet. There must also be an action of the divine will, which is not rationally predictable.

But the account of God given by the inspired prophets differs greatly from that which we derive from the use of reason. This brings us to what the medieval thinkers call the question of attributes—what terms can we properly apply to God?

The difficulties are largely reduced by the allegorical method. Biblical passages that depict God in physical form must not be taken literally. So also with utterances that describe Him as subject to human emotions. When Scripture speaks of God as now angry, now forgiving, it refers to actions which a human being would have performed out of anger or compassion. God Himself does not change.

But other difficulties remained. The Christian theologians used the theory of attributes to support their own dogma. God, His wisdom, and His power—they said—are three aspects of one Deity, and are to be identified with the three persons of the Trinity. In opposition, Jewish and Moslem teachers insisted that the attributes must be understood only in a negative sense. When we speak of a living God, we do not suggest that He has the kind of life that accompanies the physiological process; we mean only that He is not dead. When we speak of His knowledge, we do not mean knowledge like ours, acquired by observation, study, or reasoning; we mean only that He is not ignorant of anything. Even when we say that He is one, we do not use the word in the ordinary sense; we simply deny that He is plural. God's oneness is unique.

The divine knowledge presents a special problem. If God is perfect, He must know everything, the future as well as the past. But if He knows the future, He knows in advance what every human being will do. Thereby He has already determined our conduct. This seems to imply that man does not have free will. If our righteous and evil deeds have been predestined in the mind of God, how can we be praised or blamed—let alone, rewarded or punished—for what we do? And if man is truly a free agent, able to choose between good and evil, God cannot know in advance what man's choice will be—and thus God's knowledge is incomplete.

This paradox had been much debated by philosophers. The difficulty was not new in Judaism. Centuries before, Rabbi Akiba had declared, "All is foreseen, yet free will is granted." He made no attempt to resolve the contradiction. With that wise lack of system that marks Talmudic theology, he insisted on the truth of both statements. But the medieval thinkers, trained in philosophic method, were forced to wrestle with the difficulty. Most of them insisted that man has free will—otherwise, they held, there could be no moral life and no divine justice. To retain this principle without impairing God's omniscience, they resorted to a number of technical devices, none entirely satisfying.

As time went on, these attempts appeared less and less convincing; and later thinkers resorted to more drastic solutions. Levi ben Gerson, the last great Jewish Aristotelian, frankly limited God's knowledge in order to make room for man's free will. On the other hand, Hasdai Crescas, the critic of Aristotle, admitted that man's acts are determined by God's foreknowledge. But he tried to cling, somehow, to the faith that man is morally responsible, and that reward and punishment are justified.

Most of the rationalists elaborated detailed proofs for the existence and unity of God. These were usually based, in one form or another, on the proposition that an ultimate cause must be assumed for all that exists. Such proofs, insofar as they are valid at all, lead us to the Prime Mover of Aristotle rather than to the loving and commanding God of religion.

But assuming that the First Cause and the God of Sinai are one and the same, and that He has made His commandments known through the prophets, we are puzzled by the content of the Torah thus revealed. Its ethical and social legislation are indeed of obvious value—they establish order and harmony among men, and help the individual to perfect himself. But why should a rational philosophic God impose a ceremonial law upon man? The Torah itself explains the reason for some observances—for instance, the Passover is a fitting memorial of the redemption from slavery. But many laws remain without any evident purpose or value.

The rationalists never questioned the divine origin of the Torah, and insisted that we must accept and obey even those laws we do not understand. Yet they assumed that every commandment has a good reason, which they attempted to discover. Maimonides gave much attention to this problem. He explained the dietary laws, for example, as a means of disciplining our appetite and as beneficial from the standpoint of hygiene.

Especially daring was his explanation of sacrifices. When Israel left Egypt, he declared, they were so accustomed to sacrificial worship that they regarded it as the essential factor in religion. Had they not been permitted to bring offerings to their own God, they would have sacrificed to idols or demons. God therefore directed Moses to make provision for sacrificial rites within the legitimate framework of Judaism. It was a concession to the needs of the people; for God in reality does not require sacrifices. (Nevertheless Maimonides assumed that sacrifice will be restored by the Messiah, and in his code he presented the pertinent laws in full detail.)

While insisting that obedience to the moral and the ceremonial law is indispensable, Maimonides did not regard correct action as the final goal of religious living. The faithful performance of the commandments is a kind of preliminary training for the highest level, which is the serene contemplation of truth, of God's existence, unity, and perfection. Such a level can be attained only through the discipline of the commandments, the knowledge of Scripture, and the understanding of philosophy. Obviously, it is attainable only by the fortunate few. Maimonides respects the simple, unreflective piety of those who obey the Torah without questioning; but his philosophic doctrine is intended for the intellectual aristocracy. He sought to give his code wide circulation, while restricting the *Guide of the Perplexed* to those mature enough to comprehend it.

This aristocratic attitude seems also to affect his view of the future life. The usual Jewish doctrine affirmed the resurrection of the dead, which Maimonides listed in his creed (to be discussed in another chapter) as one of the fundamental beliefs of Judaism. But the *Guide* does not mention resurrection and speaks rather of spiritual immortality. Maimonides touches the subject gingerly, but he seems to deny the survival of the individual consciousness. Immortality appears to mean rather the permanent reunion of the soul with the "Active Intellect"— and this pale privilege is limited to those who have risen to the highest level in their lifetime on earth. It is not surprising that such opinions aroused vehement antagonism.

Most of the positions described in this section were first proposed in the Jewish camp by Abraham ibn Daud, but Maimonides developed them with greater clarity, precision and power. Moreover, his prestige as a master of halakah gave the *Guide* far greater influence than any other Jewish philosophic work. Thus Maimonides became the idol of the rationalists and the special target of the conservatives.

26.

An Age of Reason

(continued)

5. The Critics of Aristotle

THOUGH ARISTOTELIANISM HAD A TREMENDOUS VOGUE AMONG THE
Spanish Jews, its influence was by no means unchallenged. Even before the time of Maimonides, the poet Judah HaLevi had vigorously
denied the supremacy of "reason"; two centuries later, Hasdai Crescas
was to make a systematic attack on the foundations of Aristotle's
thought. These men were not narrow-minded obscurantists, like some
of those we shall meet in our next chapter. They had a thorough
grounding in philosophy. HaLevi even followed the Aristotelians in his
treatment of God's attributes and the problem of free will. But at the
outset of his principal work, he insisted that revelation is infinitely
more reliable and more authoritative than reason. To understand how
he did this, we must know something about the form of his book.

The first Spanish Jew to attain eminence in public life was Hasdai
ibn Shaprut (10th century), an official of the royal court at Cordova.
A devout and loyal Jew, he sought constantly to advance the welfare
of his coreligionists and to encourage the development of scholarship
and of Hebrew literature. Word came to Hasdai of a Jewish state—the
kingdom of the Chazars—somewhere in the East. He despatched a
letter of inquiry which eventually reached Joseph, the Chazar king;
and after years of delay, he received the monarch's reply.

The Chazars were a people of Tartar extraction who occupied what is now southeastern Russia. They had trade and diplomatic relations with both eastern Europe and western Asia, and so they became aware of the great Biblical religions. During the eighth century, their rulers were converted to Judaism, and most of the people followed their example. Though Judaism was the state religion, the Chazar kings treated Christians and Moslems with unusual tolerance. Hasdai and his fellow Jews learned with great joy that a considerable and prosperous Jewish kingdom existed in the East. They did not know that Joseph was destined to be the last Chazar ruler. Not long after he wrote to Spain, his kingdom was overthrown by a coalition of the Duke of Moscow and the Byzantine emperor. Freedom of conscience was banished from Russian soil, and to this day it has not been restored.

This romantic episode provided the framework of HaLevi's philosophic work, which he called *Book of Arguments in Behalf of the Despised Faith*. (But it is generally known as the "Kuzari.") It tells how the king of the Chazars was led by a dream to abandon his idolatrous religion. Consulting an Aristotelian, he was left cold and unsatisfied by his arguments. He therefore sought out theologians of the Mohammedan and Christian faiths, and was startled when they both referred to the Jewish Scriptures as proof of their claims. He had not consulted a Jew at first; he had inferred from the degraded state of the Jewish people that their doctrines must be false. Now he was driven to summon a Jewish scholar and inquire into his beliefs.

The latter replied that he believed in the God of Abraham, who led Israel out of Egypt, gave the Torah at Sinai, and inspired the words of the prophets. This astonished the king. Why do you not, he inquired, say that you believe in God the Creator of the world?—Because, replied the sage, that is a matter of speculative philosophy, the arguments for which are not entirely convincing. But a revelation that took place in the presence of six hundred thousand people, to the accompaniment of miracles, and which is attested by a continuous tradition from those who were actually present at the revelation to the present day—this cannot be refuted. Thus by validating (as he believed) the authenticity of the tradition linking his own generation to the giving of the Torah, HaLevi could dispense with philosophic proof for God's existence.

The entire work is cast in the form of a dialogue between the Chazar king and the Jewish sage. It presents a unique conception of the place of Israel and of the ceremonial law in the divine scheme. To the problem: how can a spiritual God have any relation with men of flesh and blood? HaLevi replied that there is a gradation of beings in nature. At the bottom are inanimate objects; above them are vegetable, animal, and human life. But there is still a fifth class that is as superior to the normal human being as the latter is to the beast—namely, the prophet. For the prophet is the agent through which the divine influence makes contact with man. But before this can occur, there must be a land of revelation, a people of revelation, and a background for revelation— Temple, sacrificial cult, and ceremonial law. To HaLevi, Palestine is literally a holy land, possessing supernatural qualities, since there alone the union between God and man can be consummated. Israel is "the heart of the world." When the heart is sick, the whole body is affected. Since Israel is in exile and the Temple destroyed, no prophet is available; and the whole world suffers by the withdrawal of the Divine Presence. Israel's national rebirth is therefore a prerequisite to universal salvation.

HaLevi, we see, was completely at odds with the rationalists in regard to the ritual law. They regarded the ethical commandments as of primary importance, the ceremonial as chiefly of disciplinary value. But to HaLevi, the ethical laws are but a preliminary, indispensable it is true, but only a preliminary. (Even a band of thieves must have some code.) The ceremonial law, however, which in its fullness brings God down to man, is the crown and culmination of the Torah.

HaLevi had no confidence in independent reason. In one of his poems he declared that the Greek wisdom "bore blossoms, but not fruit." Nevertheless, he admitted the use of philosophy to clarify certain teachings of religion. Quite different was the approach of Crescas, the last of the great Spanish Jewish thinkers. Crescas lived under Christian rule; and in his days, the Golden Age was drawing to a close. Terrible bloody attacks upon the Jews occurred during his later years, and the events which led to the establishment of the Spanish Inquisition and the final expulsion of the Jews were already in progress. Perhaps the thinking of Crescas was affected by the orthodoxy which dominated Christian Spain. Perhaps, too, he had discovered that a somewhat chilly rationalism was insufficient for the spiritual needs of a generation of martyrs. This, too, may explain why Crescas alone among Jewish thinkers accepted the view that our destinies are not determined by our free choice, but only by the will of God.

At any rate, Crescas set out to undermine the dominant philosophy— that of Aristotle as interpreted by Maimonides. His procedure was to analyze and attack the basic conceptions and preconceptions of Aristotle —his notions of space, time, cause and effect, and so on. The criticism is much too technical and complex for us to follow here, but thorough and powerfully reasoned. It revealed many weaknesses in the foundation on which the scholastics had built such massive rationalistic structures.

But while Crescas' philosophic method was negative and critical, his conclusions were not skeptical but orthodox. Having shown the weaknesses of rationalism, he argued that not reason, but revelation and faith must be the corner-stone of religious living. Moreover, he insisted, the final goal of religion is not intellectual contemplation—as the Maimonideans held—but simple righteousness and love of God.

6. Gabirol and Bachya

The chief issue of medieval philosophy, as we have seen, was the arbitration of the conflicting claims of reason and revelation. But there were two Spanish Jewish thinkers who centered their attention on other matters.

Solomon ibn Gabirol achieved fame among his fellow Jews chiefly as a poet. His philosophic work, the *Fountain of Life,* written in the mystical tradition of the later Platonists, had little success with Jewish readers, though it may have influenced the development of the Cabala. It has survived only in a Latin translation which was much studied by Christian philosophers. The name of the author was corrupted to Avicebrol or Avicebron, and his identity with the famous poet was discovered only in the nineteenth century.

From the most neglected book of medieval Jewish philosophy we turn to the most popular: The *Duties of the Heart* by Bachya ibn Pakuda. It has been popular because strictly speaking it is not a philosophic treatise but a handbook of personal piety. Bachya pointed out that the outward duties of the Jew are minutely regulated by the halakah, and explained in numberless legal works; but little had been done to discipline the inner life and encourage the cultivation of proper spiritual attitudes. But though Bachya was interested chiefly in such values as reverence, trust, humility, and repentance, he advocated an intelligent faith. His work begins therefore with an argument for the existence and unity of God, following much the same method as Saadia. Moreover he urges his readers to examine the wonders of the physical universe, including man himself; for in considering the divine wisdom which nature displays, we attain to a deeper and more grateful reverence for the Creator. Upon this rational conviction, Bachya bases his counsels for fulfilling the duties of the heart. His presentation is enriched by fine sayings, illustrations, and original prayers.

"Thy days are as scrolls," says Bachya. "Write on them what you want to be remembered for you." "A little truth dispels much falsehood, as a little light relieves vast darkness." A solitary saint was asked if he was not afraid to dwell alone in a desert. "I should be ashamed," he replied, "were God to see me afraid of aught but Him." And Bachya recommends this prayer: "My God, I have not been led to stand before Thee by ignorance of my own weakness and lowliness, nor by disregard of Thy greatness and loftiness. But Thou hast conferred a privilege in that Thou hast commanded me to call unto Thee and permitted me to praise Thy name according to the extent of my comprehension. Thou knowest what is for my good. I have not recited my wants to remind Thee of them, but only that I may perceive the greatness of my need, and my trust in Thee. If in my folly I have asked what is not good for me or desired what is not for my benefit, Thy most high will is better than mine, and I entrust my destiny to Thine enduring decree and providence."

7. *Summing Up*

The Jews who during the Middle Ages devoted themselves to science and philosophy played an important role in the cultural history of the West. It was Jewish translators, we have seen, who first made the classics of Greek philosophy available to the scholars of Christian Europe. Jewish thinkers also exerted direct influence on the development of Christian theology. Albert the Great and Thomas Aquinas, the two leading Christian scholastics, frequently quote Maimonides; their rival, Duns Scotus, turned back repeatedly to the views of "Avicebron." And the philosophy of Spinoza, so influential in modern times, incorporated ideas borrowed from Maimonides, and especially from Crescas.

The Jewish scholastics showed that their faith need not fear exposure to enlightenment and progressive thought. But the problem of reconciling faith and reason persists from generation to generation; for yesterday's science and philosophy are soon out of date, and each new system of thought presents its challenge to the religious believer. Thus, the synthesis of Aristotle and the Torah attempted by Maimonides could not be a sufficient guide for those who had outgrown the Aristotelianism of the Middle Ages.

Nevertheless, the philosophic movement had enduring and important results. The broad outlook and lofty spiritual courage of the philosophers provide an inspiring example of intellectual honesty and responsibility. Moreover, the work of the philosophers focused greater attention on Jewish doctrines and beliefs. Previously, in their devotion to the halakah, the most eminent teachers had left the exposition of doctrine to preachers and aggadists. Henceforth, no Jew, however little inclined by temperament to philosophize, could avoid the question: What do Jews believe?

This brings us to a new stage in our story.

27.

War among the Theologians

1. What Should a Jew Believe?

JUDAISM HAS NO OFFICIAL CREED. ISRAEL'S RELIGION AROSE IN A SIM-
ple, unphilosophic age. Its adherents regarded it not as a new doctrine
—not, indeed, as a doctrine at all—but as loyalty to the one and only
God. This loyalty had to be expressed in conduct, in the totality of
individual and group living. As they were led by circumstances to
speculate on religious theory, Jews seldom felt themselves restrained
by established doctrines. Standard rules were set up for behavior, but
not for thought.

A brief paragraph of the Mishnah denies "a portion in the world to
come" to the following: one who rejects the divine origin of the
Torah, one who denies the resurrection, and the complete unbeliever
(Epicurean). This is almost the only ancient Jewish document of a
dogmatic character. But even this statement was not used as a formal
creed which people had to profess in order to avoid penalties. Instead,
the basic beliefs were woven into the prayers of the synagogue. In
subsequent centuries, orthodoxy was tested by practice rather than by
opinion. The Karaites, for example, were excluded from the main
body of Israel not merely because of their theoretical views, but because they would not conform to the Talmudic halakah.

By the time of Maimonides the situation had changed. Jews lived
in daily contact with a Christian or Moslem majority. Scholars and
plain folk alike had to reckon with the resemblances and differences

of the three faiths. Theology was inescapable, the more so because the two younger religions placed such great emphasis on doctrinal correctness. Lengthy councils of the Christian church had been devoted to drawing up definitions of orthodox teaching; the recitation of such creeds is still a regular feature of Christian worship. In Islam, the doctrinal development was less elaborate, but there was much stress on the purity of monotheistic belief. In such a situation, the Jews, especially the simple and unlearned, needed a clear-cut statement of Jewish principles. Moses ben Maimon recognized this need.

His first major work was a commentary on the Mishnah. Into his exposition of the Law he inserted several extended essays on general themes. His preface to the Mishnah passage mentioned above is a searching examination of Jewish beliefs, concluding with thirteen principles of faith which—Maimonides held—every Jew must accept:

1. That God exists.
2. That He is One in a unique and perfect sense.
3. That He is immaterial, and not to be compared to anything else.
4. That He is eternal.
5. That prayer must be addressed to Him alone (against the Christian custom of appealing to the saints).
6. That God revealed Himself to the prophets.
7. That the prophecy of Moses is unique and superior to all other revelations. (A retort to the claims made for Jesus and Mohammed.)
8. That through Moses God gave us the Torah.
9. That God will never change or revoke the Torah.
10. That God's Providence observes our actions and our inner motives.
11. That man is rewarded or punished according to his deserts.
12. The coming of the Messiah.
13. The resurrection of the dead.

The reception accorded to this summary was typically Jewish. The thirteen principles never became an official creed. Many thinkers criticized them. Not that they questioned the truth of any of these statements; but they denied that they are all equally fundamental and important. Thus, it was argued, one might believe it possible that in the future God will change the Torah, without putting himself outside the pale of Judaism. Different scholars attempted to enumerate the basic Jewish doctrines and to distinguish between primary and secondary beliefs. In the fifteenth century, Joseph Albo popularized the view that Judaism has three fundamental beliefs—God, revelation, and retribution. On the other hand, there were teachers who objected to all such summaries, insisting that the entire Torah is fundamental, and that it is irreverent to make distinctions between what is more and less important in a religion revealed by God.

But though the synagogue did not adopt Maimonides' thirteen articles as an official creed, it did not reject them either. A rhymed version of these principles, known from its first word as *Yigdal*, was incorporated into the ritual during the fifteenth century, and is sung daily in the synagogue.*

2. *The Quarrel over Teaching Philosophy*

In 1148 Spain was invaded by half-civilized Moroccans who quickly displaced the former Arab rulers. The newcomers were members of a fanatical sect that persecuted even those Moslems who did not share their own narrow views; Jews and Christians had to choose between conversion to Islam or death. Thus, the Golden Age of the Jews in Arab Spain came to a sudden and tragic end.

The Christian rulers, however, had always kept a foothold in the northern provinces, and now gradually extended the area of their control. For three centuries they pressed southward, until the Moslems were expelled from the peninsula. For a time, the Christian kings found it expedient to treat the Jews tolerantly, especially because Jewish financiers were of great help in the prosecution of the almost constant wars. The Jews of Christian Spain maintained the great cultural tradition they had inherited, though with lessening independence and originality. No doubt the rather gloomy orthodoxy of the Spanish Catholics affected the tone of Jewish life. Then persecution gradually became more frequent and severe, and this was bound to strengthen conservative trends within Judaism.

The Jewish community in the southern French district of Provence

---

* Later still, the prayer books incorporated a Hebrew version of the creed in formal style, each article beginning "I believe with perfect faith that . . ." This creed, however, was never recited at a public service, and was included only for private devotion.

had close ties with the Jewry of Spain. This area was for a long time independent of the French crown; its rulers were comparatively tolerant and culturally advanced. The Provençal Jews shared the broad outlook of their Spanish brothers. Their most distinguished intellectual was Levi ben Gershom, famous as a scientist, philosopher, and Bible commentator. Joseph Kimchi and his more famous son, David, were also great Bible scholars; they made available in lucid Hebrew the new discoveries which Spanish grammarians and critics had published in Arabic. (A similar service was rendered by Abraham ibn Ezra, himself of Spanish birth, a witty, erratic intellectual vagabond, whose restless impulses took him to France, England, and Italy.)

But Provence also had Talmudists of a more conservative stamp, who did not care to know Arabic and the works written in Arabic, and who were darkly suspicious of any attempt to make Judaism sophisticated. Such types became more numerous also in Spain. These were the men who were to take up arms against philosophy.

The attack was delayed for a time. The writings of Maimonides were chiefly in Arabic, and the traditionalists did not at first take note of them. But his great legal code, composed in Hebrew, called forth their disapproval and criticism.

For Maimonides, in the interest of brevity, did not indicate the sources on which he based his decisions. Many conservatives deemed it arrogant and irresponsible for him to suggest that readers should rely exclusively on his judgment. He had implied—so his detractors claimed—that men need no longer study the Talmud, since his code provided all the needed information. But the conservatives were especially indignant at the opening section of this work, which expounds the beliefs of Judaism in simple, yet unmistakably rationalistic style. (It does not explicitly affirm the belief in resurrection.)

While the appearance of the code called forth paeans of praise in both the East and the West, Rabbi Abraham ben David of Posquières published a series of stinging comments on the work. He was a Talmudist of the first rank, and many of his criticisms were legitimate; but orthodox zeal (and perhaps personal jealousy) led him to use harsh and intemperate language.

Maimonides had argued, for example, that no physical body is a perfect unity. One who believes that God is corporeal therefore denies that God is truly one, and as a heretic forfeits his share in the life to come. To this Rabbi Abraham ben David protested, "How can he say such a thing? Many people wiser and better than he were led by the language of the Bible and the stories of the aggadah to suppose that God has a body." (Later Jewish tradition, despite the universal veneration of Maimonides, recognized that there was something to be said on the other side. The strictures of Rabbi Abraham are regularly printed in the margin of editions of the code.)

In the face of criticism and insult, Maimonides maintained the dignified silence of the true sage. Moreover, his prestige as a Talmudist, as well as his position at court, protected him against open attack.

Yet his very eminence as a legalist provoked added hostility. Most of the Talmudic authorities were unphilosophic, and few of the philosophers were distinguished masters of the halakah. The philosophic opinions of Maimonides had been anticipated by Abraham ibn Daud, known otherwise chiefly as a chronicler. Yet his book, *The Exalted Faith*, had aroused little controversy. But it was much more disturbing when the outstanding Talmudist and dominant personality of the age announced publicly that he was an Aristotelian. That, the fundamentalists felt, was a menace to the faith of the whole community which could not be ignored.

By the time of Maimonides' death, conditions were ripe for an open outbreak. For a distinguished Provençal family, the ibn Tibbons, had rendered into Hebrew the chief Arabic works on philosophy. The father, Judah, had translated the writings of Saadia, Bahya, and HaLevi; the son, Samuel, translated the *Guide*. The difficulties were great. Hebrew had no philosophic vocabulary, and these pioneers had to create one. Their renderings are often clumsy and difficult to follow; but the results were important. The chief classics of medieval Jewish philosophy were available to Jews in a language understood everywhere—a permanent result. And they were available for the orthodox to attack—an immediate result.

Two facts must be borne in mind. First, the conditions of Jewish life had changed. Persecution was the order of the day in the Arab areas; and in Christian Spain and Provence there was a growing intolerance which must have affected the spirit of the Jewish group. Second, many who were not hostile to speculation as such feared its unsettling effects upon the young. The allegorical interpretation of Scripture, which the philosophers had of necessity adopted, could be dangerous in the hands of inexperienced enthusiasts. Maimonides, like Philo before him, had insisted on strict adherence to the halakah. But there were others who felt that, once you understood the inner meaning of Scripture, you could be lax about its outward observance. And so Maimonides was hardly in his grave before a bitter attack upon philosophy in general and Maimonides in particular was launched in Provence, and shortly thereafter in Spain. (The conflict had repercussions throughout the world. An insulting inscription was placed on the tomb of Maimonides in Palestine.)

The orthodox sought to forbid the study and publication of the heretical works, and to punish those who publicly expounded or advocated the teachings of Maimonides. The "enlightened" party denounced their opponents as ignorant obscurantists, who blasphemed God by too literal an interpretation of His word. Representatives of both sides toured France and Spain, soliciting the signatures of outstanding leaders to documents denouncing their opponents. The excommunicatory ban was invoked so frequently by both sides that it lost much of its effectiveness.

A noble but fruitless attempt to establish peace was made by the most lovable Jewish teacher of the age, Rabbi Moses ben Nachman of Gerona. As Maimonides is the outstanding Jew of Arab Spain, so Nachmanides represents the Jew of Christian Spain at his best. In his views of religion, he was closer to the opponents of Maimonides than to his champions. Essentially conservative, a profound Talmudist, a pioneer of the Cabala, Moses ben Nachman had little sympathy with the rationalism of the Maimonideans. In one of his writings he denounces those who deny the existence of realities unperceived by the senses, and who suppose that whatever their little minds cannot grasp must be untrue! But he was too fair and generous a man to join in heresy hunting. He might disagree with Maimonides, but he revered his great predecessor for his massive scholarship and his high-minded motives. Nachmanides urged both sides to practice tolerance and restraint.

But his counsels went unheeded. Both parties had gone too far to make concessions. The fanatics of Provence took a disastrous step, in violation of that Jewish tradition they claimed to defend. They denounced the *Guide* to the Christian authorities as heretical and dangerous. The book was publicly burned, and many Jews were punished by the secular authorities. But this desperate expedient turned many loyal Jews against the conservative leadership. They could not regard the denunciation of Jew by Jew to Gentile rulers as anything but treason. For a time the excitement died down.

But it flared up afresh after a few years, until the controversy was

settled by Rabbi Solomon ben Adret, who had succeeded Nachmanides as the legal authority of Spain. In 1305 ben Adret issued a
proclamation unconditionally prohibiting the study of science and
philosophy by the young. Only those who had reached the age of
thirty and who had been properly trained in the traditional disciplines
were deemed mature enough for these dangerous studies. An exception was made for medical students only. And with this decision, the
controversy came to an end.

We moderns, with our strong devotion to liberalism and our resentment at any kind of thought control, are almost bound to approve the
stand of the Maimonideans. Yet ibn Adret and his colleagues may not
have been entirely wrong in regarding the rationalist movement as a
threat to the religious security of the people. It is certainly true that
the philosophers do not represent the mainstream of Jewish tradition.
Though Maimonides was a greater intellect, Judah HaLevi was undoubtedly closer to the spirit of the prophets and the Rabbis; and
Crescas was right in his insistence that the ultimate aim of the Torah
is not philosophic knowledge, but righteous conduct and the love of
God. However coarse his tone, Abraham ben David spoke with the
authentic voice of Judaism when he objected to reading out of the
community a pious person who failed to understand the incorporeality
of God.

3. The Disputations

Meanwhile, a new problem had arisen—the defense of Judaism against
Christian polemics. With the growing power of the Christian state
in North Spain, the Jewish position began to deteriorate. The Dominican monks, who were trained for militant evangelism, were especially
troublesome. A number of Jews—some of learning and prominence—
adopted the ruling faith. Whether in the hope of worldly advancement, or out of the genuine zeal which often marks new converts,
these apostates agitated for movements to convert the Jews *en masse*.
They constantly advocated the public disputations which became the
bane of the Jewish communities.

In these meetings, representatives of the Jewish and Christian faiths
met, supposedly to debate some question at issue between the two
religions. In practice, the Christian spokesman was allowed full license
to abuse Jews and Judaism; the Jewish representative could not speak
so frankly. Any vigorous argument against Christianity was certain to

be pronounced blasphemy, with possible disastrous results not only to the speaker but to his entire community. The judges of the disputation were themselves representatives of the Church or else the Christian king. The best that the Jews could do was to hedge, and to try to undermine the arguments of the Christian disputant. The whole procedure was humiliating to the Jews, who were usually told at the close of the debate that their representatives had been logically overwhelmed and that they should all accept the salvation of the Church.

The most notable of these disputations took place in 1263 before King James of Aragon, with the saintly Nachmanides as the spokesman of Judaism. It was held at the instigation of an ex-Jew who had entered the Dominican order and taken the name of Pablo Christiani. This man undertook to prove that the Talmud itself recognized Jesus as the Messiah. (In a disputation at Paris about a century earlier, an apostate named Nicholas Donin had attacked the Talmud on the ground that it blasphemed Jesus!)

Nachmanides displayed exceptional boldness. From the start, he insisted that he must have complete freedom of speech; and though the Dominicans restricted his liberty to some extent, his courage and tact won the admiring approval of the king and court. The Talmudic evidence cited by his opponent was readily disposed of. These citations in no way prove that the Talmud regarded Jesus as the Messiah. But even if they sustained the interpretation put upon them by Christiani, Nachmanides declared Jews would not have to accept them. For these passages are taken from the aggadah of the Talmud, narratives and sermons which are not authoritative and binding like the legal decisions of the Rabbis. (This plain statement by the orthodox Nachmanides is perhaps more daring than any utterance of the rationalists.) Above all, Nachmanides argued simple observation of life proves that the Messiah has not yet come. For both Jewish and Christian Scriptures picture the age of the Messiah as a reign of peace and brotherhood, and we are far from such a blessed consummation.

The disputations continued, with increasingly unfortunate consequences for the Jewish community. The most elaborate was held at Tortosa and lasted twenty-one months, from February, 1413 to November, 1414. By this time, the Jews of Spain were in a most precarious situation, and the Jewish participants risked their security with every honest utterance, but they bore themselves with admirable dignity.

Among those who took part in this theological pageant was Joseph Albo, a pupil of Crescas, and the last of the Spanish-Jewish philos-

28.

Judaism in Christian Europe

RELIGION IS FAR MORE THAN A THEORY: IT IS A WAY OF LIFE. FOR
this reason, in telling the story of a religion, it is necessary to do more
than mention its leaders and expound their doctrine. One must also
indicate the extent to which these doctrines were translated into action
in the lives of men.

From this standpoint, the story of Judaism in Christian Europe during the Middle Ages is no less important than that of Judaism in Arab
Spain. But the record is of a different sort. Here there was no flowering of poetry or philosophy, no science worth speaking of. The outlook
was comparatively narrow, the esthetic sense was undeveloped, superstition was wide-spread. Neither France, Germany, nor Italy produced
an eagle-like Maimonides, an encyclopedic Saadia, a genius like
HaLevi. Instead, we have the record of a whole people living with
supreme courage, indomitable persistence, and simple faith under the
constant shadow of terror and oppression, and preserving its loyalty to
Judaism and its essential sanity of spirit. This is surely no less an
achievement than the formulation of a philosophic system.

The European settlements were ancient, but they were slow to
develop any distinctive religious or cultural values. There was indeed
nothing in the environment to stimulate them. During the gaonic period and for a century or more thereafter Europe was passing through
the "Dark Ages," when illiteracy was the general rule, and superstition
flourished. What little learning had survived was confined almost entirely to the monasteries; most of the secular clergy, even, were nearly

illiterate. The Jews were thus left entirely to their own cultural re-sources: Biblical and Talmudic studies. By virtue of their interna-tional connections (prior to the Crusades, most of the trade between the East and West was in their hands) and their international lan-guage, they had a far more cosmopolitan outlook than the peoples among whom they lived. Yet in the early centuries of the Middle Ages they managed to maintain amicable relationships with their Christian neighbors in most countries.

1. *The Communities*

A large proportion of the Jews in Palestine and Babylonia had been farmers; and many of those who settled in Europe likewise established themselves on the soil. Gradually the antagonism of the Church and the pressure of the feudal system—into which the Jews could not be fitted—drove them to the towns and cities, where for many centuries they engaged in commerce and the skilled trades. Later the guilds and the local governments, with ecclesiastical backing, excluded the Jews from the trades and the more lucrative commercial fields. Eventually Jews were compelled to limit their activities to petty trade and money-lending.

It was clear from an early date that the Jews must have a community organization of their own. Such an organization was essential to the Jews themselves, if they were to make proper provision for their own religious and educational needs; it was equally convenient to the Gen-tile rulers as a means of dealing with the Jews as a group, above all for purposes of taxation. The Jewish community structure, as it devel-oped in the Middle Ages, was based on earlier precedents, adapted to new needs. For example, Jews had always turned to their own courts for the settlement of civil claims, as well as for the adjudication of marriage and family problems. This procedure was followed also in Europe, and generally recognized as valid by the governments; only if a Jew was accused of a crime, or if he was involved in litigation in which a Gentile also had an interest, did he appear before a non-Jewish judge.

In the Orient, the Exilarch had exercised authority over all the Jews in the domain of his Persian or Arab master; he appointed the local officials who were directly responsible to him. This type of central-ized organization was to be found later in Egypt, where the top Jew-ish official was called the *Nagid* or Prince. (Maimonides was the most distinguished occupant of this post.) In the various Christian and Arab states of Spain and Portugal, a similar trend to centralization (under a Nagid or Chief Rabbi) was also marked. But the Ashk'nazic Jews perceived that such a system was a danger to their freedom and even to their survival. A centralized authority made it too easy for their oppressors to collect confiscatory taxes and to enforce discriminatory laws. By refusing to recognize any "chief rabbi" appointed by royal decree, the Jews of France and Germany preserved a measure of independence for the local community.

The typical Jewish community (*kehillah*) included all the Jews resident in a city and its environs; sometimes a few cities located close together combined to form a single kehillah. Since the individual Jew had civic status only as a member of such a community, the authority of the latter was considerable. It frequently restricted the right of membership, admitting only as many newcomers to the community as was deemed consistent with the interest of the older settlers. The kehillah was responsible as a body for the taxes to be paid to the secular government; its leaders had the task of apportioning the amounts to be paid by each taxpayer, and of actually collecting the moneys. In addition, they imposed assessments for the maintenance of their community institutions.

The exact procedure for the selection of the community leaders varied greatly. In some places, there were direct elections by the taxpayers; in others, the leaders were chosen by lot; in a good many instances the voters chose electors who met to name the community officers. Both in form and in spirit, there was a considerable measure of democracy in the medieval Jewish community. At times the influence of the wealthy was strongly felt, especially if a rich man had connections at court, which he could utilize for the benefit of the Jewish group. But the chief control was in the hands of the scholars. Their moral authority and the power of the ban which they wielded usually enabled them to direct community policies.

The post of Rabbi as official spiritual head of the community emerged slowly. The Rabbi and his assistants constituted the court for the settlement of domestic and civil claims, answered inquiries about religious law and custom, and supervised the religious and educational institutions of the community. Frequently the Rabbi headed a y'shivo or Talmudic academy for advanced students. For many centuries he performed these services without pay, deriving his income from a skilled trade or from commerce (but from Talmudic times, it had been customary to allow scholars special business privileges, such as certain tax exemptions, that they might devote most of their time to the public service). Only in the fifteenth century did it become usual to provide a salary for the Rabbi—a departure from tradition that troubled many consciences.

The fullest measure of popular democracy was insured by the extraordinary custom of "delaying the prayers." An individual who had a grievance against another member of the community, even against its officials and leaders, could rise in the synagogue on a Sabbath and forbid the reading of the Torah to proceed until he had stated his grievance and received some assurance that it would be corrected. Thus the power of public opinion could be employed to defend the "little man" against the vested interests. The custom seems to have its roots in Palestine, and was practiced to a greater or less extent in most of the medieval communities. Where authority was centralized, the procedure was naturally discouraged; and obviously it could be abused by cranks and nuisances. Some rabbis objected to it on the ground that it caused disorder in the synagogue and destroyed the mood of reverential worship. But it persisted in the traditional communities of eastern Europe almost to our own day, as a safeguard of the rights of the masses.

The kehillah maintained one or more synagogues, a ritual bath, a matso bakery, a rudimentary hospital (called *hekdesh*, literally "holy place"), and sometimes a social hall or "dance house." Its functionaries included a trained singer to conduct the synagogue service (who bore the title *chazan* which in earlier centuries designated the caretaker of the synagogue), a *shochet* or ritual slaughterer, and a teacher of the young. The supervision of elementary education was a primary task of the community officials. They also administered the local charities, and determined on participation in larger philanthropic efforts when a major disaster afflicted their brothers elsewhere.

For, though the local communities were independent, they were not isolationist. They maintained constant contacts with each other through personal visits and correspondence. From time to time the representatives of various k'hillos would meet at a central point to confer on matters of common interest. By general consent, they would turn to rabbis of outstanding scholarship and character to answer their more difficult legal questions and to settle disputes that had got out of hand. Such men as Rabbi Solomon ben Adret in Spain and Rabbi

Meir of Rothenburg in Germany, though they had no special political power, acted as appeals judges for the men of their generation.

The organized Jewish community has perhaps a longer record of success in democratic procedure than any other human institution.

2. Rabbenu Gershom, Rashi, and Their Successors

Among the oldest Jewish settlements in central Europe were the communities of the Rhineland. Tranquil and prosperous, they became the seat of creative scholarly effort. Rabbenu * Gershom of Mainz (born about 960) established a great Talmudic school, to which students flocked from many countries. His great prestige (he was called "The Light of the Exile") made it possible for him and his colleagues to promulgate some important reforms.

Most important was the official prohibition of polygamy. We have seen that monogamy was the general rule in Judaism long before the close of the Biblical period; but polygamy was still legally permissible, and was occasionally practiced. Apparently some of the Jews, engaged in international commerce, maintained families in more than one country. Gershom withdrew legal sanction from such arrangements. His decree was generally accepted in Europe; but oriental Jews have countenanced polygamy up to the present.

A second decision forbade a man to divorce his wife against her will, except when she was guilty of infidelity: a further development in the protection of women by Jewish law. A special procedure was devised in the case of a wife who had lost her reason, to safeguard her against being hastily discarded, while providing some relief for the husband.

Still another ordinance, of great consequence for those days, forbade the opening of a letter by any save the person to whom it was addressed.

Among those who studied under the pupils of Rabbenu Gershom was a French Jew, Rabbi Solomon Yizchaki (1040–1105), universally known as *Rashi* from the initials of his name. After his student years, Rashi returned to his native town of Troyes, where his leadership brought him fame in his lifetime and immortality thereafter.

---

* Rabbenu means "Our Teacher"—indicating special affection and respect.

The full importance of Rashi is hard to convey by a simple record of his accomplishments. His impact on the life and mind of Jewry was greater than that of any other medieval teacher—greater even than that of Maimonides. And yet he originated little or nothing. His chief gift was an extraordinary lucidity of mind and pen.

Rashi wrote running commentaries to most of the Babylonian Talmud. These commentaries are still indispensable to the student of the Talmud text. With wonderful brevity and simplicity, Rashi explains the tangled legal arguments; frequently one or two words of comment enable the student to grasp the meaning of a passage that would otherwise be obscure. Previously, the living oral tradition of Talmudic interpretation had been the indispensable key to the understanding of the Talmud. Rashi committed this tradition to writing in superb form just at the time when new and terrible outbreaks of persecution were starting. Thus, access to this basic source of Jewish law and lore was insured.

Hardly less important were the commentaries of Rashi to the books of the Bible. Here, too, he displayed the same talent for making difficult passages clear by a few brief statements. Rashi inaugurated an independent movement to liberate the Bible from Midrashic fancies and to return to its plain and basic meaning. He and his followers did not have the stimulus of Karaite competition; nor were they influenced by the parallel movement in Spain, called forth by scientific and philosophic trends. The French scholars were not acquainted with the work of the outstanding Spanish grammarians and Bible critics, for most of the latter wrote in Arabic, and their works had not yet been translated into Hebrew. Rashi's Biblical scholarship was based solely on his clearness of intellect and his sensitive feeling for the Hebrew language. With these simple tools he and his successors succeeded to a marked degree in rediscovering the intent of the Biblical writers.

Rashi himself, especially in his commentary on the books of the Torah, manifested a strong fondness for the aggadah. As a rule he treated the more difficult passages of the Torah with scientific exactness, and ornamented the easy sections with well-chosen Midrashim. This combination made Rashi's Torah commentary for centuries a favorite work of general readers, as his Talmud commentaries were indispensable to students. His followers concentrated more and more on the plain meaning of the Biblical text.

Rashi's disciples continued his work for several generations, producing brilliant Talmudic studies and sound Bible commentaries. Then conditions of Jewish life in France (except for Provence) became intolerable, and intellectual activity dwindled.

The incisive intelligence of Rashi was directed to the correct understanding of the classic Jewish sources—Bible and Talmud. He and his pupils were brilliantly critical in discovering the exact meaning of the ancient teachers. But the scientific and philosophic problems raised by these sources—the problems which troubled the minds of the Spanish scholars—simply did not exist for the French sages. They neither knew, nor did they care to learn, the Greek wisdom. With simple and unquestioning faith they accepted as true whatever was written by the prophets and the Rabbis. This combination of keen Talmudic reasoning with a tranquil unspeculative orthodoxy was to be a far more typical pattern in Judaism than the attempt of the Spanish school to combine tradition and philosophy.

The influence of Rashi and his school on Judaism was great and decisive; the impact of his work was felt also in the wider field of western culture and religion. Nicholas de Lyra, who taught at the University of Paris some two centuries after Rashi's death, embodied a great number of Rashi's explanations in his Latin commentaries on the Bible; and Martin Luther's great German translation of Scripture was based largely on Lyra's work. Many other Christian authorities consulted Rashi, among them the translators of the Authorized Version of the English Bible, who also made extensive use of the commentaries of David Kimchi. Thus the work of medieval Jewish scholars directly influenced the language, literature, and religion of the modern Western world.

3. *Blood and Gold*

The Crusades were avowedly holy wars waged to rescue the sepulcher of Jesus from Moslem hands. But though the undertaking attracted many persons moved by high religious fervor, others joined the adventure for less noble reasons.

The First Crusade began (1096) with attacks on the Jews of France and Germany. Impelled both by fanaticism and greed, the newly assembled warriors butchered the Jews of the Rhineland cities. Three years later, Godfrey of Bouillon led his triumphant army into Jerusalem; the Jews who remained in the city were herded into a synagogue building which was set afire.

Succeeding crusades also brought disaster to the Jews in various lands. Violence once started tends to become chronic. When the Black Death ravaged Europe in the fourteenth century, the Jews were accused of causing the plague by poisoning wells, and thousands were massacred. Mobs were repeatedly roused to slaughter by the tale that Jews had killed Christian children in order to use their blood in the Passover ritual. Another recurrent libel accused the Jews of stealing and desecrating the wafers used in the Mass, which according to Catholic doctrine constitute the actual body and blood of Christ. For such imaginary crimes, thousands paid with their lives, and others escaped only by accepting baptism.

Even in relatively quiet periods, the life of the Jew was made ever more burdensome. He was required to wear a distinctive badge as a mark of shame. If summoned as witness in a court, he had to take the oath in a special and humiliating form. Heavy and discriminatory taxes were imposed on him, yet his opportunities for a livelihood were steadily restricted.

The feudal system had removed Jews from the soil; the growing guilds barred them from the practice of many skilled crafts. International trade, largely in Jewish hands during the early Middle Ages, was taken over by Christian merchants after the Crusades had opened the way for them. In many countries there was talk of expelling the Jews altogether. But these proposals did not bear fruit at once: the Jews were still needed as money-lenders.

Biblical law forbids a Jew to charge a fellow Jew interest on a loan. Though this rule dates from a period when a loan was a favor rather than an investment, it was generally obeyed. Not till a relatively late date did Jewish practice distinguish between philanthropic and commercial loans. The former were provided by free loan societies such as exist down to the present. Interest on commercial credit was made permissible through a legal fiction: the creditor was regarded as a partner of the debtor and so entitled to a share of the profit from the investment.

Though the Torah permits an Israelite to take interest from a non-Jew (since the latter may charge interest), the rabbis for many centuries prohibited the practice. To Jewish as to Christian teachers, all interest was usury, and therefore illegitimate, whether the rate was high or low.

Church law strictly forbade the Christian to lend money at interest. But the developing economy of Europe made credit increasingly necessary. The Jews, exempt from the church rule, were first encouraged and later compelled to engage in money-lending. They worked under royal or imperial supervision, and the major share of the profits went into the treasuries of the rulers. This system added to the royal wealth, and also aided the Crown in the struggle for power against noblemen and burghers, who were the chief clients of the Jewish money-lenders. While the kings took most of the gain, the Jews bore the burden of resentment against the system. Jew-hatred, already inflamed by fantastic lies, was intensified by the picture of the heartless usurer, swelling his already heavy money bags with pennies wrung from the poor Christian.

Hardly less serious was the moral effect on the Jews of involvement in an occupation so generally despised. Instead of engaging in more creative work, Jews were forced to enter a highly speculative field (for money-lending is twice as risky when the debtor is likely to organize a riot against the creditor) in which sharp practice was often indispensable for survival. This is said without apology. Despite the demoralizing circumstances in which Jews had to live and work, the integrity of Jewish character was hardly impaired—an impressive testimony to the ethical power of Judaism.

Yet even this dubious resource did not remain permanently in Jewish hands. Christians discovered that money could be loaned profitably without charging interest, if you called the interest by some other name. When Italian bankers established themselves in England, the Jews were promptly expelled (1290). The French kings several times drove the Jews from their realm and then permitted them to return; the expulsion was made final in 1394. It did not affect certain areas in southern France which were not directly subject to the Crown. In the Italian and German states there never was a general expulsion, but Jews were many times driven from one city or province to another, and were constantly harried by oppressive taxes and discriminatory laws. Many Jewish communities were forced into literal bankruptcy toward the end of the Middle Ages.

4. The German-Jewish Way of Life

German Jewry continued to produce notable Talmudic scholars, but it was even more noteworthy for the fortitude and piety of its masses. "The pious Jews of Germany" were respected everywhere. Their piety was expressed on the one side by a simple, unquestioning faith that eschewed all philosophic speculation, and on the other by a great meticulousness in regard to ritual.

The German Jews were much interested in customs (*minhogim*) which, though not recorded as commandments, had won popular acceptance. Some were peculiar to German Jewry, or even to particular communities. Others were wide-spread and undoubtedly ancient. The Talmudic teachers did not mention them because they recognized their superstitious character and did not approve of them. But they did not attack them, lest they publicize them more widely. Such customs had now acquired the sanctity of age, and were often modified or reinterpreted to adapt them to Jewish religious beliefs.

The breaking of a glass at the close of the marriage service, for example, was originally intended to drive away envious demons. It was later explained as a sign of mourning for the destruction of the Temple. *Tashlich* is the custom of throwing crumbs into a body of water on the afternoon of Rosh Ha-shono. In ancient times it was no doubt an offering to the water-spirits; now it was reinterpreted as a symbolic casting away of sins. By such adjustments the authorities were able to sanction the old customs, and the people observed them piously with little or no awareness of their original meaning.

The Ashk'nazim devised formalities to mark the attainment by a boy of his legal majority at the age of thirteen. Now that he was *Bar Mitzvah* (of age to observe the commandments), he was allowed to participate in the public reading of the Torah, a privilege from which minors were excluded. (The earlier halakah, still followed in some S'fardic communities, was less rigid on this point.) The formal Bar Mitzvah celebration emerged rather late in the Middle Ages, and remained a simple and unpretentious occasion until recent decades. Its transformation into a lavish festival is an American innovation of dubious merit.

German Jewry adopted new customs of memorial and intercession for the dead. During the frequent outbreaks of anti-Jewish violence, many had died heroically for the Sanctification of God's Name. The memory of these martyrs was piously preserved in careful records and in elegies which, though crude in poetic form, are infinitely pathetic in content. On the anniversary of the massacres, special services were conducted, the elegies were chanted, the names of the martyrs were read, and prayers were recited for the repose of their souls.

Undoubtedly this custom was suggested by the Catholic requiem mass. Gradually it was extended, so that the memory of all departed relatives—and not only those who were murdered for their faith—might be consecrated on the anniversary of their death. The observance was called *Jahrzeit* (time of the year); and this German name for the custom is employed even by the oriental Jews who gradually adopted it. Its chief features are the kindling of a memorial light in the home, and the recitation of Kaddish in the synagogue. The Ashk'nazim also introduced a service for the memorial of the dead (*Yizkor* or *Hazkoras Neshomos*) on the Day of Atonement; later it was added to the service on the second day of the festivals.*

It may seem surprising that a persecuted group should have borrowed religious ideas and customs from its oppressors, but there is no doubt that such influences were felt. Messianic and mystical movements among German Christians stimulated parallel trends in the Jewish community. Furthermore, Jewish writings of the period display a marked other-worldliness. For centuries, indeed, Jews had regarded "the world to come" as the crown and compensation of labor and suffering in the present. But this belief had not crowded out the confidence that meaning and joy can be found in this earthly life through the study and practice of the Torah, and through the grateful enjoyment of God's gifts. Now, however, we meet increasing emphasis on the vanity of this world, which is merely a painful prelude to future bliss. This pessimism is doubly due to Christian influence. On the one hand, it reflects a typically Christian mood; on the other, it was intolerance and persecution which made Jews receptive to the doctrine.

One of the special concerns of German Jewry was *musar*, edification, both of an ethical and religious character. Many books were written, not to teach anything new, but to reimpress on the reader the simple lessons of righteousness and faith. These books were often favorites of the women, for whose benefit they were rendered into German. Also popular were collections of *t'chinos*, prayers in the vernacular for private use. Particularly impressive was the custom of leaving "ethical wills." (The German Jews did not originate this practice but cultivated it effectively.) The Jewish law of inheritance is rather rigid, and does not give much choice to the testator. In earlier times, therefore, wills in the modern legal sense were rare among Jews. But many a father left his children a spiritual testament,

---

* The S'fardim developed independently a prayer for the dead recited in connection with the reading of the Torah on Sabbath and holy days.

expounding his attitude to life and exhorting them to lead noble and pious lives. The inspirational effect of such testaments must have been very great. The custom of writing ethical wills continues among Jews to the present.

Another distinctive and precious contribution which German Jewry made during the Middle Ages was in the field of religious music. The sources of Jewish music are to be found in the ancient East; the Biblical chants are very old. But these, as well as the prayer chants derived from them, are not tunes in our sense of the word. They repeat the same figures over and over, without any clearly marked rhythm. It was the nameless *chazanim* of medieval Germany who built sublime and dramatic melodies out of these ancient model materials. The "Kol Nidrei" is but the most famous of their many inspiring tunes.

Impoverished and insecure, the German Jews began to seek refuge in other lands. In 1286, the great Rabbi Meir of Rothenburg set out for Palestine with a group of emigrants. He was arrested and held for ransom by a German nobleman; but he forbade his followers to purchase his freedom and thus encourage blackmail. He died years later in captivity.

Rabbi Asher ben Yechiel (1256–1328) was more fortunate. He and his sons, all Talmudists of the first rank, escaped to Christian Spain, where he became Rabbi of Toledo. Asher proudly declared that he knew nothing about philosophy, but even in Spain this was no longer considered a blemish. Times had changed, and the S'fardic Jews were well satisfied to follow his simple devout leadership.

Asher's son Jacob (died 1340) composed an important code which brought the halakah closer to its final crystallization. Called *Arbaah Turim* (Four Rows), it lacks the breadth and magnificence of Maimonides' great masterpiece, but it is more convenient for practical use. Jacob ben Asher omitted from his work not only the philosophizing of his predecessor, but all laws which were no longer observed, and he arranged the material in such a way as to make reference simpler and easier. He also included new legal developments, especially those produced in the schools of western and central Europe.

A brief word must be devoted to Italy, where the Jews had a comparatively untroubled existence. Under the papal authority, major persecutions were forbidden, though the Jews were hedged about by many restrictions and were not entirely happy. The Jews of Italy had more contact with secular culture than those of Germany, but did not produce original thinkers comparable to those in Spain. Nathan ben Yechiel of Rome, compiler of a valuable Talmudic dictionary, was the only first-rate Italian Jewish scholar of the Middle Ages.

* * *

By the time that the Christian Middle Ages reached their high point, in the thirteenth century, Judaism had entered far into decline. The Jews were impoverished, battered by incessant persecution, and culturally on a far lower level than in previous centuries. But they were by no means beaten. Their spirit was staunch, and before darkness settled over them, there was to be one more creative outburst. This will be the subject of our next chapter.

29.

The Cabala

SOME MEN HAVE A NATURALLY INDEPENDENT AND INQUIRING MIND; they want to reason problems through by cool, logical analysis. Others are ruled more by emotion and intuition: they are the romantics, dreamers, and poets. Both types—the rationalists and the mystics—exist in every generation; indeed, most individuals are a combination of both. But the circumstances of life may stimulate and accentuate one trend or the other in an individual or in a generation.

The material prosperity and social tranquillity of Arab Spain, and the scientific and literary flowering that resulted, naturally encouraged the self-reliant, independent thinking of the great Jewish philosophers. But as these favorable conditions disappeared, as tragedy after violent tragedy wrecked the Jewish communities of Europe, as life became increasingly grim through poverty and oppression, a new religious mood was required. The dry abstractions of Aristotelian thought, already worn somewhat threadbare, did not give men a faith sufficiently vivid and intense to sustain them in their dark hours. They wanted a warmer assurance of God's nearness and help, and a more concrete promise of the coming redemption. And so a great mystical movement arose and spread among the Jews of Europe, the movement called Cabala.

Jewish mysticism, as we have seen, was not something new. Its roots are in the visions of the prophets and the deep personal piety of the Psalms. The ancient apocalyptic books and the writings of

Philo contain ideas that recur in the works of the Cabalists. Many of the Talmudic Rabbis were adept in the secret lore of "God's chariot throne" and the mysteries of creation; and there was an extensive mystical movement during the gaonic period. The medieval mystics were fully justified in calling their doctrine Cabala—that is, tradition.

This name was not, however, applied to the mystical teaching until about the eleventh century, when the mystical movement was transplanted to Europe and acquired new forms and expressions. It is true, likewise, that the Cabalists exaggerated the antiquity of their lore. The gaonic Book of Creation had been attributed to Abraham; medieval cabalistic writings were ascribed to Rabbis of the third century. Yet it would be wrong to suppose that the Cabala was just a late fabrication.

The basic element of mysticism is a profound inner experience: a sense of union with God, or at least an immediate vision of the divine. To attain and prolong this experience, the mystics have often developed techniques of self-discipline and contemplation. They have also been impelled to give some account of their mystical enlightenment and its meaning, though they have constantly complained that words are insufficient to convey the reality they have experienced. And so they have frequently had recourse to symbols. This is especially true of the Cabala. Its exponents set forth their doctrine through complicated symbolisms, usually cryptic and often fantastic. These strange modes of expression make many of the cabalistic writings hard to comprehend, and have caused grotesque misunderstanding by those who did not distinguish between the symbol and the reality it is intended to suggest. Cabala, then, is not only mystical piety: it is a kind of philosophy rooted in the mystic experience. It includes new methods of scriptural allegory, and a novel approach to the ceremonial law.

The rational philosopher seeks to approach the truth by his own mental exertion. The mood of the Cabalist was rather that of humble expectation; he waited hopefully for the divine illumination. In such a mood, the critical faculty is held in check. Ideas or practices that seem strange or superstitious are not challenged: perhaps they veil profound mysteries as yet unrevealed. Thus it happened that many trivial and superstitious elements, foreign to the spirit of true mysticism, attached themselves to the Cabala.

The Cabala was drawn from many sources—ancient Jewish tradition, Alexandrian mysticism, medieval philosophy, and perhaps to some extent Christian thought. These materials were variously chosen and combined into a variety of cabalistic systems. At one extreme was the "prophetic" Cabalist, Abraham Abulafia. To him the Bible was one huge cipher. He was able to rise to heights of ecstasy by concentration on the letters of Scripture—not on words and sentences, but on individual letters, combined and recombined in an infinite number of forms. Abulafia seems to have nursed messianic ambitions. In 1280 he actually went to Rome to confer with the Pope—an adventure which all but cost him his life. At the opposite extreme were other Spanish Cabalists, who combined depth of feeling with genuine profundity of thought, and with a talent for beautiful poetic symbols.

1. *The German Cabala*

The mystical traditions of the Orient were brought to Italy in the ninth century. Before long the visionary lore had been transmitted to Germany, where it was cultivated intensively in small but enthusiastic groups.

From ancient times it had been agreed that the "secrets of the Torah" must be handled with utmost discretion. They should be taught only to the well-prepared and spiritually mature student, and then only by guarded hints which he is able to follow up for himself. They are too holy to entrust to the average man, and too dangerous—like a strong electric current or a powerful chemical in the hands of one without proper training. These injunctions were carefully heeded by the German mystics. Their visionary experiences and their reflections upon these experiences were confided only to chosen disciples, and were written down in rare manuscripts, most of which remained unpublished till recent times.

Yet these teachers were close to the masses, and shared with them as much of their doctrine as they felt was permissible. They taught an austere and simple piety of scrupulous moral behavior, fervent prayer, midnight vigils, and ascetic self-denial. Their ideal (which they achieved to a remarkable degree) was an entire community dedicated to saintliness (*chasidus*). One of the most remarkable documents of Jewish literature is the Book of the Pious (*Sefer Chasidim*), produced by the school of Rabbi Judah the Chasid, the outstanding leader of the German Cabala (twelfth century). This book is not a mystical work at all but a rambling guide for the conduct of the average man. It contains many quaint and touching stories, designed to glorify virtue and to warn men of the terrible consequences of sin. It sometimes reflects popular superstitions, often of non-Jewish origin. Yet it constantly implies the intense visionary background of those who composed it. And it profoundly affected the life of many generations.

The masses admired and revered their leaders but did not fully understand them. Rabbi Judah and his followers became the subject of innumerable legends in which they performed miracles for the benefit of their people. The secluded habits of the mystics, their nocturnal vigils, their unmistakable reticence about their doctrine, made them the objects of popular wonder. In time, the German Cabalists themselves accepted the popular view of their function and began to dabble in magic.

Essentially, mysticism and magic have nothing in common. Mysticism seeks spiritual bliss; magic is an attempt to control the material world. Its objectives are the cure of disease, the attainment of wealth, the defeat of enemies, and so on. Many of the Gentile sorcerers engaged in "black magic"—that is, they tried to use diabolic powers. In explicit (though secret) rebellion against Christianity, they chose Satan as their master and sought to exploit his might for their own ends. But they also knew of "white magic," which employed more beneficent agencies.

The Jewish magicians dealt only in white magic, though they did not use the term. They operated either with the letters of the Hebrew alphabet (which were widely believed to possess mysterious powers) or more especially with the names of angels. By such means they were thought to protect the community against persecution and plague, and to confer benefit on individuals. At this time, amulets inscribed with "holy names" acquire a more prominent place in Jewish life; sometimes they were worn on the person, sometimes displayed in the home. They were especially sought for protection against Lilith, a malevolent female demon who threatened infants and women in childbirth. Not that these superstitions were new, but through their association with the Cabala they acquired more dignity and respectability than before.

But though such matters occupied a large place in popular notions about the Cabala, they were not the concern of the great mystics, either in Germany or in Spain.

2. The Spanish Cabala

At the same time that Rabbi Judah the Chasid was active in Germany, a school of mystics appeared rather suddenly in Provence. Rabbi Abraham ben David, who so bitterly criticized Maimonides, was among the leaders of the group; he is said to have received revelations from the prophet Elijah. Attracted by reports of the new doctrine, students came to Provence from Spain, and soon an important center of Cabala arose in the Spanish town of Gerona. Here, especially under the influence of Azriel ben Solomon, the Cabala assumed a more rational form. The Provençal mystics had taught a doctrine that may be called mythological; the Spanish teachers restated the doctrine in philosophic terms. Nachmanides may have been a pupil of Azriel. In his Torah-commentary he makes many references to the Cabala, but always in brief enigmatic terms, which he frankly tells the uninitiated reader he is not intended to understand. While Nachmanides was hardly a teacher of the Cabala, his enormous prestige as a Talmudist and as a personality undoubtedly helped to spread the new lore.

As time went on, the Cabala became less and less a secret doctrine. Darkness was spreading over Spanish Jewry, and men found ever greater need for the solace and inspiration which the new teaching offered. Even writings intended for popular consumption presented the ideas of the Cabala with little reticence.

The climax of the cabalistic movement was the appearance in the thirteenth century of the *Zohar*, The Book of Splendor. It is in the form of a bulky Midrash on the Torah (with shorter sections on Ruth and Song of Songs), and it is made up chiefly of expositions and discussions by Rabbi Simeon ben Johai and his disciples—Palestinian teachers of the second Christian century. Rabbi Simeon was a unique personality who had to spend many years hiding from the Roman soldiery. As the ancient sources indicate, he was something of a visionary. The Cabalists have generally regarded him as the author of the Zohar, and his tomb in Galilee is to this day a sacred shrine of the mystics.

The Zohar was put before the public by Moses de Leon, a well-known Cabalist; and from the start there were those who asserted that Moses had not "discovered" the Zohar, but had written it himself. Ever since, critics of the Cabala have accused Moses of being a charlatan and forger. Careful analysis makes it all but absolutely certain that Moses de Leon was indeed the author of the Zohar; but there is no evidence that he ever sought or received any personal advantage from its publication. The Zohar was patently composed in moments of exaltation and high emotional stress; its author no doubt believed himself to be writing under direct divine guidance. Apparently he followed the example of the old apocalyptic writers, who attached the names of ancient worthies to their visions, and for the same reason—so that readers would approach these revelations with greater seriousness and respect.

The Zohar is a work of genius, but it is difficult to characterize. Its contents range from the sublime to the grotesque, from the profound to the silly and the simply incomprehensible. It contains brilliantly original interpretations of Scripture, beautiful sayings and parables, and fantastic myths. In one form or another, it deals with all the problems and interests of the Cabala. For centuries, it was reverenced as one of the basic sources of Judaism; by many it was exalted even above the Talmud and regarded as second only to the Bible. Indeed, all Judaism from the fourteenth century to the end of the eighteenth was permeated by cabalistic ideas, largely through the influence of the Zohar.

Now let us see a little more closely what the Cabala is about.

3. The Structure of the Spiritual Universe

The classic doctrine of mysticism was elaborated in second century Alexandria by a pagan Platonist named Plotinus. According to this doctrine God (or The One) is the only true reality. But from His being a secondary reality emanates, as light radiates from a lamp or water flows from a central fountain. The further one moves from the flame, the dimmer the light and the greater the admixture of darkness; just so, the process of emanation eventuates in beings who are touched but faintly with the light of divine reality. Matter is a kind of non-being; evil, which is associated with matter, is thus no more than the absence of good. Nevertheless, mortal man contains a dim spark of the divine spirit, which yearns for its source. The mystic way is the reverse of the process of emanation, and is fulfilled when the soul is reunited in ecstasy with The One.

This doctrine had great influence on Christian thought and considerable effect likewise on Moslem and Jewish philosophy. It was adopted in part by Ibn Gabirol, and in the Cabala it recurs in a specialized form.

The Jewish mystics refer to God as *En Sof*, the Infinite. Of God in Himself we can know nothing; to our dull vision, the En Sof is eternal darkness. But from the being of God emanates a series of spiritual powers or beings, through whom God's divinity is made manifest, and through whom the world of matter came into existence. These intermediary beings are the *Ten S'firos,* which bear such names as Wisdom, Mercy, Majesty. The Cabalists discuss at length the functions of the various S'firos, their relationships to one another, and the channels of communication between them; for our purpose it is sufficient to understand that through them the moral values inherent in God's nature are made available to the world. The S'firos are not conceived as persons—they are rather instruments for God's self-revelation. Perhaps we might picture them as bays or straits, filled with water from the boundless ocean—they are not the ocean, yet not apart from it.

The divine light is transmitted to man through the S'firos; but there is an upward as well as a downward movement. Man aspires toward God. The process of self-purification and contemplation leads man through the S'firos toward the Infinite. The S'firos constitute a Jacob's ladder on which the messengers of God descend and by which the mystic rises rung by rung toward God.

But this is not all. The structure of reality here described suggests that man and God are interdependent. Man could not exist without God; but the spiritual forces of the divine world are conserved and enhanced by man's righteousness and piety, and dissipated by man's sin. By prayer and good deeds, the Zohar declares, man creates hosts of angels; by wrong-doing he multiplies the destructive spirits. Thus man's smallest action is not only of concern to himself and to society: it has cosmic consequences.

4. The Source of Evil

Through the centuries, the serious monotheist has had to struggle with the problem of evil. How is it that a good God, who is the Only God, tolerates the existence of so much suffering and wickedness? This problem, posed with unequaled power and intensity in the Book of Job, still continues to trouble both the minds and the hearts of men. Rabbinic Judaism assumed generally that suffering is a punishment for sin; and the seeming inequities of this world are corrected in life beyond death. Indeed, the Rabbis suggested that the righteous suffer in this world so that, having expiated their few offenses, they may enter into unalloyed bliss; whereas God squares accounts with the wicked for their few merits by giving them prosperity in the here and now. Their punishment will come hereafter.

But such a solution does not even attempt to meet the darker mystery: how can there be evil at all in a world that is the creation of a good and loving God?

The medieval Jewish philosophers had touched upon this problem, and had disposed of it by answers that were neither original nor satisfying. One of the solutions offered is that evil has no positive existence: it is merely the absence of good. God did not, therefore, have to create evil, since it is not an entity but only a lack. Another answer is that evil, while real, is only apparently bad; in the long run (if we had but vision to understand) it serves a good purpose. Such explanations (and there were others), however they differ in form, are alike in that they minimize the seriousness of the problem.

The Cabalists lived in an age that could no longer shrug off the realities of human wickedness and human agony. Though a few of the more philosophic Cabalists were inclined to accept the Neo-Platonic view that evil is non-being, most of the mystics saw a genuine and terrifying reality in evil, whose origin is in the cosmic process itself. This is expressed in a variety of striking symbolisms.

Every process, physiological or industrial, produces waste products. The existence of such unpleasant substances does not imply that the original material was bad; the waste is an inevitable accompaniment of the essential process.

A more familiar form of this symbolism describes the forces of evil as "husks." The shell of a nut has neither taste nor nutritive value; but somehow, the nut cannot grow without it.

Another type of symbolism derives ultimately from ancient Christian heretics, who identified good with the right side and evil with the left (sinister). One of the commonest diagrams of the Ten S'firos arranges them to correspond with the parts of the human body; the Ten S'firos together form the "Primordial Man." In this pattern, the S'firos that correspond to God's qualities of strict justice and punishment are placed on the left side of the cosmic body: and it is through them that suffering enters the cosmos.

A more radical version of this symbolism supposes that just as the Ten S'firos of holiness emanated "to the right," so Ten S'firos of impurity emanated "to the left." This comes dangerously close to the dualism of ancient Persia. However, the Cabalists insisted that the leftward

emanation is inferior in origin and dignity to the holy rightward emanation. The S'firos of impurity are not in equal opposition to the holy
S'firos, but are rather a parody of them. Evil is always inferior and
subordinate to good.

What is common to all these interpretations is the notion that evil
has roots deep within the structure of God's own life and world. It will
not be fully overcome until the final redemption. The Messiah, in
cabalistic thought, is a cosmic figure as much as (or more than) he is
a national liberator. There is much apocalyptic material in the Zohar,
but the full and tragic flowering of mystical Messianism came later.

The cabalistic account of the source of evil is a profound one; yet it
was linked with some of the crudest survivals of primitive mythology
and superstition. The "husks" of the cosmic process, the "left side" of
the double emanation, were identified with a host of demons and evil
spirits, including not only Satan and Lilith, but many more with odd
names and grotesque characteristics. Thus the way was open for the
burgeoning of superstitious fears and of customs designed to allay them.

5. Prayer, Study, and Commandments

The mystics laid great stress on prayer. Whereas, some of the Talmudists and philosophers, while following the prescribed order of prayers,
had regarded study as more important, the Cabalists restored prayer to
a central place. Long before, the Rabbis had insisted that prayer requires *kavono*—concentrated attention. "When you pray," said Rabbi
Eliezer, "let it not be a matter of routine, but a plea for mercy and
grace before God." This ancient doctrine was now vigorously stressed;
but the Cabalists gave a new meaning to the word kavono. Before the
most important sections of the daily prayers, they inserted introductions
on which the worshipper was to meditate before he recited the prayer
in question. Some of these kavonos are noble and inspiring; others are
no more than incantations designed to bring the angels near to receive
and transmit the prayer.

Many mystics—since the days of the apostle Paul—have been impatient of law, and especially of ceremony. They have supposed that one
who knew God by direct experience would serve Him spontaneously
and did not need to bind himself by petty rules. This was not the view
of the Cabalists. Holding that every item of man's conduct has its effect
for good or bad in the heavenly levels, they were even more precise
than the Talmudists in matters of ritual. Secret meanings were read

into every ceremonial detail. The first page of the Zohar prescribes that one who recites Kiddush on Sabbath or festivals should grasp the wine cup with all five fingers. Thus he is reminded of the five-petaled rose of Sharon, to which the Bible compares Israel. The mystics also introduced some new customs, notably the Midnight Ritual, in which the pious mourned for the lost Temple and prayed for its restoration.

Thus, while Maimonides had attempted to find a rational explanation of the ceremonial commandments, the Cabalists invested these observances with imaginative and poetic meanings.

Their approach to the stories of the Bible was similar. Like the philosophers, they were not satisfied with a simple literalism. The narratives of the Torah, they declared, cloak inner truths which the spiritually discerning can perceive; this inner truth is the soul of the Torah, of which the stories constitute the body. But the cabalistic allegories were far more complex and often more interesting than those of the rationalists. The latter regarded the Biblical characters as personifications of abstract religious and ethical concepts. Thus they reduced many a dramatic story to a rather insipid moralistic parable. In the same stories, the Cabalists found the secrets of the S'firos, hints of God's self-revelation, suggestions for new and surprising symbolism. Such interpretations assuredly helped no one to understand the Bible as such; yet they at least stimulated awe and wonder in the presence of Scripture—a mood that the philosophers sometimes explained away.

In attempting to estimate the value of the Cabala, we must recognize first that for four centuries it dominated Jewish religious thought. A doctrine that so greatly met the inner needs of scholars and plain folk alike through so many dark years cannot be lightly dismissed. There was a sharp reaction against Cabala in the nineteenth century; and it is only in recent generations that Jewish scholars have begun again to study it with open-minded and sympathetic understanding.

Second, the average individual has little access to the most important aspect of the Cabala—the inner experience of the mystics who, following the doctrine in theory and practice, ascended through the S'firos to spiritual union with the Infinite. From the exterior of a planetarium, one could hardly imagine the inspiring experience of those who attend the performance inside.

Yet one need not be a mystic in order to see the value of a movement that stressed warmth of piety and ardor in prayer. Scattered through the cabalistic writings, amid much that is unintelligible or unimportant, are many quaint and poetic thoughts inspiring to the modern reader.

The Cabala 207

Echoes of cabalistic doctrine appear in the writings of Spinoza; and the doctrine that man's conduct can strengthen or weaken the divine world recurs in present-day philosophies.

But in its time, the Cabala was literally a weapon for survival. A crisis was brewing which would allow the Jews little time for contemplation, whether of philosophic concepts or of mystical secrets. The hour of complete tragedy was at hand.

Part 5.
Within Ghetto Walls

30.

Darkness at Sunrise

THE CHRISTIAN MIDDLE AGES REACHED THEIR IMPRESSIVE CLIMAX IN the thirteenth century. An intellectual awakening, stimulated by the scientific and philosophic activity of Arabs and Jews, led to the establishment of universities. Great cathedrals were reared in majesty, and Thomas Aquinas produced his no less monumental synthesis of Christian doctrine.

But by the end of this wonderful thirteenth century, to whose cultural achievements the Jews had contributed so much, European Jewry was in tragic decline. The Jews had been expelled from England and were shortly to be banished from France. In the German states massacre, humiliation, exorbitant taxes, and periodic expulsions had destroyed all sense of security, and the Jews were seeking new homes. And dark clouds were gathering over the great Jewish community of Spain.

Gradually, a new cultural outlook developed in Europe. Medieval life, dominated by the Church, had been largely concerned with the means of escaping hell and entering heaven. Now men began to devote themselves more to human values, to the enjoyment of both physical and intellectual delights in the here and now, and to the cultivation of secular literature. There was a great revival of interest in the Latin classics—a revival which was perhaps both a cause and a result of the new spirit. The Renaissance began in the fourteenth century in Italy, and gradually spread its light throughout western Europe. In 1453 the Turks captured Constantinople, and many of the Byzantine scholars fled westward, bringing with them the surviving masterpieces of Greek literature. A great enthusiasm for the classic culture of antiquity was kindled, and men began eagerly to study and to imitate all its phases —literature, philosophy, science, sculpture, architecture, and the enjoyment of life. Thus, the Renaissance was a revolt against medieval authority, an increasingly confident assertion of man's mental and spiritual independence, and (in some degree) a return to joyous paganism.

There was also a Hebraic side to the Renaissance. Though the major enthusiasm of students was for the Greek and Latin classics, many Gentiles were also attracted to Hebrew. Jewish scholars instructed Christian intellectuals in the grammar and text of the Bible, and even guided some into the rockier pathways of Talmud and Cabala.

In 1509 a Jewish apostate named Pfefferkorn began, after the traditions of his sort, a campaign for the suppression of the Talmud, which he declared was full of wicked anti-Christian teachings. The Dominican monks backed his efforts, and the Jews of Germany had real cause for anxiety over the fate of their sacred texts. But it was the great Christian humanist, Johannes Reuchlin, who answered the charges of Pfefferkorn and defended the Talmud. This was indeed something new, a far cry from the day when twenty-four cartloads of Talmud manuscripts were burnt at Paris because of the slanders of an apostate.

Reuchlin and other scholars of the Renaissance were fascinated in particular by the Cabala. Certain symbolisms of the Zohar seem somewhat akin to the doctrine of the Trinity; and Christian students hoped to find in the Cabala a confirmation of their own beliefs and perhaps a means of bringing the Jews into the Church.

From this time on Hebraic studies have been cultivated by Christian scholars in many of the great universities. The Christian Hebraists have usually concentrated on the Bible, though not a few have also mastered the later Hebrew literature. Such knowledge has not invariably generated sympathy for Jews and Judaism; some Hebraists have used their learning as a weapon against the people and faith of Israel. But they have been the exceptions.

Thus the Jews exerted a significant though limited influence on the Renaissance. In turn, Jewish life, especially in Italy, was affected somewhat by the new trends. Though the name and the institution of the ghetto had their origin in Italy, its Jews enjoyed comparative tranquillity for many centuries. Some of the Renaissance popes were themselves pagan at heart, and disinclined to persecute others for their beliefs. For a long time there were friendly contacts between Jew and Christian.

Immanuel of Rome, a Hebrew poet of pleasant if minor talents, was a contemporary of the great Dante. He composed a Hebrew imitation of the *Inferno* and *Paradiso,* not to be compared to the original in either length or quality. Yet Immanuel's poem, in consonance with his Jewish background, displayed a breadth of tolerance which Dante could not attain. The *Divine Comedy* consigned the greatest pre-Christian saints to the nether regions, in accordance with the doctrine that outside the Church there is no salvation. Immanuel, however, found a place in heaven for the pious Gentiles, including a departed friend called Daniel. But the tempting theory, once widely held, that Dante and Immanuel were personally acquainted, seems untenable.

There was indeed a liberal spirit in Italian Jewry. A fourteenth century rabbi, resident in Rome, was bold enough to compose a genial parody on the Talmud, as a diversion for the Purim festival. A century later, Elijah del Medigo was defending the propriety of scientific and philosophic studies against the protests of the official rabbinate; he was permitted to lecture at the University of Padua.

Elijah Levita,* who instructed eminent churchmen in Hebrew, proved that the Hebrew vowel points were not invented until after the completion of the Talmud (1538). This was a revolutionary view for his time, because it challenged the antiquity of the Zohar, the most sacred text of the Cabala. For the Zohar, then generally accepted as a product of the early Talmudic period, makes repeated reference to the vowel signs.

About forty years after Levita, Azariah dei Rossi published the first work on Jewish history to be written in the scientific spirit. Azariah utilized non-Jewish sources and non-Hebrew Jewish writings—such as the Apocrypha and Josephus—to elucidate the history of the Jews, and he is the first Hebrew writer to mention the name and work of Philo. And Judah Moscato, the Chief Rabbi of Mantua, did not hesitate to adorn his sermons with quotations from Gentile authors and allusions to classical mythology as well as references to the Midrash and the Cabala.

Even during the ghetto period, these tendencies persisted. The Italian Jews were concerned with elegance in manners, speech, and literature. They continued to write secular poetry in both Italian and Hebrew. Their beautiful ceremonial objects were sometimes decorated with human figures, in contravention of the letter of the law.

A vigorous conservative party opposed all such worldly vanities.

---

* Levita was of German birth, but lived a great part of his life in Italy.

Azariah dei Rossi was bitterly attacked for his unorthodox views, despite earnest and repeated assertions of his loyalty to the Torah. But outside Italy there were no such figures at all.

One event of the Renaissance had a great effect on all Judaism: the invention of printing. The new art was hailed with delight by Jews, so long devoted to learning. A high proportion of the oldest printed books are in Hebrew. Several early printers were Jews, but here politics and prejudice interfered. The beautiful Hebrew books published in Venice —for many years the world's printing center—came from the presses of Christian publishers, who alone could obtain the necessary license.

Printing developed in an age when the Jews were on the economic downgrade. By providing a relatively cheap and plentiful supply of books, it helped greatly in the maintenance of cultural traditions when time and money for the copying of manuscripts were getting tragically scarce.

An important effect of this new invention was the crystallization of the Jewish prayer book. The main features of the liturgy had been fixed long since; but there was still a great deal of variety. For the holy day service in particular, each locality had its own selection of *piyyutim* or hymns, which surrounded and embellished the standard prayers. The chazanim, in addition to composing the music of the synagogue, were frequently authors of piyyutim. While some of them produced fine hymns, other "creative" spirits cluttered up the service with lengthy, obscure and ungrammatical compositions. The invention of printing put a stop to this whole trend. The particular copies which happened to be given to the printer became the set forms of prayer. Not that a single standard version was ever universally accepted. The S'fardic and Ashk'nazic prayer books are materially different, the former being shorter and simpler. The Ashk'nazim adopted more of the piyyutim, including long and difficult poems by Kalir and his imitators, whereas the Spanish Jews utilized the shorter and more beautiful hymns of their own great poets. Within these two divisions there were still a good many local variations, but these were few in proportion to the situation before the prayer book was printed. And henceforth there were few additions to the service.

* * *

As Christian Spain grew stronger and the Moors were driven further to the south, the Jews became less essential to their masters and their lot grew steadily worse. The peculiarly gloomy and fanatical form of Catholicism characteristic of Spain was increasingly evident under the special guidance of the Dominican order. The popes had usually tried to protect the Jews against the grosser forms of violence, had repeatedly if ineffectively forbidden the blood libel, and had denied the propriety of forcible baptisms. But these papal rulings were disregarded by the Spanish enthusiasts. In 1391 the storm broke. Roused by the preaching of a fanatical priest, Ferrand Martinez, the mobs broke loose throughout Spain, and within a few months, fifty thousand Jews were massacred. More than double that number were dragged into the churches and forcibly converted. Children were torn from their parents and baptized. The great Spanish Jewish community had been destroyed: the next hundred years is simply the record of a dreadful death agony.

These mass conversions created a novel problem, which issued in one of the strangest and most pathetic episodes of human history. For ecclesiastical law as interpreted in Spain regarded these baptisms—however insincere, however much the result of intimidation or physical force—as valid and irrevocable. The unbaptized Jew was a proper object of persecution, but he was not under the direct supervision of the Church. Once touched with the baptismal waters, however, he was a Christian. Any attempt to abandon his new faith was heresy and mortal sin. And so the Marranos come into existence, Jews by birth and conviction, forced to maintain the appearance of conformity to the Catholic religion.

For a time the Marranos enjoyed considerable well-being. No longer officially Jews, they were free from all the galling restrictions which fettered Jewish initiative and ability; and they rose rapidly in commerce, the professions—including the Church!—and the service of the state. In many cases their adherence to Catholicism was hardly more than nominal, and they maintained contact with their sympathetic brother Jews.

But this soon became a public scandal. It is hard to say how much of what followed was due to resentment at the success of the Marranos and how much to genuine dismay at the insincerity of their Catholicism. At any rate, conditions changed radically. Various restrictions were placed on the activities of the "New Christians" and severe religious checks were instituted. As these seemed inadequate, the papal permission was secured in 1480 for the establishment of the Holy Inquisition in Spain.

We need not relate here the history and activities of this sinister organization, the tortures, burnings, confiscations, the trials conducted without a semblance of justice, and the autos da fé, at which men and women were burned to death amid elaborate pageantry. Hundreds died and thousands escaped with their lives only after horrible torture, humiliating recantations, and the loss of all their property. Year after year the tortures and the burnings continued; among the victims were many who were mighty in the state and even notable figures of the Church.

Finally the Grand Inquisitor, Tomas de Torquemada, decided that the New Christians would never become sincere Catholics so long as they had the evil example of professing Jews before their eyes. The Jews must therefore either convert en masse or go into exile. This decision dovetailed nicely with the conquest of Granada, the last Moslem stronghold in Spain. Now that the entire peninsula was in Christian hands, Jewish financiers could be dispensed with. The decision was forced by Torquemada, through his influence on the gloomy but pious Queen Isabella. King Ferdinand was somewhat hesitant, especially when his Jewish treasurer, Isaac Abrabanel, offered huge sums for the withdrawal of the decree. But fanaticism prevailed, and the Jews had to go. Few sought refuge in conversion—the experience of the Marranos had proved that baptism was a bad bargain. In August, 1492, the grief-stricken exiles left the shores of Spain, many to find no refuge anywhere except—after unspeakable hardships—in death. A large proportion, however, were able to establish new homes in the East. In Constantinople and its hinterland, as well as in the cities of Greece that were under Turkish rule, the Jews were decently received.* Other exiles found homes in Africa; many, including Abrabanel, in Italy. Here this eminent statesman and man of affairs wrote a fitting epitaph to the glories of Jewish Spain by composing voluminous works on the Bible and on various religious questions. Learned and pious, he showed no special originality; yet he closed with dignity and honor the glorious chapter of Spanish Judaism.

But the expulsion of the Jews did not solve the Marrano problem as Torquemada had expected. Even when the royal houses of Portugal and Spain were united in marriage, and in accordance with the terms of this union the Jews were expelled from Portugal with horrible cruelty,

---

* The S'fardic exiles generally formed their own communities, through which they preserved not only their distinctive religious forms, but also their Spanish speech. This Judeo-Spanish dialect includes many Hebrew words and is usually written in Hebrew characters. It is called *Ladino.*

the New Christians still held fast to the secret practice of Judaism. The fires of the Inquisition continued to burn and were even to be kindled in Mexico and Peru. Meantime, new havens of refuge appeared. The great Jewish centers of the Western world—Holland, England, America —were established by Marranos who fled from Spain and Portugal and returned to Judaism some three centuries after their ancestors had been baptized. More astonishing still, some half-remembered, oddly distorted remnants of Judaism persisted among the Portuguese Marranos to the twentieth century, when a Jewish engineer prospecting in Portugal discovered their existence. The surviving Marranos have now openly returned to Judaism and there are synagogues in the chief Portuguese cities.

A different fate befell the Jews on the Island of Majorca. These, too, were forced to adopt Christianity, and their conversion seems to have become ultimately sincere. But the anti-Jewish prejudices of their Gentile neighbors continued even after they were both in name and spirit adherents of the Church. To this day the New Christians of Majorca are a segregated group, who marry only among themselves, and who bear the opprobrious name of Chuetas—pigs!

With the Spanish Expulsion a darkness settled over European Jewry that—save for occasional fitful gleams—was not to be dispelled for nearly three hundred bitter years. The age of the ghetto had arrived.

31.

The Ghetto Days

THE PROTESTANT REFORMATION WAS THE RESULT OF MANY FORCES, social, political, and intellectual as well as religious. On the theological side, it was a challenge to the apostolic tradition on which the Catholic Church based her authority. Instead, the reformers turned directly to Scripture, as the Karaites had done within Judaism centuries before. The various Protestant sects arose largely out of disagreements over the interpretation of the Bible.

Early in his career, Martin Luther professed friendship for the Jews: they could not really be blamed for rejecting Christianity in the Roman version. But his hopes that they would accept his purified form of the Christian faith were not fulfilled. In his later writings, Luther repeated the old anti-Jewish slanders with unrestrained bitterness, and many other Protestants followed his example. The religious wars which came in the wake of the Reformation constantly terrorized the Jewish communities of Germany.

But the consequences of the upheaval were even more serious for Jews in lands that remained Catholic. The Reformation had begun as a protest against indifference, cynicism and corruption within the Roman church. The defenders of the papacy would not yield an inch to the claims of the reformers, but they recognized that a lax and insincere leadership could not hold the loyalty of the people. Through the Counter-Reformation, order and discipline were restored to the Catholic Church. Christian doctrine was precisely defined, and uncompromising adherence was demanded. The mood of Catholicism was more rigid and severe in the sixteenth than in the thirteenth century.

In the opinion of many clerics, the Jews were to blame for the Protestant heresy. There was this much truth in the charge: the study of the Hebrew Bible, made possible by Jewish instructors, had been one factor among many in bringing on the Reformation. The Catholic leaders, determined to establish complete religious uniformity in their domain, took steps to prevent the masses from being influenced by Jewish ideas. The ghetto decrees went forth.

The resulting system was not basically new: What made it so horrible was its consistent, unrelenting enforcement.

From the earliest days of the Diaspora, Jews had tended to live in the same section of a city, just as they do today in many places. The natural impulse to congregate with their own kind was supplemented by two practical necessities—to be within walking distance of a synagogue or at least of a religious quorum (*minyon*), and to provide mutual protection against enemies.

For centuries, moreover, the rights of Jewish residence had been subject to restrictions. Whether out of social hostility, the desire to simplify the collection of special taxes, or the religious purpose of keeping Christians (or Moslems) free from Hebraic contamination, special quarters had been set aside in many communities for Jewish residence. But as a rule, these regulations were not absolutely ironclad. Where Jewish populations grew and prospered, they were often able to increase the area set aside for them, and they were never entirely segregated from their non-Jewish neighbors.

Likewise, there had been in existence for centuries decrees of the Church and the states, requiring the Jews to wear a distinctive dress or badge. But these decrees had seldom been rigidly enforced; indifference on the part of the Christian authorities, plus a little bribery or wire-pulling, had enabled the Jews to evade these humiliating measures.

But now the Church, with full cooperation from civil authorities, set out efficiently and systematically to segregate and degrade all Jews. In those cities of Germany, Austria, and Italy, where they were still permitted to live at all, a limited area was set aside for them, generally in the most unhealthy part of the city. In Germany this area was called simply the Jew's street (*Judengasse*); in Italy it received by accident the special name of ghetto.* It was separated from the rest of the city by walls and gates, within which all Jews had to withdraw by nightfall,

---

* The quarter first set aside for the Jews of Venice was near a cannon foundry (*geto* or ghetto).

and in which they were locked all day on Christian church holidays. The effect of the walls was likewise to prevent the Jews from extending their quarter, no matter how much their numbers increased. The ghetto thus became more and more overcrowded, with inevitable damage both to health and to the general tone of life. Since all Jews had to live within these restricted areas, since there never was sufficient space, and since the ghetto real estate was frequently owned by Gentiles, there was danger that rents would be forced steadily upward. The rabbis, therefore, applied the principle of *hazakah*—possession—forbidding any Jew to offer a higher rent for a dwelling occupied by another Jew, and permitting the transmission by inheritance of the right to a lease.

When the Jew left the ghetto area for any purpose he had to wear the yellow badge, so that he might be immediately recognized and singled out. This provision, humiliating in itself, was also an invitation to toughs to attack or insult him with impunity. The exorbitant taxes Jews had to pay for "protection," the laws limiting the number of Jewish marriages and excluding Jews from productive occupations, the oath in the Jewish fashion required of Jews who appeared in the courts, which implied that every Jew was an inveterate liar and cheat— all this constituted a complete apparatus of mental torture.

Physically, the Jew lost ground in the ghetto. The unwholesome conditions, the lack of light and air, shortened his stature and lessened his physical sturdiness. These factors, combined with the systematic humiliation to which he was subjected, caused some decline of morale. One should not read too much into this statement. The ghetto Jew was neither a coward nor a crook. That the people managed to preserve its moral decency through these centuries of degradation is testimony to the soundness of the stock and to the ethical magnificence of the religion. It is a great glory and little short of a miracle that the Jews came through this ordeal so well. But they would not have been human had they emerged entirely unscathed. In the recorded actions and in the writings of the ghetto period there is less boldness and independence than in previous centuries. Nor is it surprising that, excluded from most of the normal ways of livelihood, economically handicapped and then insanely overtaxed, some Jews should have cracked under the strain and resorted to devious business methods. There is no need to offer excuses. The moral decline in Judaism—limited though it was—is the shame of the oppressor, not of the oppressed.

From the standpoint of Judaism, the chief result of the ghetto conditions was to insulate the religion from contact with new trends in life and thought. The ghetto Jews in their enforced isolation even developed dialects of their own, notably in Germany, where the Judeo-German dialect preserved archaisms that disappeared from the general speech, and had its own peculiarities of idiom and pronunciation, as well as a large vocabulary of Hebrew words. Even Jewish leaders and teachers knew and cared little about the thought currents of their time. The flowering of the Renaissance hardly touched the Jews outside of Italy. The great names of seventeenth and eighteenth century science and philosophy—Newton, Descartes, Harvey, Leibniz, Locke—meant nothing to them. For the best part of three centuries Jewish life was static.

But there is no such thing as static life. Where there is no progress, there is retrogression. Judaism in the ghetto period not only failed to keep abreast of the times—it receded from its own highest achievements. The liberalism of the Golden Age was neglected and even condemned; a narrow Talmudism was generally dominant.

The halakah received its last authoritative formulation in the code known as the *Shulchan Aruch* or Set Table. Its author, a S'fardic exile, Joseph Karo, had written an immense commentary on the *Four Rows,* the code of Jacob ben Asher. In this work, he subjected every item of the current halakah to a profound critical analysis, clarifying both the principles and the details of the law. Karo then decided to compile a briefer and simpler code for the use of students. The *Shulchan Aruch* (first printed in 1567), a sort of popular version of the *Four Rows,* had a fate similar to that of the Mishnah in its time. Designed chiefly for educational purposes, it became an authority. To this day Karo's code is standard in Orthodox Judaism.

Some rather pointless abuse has been poured upon the *Shulchan Aruch* by certain Jewish modernists. It lacks indeed the philosophic breath and the universalistic spirit that mark the code of Maimonides, but then over three hundred years of bloody persecution had intervened between the production of the two works. The substance of all halakic codes is the same—the Talmudic law, with its admitted limitations and its very great virtues.

Nor was it the fault of Karo and his work that the law had crystallized so rigidly. The code was a result rather than a cause of this situation. The halakah had become less and less fluid through the centuries. The bold creativeness of Hillel and Akiba had long since disappeared. The halakists of succeeding centuries continued to operate with the same material, and after a time its ultimate implications were pretty thoroughly worked out. Almost every imaginable practical issue had been solved, so far as was possible within the framework of Talmudic law. Progress in the halakah would have required the introduction of new elements and creative methods—such as the early giants of the Talmud had supplied. But each succeeding generation of scholars grew more timid in its adherence to the precedents and customs of earlier days. The work of Alfasi, Maimonides, and the other codifiers hastened the process of which the *Shulchan Aruch* marks the culmination.

The ghetto period, then, was a period of unmistakable decline. The Jews, who previously had been abreast and frequently ahead of the cultural life of their time, had almost no share in the development of the new European civilization. Their outlook was narrowly conservative, often obscurantist. Yet they clung with stubborn fidelity to a heritage that insured their spiritual survival. Their lofty traditions of family life provided warmth and cheer; the commandment to study the Torah preserved their intellectual vigor and sanity; and despite sordid poverty, they kept intact their communal and philanthropic institutions.

Another instrument of survival that should not be overlooked was the Jewish sense of humor. Much of the characteristically Jewish humor reflects the frustrations of ghetto life. Its typical figures are the *shlemiel*, the well-meaning individual who may be good at book learning, but always does the wrong thing in practical matters, and the *luftmensch*, whose head is full of grandiose schemes while his pockets are empty. These types were the inevitable products of the abnormal economic position of the Jews.

Yet strangely, during the ghetto period, the largest number of Jews did not reside in literal ghettos: the ghetto in the strict sense was found only in Italy and central Europe, and in the backward countries of North Africa. (The Moslem version of the ghetto was called the *mellah*.) Nevertheless, this was a ghetto period for nearly all Jewry, as we shall see in the next chapter.

32.

New Centers

1. Holland

THERE WAS ONE JEWISH COMMUNITY DURING THE GHETTO CENTURIES
which could be called truly fortunate. It was established at the beginning of the seventeenth century in the Netherlands, and was concentrated largely in the city of Amsterdam. The success of the Dutch in
driving the Spaniards from their little country and setting up a quasi-
republican commonwealth thrilled many Spanish and Portuguese Marranos who, despite two centuries of outward conformity, were still Jews
at heart. At the risk of their lives and the sacrifice of their fortunes,
they slipped away, came to Amsterdam, and there openly returned to
their ancestral faith. Once assured that these immigrants were not
Catholic spies, the Dutch gave them a friendly reception. Holland is the
only European nation with a substantial Jewish community that has
never persecuted its Jews. Not, of course, that the Jews were granted
full rights of citizenship; but they had security and the opportunity to
make a living and to practice their faith without molestation—and they
proved with distinction that fair treatment of the Jews benefits the
country of their abode.

At the start, the community was faced with considerable religious
difficulties, even after they had secured permission to conduct services
and bought a place for a cemetery. For the majority of these ex-
Marranos, however persistent their loyalty to the faith of their fathers,
had only the vaguest notions about it. They secured the services of

several rabbis and, under their leadership, gradually readjusted themselves to the forms of Jewish life. Chief among the early leaders was Rabbi Saul Morteira, a stern disciplinarian, who literally whipped the Jewish community into shape. His harshness is comprehensible when we realize how little some of his charges understood the spirit of Judaism, supposing—for instance—that they might atone for their sins by confessing them to the rabbi, as they had done once to the priest! It is in this light that we must understand Morteira's policies regarding the two famous heretics of the community, Uriel Acosta and Baruch Spinoza.

The first of these men was a truly pathetic, the second, a truly admirable figure. Beside them, Morteira appears as the narrow bigot— a judgment something less than fair.

Acosta was a Portuguese Marrano, unstable and hypersensitive, who even before he could return to Judaism had worked out a Jewish philosophy of his own. His notions were somewhat akin to those later promulgated by Reform Judaism. He professed a religion of prophetic idealism, with little concern for the authority of the halakah. When he arrived in Amsterdam, and openly returned to the ancestral faith, he was deeply disappointed to find that the Judaism of reality was a more pedestrian discipline than he had imagined.

He found himself caught in a situation from which he lacked the spiritual strength to escape. He could not submit to the rabbinic authority and conform to Jewish law without question; nor could he make a clean break from the community, for the fellowship of which he yearned. Twice he was expelled from the synagogue for unmistakably heretical utterances; twice he was readmitted after recantation and penance of an extremely humiliating character. Finally, he poured out his despair in a touching autobiography and committed suicide.

These weaknesses were not found in Spinoza, who knew exactly where he stood, and was fully prepared to accept the consequences of his decisions. For Spinoza was a philosopher in action as well as in thought. The son of a Marrano family, he was born in Amsterdam and received a good grounding in Jewish lore. Nor did his teachers object to his interest in secular studies as such; but when he began to voice unorthodox opinions, they were deeply troubled. Regretting perhaps the tragic results of their severity toward Acosta, they tried to arrive at an understanding with him: they would leave him undisturbed if he would conform outwardly to Judaism and refrain from expressing his radical views to the youth of the community. Spinoza was unable to accede to these terms. As he himself said later, his excommunication did not change his status: for he had already put himself outside the Synagogue.

One cannot but regret the vehemence of the curses called down upon his head for following the dictates of his own mind and conscience, as one cannot but wish that the Rabbis had been gentler to the sensitive Acosta. But essentially they were justified and their instinct was sound. Their responsibility was to gather the scattered sheep of Israel and to lead them in the way of the Torah. The root principle of traditional Judaism is that the Torah is God-given and hence authoritative. To have tolerated within the Jewish community men who openly challenged this principle would have been the most flagrant dereliction of duty. Morteira could not know, and would not have cared, that the errant pupil whom he had loved so much was to become a titanic figure in the history of philosophy. But the soundness of his judgment is vindicated by the fact that the Amsterdam Jewish community which he so largely created was for centuries a model of honor, learning, and piety; in particular, the charitable and the educational systems of the community were unsurpassed.

We shall not attempt to present fully the philosophic doctrines of Spinoza, because of a definite conviction that they do not belong to the history of Judaism. True, some people insist that Spinoza's doctrine is Jewish, even that it represents the most perfect interpretation of Judaism; but less partisan students find a basic contradiction between Spinozistic philosophy and Jewish religion. It is likewise true that Spinoza drew to a considerable extent on his Jewish background. He was the first openly to challenge the Mosaic authorship of the Pentateuch; but as he freely admitted, his Biblical criticism was based on the hints of Ibn Ezra, who reproduced the opinions of Moses ibn Gikatilla. In his philosophic thinking, he shows unmistakable traces of the influence of Maimonides, Crescas, and even the Cabala. Yet the total effect of his work is thoroughly un-Jewish.

Spinoza was a pantheist—he identified God and the world. Such a doctrine was not unknown in Judaism, before and since, but with a difference. The Cabalists, for example, regarded the universe as a living manifestation of God. It is pervaded with divine influences, but it is not identical with En Sof. But to Spinoza the world *is* God. The mental and spiritual life of man is just as much part of God as the rocks or the sea; but Spinoza's God has no conscious purpose, no relationship to humanity. He is not a loving Father; prayer cannot be addressed to Him. As we have seen, Jewish monotheism is fundamentally ethical. Between the two outlooks there is a basic and un-bridgeable gap.

Second, Spinoza's outlook on human life is different from that of Judaism. Jewish ethics have a dynamic quality and are directed toward the achievement of a noble society. The ethic of Spinoza is thoroughly intellectual and lacks that intense upward striving that derives from the prophets. There is no revolt against the world as it is, no messianic hope, even in the most rarefied form. Spinoza is the preacher of resignation. The individual finds salvation by freeing himself from outward ambition and inner emotional turmoil, and by adjusting himself to the universe as it is. Even repentance is bad, because it disturbs one's philosophic balance. The ultimate goal is the "intellectual love of God." This term does not mean that burning devotion to God that produced the martyrs of Israel, but an intellectual assent to the universe and a detached contemplation thereof. One cannot reconcile the athleticism of Jewish ethics—which may be called the ethics of protest —with the pallidly beautiful submissiveness of the philosopher.

Finally, Spinoza himself regarded his doctrine as a complete break with Jewish tradition. True enough, the Jewish reformers of a later century were to agree with him in denying that the Bible and the halakah were supernaturally ordained. But they consciously sought to reinterpret and revitalize the essential elements of the Jewish tradition, whereas Spinoza turned his back upon it. Nor are his writings entirely free from unfair and unfriendly references to the Jewish people and their faith. Even his saintly character occasionally betrayed its human limitations. And so, while Jews may take pride in the fact that this wise and noble spirit issued from the Jewish group, Spinoza cannot—any more than Paul—be classed among the spokesmen of the Jewish spirit.

The Amsterdam community was noteworthy more for its generally high standard than for unusual accomplishments or original thinkers; but one personality must be mentioned, of a type new to Jewish life, Rabbi Menasseh ben Israel. He was the first famous Rabbi whose prestige was not based primarily on his attainments as a Talmudist. Menasseh was a popular preacher, a writer in several secular tongues, and an ambassador to the Gentiles. Menasseh's particular interest was Messianism, which—as we shall see—was coming to the fore again; and from this interest arose his famous mission to England.

For Menasseh was convinced from his study of the Biblical prophecies that the arrival of the Messiah must be preceded by a dispersal of the Jews in all the lands of the world. A few had recently emigrated to the Dutch colonies in South America, and—so he was convinced—Britain was now the only land which completely barred them. In 1655 he went to England, and by published writings and personal contacts tried to have the edict of expulsion revoked. Despite the sympathetic interest of Cromwell, mercantile and religious opposition prevented Parliament from approving the plan. (But as a matter of fact, there were already some Marranos living in London whose presence was an open secret; and from the time of Menasseh their number increased without hindrance. Formal recognition of the right of Jews to live in Britain was not, however, accorded till 1688, when the Dutch ruler, William of Orange, ascended the English throne.) Menasseh's arguments were based both on his Biblical theories and on the practical usefulness of the Jews to the state; and he was the first Jew to defend in Latin and several modern languages the character and worth of his fellow Jews.

Some of the S'fardic exiles of 1492, as we have seen, found refuge in various Italian states which had comparatively liberal policies. Subsequently, a good many Marranos were able to settle in Italian cities, and even to return openly to Judaism. Despite ghetto regulations, a surprising degree of modernity prevailed among Italian Jews. Several Jewish poetesses were numbered among the inhabitants of the Venice ghetto. Its most famous preacher, Leo da Modena, whose sermons attracted even Gentile tourists, was a complex and baffling personality. Brilliant, learned, and versatile, he was yet of unstable character, an inveterate and unsuccessful card player, and a chronically unhappy man. His many writings include a short treatise in Italian on Jewish customs and ceremonies, intended for Gentile readers.

2. Turkey

But the main trend of Jewish population was eastward. German Jews, as we shall see, were moving into Poland. The chief refuge of the S'fardim was the Turkish Empire, which included most of the Balkan area. The Turkish rulers were generally tolerant, and they recognized that the newcomers were an economic asset to their realm. Because of their skill in finance and public affairs and their attainments in secular and Hebraic culture, the Spanish Jews soon dominated the Jewish life of the Levant.

Their outstanding representatives were the fabulous Nasi family.

These wealthy, able, and courageous Marranos had lived for a time in Antwerp, where they directed an international "underground" to help New Christians escape to lands of freedom. For many years the head of the family was a woman, Doña Beatrice Mendes. From Antwerp she went to Italy, where she formally returned to Judaism as Doña Gracia Nasi. Eventually she settled in Constantinople; there she was joined by her nephew and co-worker, Don Joseph Nasi.

Doña Gracia and Don Joseph soon became welcome figures at the Turkish court and the commanding personalities of the Jewish community. "The Señora" continued her munificent help to the victims of persecution, and generously supported Jewish scholarship and literature. It was she who took the initiative in an extraordinary attempt at Jewish self-defense.

A considerable Marrano colony had grown up in the Italian port of Ancona. Under the stern direction of Paul IV, the Pope of the Counter-Reformation, these refugees were condemned and burned to death for abandoning Christianity (1556). When news of the tragedy reached Turkey, Doña Gracia organized a boycott of Jewish merchants and shipowners against the port of Ancona, which all but ruined the city. The boycott was not wholly successful; there were conflicting economic and political interests, and the rabbis disagreed as to the legal and moral justification of the proposal. But the incident is noteworthy because for once, the Jews protected their interests not by pleading or bribery, but by direct action—the first such instance perhaps, since the Bar Kochba rebellion.

For many years, Don Joseph was one of the most powerful men in the Turkish Empire. Suleiman the Magnificent made him ruler over the Palestinian city of Tiberias and its environs (though Joseph did not live there himself), and his son Selim II gave him the title of Duke of Naxos. No professing Jew had wielded such political power since the days of the independent Jewish commonwealth. To the end of his days, Joseph was the ardent advocate of Jewish interests.

But the Turkish Empire began to decline soon after the new immigrants arrived, and this decline was gradually reflected in the tone of Jewish life. Though there were some outstanding Talmudists among the Turkish rabbis, and the press of Contantinople produced many Hebrew works of value (in beauty they did not equal the exquisite Venetian prints), a mood of apathy gradually settled upon Turkish Jewry. It was to be broken only by a brief dramatic episode, which will be related in another chapter.

3. *Poland*

The greatest number of the Jews lived in the kingdom of Poland. They had flocked eastward in the fourteenth and fifteenth centuries, driven by the intolerable conditions in Germany and by the opportunities which this as yet undeveloped country afforded.

They found there a nation divided into two classes—the large body of arrogant, undisciplined, and uncultured nobility, and the far larger body of downtrodden and utterly ignorant serfs. There was no middle class, and to supply this need the Jews were welcomed by the Polish rulers. But because of this situation they were never more than slightly assimilated into Polish life. The nobility would not associate with them, save to employ them as stewards and business agents. With the illiterate bondmen of the soil, they could not meet on even terms. Thus the Jews in Poland formed a distinct group not only religiously, but economically, socially, and linguistically. The German dialect which they brought with them remained their daily language; they had no occasion to learn any more Polish than they needed for business purposes. Yiddish, as it has come to be called, became the spoken language, not only of the Jews of Poland, but of the related areas of Lithuania and the Ukraine. Written in Hebrew characters, it has remained an important factor in the life of world Jewry to the present day.

The economic advantages and the security afforded by royal charters resulted in the growth of numerous Polish-Jewish communities, many of them very large. And before long, this material well-being found its complement in an active intellectual life. But the lack of any cross-pollination by external contacts produced a sort of cultural inbreeding. The Jews of Poland lived in a spiritual ghetto, the result not of persecution but of the peculiar conditions in that backward country.

Thus the Jewish culture of Poland was limited to the Talmud, its commentators, and codifiers. In this field the Polish Jews had no rivals. Before long, Germany and Italy got their rabbinic leaders from Poland, or else sent their own promising students to the Polish academies for advanced study. The *Shulchan Aruch* won general acceptance only after the "Set Table" had been spread with a "Table-Cloth" by the Polish Rabbi, Moses Isserles, containing the Ashk'nazic decisions and customs. Some of the Polish Talmudists produced works of permanent value; but many of them were dazzled by a new approach invented in Germany towards the end of the Middle Ages, and known as *pilpul*. The word means "pepper." It is a method of studying the Talmud not for knowledge or inspiration, but to find complications, and then to solve these by involved and subtle argument. Because of its essential artificiality and its stress on intellectual gymnastics, pilpul was by no means wholesome for the mental outlook of young Jews.

Most remarkable was the popularity and extent of Polish Jewish scholarship. There never was a period when so many really erudite Jews were to be found. The Jewish boy who showed aptitude was afforded almost indefinite opportunity to pursue advanced studies, without charge if he could not afford to pay. After reaching his religious majority (Bar Mitzvah) at the age of thirteen, the studious boy left home and sought out some eminent Talmudist under whom he continued his studies. (Such *Wanderjahre* were deemed desirable even when there was an academy in his home city.) If his parents could not support him, he was fed and lodged—not well perhaps, but after a fashion—by the residents of the town in which he was staying. The laity prided themselves on the number of students which the local rabbi could attract, even at increased expense to his community. The young man often continued his studies until he was married; and if he displayed unusual talent, he was almost sure to make an advantageous match, however poor and obscure his origins. Frequently, his wife's parents enabled him to continue his studies for a few years after his marriage, before he was required to assume the financial burdens of family life.

These studies were carried on in the Talmudic spirit, "for their own sake." Comparatively few of those who undertook them sought the diploma of ordination, nor did all of the ordained accept posts in the official rabbinate. But no man could aspire to high regard in communal life unless he had a good Talmudic background. When a scholar married the daughter of a rich ignoramus, it was the scholar who condescended.

The Polish Jewish communities governed themselves for over a century through a representative body, known as "The Council of the Four Lands." This body was vested with the responsibility for collecting the taxes of the Polish Jews and transmitting them to the government; but it derived its prestige among the Jews less from this power than from the personal authority and influence of its members.

The laymen as well as the rabbis who were elected to the Council were men of learning and probity, and they directed the material and spiritual affairs of Polish Jewry with marked success. Again, when the chance was afforded, the democratic spirit of Judaism expressed itself with honor.

The educational set-up we have described continued, to a considerable extent, well into the nineteenth century. But the palmy days of Polish Jewry did not last so long. The decline began with the Counter-Reformation. Although the Lutheran movement did not spread very far in Poland, the Catholic authorities were fearful about it, the more so because the Poles had been converted from paganism but a few centuries since. The Jesuits were sent to take over the educational system of the country; and they went about the task aggressively. Their influence soon showed itself in the withdrawal of many privileges which the Jews had enjoyed for centuries; and though Jews and Poles had lived previously on amicable terms, popular outbreaks against the Jewish communities began and became more and more frequent.

A massive tragedy struck in 1648. A large section of western Russia had long been under Polish rule. In that terrible year the Cossacks, with the aid of Tartar allies, revolted and invaded Poland. Though presumably rebelling against the Polish nobility, the Cossack hordes made the Jews their special victims. The record is almost too horrible to read; its only redeeming feature is the heroism of the Jewish victims. This heroism found its most glorious and heartbreaking expression at Tulchin.

Tulchin was a fortress city defended by a few hundred Poles and some fifteen hundred Jews. The Cossacks feared a long and costly siege; they offered the Poles immunity if they would surrender the Jews to them, and the latter were ordered to lay down their arms. The Jews, enraged at this treachery, were going to slaughter the Poles whom they so greatly outnumbered; but their rabbi pointed out that such an act might lead to terrible reprisals by the Poles against their fellow Jews. And so the Jews surrendered. Not a single soul responded to the invitation to save his life by baptism; they were butchered for the Sanctification of the Name. Only a few hundred pitiful survivors escaped. (The treacherous Poles were also massacred.)

It is not our task to recount the succeeding disasters and persecutions which plagued the greatly reduced and weakened Jewry of Poland. They did not change the essential temper of the people, save perhaps to stimulate the cultivation of cabalistic studies in addition to Talmudic learning.

The Jewish Middle Ages—from the fifteenth to the end of the eighteenth century—were almost uniformly a period of gloom and decline. That the Jews and Judaism went backward is not strange. That they held on so well, that they did not slip into complete disintegration is amazing. That here and there, converts still came to them—at the risk of their lives—is nothing short of miraculous. Yet even under the strained and terrible conditions of those days, the creative power of Judaism was not dead. In strange, sometimes fantastic forms, it came to light again in the last days of the ghetto period. This will be the subject of our next chapter.

33.

Dreams

1. The Question of Ordination

AFTER MORE THAN A THOUSAND YEARS, THE SCENE SHIFTS BACK TO Palestine. The Jewish community of the Holy Land had dwindled during the gaonic period, until the Crusaders could easily massacre the few survivors. But when the Saracens conquered the country, Jews began to return, and under Turkish rule their numbers became larger. The great Don Joseph Nasi tried to promote the systematic colonization of his province of Tiberias—a project that foreshadows the later efforts of the Zionist movement—but the undertaking did not succeed.

In the sixteenth century the town of Safed, in the hills of Galilee, became an extraordinary center of learning and piety. Here Talmud and Cabala were studied with equal zeal. It was probably this combination that attracted Joseph Karo to Safed rather than to Jerusalem. For this brilliant legal intellect had a mystic dreamy side to his nature. He often received revelations from an inner voice, who announced herself to him as the spirit of the Mishnah. (Strikingly, this genius guided Karo only in the conduct of his personal life; questions of halakah were left entirely to the workings of his conscious mind.) The *Shulchan Aruch* was completed after Karo settled in Palestine.

One of Karo's older colleagues in Safed was Rabbi Jacob Berab, an aggressive and independent personality. Encouraged by the growth of the Palestinian community in numbers and scholarly prestige,

Berab made a startling proposal—that ordination be revived. To understand this proposal, we must review its background.

The ordination of rabbis, as practiced during the Talmudic period, was considered the direct continuation of that divinely authorized leadership which began when Moses appointed the seventy elders (Numbers 11:16). This dignity was conferred, as in the Bible story, by "laying hands" on the head of the candidate; and this ceremony was performed only by the Patriarch or his duly accredited representative. Those so ordained were privileged to sit in the Sanhedrin, the supreme religious authority in Jewish life.

The Palestinian leaders would not ordain residents of the Diaspora. They would authorize non-Palestinian scholars to decide ritual and other legal questions, but withheld certain powers (including the right to impose fines) which were conferred by full ordination. To indicate this distinction, the Babylonian teachers were called Rab, not Rabbi. The old ordination lapsed when the Patriarchate was abolished.

During the Middle Ages, scholars again resumed the title of Rabbi —it is said, as an anti-Karaitic gesture. It became customary for young students to present themselves for examination in Talmudic law to one who already bore the title; and if they proved their competence, they were given a diploma attesting that fact. The conferring of this degree was still called ordination (s'micho), but its recipients possessed only limited powers. They were merely reporters and teachers of the recorded halakah, not its molders as the Tannaim and early Amoraim had been. At first they derived their judicial powers from their appointment by the Exilarch; later on, especially in Europe, the authority of the scholars both as judges and legislators was based on the implied or explicit agreement of the community to accept their decisions. But Maimonides declared in his code that the earlier form of complete ordination could be restored by the unanimous agreement of all scholars resident in Palestine.

In 1538 Jacob Berab attempted to secure such agreement. With the revival of ordination, he argued, it would be possible to reconstitute a Sanhedrin qualified to legislate for all world Jewry. This body would provide a central authority and rallying point for the scattered people, and would be able to deal far more boldly with many vexing legal problems than an individual rabbi might dare.

What results would have followed if Berab's plan had succeeded? Would the world Jewish community have been unified? Could the halakah have been revitalized to meet changing circumstances? These questions, though fascinating, remain academic. For the Chief Rabbi of Jerusalem withheld his assent to the proposal. The scholars had become timid, and were not prepared for original, creative action. Israel remained without a central religious authority.

2. *The New Cabala*

Safed is famous chiefly as the new center of Jewish mysticism. Many distinguished Cabalists settled there, but they were all overshadowed by the awesome and mysterious figure of Isaac Luria. He was of Ashk'nazic origin, grew up in Egypt, and settled in Safed while still in his thirties; he died only a few years later. Yet even such a master as Karo treated the young man with respect verging on reverence, and his disciples regarded him as no mere saint, but a truly supernatural being. We know about him chiefly from their reports, for he himself wrote little. His doctrine was transmitted by word of mouth and for a long time it was guarded in strictest secrecy.

Luria made some original contributions to cabalistic theory, in particular to the problem of creation; but we shall have to pass by these difficult themes. For to Luria, Cabala was not primarily a philosophic doctrine nor a technique of timeless contemplation, but a means of redeeming the world from evil and Israel from exile. The messianic emphasis was not new in the Cabala, but now it became the dominant motive—a natural trend in view of the Spanish-Jewish tragedy.

What is the nature of the world's plight? To this question, Luria replied that good and evil have become intermixed and confused—in his own mixed metaphor, sparks of divinity are scattered among the husks of evil. This disaster occurred in the very process of creation. As light poured forth from the En Sof, the Infinite God, the channels or receptacles through which the light should have flowed were not able to contain it. Some of the S'firos burst, and thus light and darkness, good and evil, were mingled in disorder.

The redemption of mankind is therefore to be accomplished by drawing out the scattered sparks of godliness from the unclean residue, uniting all the elements of light in perfect righteousness and purity. When this process is accomplished, the Messiah will appear.

But a single human life is inadequate for this purpose. The most earnest and sincere individual finds himself a mixture of good and evil impulses, of spark and husk. Therefore, Luria introduced the theories of reincarnation and transmigration of souls. These ideas originated, so far as we know, in ancient India, but had long been current in the Western world. When they first penetrated Jewish life is hard to say; but they were familiar to many Cabalists. Only with Luria, however, did reincarnation become a basic doctrine. In order to continue and complete the process of separation between good and evil, he taught that the souls of the dead are returned to new bodies. The character of the new body is dependent on the quality of the previous life. The righteous return in the bodies of saints, the wicked may be degraded to the form of beasts.

But this process alone affords no promise of ultimate redemption. The tendency toward degradation, toward the more catastrophic mingling of spark and husk, is just as likely to predominate as the trend to redemption. Therefore, Luria added to the doctrine of transmigration a feature original with himself. When God perceives that a given soul is inadequate to its task, His mercy leads Him to join two (or even three) souls together in a single body. By this united effort, the scales are turned in favor of the positive process.

The practical means by which Luria led his disciples along the path of redemption were a scrupulous concern with all issues of personal and social morality, and the practice of ascetic piety. Fasting and other forms of self-denial, constant prayer, frequent ritual bathing, and midnight vigils made up the regimen of Luria's followers. Only on the Sabbath was the austerity relaxed; the holy day was dedicated to joyous meditation, study, prayer, and song.

Each Friday afternoon, as the sun declined, the members of the fellowship performed their ritual bath, garbed themselves in white, and walked out over the hills of Galilee to greet the Sabbath. On such occasions they no doubt sang the hymn "L'cho Dodi" ("Come, my beloved, to meet the bride") by Solomon HaLevi Alkabetz, a friend of Karo. This hymn is perhaps the most durable product of the mystical revival. It was quickly adopted by communities everywhere as part of the Friday evening service. Some three thousand settings have been composed for it—more than have been written for any other lyric in world literature.

The immediate disciples of Luria were relatively few; even his personal followers were divided into two groups, the beginners and the initiates. But the general tone of his teaching rapidly permeated the Jewish world. The manuals of piety which multiplied during the period stress a gloomy other-worldliness, and advocate stringent penitential practices; they also make frequent reference to reincarnation. Above all, the messianic goal of Luria's doctrine was constantly in the minds of men. Legends circulated among the people concerning desperate men who tried to force God's hand and unleash supernatural powers which would bring the Messiah at once. In the century that followed Luria's death (1572), the emotional tension of Jewry mounted steadily; messianic agitation reached a climax—then literally blew up.

34.

Nightmares

WAVES OF MESSIANIC EXCITEMENT HAD FREQUENTLY SWEPT BOTH the Jewish and the Christian world. In 1524 an enigmatic figure appeared in Venice, calling himself David Reubeni. He claimed to be an emissary of the "Ten Lost Tribes," dwelling somewhere in Arabia; he had come, he said, to form an alliance between the Christian powers and his brother, king of the Tribe of Reuben, in order to drive the Turks from the Holy Land. And for a time, he received respectful attention from the pope and the king of Portugal.

Reubeni seems to have been a deliberate impostor; but among those he attracted was a nobly sincere and gifted young man, a Portuguese Marrano, who at the risk of his life returned to Judaism under the name of Solomon Molcho. Molcho lived constantly on a plane of high religious enthusiasm; he was sure the Messiah was at hand, and at times suspected or hoped that he himself was the chosen redeemer. But throughout the course of his fantastic adventures, he displayed such a lofty faith and such purity of motive that he was everywhere loved and trusted. For a time he, too, gained the ear of great men; but ultimately he and Reubeni were arrested. Reubeni died in prison. Molcho was condemned by the Inquisition and went to the stake triumphantly, rejoicing that he might give his body as a "burnt offering" to God.

This episode was one of the most spectacular in the long history of pseudo-Messiahs. Many such had appeared in the course of Jewish history. Some were sincere; others were charlatans seeking to profit by the gullibility of the masses. But the most fantastic of them all was the Turkish Messiah, Sabbatai Zevi.

Born in Smyrna in 1626, Sabbatai was a man of handsome appearance and unusual charm. But his sensational success was due not only to his personal qualities but also to the circumstances of the age, which provided an effective "build-up" for his messianic pretensions. For decades, the doctrines of Isaac Luria had been spreading through the Jewish world, churning up the hope of redemption in the souls of the pious. According to a widely accepted computation of the Cabalists, 1648 was to be the year of the messianic advent. That was the terrible year of the Cossack and Tartar massacres in Poland. The ancient apocalyptic visions had always predicted that the birth pangs of the Messiah would be agonizing; the redeemed would first have to pass through a period of dark tribulation. The prophet Ezekiel had foretold that just before the final deliverance, the saints would be attacked by the barbarous hordes of Gog from the land of Magog. This prophecy was generally thought to have been fulfilled by the tragedy in Poland. Indeed, the terror of the victims was mingled with a strange ecstasy, so sure were they that their suffering was but the prelude to the messianic dawn.

These trends within Judaism were reinforced by similar phenomena in the Christian world. The same seventeenth century that produced the science of Newton and the philosophy of Spinoza also had its credulous side. In England, especially, messianic cults were strong. The father of Sabbatai Zevi was engaged in trade with British merchants; and in his boyhood, Sabbatai probably heard of circles which expected the second coming of the Christ in the year 1666.

The young man, a devoted student of Cabala, began to indulge in practices that kindled the hopes of enthusiasts, while rousing the suspicion and anxiety of the conservative. He publicly pronounced the Name of God, so long unuttered. He refused to live in wedlock, but celebrated his marriage to the Torah. Later, indeed, he took a human wife—a Polish Jewess named Sarah, who had been declaring for many years that she was to be the bride of the Messiah. In the course of his travels, Sabbatai acquired a following of visionaries and fanatics, whose firmness of purpose strengthened his faith in himself and provided the drive that carried him through moods of wavering and doubt.

In the fall of 1665, Sabbatai returned to his native city and publicly announced himself as the Messiah amid scenes of hysterical joy.

The news spread like wild-fire, throwing the Jewish communities of Europe and the Near East into utter confusion. The saner spirits who doubted that he was the Messiah, or even denounced his utterances as blasphemy, were rejected and persecuted by the excited people. Thousands sold their belongings for a song, that they might respond to the summons of Sabbatai and join him in Palestine. Many came to grief on the way, but a great host arrived in the Holy Land, where Sabbatai had gone to meet them. Odds of ten to one were offered on the London Stock Exchange that the Jews would establish a kingdom of their own.

Sabbatai set out for Constantinople, accompanied by hundreds of his followers. The Turkish authorities, eager to avoid violence, acted with forbearance. Sabbatai was arrested, but treated courteously. His disciples were permitted to visit him, and in his prison they continued to pay him royal honors. At last the Turkish court decided on a showdown. Sabbatai was offered the choice between death and Islam. In the critical hour his nerve failed. Docilely, he donned the turban which signified his acceptance of the Moslem faith. He and Sarah lived henceforth in seclusion as pensioners of the sultan.

Thousands of unfortunates found themselves stranded and penniless, crushed by disillusionment and despair. Rarely had there been a worse blow to the morale of world Jewry. But a fanatical conviction is all but indestructible. The stalwarts of the movement refused to abandon their hope. For over a century Jewish life was disturbed by a persistent and vigorous Sabbatian sect.

The doctrines of Luria supplied an explanation and excuse for Sabbatai's apostasy. The redemption, it will be recalled, cannot take place until all the sparks of divinity have been withdrawn from the "husks" among which they are scattered. Sabbatai, his disciples argued, had entered the realm of impurity in order to rescue the fragments of heavenly light imbedded in Islam. When this process was completed, he would return and manifest himself in his full glory.

A number of Jews followed the example of their Messiah and outwardly adopted Islam. Up to the present a small group of these secret Jews, known as Dönmeh, have survived in the cities of Turkey. The rest of the Sabbatians remained within the framework of Jewish life, cherishing their faith in Sabbatai privately, and voicing it only when circumstances favored.

For their opponents quickly regained the upper hand in most of the Jewish communities; and the authorities worked vigorously to suppress what they regarded as a dangerous and intolerable heresy. Their bitter opposition was indeed fully justified.

For the Sabbatians had adopted an approach to religion that was incompatible with the fundamental teachings of Judaism. It was not merely that they believed that Sabbatai was a genuine messianic figure, and that he would return in a new incarnation, or that some successor of his would bring in the final redemption. They had a radical new view about God and about the conduct of life.

They denied that the God of reason and the God of revelation are one and the same. That the First Cause, the God of the philosophers exists, they held to be self-evident. But nothing is known or can be known of this God, except that He exists; He cannot be worshipped. From the Unknown God, there emerged the God of Israel, who revealed Himself at Sinai. It is with this secondary God alone that we are concerned; our prayers can only be addressed to Him, and it is through Him that the Messiah was sent to us. Thus the Sabbatians compromised the basic Jewish teaching of the oneness of God.

They also adopted an ancient view that in the messianic age the commandments of the Torah would be abrogated; and this tradition was combined with the speculations about the sparks and the husks. Some Sabbatians were prepared to follow the example of their leader and to triumph over evil by practicing it. They deliberately violated the hallowed practices of Judaism, feasting on fast days, eating forbidden food—not out of indifference or neglect, but in the conviction that these transgressions constituted a religious act in some higher sense. The extremists rejected even the moral law and abandoned themselves to licentiousness. Thus the orthodox had no choice but to fight bitterly against every Sabbatian trend, and to excommunicate the prophets of the sect who appeared from time to time in various communities, preaching extravagant doctrines, and claiming to be Sabbatai's legitimate successors.

Some sad and sordid events followed. Moses Hayyim Luzzatto of Padua was a gifted Hebrew poet, and a noble, devout personality. But when he became the leader of a group that studied Cabala with intense excitement, the German and Italian rabbis became alarmed. Quite unjustifiably, they suspected the young man of Sabbatian leanings, and they were not satisfied even when he submitted humbly to their discipline. He was forced to leave Italy and found refuge in Amsterdam; at length he migrated to Palestine, where he died in 1747.

Shortly thereafter the community of Hamburg (which included the nearby cities of Altona, in Danish territory, and Wandsbeck) was torn by scandal. Its brilliant Rabbi, Jonathan Eybeschütz, was accused of Sabbatian heresy. The charge came from the learned and cantankerous Jacob Emden, whose father before him had been an arch-foe of Sabbatai's followers. To this day the facts of the case are disputed. But the immediate results were plain and tragic. The community was so torn by dissension that the Danish court and the Senate of Hamburg had to intervene. The controversy spread throughout central Europe, impairing the dignity of the rabbinate and causing further decline in Jewish morale.

The final episode centers around the worst rogue in Jewish history, known as Jacob Frank. Of Polish origin, he spent some years in Turkey; then returning home, he organized a cult that paid him royal honors. Within this cult, immorality was elevated to the level of a religious commandment. Excommunicated by the Jewish leaders, Frank began to intrigue with the Catholic clergy, furnishing them with libels against the Talmud and even reviving the old charge of ritual murder. As a result, public disputations concerning the Talmud were held at Lemberg in 1757 and 1759—the last of a long and painful series. Frank and his followers were then baptized, but the church leaders soon discovered his dishonesty and he was imprisoned for many years. He ended his days in Germany, a swindler to the last.

Thus, after a bitter struggle, the messianic heresy was wiped out. As a result, the hope for the coming of the Messiah lost most of its dynamic influence in Jewish life. Though Orthodox Jews have continued to pray for the advent of the son of David, the belief has been a dim and formal hope for the indeterminate future.

This does not mean that Messianism in its broadest sense—as faith in a better future—has disappeared from modern Judaism. Quite the opposite. But this faith has expressed itself in new terms and has evoked new programs of action.

35.

The Rebirth of Joy

FROM THE DARK MYSTERIES OF THE LURIAN CABALA AND THE LURID excesses of the Sabbatians, we turn with relief to a new kind of mystical movement, which sought to shed the divine radiance on the simple patterns of normal living. It was addressed not to the select few who could grasp the intricacies of Cabala, but to the entire Jewish people, especially to the poor and discouraged masses. Instead of diverting their minds from present realities to a garishly colored messianic dream, it heightened their consciousness of the meaning and beauty in daily existence.

This popular mystical movement, called Chasidism, began with a certain Israel ben Eliezer, known as the Baal Shem Tov (the good master of the Name *), and from the initials of this title, the Besht. Though he lived but two centuries ago, he seems to belong to a remote and ancient time. The Besht was a wandering teacher and teller of tales. He did not found an organization, nor did he write books. We see his personality and teaching through the eyes of his disciples and apostles; the few ascertainable facts of his life are obscured by clouds of miraculous legend.

He was far from unlearned; but he relied less on books than on his own experience, especially during years of quiet and solitary com-

---

* Baal Shem means one who performs wonders by using the name of God. Such men were half-revered, half-distrusted; but R. Israel was a good Baal Shem.

munion with nature. As his thinking matured, he began informally and unpretentiously to teach the people in the rural districts of eastern Poland. His doctrine was in a sense a reaction to the gloomy asceticism of Luria and a prophylactic against the Sabbatian excesses. (Rabbi Israel was one of the Jewish representatives at the disputation with the Frankists in Lemberg.) But chiefly, Chasidism was a protest against the narrowly intellectual Talmudism which was the dominant interest of educated Polish Jews. The scholarship of the day was devoted to the mental gymnastics of pilpul. It left even the learned spiritually cold; it offered nothing to those who lacked the agility of mind for this exercise, or who could not acquire it because of poverty, or because they lived in country districts isolated from the great centers of Torah.

To this group—economically underprivileged, discouraged by the collapse of the messianic hopes, neglected and scorned by the scholars —the Baal Shem brought a message of comfort and inspiration. Learning, he assured them, is not the only way to God, not even the best way. He is to be found not by the intellect, but by the heart. God is not remote. He is everywhere. It is His universal presence which alone gives life and beauty to the world.

God is to be served by the practice of humility, enthusiasm, and joy. Our love for God must be a genuine passion. Our prayers are made effective not by decorum but by thrilling intensity. The Besht encouraged his followers—the Chasidim or pious, as they began to call themselves—to utilize music and dancing in their worship. Their songs were usually tunes without words, intended to create a mood of aspiration without the interference of mental concepts. (This is the function of the organ in modern houses of worship.) By their dancing they induced a positive frenzy of devotion. It was said of a famous Chasidic leader that anyone who saw him dance was instantly stirred to repent his sins!

Equally important is the spirit of cheerfulness. Here the Baal Shem restored a basic Jewish value, which had been largely lost during the long dreary centuries. You cannot properly serve God, he taught, in a mood of gloom; for if you are conscious of God's nearness and love, you must perforce be happy. Even in repenting for sin, one should not linger too long over morbid thoughts: they are a device of Satan to bar us from God's presence. Excessive fasting and self-denial are not desirable: it is better far to enjoy God's blessings in humble gratitude. Material goods should not be rejected, but sanctified. "The smoke of my pipe," said the Baal Shem, "can be an offering of incense to God."

Such truths were expounded by the Besht in terms that the people could readily understand—in simple, homely sayings, parables, and tales. He drew his illustrations, not from hackneyed literary sources, but from the familiar circumstances of the life about him. This method was followed by his great successors who created a large body of fresh and stimulating lore.

A Chasidic leader, for example, feared that one of his well-to-do followers was growing self-centered and indifferent to the needs of others. He called the rich man to his house and asked him to look out the window. "What do you see?" he asked, and the disciple replied, "I see several people." "Now look into this mirror," went on the teacher, "and tell me what you see." "I see myself," was the reply. "They are both glass," explained the sage, "but the one is backed with silver. This prevents a man from seeing others when he looks into it."

A more recent teacher explained to his Chasidim the spiritual truths suggested by modern inventions. "The train teaches us that everything can be missed in a single moment. The telegraph reminds us that all our words are counted and must be paid for. The telephone suggests that what we say here is heard there."

The Chasidim loved to tell stories about simple and unquestioning faith—like the story of the ignorant man who did not know the prayers well. So he recited the alphabet to God, and asked Him to combine the letters in the way that pleased Him best.

The Besht acquired many followers, some of them distinguished scholars, in whom he satisfied a long-felt inner hunger. It was such men who became in time the leaders of the Chasidic movement. But knowledge alone did not fit a man for Chasidic leadership. The primary requirement was an electrical inner power which could rouse a response among the people. The Baal Shem glorified the righteous man (tsadik) as the channel through whom divine inspiration is transmitted to the world. Soon tsadik became the regular title of the Chasidic teacher (he was also called rebbe, a diminutive of rabbi, or guter Yid, good Jew). The tsadik lived on terms of affectionate intimacy with his Chasidim who accorded him complete veneration. He was their confidant and guide. His prayers brought God down to them and made Him real. Many of the tsadikim, beginning with the Besht, were credited with the performance of miracles.

In Chasidism the word Torah came to have a special meaning—it included the personal sayings, teachings, and acts of the tsadik. His life, no less than the ancient Scripture and tradition, was an embodiment of the eternal Law. Profound meanings were discovered in his most casual remarks. His behavior was observed in fullest detail and awesomely reported from group to group.

After the Baal Shem's death, his followers undertook a more systematic program to spread the new doctrine both by the spoken and the printed word. And now opposition began to rise rapidly. Those who were unaffected by the enthusiasm of the Chasidim ridiculed and resented their disorderly, even orgiastic services. (They had also made some minor changes in the prayer book.) More serious thinkers sensed a dangerous trend toward pantheism in the teaching of the Baal Shem, and demanded a clearer distinction between the world and God as its Ruler. But the chief objection was to the Chasidic attack on scholarship. The Baal Shem was no enemy of learning. He had argued only that a cold intellectualism is not adequate to the service of God, and that a burning enthusiasm—even without great knowledge—is preferable. But this view was sometimes distorted into an active dislike and contempt for scholars. It was not surprising that in the urban centers, where the great y'shivos were located, the Chasidim should meet opposition and even persecution.

The counter-movement reached its height in the Lithuanian city of Vilna, which had become the outstanding home of Talmudic scholarship. Its brightest jewel was Rabbi Elijah ben Solomon, known as the Gaon* of Vilna. Technically he was just a private citizen who devoted himself to study in the company of a chosen group of friends, but his prestige and influence exceeded that of the official rabbinate. He was in fact a profound and creative scholar. He had turned from the artificial and unproductive pilpul to a penetrating study of rabbinic texts, to determine what the authors had really meant. Not only the Babylonian Talmud and its commentators—the usual area of interest—but also the long-neglected Palestinian Talmud and other early rabbinic works were carefully studied. The Gaon insisted on a sound grammatical foundation, corrected the printed texts by consulting old manuscripts, and admitted cautiously such secular subjects as mathematics, which shed light on portions of rabbinic lore. This does not seem

---

* No longer an official title but a term of highest respect.

revolutionary to us, but it was novel for the time and place. The researches of the Gaon, and of his disciples and successors, have been of continuing value to modern students.

Rabbi Elijah, for all his fabulous learning and deep sincerity, was a rather harsh and distant personality. He had deliberately avoided involvement in public affairs; but the Chasidic movement seemed to him a challenge he could not disregard. The rebels had made changes in the forms of worship; worse, they had denied the primacy of scholars and scholarship in Jewish life. The Gaon emerged from his secluded study to lead the anti-Chasidic forces. With his backing, the Lithuanian rabbinate issued a ban against the Chasidim. In areas where the *misnagdim* (opponents) held the upper hand, many of the mystics suffered real hardships.

Two of the most learned Chasidic leaders went as a deputation to Vilna, humbly requesting an interview with the Gaon, that they might explain their position and clear away misunderstandings. But, though the emissaries were Talmudists of established fame, the Gaon would not even admit them to his house. One of these scholars, Rabbi Shneur Zalman, was actually denounced to the Russian government as subversive, and put under arrest; but not even the agents of the tsar could find a taint of revolution in this gentle pietist.

And the movement grew, even where the misnagdim were powerful. Rabbi Shneur Zalman, the chief leader in the Lithuanian area, gave a more philosophic turn to the teaching of the Baal Shem. In his school both learning and piety were stressed, and the tsadik was regarded more as sage than as wonder worker. Despite his humiliation at the hands of the Gaon, he forbade his Chasidim to speak of the great master with disrespect. The Gaon had been misinformed, he asserted; we must venerate him for his great powers of mind and spirit.

Polish Chasidism (which spread also into Hungary and Rumania) had a less sophisticated character. There was no single center or authority. In different cities and towns, groups clustered about their favorite tsadik. Many of the early teachers possessed unusual gifts and substantially enriched the treasury of Chasidic lore. Among these arresting personalities, we may mention Rabbi Levi Isaac of Berdichev, the impassioned champion of the people of Israel. In one of his songs (in Yiddish, the folk language), he took God to task for demanding too much of his poor people. He had given them a bulky Torah which is hard to observe, and had punished them severely for every infraction. It is time

The Rebirth of Joy 247

for God to recognize that they are trying to do their best, and that He should forgive and redeem them!*

But this glorification of the tsadik soon led to abuses. The kindling power of a vibrant personality can greatly advance any human endeavor, and is especially effective in the field of religion. But too much devotion to the personality of the leader can become idolatrous. Centuries before, prophet and Pharisee had struggled to reduce the importance of priestly intermediaries and to give the individual direct access to God. The acceptance of the tsadik as God's visible representative was a step backward. In practice it was even more unfortunate than in theory, for the Chasidim were largely uneducated, and therefore credulous and superstitious. They were sure the tsadik could perform miracles. They expected him to provide amulets for the relief of disease and childlessness, to locate lost articles, and to give infallible advice on all personal affairs. The fellowship of the Sabbath meal, which all the Chasidim ate in the company of the rebbe, was transformed into a magical sacrament. Every dish which the rebbe's hand touched was considered sanctified, and the Chasidim would scramble for a crumb of the holy food. Many of the faithful left their homes and families to spend long periods in constant association with a beloved teacher, and abjured all personal freedom in favor of implicit obedience to his word.

The rebbe's household was organized as a royal court and his son usually succeeded to the throne. Rival dynasties competed for popular support. The adherents of each tsadik glorified their own master and disparaged all others. Unscrupulous tsadikim exploited their position for its honors and emoluments, and lived in luxury on the contributions of their pitiful followers. Sometimes a sincere and unworldly saint became the tool of cynical and greedy "court" officials. The pressure of the believers even forced the tsadik to assume the role of miracle-monger even against his will. If he insisted that he had no supernatural powers, the people dismissed his protest as an evidence of his deep humility, and awaited marvels with redoubled confidence. Of course, faith cures did occur: they always do among people who expect them to occur.

Within half a century of its beginning, the Chasidic movement was in deep decline. It had become grossly superstitious and obscurantist. The Chasidim opposed every effort at enlightenment and progress. They objected even to such seemingly harmless developments as the intro-

---

* The famous Kaddish of Rabbi Levi.

duction of modern sanitary and medical methods, and to the slightest tincture of secular education. Characteristically, a tsadik of the early nineteenth century, a man of singular poetic genius, declared flatly that Maimonides did not write the *Guide of the Perplexed*. For Maimonides was a great and pious Rabbi: he could never have composed so blasphemous a book! And in the subtropical climate of Israel, Chasidim continue to wear the heavy garments and big fur hats that were appropriate (and fashionable) in eighteenth-century Poland.

Because, for many decades the Chasidim were the arch-reactionaries, the bitter foes of any social or cultural advance, the spokesmen of modernism responded with bitterness and contempt. Today we are better able to recognize the virtues of the Chasidic movement. Even in its decline, the spark of inspiration was never wholly extinguished. (There are Chasidic colonies in Israel and New York City.) During its brief classic period, Chasidism did much to arouse the flagging spirit of the masses scattered through the villages of eastern Europe. It revived the consciousness of the world of nature, introduced a kind of piety that was both earnest and gay, and provided charming and poetic additions to Jewish folklore. The best of the Chasidic teachings constitute an original and moving expression of ethical and religious truth. Contemporary poets, artists, musicians, dancers, and dramatists have drawn heavily on Chasidic lore and life.*

---

* An outstanding example is An-sky's play, *The Dybbuk*, which has provided a libretto for two operas; Ernest Bloch has composed a Baal Shem Suite for violin and piano. A full list of such works would be lengthy.

Part 6.
Era of Hope

36.

Crossroads

UP TO THIS POINT WE HAVE BEEN TELLING THE STORY OF A VANISHED past. It is a past that still affects our lives, but it is so remote from us that it requires a large effort of imagination to understand its character and spirit. The Baal Shem Tov lived in a simple, medieval world. Moses Mendelssohn was born only thirty years after Rabbi Israel, but he belonged to the new age that produced the American and French Revolutions. Despite enormous changes of outer circumstances and mental climate since Mendelssohn's day, the problems he discussed are still our problems: the adjustment of Jews to modern life and of Judaism to modern thought. One instance will suffice. Mendelssohn was the first Jew who ever tried to define Judaism; since his time, many diverse definitions have been offered.

The Biblical and Talmudic periods may be called the *creative era of Judaism*. The great universal ideals of the prophets were fused with the ancient popular and priestly traditions. The absolute unity of God was affirmed and a noble ethical standard was established as God's first demand upon His creatures. The Torah translated these principles into a concrete discipline, and ritual forms were utilized to foster spiritual aims. The synagogue, the Sabbath, the sanctification of the home by worship and observance, the emphasis on education for young and old, provided stamina for Jewish survival and instruments for the transmission of spiritual values. The democratic principle, the leadership of the learned, the standardization of practice combined with broad latitude on questions of belief, a sane human outlook vitalized by an intense messianic optimism—such were the basic values that permeated all Jewish existence.

The twelve centuries that followed the completion of the Talmud may be called the *period of preservation*. Judaism was less creative, but it still remained very much alive. It reacted vigorously to new ideas and customs current in the outside world, absorbing and adapting some of them, rejecting others. New sects arose, some finding permanent lodgment within the family of Israel, others finally breaking with the mother faith.

Mounting waves of persecution gradually reduced this flexibility. Those who had to defend their right to live as Jews against steady and hostile pressure, who were summoned even to die for the Sanctification of the Name, were not likely to make concessions and compromises. Self-criticism was hardly possible. Legal authorities became increasingly hesitant to modify existing rules. Free inquiry was discouraged.

These trends were enormously strengthened by the destruction of Spanish Jewry and by the establishment of the ghetto system. Church and State joined in the policy of segregating and degrading the Jews. Physical, legal, and social barriers excluded them from a share in the rich intellectual developments of the sixteenth and seventeenth centuries. The masses who had migrated to eastern Europe were isolated from the advancing culture of the West by simple distance and by the backwardness of their environment. Eventually they too were beset by savage persecution. The Jews of the Turkish Empire, less cruelly oppressed, suffered from the cultural stagnation about them. In northern Africa, the Jews were confined in sordid and filthy mellahs.

Judaism never became completely static. The great scholarly revival led by the Vilna Gaon and the mystical awakening of Chasidism were evidences of continuing vitality. Yet this period was, especially in its latter centuries, a period of decline. The pattern of Jewish life was rigidly fixed, and few deviations were permitted in the tightly organized communities. Jewish loyalty, however, remained intense, piety was simple and sincere. There was a dogged determination to hold on until the day of redemption should come.

The last two centuries of Jewish history may be rightly called the *period of confusion*. Emancipation suddenly ended the segregation and catapulted thousands of Jews into the whirlpool of modern life. Even where the liberation of the Jews was incomplete, or where reactionary governments tried to block it altogether, the *hope* of freedom and equality generated radical changes in Jewish thought and behavior.

The opportunity for secular education and contact with modern thought dangerously breached the hitherto intact structure of Judaism. During the ghetto period, a new scientific outlook had arisen, which challenged the authority of all revealed religion. Many Jews now were led to question or reject the basic doctrine that the Torah was of divine origin. The authority of the halakah was undermined. The future of the Jewish religion was in jeopardy.

Judaism, as we have seen, has adapted itself to many different intellectual climates. It is certainly less difficult to adjust the simple teachings of Judaism to modern philosophy than to do the same for the more complicated Christian theology with its doctrines of the incarnation and the Trinity. But the task was made doubly hard for Jewish teachers because Judaism had so long been isolated from the new trends. A very large adjustment had to be made quickly. To the first generations of the emancipated, Judaism appeared hopelessly behind the times.

Moreover, the vast opportunities that opened before them were so dazzling that many were distracted from Jewish interests. Now that they could range at will in the vast fields of learning provided by the universities, or revel in the hitherto unknown delights of literary, plastic, musical, and dramatic art, they turned aside indifferently from their Jewish inheritance.

But the practical problems of Jewish living in the modern world were even more difficult. As long as Jews lived in ghettos, and were restricted to a few specifically "Jewish" occupations, it was not hard for them to observe the Sabbath, festivals, dietary laws, and so forth. Now the compact, well-organized Jewish community broke down. It could no longer enforce its discipline upon the individual. And even the Jew who wanted to abide by the tradition found it harder and harder, the more he entered into the general economic life of the nation, to observe the ancient rest days and the other religious laws. The Industrial Revolution, which was beginning at about the same time as the movement for Jewish emancipation, tended to speed up this disintegration of old patterns. And the great Jewish migrations of the nineteenth and twentieth centuries, which uprooted millions from their former homes, disrupted still more the continuity of the tradition.

The movement for emancipation had hardly begun, moreover, when a vigorous anti-Jewish reaction appeared. It rapidly acquired a secular form. Jew-hatred, now called anti-Semitism, justified itself not on the old religious ground, but by means of new racial theories. Thus even the refuge of baptism was denied its victims. This movement reached its horrible climax in the greatest tragedy of all Jewish history—the destruction of six million Jews by Hitler Germany.

The modern age is one of the most violent and startling contrasts. Individual Jews have achieved greater power, fame, and influence than ever before. Their contribution to every field of modern life has been phenomenal. Entire Jewish communities, above all that of the United States, have attained a degree of acceptance, prosperity, and prestige without parallel. And this in a period when elsewhere Jews have suffered more bitterly than in the darkest of the dark ages.

The authority and relative uniformity of Jewish religious life have broken down. Many Jews have adopted the dominant faith, not as in the past under the threat of torture or death, but out of professional or social ambition, or out of simple ignorance and indifference. Large groups who continue to identify themselves as Jews have consciously or otherwise abandoned religious loyalties; and several secularist philosophies of Jewish life have been constructed. Yet a vigorous spiritual life has been maintained. New interpretations of Jewish religion have revealed hitherto unsuspected possibilities for growth and creation within the framework of the tradition. Magnificent synagogues have been built, great religious music composed, outstanding works of Jewish scholarship and original thought have been produced.

The Hebrew language has been revived both as a literary and a spoken tongue. And in the very decade when the worst disaster fell, an independent Jewish state was established on the soil of Palestine.

These are but the most sensational of the contradictory phenomena in Jewish experience of the past two centuries. The reader should therefore not be surprised if he finds the effect of the ensuing chapters somewhat confusing. But the confusion, though great, is not meaningless. Certainly it affords no reason to think that the story of Judaism is approaching an unhappy termination. Important positive trends are gradually coming into sharper focus. Indications of a great spiritual rebirth are growing plainer. Judaism still has much to offer to the Jewish people and to mankind. To the stout of heart, the Jewish faith presents a magnificent challenge and a thrilling opportunity.

37.

Another Dawn

THE EIGHTEENTH CENTURY WAS AN AGE OF REASON. WE APPLIED THIS
term to the flowering of scholasticism some six hundred years earlier;
but there is little resemblance between the two periods. Medieval
rationalism was rooted in the rediscovery of ancient philosophy; the
"Enlightenment" of the eighteenth century was based on solid new
achievements in mathematics, astronomy, and other sciences. Reflect-
ing the rigid structure of feudal society, the thinking of the Middle Ages
was predominantly authoritarian. The scholastics attempted no more
than to harmonize reason and faith; revealed religion was not only sustained by the state but exercised full sway over the minds and souls of
men. In the eighteenth century, the feudal aristocracy was an anach-
ronism and the institution of monarchy was getting shaky. The commercial middle class was gaining in power and self-confidence, and the
beginnings of the Industrial Revolution were not far away. Reason was
no longer the handmaid of faith but a powerful challenge to all entrenched authority.

The churches and their doctrines were boldly criticized. Scientific
and mechanistic atheism was revived, especially in France. But a more
typical expression of the Enlightenment was *deism*: an abstract, non-
institutional belief in a creative God. This deism was neither profoundly
philosophic nor intensely religious; but it was sane and ethical. Far removed from all sectarianism, it demanded just and equal treatment for
man as man, regardless of nationality or creed. It provided a basis
for the belief in progress, a conception which now became popular for

perhaps the first time. Only ignorance, it was said, has barred mankind from the earthly paradise. The advance of science, the spread of education, and the growth of liberty will bring man and mankind ever closer to perfection.

The Enlightenment thinkers were not the greatest philosophers. Their faith in the power of reason was unduly optimistic. But it was a generous and noble faith, and it led directly to the French and American Revolutions. Perhaps its finest expression is in Jefferson's words: "We hold these truths to be self-evident: that all men are created equal; that they are endowed by their Creator with certain unalienable rights; that among these are life, liberty, and the pursuit of happiness."

In this tolerant era, for the first time in many centuries, men began to suggest some improvement in the status of the Jews. The vested interests, governmental and ecclesiastical, who opposed any innovation, naturally objected to all such proposals. But even the friends of the Jews advocated only small changes at the start. They did not propose that equal rights be given at once to the ghetto-dwellers—they were too backward and degraded for that! But they maintained that the backwardness of the Jews was due only to the oppressive conditions under which they were forced to live. Give them a chance for education, admit them to more productive callings, treat them as human beings and not as pariahs—pleaded the liberals—and the Jews will soon prove themselves worthy of citizenship.

At the center of the new trend stands a strangely winsome personality, a little hunchbacked gnome of a man named Moses Mendelssohn (1729–1786). As a poor, frail boy from Dessau, he barely succeeded in getting admission to Berlin. He had a solid grounding in Hebrew lore; now he discovered the vast realms of western culture. With only a minimum of help from others, he mastered the classical and modern languages, read widely in literature and philosophy, and became an outstanding German stylist. His own critical and philosophic writings were widely admired; his personal charm won all hearts. Frederick the Great granted him favors; and Lessing, the noblest figure of the German Enlightenment, became his intimate friend. Lessing was the first modern author to depict Jews sympathetically; the hero of his poetic drama, *Nathan the Wise*, is modeled after Moses Mendelssohn.

While acquiring a great reputation in the Gentile world, Mendelssohn remained a loyal and strictly observant Jew. But he did not take an active part in Jewish affairs until roused by an event which created a sensation at the time. A Swiss pastor, Johann Christian Lavater, was one of his admirers. In 1769 Lavater published a book on Christian evidences, translated from the French, with a dedication to Mendelssohn. The dedication challenged Mendelssohn (in the friendliest terms) to refute the arguments of the book, or else in honesty to acknowledge their force and become a Christian.

Mendelssohn was in a delicate and embarrassing position. It was difficult either to accept or to refuse the challenge. His public reply to Lavater was a masterpiece of courage and of tact. Surely, he argues, I must be strongly convinced of the truth of Judaism: why else should I continue to endure the disabilities imposed on the loyal Jew? (And with telling irony he noted that Swiss law forbade him to visit Lavater in Zurich.) The arguments of the book are convincing only to those who already believe the Christian doctrine; but Mendelssohn has no desire to point out their weaknesses. His Jewish religion does not doom to perdition the honest adherents of other faiths. "The righteous of all peoples have a share in the world to come." Let Jew and Christian each strive to exemplify the highest ideals of his own religion.

This honest and gracious response won the applause of men of good will. Lavater publicly apologized to Mendelssohn for his ill-considered act. But the bigots were stirred up by the episode, and several hateful pamphlets were directed against Mendelssohn and the Jews. As a result, the Berlin sage was stimulated to productive work in and for the Jewish community.

He published several writings urging the removal of the oppressive laws against the Jews, and persuaded his Gentile friends to enter the struggle. The question was extensively discussed, but little progress was made against the stubborn opposition of the German rulers. On several occasions, however, Mendelssohn's influential connections helped protect Jews against exceptional persecution.

Confident of eventual success, Mendelssohn sought to prepare his coreligionists for entrance into European life. They were indeed a bedraggled and discouraged group. Except for a small mercantile class who enjoyed special privileges, they were still segregated, oppressed, despised and poor. They spoke a Jewish dialect, akin to the Yiddish of eastern Europe (which they wrote in Hebrew characters), and knew little even of the superficial aspects of German culture. The standard of Jewish learning had likewise declined; it was frequently necessary to import rabbinical leaders from the y'shivos of the East. Few even of the best Talmudic scholars were prepared to assume leadership in the new day that was unmistakably approaching.

Another Dawn 259

Mendelssohn took a prominent part in establishing a school for Jewish children in Berlin, which served as a model for several others. Here the secular subjects were taught along with Jewish studies; moreover, the religious training included not only the reading of Hebrew texts, but some instruction in the general principles of Judaism. For now that Jews were coming into more frequent contact with Christians, they must better understand the underlying ideas of their religion, and be able to explain them to others. Mendelssohn was also interested in vocational guidance and training.

Another important contribution was his translation of the Torah into German, which was published in Hebrew characters and thus made more accessible to the average Jew. Though an excellent rendering of the sacred text, and furnished with a clear Hebrew commentary prepared by Mendelssohn and several co-workers, this translation did not greatly stimulate Biblical studies. Its importance was that it introduced the Jewish masses to a specimen of standard German, and so influenced them to discard their distinctive Jewish speech. It thus opened the way to a knowledge of western culture, and in later generations it served a similar function for the Jews of eastern Europe. For this reason, the ultra-orthodox authorities viewed the translation with stern disapproval.

Of Mendelssohn's other writings on Jewish themes, the most notable is *Jerusalem*. The first part of this work argued eloquently for freedom of philosophic inquiry and expression, and insisted that the State should not concern itself with matters of dogma which belong to the individual conscience. Christian critics replied to Mendelssohn's argument: How could he, an adherent of a revealed religion, take so irresponsible an attitude toward religious doctrine? So in the second part of his work, Mendelssohn undertook to expound the character of Judaism.

Judaism, he held, imposes no irrational dogmas. Its basic theological tenets—the unity of God, the moral law, human freedom and the immortality of the soul—are rational concepts which (according to the thinking of the Enlightenment) can be demonstrated by logic. The Bible contains no commandment "Thou shalt believe." Judaism is not revealed dogma, but *revealed legislation*. It is distinguished from deism by the network of practices and ceremonies which are incumbent only on Jews, but are eternally binding on them.

Mendelssohn therefore called on his fellow Jews to be rational in faith, sturdily orthodox in practice, and German in culture. And in these terms he felt he had pointed to a solution of the problems that were beginning to trouble his generation.

Actually, he had not solved the problem but only stated it. The real question was: *How* can one be at the same time loyally German, traditionally Jewish, and fully modern? It was not easy for everyone to harmonize the findings of science with faith in a revealed religion. True, Judaism does not impose a rigid and elaborate creed upon its adherents, and in this sense Mendelssohn argued rightly that it is not "revealed dogma." Yet the very phrase "revealed legislation" implies some sort of belief in revelation. One cannot readily demonstrate by logical argument that the ceremonial law is forever binding on Jews.

Just as Mendelssohn failed to recognize the seriousness of the basic philosophic problem, so also he underestimated the practical difficulties of observing the traditional law under modern conditions. Mendelssohn had become prosperous and did not find it hard to keep the Sabbath and dietary laws. But as the Industrial Revolution progressed, the observant Jew was to encounter increasing difficulty in holding fast to his traditions.

Moreover, Mendelssohn's own virtues led him to discount the frustrations which his fellow Jews would encounter when they left the ghetto (which was a shelter as well as a prison) and came into fuller contact with a still hostile Gentile world. He apparently assumed that his accomplishments were not extraordinary and that any Jew who made the effort could duplicate them. He did not recognize that his own success had been due to his exceptional talents and charm, and that doors which opened to him would remain closed to other Jews. His genuine saintliness enabled him to rise serenely above slights and insults; the bigots could not upset his essential dignity and his unfailing sense of humor. But not every man can be a sage and a saint. Most of us can be hurt by scorn, even from those we consider our inferiors; and to keep silent then would not be saintliness, but cowardice.

The times called for a leader of the first magnitude—for a new Johanan ben Zakkai or Saadia. Mendelssohn was not a man of such caliber. He achieved a unique personal success, and remained unspoiled by it, sincere, humble, and kind. But he never perceived the tremendous and even tragic character of the problems confronting Jewry in the new age, and so it is not surprising that he contributed little to any basic solution of them. Paradoxically, this man who wrote with such elegant clarity of style left spiritual confusion behind him.

This is not, let us emphasize, to his discredit. We can hardly blame him because, at the very outset of the modern period, he could not solve riddles to which no answer has yet been found.

The period following Mendelssohn's death is one of the saddest in German Jewish history. There were many who had hailed Mendelssohn as their master and model; but, though they were zealous in adopting the externals of German culture, they did not emulate their hero in intellectual seriousness, ethical idealism, or Jewish loyalty. Rebuffed in their attempts at professional and social advancement, many took the easy route of baptism. It was especially the prosperous and educated, whose ambitions were highest, and whose disappointments were consequently the keenest, who most often paid this price for acceptance. Among them were the children of Moses Mendelssohn.

38.

Morning—with Clouds

THERE WAS MUCH TALK ABOUT IMPROVING THE LOT OF THE JEWS, but little action. Then the ideals of freedom and equality won a magnificent victory in the New World. The Jews were full citizens of the United States from the time the nation was established. The American Revolution prepared the way for the French Revolution, and the French National Assembly which enacted the great reforms of 1789 soon turned to consider the "Jewish question."

The Jews had been expelled from France in 1394, yet at the end of the eighteenth century the French Crown had a considerable number of Jewish subjects. Most of them lived in the partly German areas of Alsace and Lorraine, where they were the victims of both official and popular oppression. There was also a smaller community in southern France, chiefly of Marrano origin; its members had achieved a rather comfortable economic and social status.

In the debates over Jewish emancipation, the great revolutionary leader Count Mirabeau (an enthusiastic student of Mendelssohn's writings) and the Catholic Abbé Grégoire pleaded eloquently for the abolition of all discriminatory laws. The opposition was voiced in the Assembly by deputies from Alsace, and was supported by petitions from the aristocratic S'fardim of the south who considered themselves a different breed from other Jews. Eventually the spirit of the Revolution won out, and all the Jews of France entered with enthusiasm upon their new rights and duties.

From France the new ideas spread not only by their own persuasiveness, but by French military victories. In the Netherlands, where the Jews had lived happily for nearly two centuries, the proposal to grant them full citizenship evoked some objections. The opposition came not only from the more conservative of the Dutch Christians but also from certain Jewish leaders. Too much freedom, they feared, might undermine the loyalty of Jews to their Judaism. Nevertheless, the Dutch Jews were soon participating actively in public affairs.

French forces occupied the western part of Germany, and here too the bitter anti-Jewish laws were abrogated. And when the French armies entered Rome, the walls of the ghetto were razed.

A few years later Napoleon made himself emperor of France. Ruthless dictator that he was, he was still in many ways a child of the Revolution. Certainly he was the foe of the old aristocracy, with its traditional prejudices. In the kingdom of Westphalia, which he carved out of western Germany for his brother Jerome, the Jews enjoyed the same privileges as the Jews of France.

But how extensive were these privileges to be? Napoleon was neither a thoroughgoing liberal nor a cordial friend of the Jews. His own inherited suspicions were intensified by steady anti-Jewish propaganda in France. Finally he hit upon a scheme that was intended to resolve his own doubts, and at the same time to indulge his love for dramatic pageantry. In 1806 he summoned an "Assembly of Notables," consisting of Jewish laymen and a few rabbis from France and the imperial territories. They were confronted with a series of questions concerning the loyalty of Jews to the countries in which they lived, their attitude toward non-Jews, and their views on polygamy, usury, and intermarriage. The tone of the questions was unfriendly, and seemed to imply that the civic loyalty of the Jews was dubious and their moral standards inferior.

The notables could answer most of these questions with complete candor. They quoted, from ancient and modern Jewish sources, abundant proof that Judaism commands fidelity to the State and obedience to its laws, brotherhood to all men, and high standards of integrity and kindness. But on the subject of intermarriage, they were constrained to answer evasively. Jewish authorities, they stated, accept as binding all marriages sanctioned by the civil law. They glossed over the fact that Judaism (like other faiths) opposed intermarriage because of religious considerations. We cannot, however, be too harsh on the notables for their timidity; they realized that their communities would be in serious trouble if they provoked the anger of the dictator.

Napoleon was in fact much pleased with the replies he received. He now announced his decision to revive the ancient Sanhedrin, which would give more binding authority to the pronouncements of the notables. Accordingly, in February, 1807, a gathering of seventy-one distinguished rabbis and laymen met in Paris, called itself the Sanhedrin, and with impressive ceremonial ratified the statements adopted the previous year. But this was all empty pageantry. The Sanhedrin could not lay rightful claim to this high-sounding name; it did not represent world-Jewry, but was made up only of persons subject to Napoleon. It did not even begin to consider the vexing problems of Jewish law which a real Sanhedrin would have had to face. And despite its servility, the Napoleonic Sanhedrin was unable to overcome the pressure of anti-Jewish forces at court. The decrees issued about a year later imposed a number of humiliating restrictions on the Jews. The Sanhedrin never met again.

The Napoleonic law established a system of Jewish community organization which (with considerable later modifications) has continued in France to the present. The congregations of each district were to be governed by a body known as the consistory, whose members, originally designated by the government, were later elected by the members of the synagogues. The local consistories in turn were subject to direction by the central consistory in Paris, with a Chief Rabbi at its head. The rabbis chosen by the congregations had to be approved first by the central consistory and then by the government. Though this systematic procedure assured order and dignity in religious affairs, it also tended to suppress spontaneity and vigor. Only in comparatively recent times has the spiritual life of French Jewry regained some measure of creative energy. Official control over the personnel (and also the finances) of the Jewish religious community ended in 1905, when Church and State were legally separated.

The full equality which Napoleon had withheld was formally granted to French Jewry in 1831. Throughout the nineteenth century, Jews took an active and often leading role in all phases of French life.

39.

The Beginnings of Reform

THE GERMAN JEWS SEEMED TO HAVE MADE A BAD BARGAIN. THE advocates of emancipation, Jewish and Gentile, had proposed a double program. The governments were to treat the Jews more fairly; the Jews should prove themselves worthy of this favor by fervid patriotism, by surrendering their old distinctiveness, and by acquiring a modern education. The Jews had done their part enthusiastically. But the German states had never agreed to the bargain, and remained coldly hostile.

As long as Jerome Bonaparte ruled in his kingdom of Westphalia, the condition of his Jewish subjects was distinctly improved. Not so the rest of German Jewry. During the War of Liberation against Napoleon —in which many of them took an active part—the Jews were allowed to think that emancipation would soon be proclaimed. But when Napoleon fell, the Jews of the Westphalian domain were again subjected to the ghetto laws, and those in the rest of the country found themselves no better off. The weary fight had to begin all over again.

These defeats were a crushing blow to Jewish morale, already so much weakened from within. Many families and individuals who had acquired wealth and some measure of general culture found themselves barred from social acceptance and from professional or public careers because they were Jews. In their zeal to advance in the German world, they had neglected Jewish faith and knowledge. The easy solution to their problem was baptism. Many Jews who could not bring themselves to take this step had their children raised as Christians.

Though the mass of German Jews remained adherents of the Synagogue, their Judaism was static and lacked fire. The synagogue buildings were dingy, the service unbeautiful and spiritless. Few of the rabbis had the ability to make the religion meaningful to their people. The German y'shivos were in decline. Many rabbinical posts were left unfilled. In other cases, rabbis were imported from eastern Europe; but their Talmudic learning did not fit them to meet the challenges of a new age.

In various quarters, a call was heard for "Reform." It was suggested that many Jewish customs, oriental in background, were repulsive to the esthetic sense and out of keeping with modern culture. Protests were heard against certain passages in the prayer book which were deemed unsuitable for an age of enlightenment and growing brotherhood. The prayers for the return to Palestine and the restoration of the Davidic monarchy were specially disturbing to those engaged in the struggle for the rights of citizenship. Sometimes the discussion dealt with more basic issues. Men called for a revival of religious fervor and ethical idealism. In the spirit of the Enlightenment, it was asserted that the essence of religion is the belief in God, human freedom, and immortality, and the practice of the moral law. Ceremonial is of secondary importance.

Such ideas were in the air for some time before they led to any concrete results. The first practical consequence was the establishment of elementary schools where Jewish children received a secular training combined with education in religion. These schools were established by disciples of Mendelssohn in several German cities; in Austria, a reform of Jewish education along similar lines was encouraged by the relatively tolerant Emperor Joseph.

The new school in Berlin was founded by the wealthy and philanthropic David Friedlander, a devoted follower of Mendelssohn and an early champion of Reform. But despite his good intentions he was badly confused. This was evident from an anonymous but public letter which he addressed in 1799 to Pastor Teller, an official in the Prussian ministry of religion. The letter suggested that the writer and his family, with other Jews of Berlin, would like to become Protestants, on condition that they did not have to accept the divinity of Jesus! The Lutheran authorities naturally refused to consider such a deal, and Friedlander remained a Jew. But his children were baptized without reservations.

The Reform movement in Judaism really began with Israel Jacobson. Like Friedlander he was a man of means and an exponent of the Mendelssohn viewpoint; but Jacobson was far more energetic and aggressive, and much more ardent in his Jewish loyalties. As a young man, he had acquired wealth and influence in the west German Duchy of Brunswick. In the little town of Seesen he established a boarding school which enrolled both Jewish and Christian children. As part of the educational program, the school conducted "worship assemblies," in which prayers were recited quietly and with decorum, hymns were sung, and addresses (sometimes prayers as well) were delivered in German. This experiment appealed both to the children and to many adults; and Jacobson was encouraged to build a little "temple" on the grounds of the Seesen school, and to equip it with an organ. This was in 1805.

Two years later Jerome Bonaparte became king of Westphalia—a territory that included Brunswick. The Jews of the kingdom were organized into a consistory on the French pattern, except that the head of the consistory was not a rabbi, but Jacobson himself. Now he had the authority to extend his plans for reform, yet he wisely refrained from attempting radical changes. He brought into the consistory rabbis and laymen of moderate and even conservative views. Jewish education was regulated and given a more modern tone. There were plans for a seminary to train rabbis and teachers. Rabbis were instructed to stress ethical themes in their preaching, and especially to inculcate the duty of patriotism. Eventually, the consistory made a number of decrees regarding practice in the synagogue and at weddings. To enhance the dignity of the services, several old customs were abolished, and when some conservatives objected, Jacobson used the authority of the State to enforce compliance.

In 1810 the Seesen temple was dedicated with the first public Reform service. The chief departure from tradition was the singing of German hymns with organ accompaniment. Jacobson's sermon on the occasion stressed his positive religious aim: to make Judaism more inspiring by giving synagogue worship greater beauty and dignity. In fact, most of Jacobson's work was not incompatible with Orthodoxy. Though on a few occasions he gave utterance to radical views, his practical reforms dealt chiefly with the externals of Jewish worship. In his personal life he observed the ceremonial law conscientiously and lovingly.

In 1813, with the fall of Napoleon, the kingdom of Westphalia crumbled, and Jacobson's plans for revitalizing Judaism by reform were completely frustrated. Soon thereafter he settled in Berlin.

Here he began to hold Sabbath services in his own home. They soon attracted a large following, especially as several brilliant young intellectuals took turns as preachers. When Jacobson's house could not accommodate the worshippers, the service was moved to the mansion of Jacob Beer, father of the composer, Meyerbeer. But the Prussian government intervened, probably at the instigation of the Orthodox. The new service was forbidden on the ground that preaching in the language of the country was contrary to Jewish tradition. Prussia wanted no innovations! Indeed, the king is reported to have said quite frankly that he objected to the modernized service because it might check the trend toward baptism. Thus, the authority of the government, which Jacobson had once employed on behalf of reform, was now used against him.

For a time the service in Beer's home was resumed on the pretext that the community synagogue was closed for repairs; and the religious apathy of the Berlin Jews is revealed by the fact that the repairs were not completed for several years. But the new trend could not make much headway against official hostility. More positive results were achieved in the free city of Hamburg, to which one of Jacobson's followers, Eduard Kley, came as an educator in 1817. His energetic support of reform led to the establishment of the Hamburg Temple, dedicated the following year. Kley shared the task of preaching with Rabbi Gotthold Salomon, and their work evoked much enthusiasm as well as sharp opposition. The attacks became much more bitter and vocal when, some years later, the Temple published a new prayer book. Its most radical feature was the elimination of some (not all) of the prayers for the coming of the Messiah and the return to Zion. Most of the other reforms attempted at Hamburg and elsewhere at this time were external, intended to make the service more appealing and beautiful. Some of the reformers, in fact, sought justification for their proposals in the Talmud, and even professed to find precedents for introducing the organ into the synagogue.

But when the Hamburg reformers changed the text of basic prayers that had been part of the service for some seventeen hundred years, they challenged the authority of the oral Torah. The Orthodox were bound to react with violent disapproval. The authors of the prayer book were denounced as heretics, blasphemers, and apostates. The language seems to us intemperate; yet the Orthodox correctly perceived that basic issues were at stake.

The advocates of the new prayer book justified the changes they had made on grounds of intellectual honesty. They no longer cherished Jewish national ambitions. Hamburg was their Jerusalem; their new temple was the only temple they wanted.* Why should they continue to mouth prayers for a return to Palestine and the restoration of sacrifices, when they did not want these things?

Obviously, the changes in the prayer book were connected with the struggle of the Jews for citizenship; but there was nothing discreditable in this. The Hamburg reformers were not suppressing their real sentiments in order to conciliate the Gentile world: they were giving outward expression to their own very deep convictions.

Yet even on this point, the Hamburg prayer book was not altogether consistent. Throughout the early period, Reform was groping for a clear viewpoint. Its leaders did not always recognize fully the implications of their own program. They required a more adequate ideology than the rationalism of the Enlightenment, which by the beginning of the nineteenth century was already passé. Most of the leaders were laymen, equipped with limited Jewish knowledge and little formal training in modern thought. Though many of their practical experiments were successful and have found permanent acceptance in the Reform synagogue, such men were at a great disadvantage when they tried to articulate broad general principles.

This was made most plain when, in 1843, a group of laymen in Frankfort, who called themselves "Friends of Reform," published a statement of their beliefs. It was largely negative, repudiating the authority of the Talmud and the belief in the Messiah; its only positive item was a vague declaration that "the Mosaic religion is capable of unlimited development." By the time this strange utterance was promulgated, there was already a group of competent rabbis who had espoused Reform; and they criticized this negative platform sharply. The time had come for a new stage in the movement, based on the use of a new instrument—the Science of Judaism.

Nevertheless, full credit and honor must be given to the Jewish laymen for their pioneer attempt to modernize and thereby revitalize the Jewish religion. Their activity stimulated the more learned and philosophic leaders to provide a firmer foundation for Jewish modernism.

One of the most successful innovations of Jacobson was the cere-

---

* It has been supposed that this is the reason the name "temple" was now applied to Reform synagogues. It should be observed, however, that in Hungarian and other Balkan languages, cognates of the word temple are used for all houses of worship.

mony of Confirmation. It was introduced first for boys—apparently the routine of Bar Mitzvah was deemed insufficiently meaningful—and was at the start associated with the school rather than the synagogue. The name and some of the forms of the service were borrowed from Protestant practice. The first Confirmation of boys and girls *in the synagogue* was held at Hamburg in 1822. Despite much opposition, the rite rapidly became popular, and was adopted in many congregations whose practices were otherwise traditional. It provided an impressive climax to the program of religious education, an inspiring occasion for the youth to declare their loyalty to Judaism, and an opportunity for girls to take part in an important synagogue ritual. This last expressed the growing conviction that women were entitled to a larger role in religious matters. Observed at various occasions during the year, Confirmation was finally associated with Shovuos, the traditional anniversary of the giving of the Torah.

For a time, the trend toward affirming the equality of the sexes was limited to providing opportunities for the religious education of girls and to Confirmation. Despite some general statements on the dignity and rights of women, made by distinguished Reform leaders, the abolition of the women's gallery in the synagogue and the election of women to congregational offices came about only after a delay of some decades, chiefly in the United States.

40.

The Science of Judaism

EUROPEAN CULTURE IN THE EIGHTEENTH CENTURY WAS GREATLY IN-
fluenced by advances in mathematics, astronomy, and physics. The
philosophy of the Enlightenment period was therefore rather abstract,
rationalistic, and cosmopolitan; art and literature were characterized
by classic balance, restraint, and elegance.

But the early decades of the nineteenth century witnessed a radical
change of intellectual climate. The Napoleonic wars stimulated the
spirit of nationalism in almost every part of Europe. At the same time
the movement we call romanticism arose in literature, the arts, and
in life itself. In rebellion against the measured classic tradition, the
romantics gave preference to the extreme, the bizarre, and the violently
emotional. Both nationalistic ardor and romantic passion led men to
glorify the far away and long ago. There was a new enthusiasm for
medieval art and culture, and a revival of Christian sentiment, esthetic
as well as theological in its motives.

In such an atmosphere there was a greater awareness of history; and
the universities, especially those of Germany, experienced a great rebirth of linguistic and historical studies. Both the ancient and the more
recent past were investigated with intensive thoroughness; the languages of Europe and Asia were examined by new comparative methods. The rich literature of the Orient was, for the first time, made
available to the European world; and neglected areas of European
culture—for example, the old Teutonic and Norse epics—were given

greater attention. Even folklore became, for the first time, a subject for scholarly inquiry.

This concern with history, in the broadest sense of the term, was soon felt within Jewish life. It gave birth to the movement called by its adherents *Die Wissenschaft des Judentums*—literally "the science of Judaism"—that is to say the investigation of the entire Jewish past by modern methods of literary and historical criticism.

Exact scholarship, of course, was not new in Jewish life. The Hebrew grammars and dictionaries produced in Spain, the Bible commentaries of the Spanish and French schools, Rashi's great exposition of the Talmud, are enduring masterpieces both of learning and of critical insight. At the beginning of the modern period, the Gaon of Vilna discarded the artificial system of pilpul, and taught his followers to establish correct texts by the use of manuscripts, and to interpret them by simple grammatical methods.

Such studies were philological and literary rather than historical; but a few Jewish scholars had also tried to penetrate into the facts about the past. Jacob Emden, the foe of mysticism, presented convincing proofs that the Zohar was not nearly so ancient as its admirers supposed. Still more independent was the work of Azariah dei Rossi, whom we met in our account of the Italian Renaissance. For questioning the accuracy of a few Talmudic legends, Azariah was severely criticized by the conservatives of his day; and not till nearly four centuries later did he have an important successor.

The name of this successor was Nachman Krochmal. He lived in Austrian Poland (Galicia), where the Jewish community, still engaged in Talmudic studies after the old tradition, was yet beginning to feel the modern influences that issued from the West. The Austrian rulers were introducing secular studies into the Jewish schools, and the prestige of Mendelssohn and his group had awakened an interest in German literature.

Krochmal, a profound thinker and saintly personality, achieved in his own mind a remarkable harmony between the old and the new. He did not rebel against the Talmudic tradition, but sought to give it enrichment and new life. He had taken his first steps in philosophy by studying the philosophic portions of Ibn Ezra's Bible commentaries; he learned much about the method and subject matter of historical scholarship from Azariah dei Rossi. Later on he read widely in the philosophic, literary, and scholarly works of the Germans.

He occupied no official position, and wrote comparatively little. His greatest achievement was to inspire a band of disciples whom he guided into new paths. Some, in accordance with their talents, were encouraged in literary endeavors. Others he trained in scholarly research, chief among them Salomon Judah Rappoport. Rappoport made notable studies of Talmudic and medieval lore, and wrote the first biography of Saadia Gaon, of the mysterious hymn-writer, Kalir, and of other Jewish worthies. His most important work was produced in his spare time while employed in a clerical position by the Jewish community of Lemberg. Later, his great talents brought him recognition, and he was made Rabbi of Prague; but his official duties thereafter limited his scholarly productiveness.

Krochmal and Rappoport wrote in Hebrew. A new phase of the movement began with the appearance of scholarly Jewish works in German. Isaac Markus Jost had received a modern education and became in turn the head of the Jewish school at Frankfort. In 1820, he began the publication of a *History of the Jews,* and throughout his career continued to extend and enrich the study of Jewish history. His works, published in the German language, are an excellent pioneer attempt at a task so long neglected—for Jost was the first important Jewish historian since Josephus! Obviously, the work of a pathfinder could not be either complete or free from mistakes. Jost was a conscientious, though not a brilliant student; the tone of his history was somewhat dry and matter of fact. Thus his works were supplanted in popular favor by the great history produced a generation later by Heinrich Graetz, whose preparation was more adequate and who imparted greater drama and excitement to the story. (Yet students today view Jost's work with great respect, and find his treatment of the modern period far more accurate and impartial than that of Graetz.)

But the giant of the period was Jost's schoolmate, Leopold Zunz, the first professing Jew to graduate from a German university. (It was he who coined the phrase, Wissenschaft des Judentums.) While a student in Berlin, Zunz had been a leading spirit in what was called the Society for the Culture and Science of the Jews. This was a group of young Jewish intellectuals who had formulated a grandiose program. They planned to spread general culture among the Jewish masses and offer vocational guidance to the youth. At the same time, they would give Jews a fuller knowledge and appreciation of their own background by means of lectures, study groups, and popular publications.

These pretentious ambitions came to almost nothing. The immense apathy of the Berlin Jews soon discouraged the leaders of the Society. Few of the intelligentsia cared to learn about Judaism; the pious viewed anything new with tight-lipped disapproval. Eduard Gans, the leader of the Society, took the easy way of baptism. Heinrich Heine, already becoming famous as a poet, had also belonged to the group; in a short poem, he poured out his contempt for Gans's surrender, but soon after surrendered in his turn. Zunz, undaunted, stuck to his own plans. Though almost no one in his own country cared about Jewish scholarship—his chief source of encouragement and inspiration was his correspondence with Rappoport—he resolved to devote his life to the science of Judaism.

He experimented briefly with the rabbinate and found it distasteful. The rabbinical office had lost its prestige. The communities were dominated by prosperous businessmen who had no tincture of letters and did not even know enough to respect scholars—another new and alarming symptom. Zunz earned his bread by teaching and journalism, and embarked on his real life work with sacrificial dedication.

He had already published a pioneer biography of Rashi. Now he attempted something broader. Zunz had been one of the young men who preached at the service established by Jacobson and Beer. This service had been suppressed on the ground that regular preaching was not native to the synagogue, but an innovation borrowed from the church. Zunz now undertook to prove the reverse. Preaching was in fact an ancient Jewish institution, which had flourished through the centuries; it had passed from the synagogue to the church.

But this could have been adequately demonstrated in a short pamphlet. Zunz's purpose was much larger. He undertook to show how the spoken word had been a source of instruction and inspiration in Israel from the days of the prophets. He traced the development of preaching in the synagogue, and described with rich and detailed learning the various works of Midrash and aggadah. After a briefer section on medieval Jewish preaching, Zunz concluded his work with a discussion on contemporary conditions. To counteract the decline of Jewish public worship, he declared, the service must be revitalized, above all by the spoken word of the preacher instructing the ignorant and arousing the indifferent. Thus Zunz linked a work of prodigious and original scholarship to living issues.

The preface to this masterly volume (*The Devotional Addresses of the Jews*) was suppressed by the Prussian government. In it Zunz demanded justice for the Jew—not "rights," as he put it, but right. But such justice cannot be won without effort. The Jew's inferior social and political status is due, at least in part, to the belief that he is culturally inferior. The Gentile world has no conception of the vigorous, creative intellectual life that has flourished among the Jews since the end of the Biblical period. Yet surely the history and literature of the Jews are just as worthy of study in the universities as the culture of Persia and China! It is therefore necessary to emancipate not only the Jew but Judaism, to release the science of Judaism from its cultural ghetto, so that it may be recognized by all educated men as a significant branch of human knowledge.

Zunz therefore had a special reason for writing his book in German rather than Hebrew. He wished his researches to reach the entire learned world, not only Jewish scholars; and indeed many Christian savants recognized the merits of his work. We may add that Zunz's hope for the emancipation of Jewish culture has been partially, though slowly, realized. Several European and American universities have chairs of Jewish Studies and have sponsored publications in the field of post-Biblical Jewish literature.

We need not review in detail the rich accomplishments of Zunz's long and productive career, nor the work of the many scholars who caught the spark from him and in the ensuing decades extended every phase of Jewish knowledge. The labors which Zunz undertook singlehanded and without help flowered into a vigorous movement. The rabbinical seminaries founded during the course of the century became centers of Jewish science. Not only the professors of these institutions, but many of their graduates, engaged in systematic and original research. Learned periodicals in Hebrew, German, and other languages were established, so that the findings of the investigators might be published promptly; and various foundations gave financial aid for the publication of more ambitious and expensive works.

Within a few decades after Zunz began his work, there was a wellknit (though comparatively small) body of Jewish scholars, many German born, mostly German trained, enthusiastically delving into the Jewish past. Great works of Jewish literature were printed for the first time or republished in more accurate editions; Hebrew libraries were catalogued; bibliographies were compiled; detailed monographs and massive reference volumes were produced. The groundwork was laid for understanding the manner in which the Jewish people and religion developed against the background of world history.

What were the new subjects treated by the masters of *Jüdische Wissenschaft*? First, history—including the economic and social, as well as the religious and cultural history of the Jews. Second, biography—a field utterly neglected by ancient and medieval Jewish writers. Third, the varied field of Jewish literature, both secular and religious. Zunz was a pioneer in the study of the prayer book in its many versions and of the vast treasury of Hebrew hymnology. Other scholars edited the poetry of the Spanish Golden Age. The long-neglected writings of the medieval philosophers were again studied in the Arabic originals and in conjunction with the writings of the Christian and Moslem scholastics. There were stirrings of interest in the history of Jewish music and art. The new historical approach was extensively applied to Talmudic studies; but few of the masters of "Jewish science" engaged in original research in Bible. (During the century, however, many translations of the Bible into modern languages were made by the Jews in various countries.)

The approach of the scholars to their material was also new. The older method was to study, let us say, the dietary legislation of the Talmud in order to determine the halakah. The modern scholar might examine the same material in order to determine how much the ancient Rabbis knew about animal physiology, and to compare their knowledge with that found in Greek or Latin writings of the same period. In the same way, the rabbinical responsa were investigated not only for the legal decisions they contain, but because of the incidental information they offer about the occupations of Jews or the social conditions in various lands and centuries.

Extensive use was also made of non-traditional sources. The many Greek, Latin, and Persian words found in Talmudic literature, as well as many cultural borrowings, were now explained through classical and oriental studies. The reports of pagan historians and of Christian church fathers, the decrees of popes and secular rulers, the legal and administrative decisions preserved in medieval records, and the researches of Christian scholars greatly enriched our knowledge of the Jewish past. Such long-neglected Jewish sources as the Septuagint, the Apocrypha, and the writings of Philo and Josephus were now carefully examined by Jewish scholars. Even the tombstones in old Jewish cemeteries provided important data for the inquiring student.

The devotees of the new discipline varied greatly in their personal approach to Judaism. Moritz Steinschneider, who devoted his long life to the sacrificial task of creating the science of Jewish bibliography,

41.

The Progress of Reform

WRITERS OFTEN DISTINGUISH TWO STAGES IN THE HISTORY OF
German Reform Judaism—the early period, when laymen took the lead
in modifying the externals of worship; and the second period, guided
by rabbis, who dealt with more fundamental issues. The distinction,
though useful, should not be pressed too far. Many of the laymen had
formulated principles, though perhaps imperfectly; and almost from
the start, some rabbis lent their support to the new movement. We have
mentioned Gotthold Salomon, the preacher of the Hamburg Temple;
another early partisan was Aaron Chorin, Rabbi at Arad, Moravia. In a
region where the old orthodoxy was still dominant, Chorin coura-
geously maintained the position of Reform in several Hebrew volumes.
In 1833, the Chief Rabbi of the duchy of Westphalia (where, perhaps,
the memory of Jacobson's efforts lingered) introduced some mild
reforms into the synagogues of the area. This Rabbi, by name Joseph
Abraham Friedlander, was nearly eighty years old at the time; his reforms, though hardly radical, evoked complaints by the Conservatives
to the government.

But a new generation of rabbis was coming to the fore. Graduates
of universities, they had learned from their professors, and from the
example of men like Zunz, to apply the methods of historical criticism
to the Jewish past. In the Wissenschaft des Judentums they found a
powerful tool for their purpose.

The more scholarly reformers had already tried to justify their innovations by appeal to the past. They pointed out that the Talmud and

279

codes permit one to pray in the language he understands best, and in the same way found precedents for other changes. But such a method could not long be satisfactory. Reform was a revolt against the unquestioned authority of the past. It vindicated the claims of reason, and often appealed to the "spirit of the age." You cannot quote authority to justify the rejection of that authority. Nor can you rely on certain ancient texts that support your contention, while disregarding others that do not please you. Some of the reforms were entirely compatible with Jewish tradition. There were soon strictly Orthodox synagogues where the service was conducted with decorum and the rabbis preached in elegant German. But while tradition might sanction reforms, it could not sanction Reform. If the appeal was to ancient precedent, the Orthodox were bound to have the best of the argument.

The method followed by Zunz in *The Devotional Addresses* was more novel than it seemed. He did not quote old authorities to prove that his suggestions were *permissible*. He turned instead to broad historic experience. Not merely was preaching customary in the ancient synagogue, not only had great Rabbis authorized it, but the spoken word had brought vitality and inspiration to Jewish life. If modern Judaism is to be revitalized, the spoken word must be restored to the synagogue. Research into the past, in short, clarifies the true nature of Judaism, and helps us to plan for the present and future. But after he had published his first masterpiece, Zunz withdrew from activity in practical religious affairs, to devote himself to pure research. Of the scholarly Rabbis who now undertook to justify and to direct the Reform movement, the outstanding figure was Dr. Abraham Geiger.

A master of Hebrew learning, Geiger included in his researches the whole sweep of Biblical and post-Biblical Judaism. He was especially interested in the development of religious ideas and in the history of the sects, and he did much to correct the unfair estimate of the Pharisees which had been current through the centuries. But as he delved deeply into the past, Geiger also stated with utmost clarity and courage the implications he drew from his studies for the belief and practice of his own day.

The old concept of absolute revelation, he felt, could no longer be maintained. The very text of the Bible has been repeatedly modified. Analysis of Biblical material and of post-Biblical sources reveals that religious ideas and practices have constantly been subject to change and revision. The scientific outlook no longer permits a naive faith in miracles. It is now possible and necessary to recognize that the Bible, for all its sublimity, contains primitive and even morally dubious elements. We can no longer dispose of such difficulties by the allegorical method employed by Philo and Maimonides, for this procedure has been outlawed by exact linguistic science.

It was indeed no novelty for anti-clerical skeptics to challenge the authority and even the ethical value of Scripture. But only in the nineteenth century was an independent approach to the Bible adopted by *devotees* of religion. To Geiger, the new methods were not a means of undermining the faith, but an instrument for enriching, purifying, and strengthening it.

Instead of one fixed and changeless revelation at Sinai, Geiger proclaimed a progressive revelation, which continues to the present in the discoveries of science and the insights of wise men. The Bible and Talmud are glorious and permanently valuable records of an early and decisive stage in this process. But since the revelation came from God *through* men, all the documents of revelation are a mixture of the divine and the human, of the eternally valid and of the temporary and transient. Judaism is a living, growing organism, evolving gradually from earlier and more primitive forms to the full flowering of its universal spiritual message.

Central and changeless is the belief in the one and holy God, who is to be served through righteousness and mercy. God's law is basically ethical; ritual and ceremony, as the prophets declared long ago, are not of the essence of the religion. Moreover, historical study reveals that ceremonial practice has been constantly subject to change. Ritual is, indeed, not without value: it is a means of making religious truth more vivid and inspiring to the worshipper. But the forms are not sacrosanct. If they fail to instruct and uplift those who practice them—still more if they repel or disgust—they may be modified or discarded.

Like most of his generation, Geiger stressed the universal ethical aspect of Judaism and rejected the national aspirations of the Jewish people. The hope for a personal Messiah-king, for the establishment of a Jewish nation in Palestine, for the restoration of Temple and sacrifice were explicitly negated. The Jews are, and should remain, citizens of the various nations among whom they live, distinctive only by virtue of their religion. Instead of the faith in a personal Messiah, Geiger looked forward to a "messianic era" of universal righteousness, brotherhood, and peace. Such an ideal had been voiced in some of the noblest pages of the prophets, and had been affirmed by the Rabbis under the name of "the kingdom of heaven." In Geiger's time, this faith took on a somewhat new character through the influence of theories concerning evolution and progress. Particularly in the first half of the nineteenth century, a period of advancing freedom and of rapidly expanding scientific invention, men felt that the Golden Age of humanity was rapidly approaching.

Yet, though he wished the Jews to differ from their fellow citizens only in religion, Geiger regarded the persistence and survival of the Jewish religious group as a most sacred and urgent obligation. The Jewish people have a mission to mankind, a mission ordained of God. They are the witnesses of the one God, as the great prophet of the Exile taught. Men have not yet adequately acknowledged the unity and holiness of God, even in words. But the task of Israel is not merely to correct a faulty theology: it is to persuade mankind, through teaching and example, to acknowledge God's unity by obedience to His law. The mission will not have been fulfilled until righteousness and peace prevail everywhere. Until that messianic consummation, the Jews must survive as a priest-people dedicated to the service of God and of humanity.

The fulfilment of the mission, in Geiger's view, requires that the Jews live among the various peoples of the earth. Their dispersion was therefore not a punishment, as earlier generations had supposed, but a providential dispensation.

Geiger and his associates boldly proclaimed these principles of Reform from their pulpits, and made full use of the printed word as well. This age saw the establishment of numerous Jewish periodicals; some were primarily for scholars, but many were addressed to the general reader and exercised considerable influence. Despite wide-spread and often heated discussion of the new ideas, however, their practical implementation proceeded slowly.

The Reform Rabbis, we must remember, were not the ministers of Reform congregations, with a free hand to experiment. Each was the official leader of an entire community, with obligations, both legal and moral, to the traditionalists as well as to the Progressives. The communities, moreover, were subject to the control of the various German states in which they were located: and many of the rulers still took a hand in regulating internal Jewish affairs, especially when complaints were made to them by dissatisfied groups. Thus, the strongly conservative views of some of these rulers, and the desire of others to modernize the education and behavior of their Jewish subjects, tended to delay or to accelerate the changes in various parts of the country.

The problem was dramatically illustrated in the case of Geiger himself when, in 1838, he was called from Wiesbaden to be Rabbi in Breslau. For Breslau already had a Rabbi, the elderly S. A. Tiktin, who was an uncompromising defender of Orthodoxy. Tiktin, quite naturally, refused to accept the heretical Geiger as an associate; and the bitter controversy which ensued lasted several years. Ultimately, the supporters of Geiger were victorious, and he was confirmed in his office; yet Reform made little progress in Breslau. Geiger's modernist sermons were delivered during services which followed the traditional ritual; and he was frequently required as Rabbi of the community, to render decisions on the halakah!

There was indeed one man who found a constituency where he could bring theory and practice into full harmony. Samuel Holdheim (1806–1860) had grown up in the old-fashioned Talmudism of the East, had reacted against it violently, and had become the most radical of the reformers. All the progressives had stressed the distinction between the universal and the national elements in Judaism; Holdheim carried this distinction to the furthest extreme. The national elements, he taught, were designed for the period when there was a Jewish state, and they lost their validity forever when the state was destroyed. Not only the laws of kingship, temple, and priesthood, not only the provisions of civil and criminal jurisprudence, but also the regulation of marriage and divorce and many of the distinctive observances of home and synagogue were classified by Holdheim as nationalistic and therefore obsolete. The enduring core of Judaism included little more than a creed and an ethical code; Holdheim regarded Judaism as a doctrine rather than as a discipline of life.

The Sabbath problem, which was troubling all serious Jewish thinkers of the time, was met by Holdheim with the simple, bold proposal to transfer the Sabbath to Sunday, the day of rest observed by the majority and recognized by the law of the State. Several of the festivals were discarded because of their nationalist implications. Holdheim could officiate without qualms of conscience at marriages between Jews and Gentile "monotheists."

These theories were advanced by Holdheim while he was Rabbi in Schwerin. Meantime a group of educated laymen in Berlin were growing increasingly impatient over the slow progress of the Reform movement. They avoided the arrogant and negative approach of the Frankfort "Friends of Reform." Instead, they addressed appeals to the rabbinical conferences (to be described shortly), urging concrete action to stimulate a spiritual revival. Eventually, they established a Reform congregation independent of the Berlin Jewish community (of which by law they had to remain members) and invited Geiger to lead them. But though Geiger was the target in Breslau of both the indignant Orthodox and the impatient progressives, he was unwilling to identify himself with a separatist group. The Berlin reformers then turned to Holdheim who became their enthusiastic leader and spokesman. The Berlin Reform Congregation, throughout most of its history, held its weekly services on Sunday. They were conducted in the German language, except for a few Hebrew sentences; the men prayed with uncovered heads and women were seated on the same floor. But this explicitly untraditional congregation found no imitators in Germany—in part, perhaps, because the adherents of such groups had to pay their assessments to the official Jewish community and also to provide for the support of their own synagogue. Only Berlin had a large group that was willing and able to assume this double burden.

The German reformers, we have seen, rejected the national aspects of Jewish tradition, especially the prayers for the return to Palestine under a Davidic king. This trend was certainly affected by the struggle for equal rights which had to be resumed in the several German states after the downfall of Napoleon. The opponents of Reform have sometimes asserted that these changes in worship were motivated by nothing better than expediency: the reformers, it is declared, watered down their own convictions in the hope of deriving political and social benefits.

The unfairness of this charge is demonstrated first of all by the positive religious achievements of Reform. The mass movement toward baptism declined sharply; the apathy and ignorance of which Heine and Zunz had complained were remedied in considerable measure. Good Jewish books and periodicals in German multiplied and were widely read. Fine synagogue buildings were erected, and they attracted large groups of worshippers. The spiritual revival which Reform sought to stimulate was felt not only by the adherents of the new movement but by its opponents as well.

The positive character of the movement was also seen in the spirit with which the struggle for Jewish rights was carried on. Outstanding in this field was a remarkable layman, Gabriel Riesser of Hamburg (1808–1863). As a young man, he found his plans for a legal career blocked by discriminatory laws. But unlike many of his contemporaries, he scorned the easy solution of an insincere baptism. He threw himself wholeheartedly into the struggle for the full emancipation of all the Jews of Germany.

Riesser was a vigorous champion of the Hamburg Temple. But he was careful to explain that Reform must be undertaken for its own sake, not as a device for political emancipation. The status of the Jews must be rectified as a matter of justice and humanity. The Jewish community could not be required to modify its beliefs and practices as a price for those rights to which its members were fully entitled.

To advance his cause, Riesser established a periodical, which he bluntly called *Der Jude* (The Jew), though this word had such unfavorable associations in German culture that it was avoided by the Jews themselves. On one occasion, when the finances of his journal were at a low ebb, Riesser received an offer of support from the Vienna Rothschilds, on the condition that the name of the publication be changed to *Der Israelit*. He responded with a scornful editorial, in which he recalled an old Jewish custom of changing the name of a person who is desperately sick, in the hope of deceiving the Angel of Death. We smile at this superstition, he remarked; but is it any more foolish than the notion that we can appease our enemies by calling ourselves Israelites instead of Jews?

Riesser understood that the struggle for Jewish emancipation was part of the larger struggle for liberty and democracy in all German life. The enemies of the Jews were precisely those aristocratic, military, and clerical parties that were trying to hold back the march of freedom in Europe. Hence, he took an active part in the liberal movements which came to a climax throughout the continent in 1848. In that revolutionary year, an all-German parliament was held at Frankfort in the effort to create a unified Germany under a liberal constitution. There were several Jewish delegates to this body; Riesser was elected one of its vice-presidents, and served on the delegation which offered the German crown to King Frederick William IV of Prussia. But the Prussian autocrat would not assent to the democratic constitution under which he would have had to reign. The high hopes of 1848 were soon dissipated. The reactionaries regained control; and the succeeding decades saw a large migration of freedom-loving Germans (Jewish and Christian) to the United States. Yet, during 1848 most of the legal disabilities of the Jews were removed by legislative enactment; in practice, however, discrimination continued in many areas up to the end of the First World War.

This change of political climate may explain in part the decline of enthusiasm for Jewish religious reform. A liberal congregation was established in the Hungarian city of Pesth amid the revolutionary fervors

42.

Philosophies of Judaism

1. *The Kantians*

MOSES MENDELSSOHN ONCE WON A PRIZE FOR AN ESSAY ON A philosophic subject; Immanuel Kant's entry in the same contest received honorable mention. Mendelssohn's essay was marked by clarity and elegance of expression; Kant's contribution was more profound in substance. Kant, indeed, always referred to Mendelssohn with great respect, and warmly praised his *Jerusalem*. Nevertheless, Kant was one of the giants of philosophy and Mendelssohn a minor figure in the history of thought.

Mendelssohn clung to the comfortable Enlightenment view that the basic truths of religion can be proved by reasoned argument. Kant, who started out with the same conviction, soon found it untenable. Thus, he was led to a searching inquiry into the character of human knowledge. He concluded that man's mind is an effective instrument for scientific research, but not for the discovery of those realities that lie beyond the limits of our experience. The mind does not (to use a modern term) photograph external reality. It molds our impressions and perceptions into a coherent structure of its own. Such concepts as time and space, cause and effect, are not derived from observation of the universe—they are inherent in the structure of the human mind. We know only phenomena. Behind these phenomena, indeed, is the ultimate reality, "the thing in itself"; but our reason cannot discover it. When we try, for example, to prove the existence of God, our results are not only inconclusive, but self-contradictory. Kant concludes that we cannot logically demonstrate the reality of God, human freedom, and immortality.

But the religious believer need have no regrets at this conclusion; for it rules out equally the possibility of *disproving* the basic tenets of faith. And while we cannot by scientific method arrive at the "thing in itself," we have another means of approaching ultimate reality.

For man is a moral being. He feels the obligation to do right, not because it is advantageous, but simply because it is right. He is capable of recognizing the command to act in such a way that his conduct may serve as a rule for all men. Two things, said Kant, fill me with awe: the starry heavens without, and the moral law within. But man, he argued, cannot be truly moral unless he has free will to choose the right and reject the evil. His ethical strivings would be futile if there were not an eternal life in which he can make good the failures and frustrations of earthly existence. And his moral purpose attains full validity only if there is a God who is both the Source and Goal of his aspirations. These beliefs, though not logically proved, are in Kant's view the indispensable requirements of man's moral nature.

The philosophy of Kant, stressing the intimate connection between ethics and religion, was peculiarly sympathetic to Judaism, which from the days of the prophets had emphasized conduct rather than dogma. Many Jewish thinkers up to the present day have drawn heavily on Kant's ideas. And from the very start, Kant found numerous disciples and expositors in the Jewish community that was just emerging from the ghetto.

Such expositors were needed: for Kant had expressed his revolutionary ideas in difficult technical terminology. His early Jewish followers ranged from the wealthy amateur, Markus Hertz, to the intellectual vagabond who called himself Salomon Maimon. Maimon was literally a refugee from east European Orthodoxy. He had rebelled violently against the rigid Talmudic discipline. He had dabbled in Chasidism, and been disillusioned by the superstition of its adherents. Finally, he settled in Germany, where he acquired a profound mastery of European philosophy. His autobiography is a vivid, though bitter and one-sided picture of Jewish life in eighteenth-century Poland. All his life he remained rootless and dissatisfied, and in his later years he was remote from Jews and Judaism. He made some brilliant contributions to the development of Kantian thought.

In 1835 Salomon Ludwig Steinheim, a physician, published the first part of a work called *Revelation According to the Doctrine of the Synagogue*—the fourth and final volume did not appear till 1865. Though he was an amateur in philosophy and a tyro in Jewish knowledge, Steinheim had a fresh and original outlook. He rebelled vigorously against the cool rationalism of Mendelssohn and his school. The Judaism of the Bible, he insisted, is intense and heart-warming. It is not an inference from scientific data or intellectual presuppositions, but a revealed religion. Yet his notions of revelation were hardly orthodox. Modern interpreters have seen Kant's influence in his thinking: the indwelling moral law (they infer) is similar to, if not identical with, what Steinheim meant by revelation. But Steinheim made little effort to propagate his ideas, and held himself aloof from organized Jewish life; and his writings had little immediate influence.

2. *Idealism*

Meantime, a new philosophic school arose in Germany, which for a time overshadowed Kantianism. Kant had denied that we can acquire a knowledge of the "thing in itself." His successors argued that since the "thing in itself" cannot be known, we need not assume that it exists. The only world we know is that which the mind constructs. To know the world is to understand the structure and content of the mind, and vice versa. All existence is logically comprehensible. God is not a Being outside this system, but the Absolute, the totality of all mind and all ideas apprehended by mind.

This position, expounded by a series of philosophers, reached its culmination in G. W. F. Hegel, who in his own time was the monarch of the philosophic world. Hegel pictured all existence as a kind of evolution or development. This kind of thinking was in the air long before Charles Darwin gave it scientific demonstration. But to Darwin evolution was a hypothesis based on the study of specific data. Hegel's evolution, however, was founded on abstract and theoretical principles. He held that every force in life generates its own negation. Tyranny begets revolution, superstition breeds skepticism, and so on. Out of the conflict of these opposites, a new synthesis is born; and this in turn generates its opposing force. Hegel applied this pattern especially to the study of human institutions and ideas. He used it, however, not to predict future developments, but to explain and justify what had already happened. Hegel seemed to imply that the evolutionary process had reached its peak on the political scene with the Prussian monarchy, in religion with Lutheran Protestantism, and in philosophy with the Hegelian system!

For a time Hegel's brilliance dazzled all minds. Geiger and his fellow reformers were much influenced by his thought, though they were interested in historical research rather than in formal philosophy. There were, however, several Jewish thinkers who consciously adopted the idealistic position. And here we must turn back to the Galician sage, Nachman Krochmal.

We have already noted his great contribution to the creation of Jüdische Wissenschaft; he was equally interested in philosophy. He was not, as is sometimes said, a follower of Hegel, whose writings he saw only in his later years; but he was familiar with the mood of German idealism, which provided a background for his own speculations. Krochmal sketched a philosophy of Jewish history, almost the first such attempt since the days of Judah HaLevi.

Man, essentially a social being, constructs increasingly elaborate social forms—family, tribe, nation. But, said Krochmal, the cohesive force in any society, primitive or advanced, is spiritual. A living society shares values, expressed in morality, law, the arts, education, and religion. The spiritual character of a people is clearly recognized and strongly felt in the days of national growth and expansion, and is most fully expressed when the nation reaches political and cultural maturity. But power and prosperity weaken the national fiber. Selfishness and love of pleasure cause decline. The ideals of the nation are neglected or corrupted, or replaced by foreign borrowings. Eventually the nation, having lost its ideals, loses its existence. The spiritual values it once cherished may survive through adoption by some other people, or they may become part of the common heritage of mankind.

The ideal of each nation reflects the dominant interest of the people —war, commerce, law, art, and so forth. Because such ideals are finite, the history of each nation is limited in time. One after another, the nations of mankind have grown, flowered, declined, and disappeared.

But the ideal of the people of Israel is no such partial manifestation. They are consecrated to the Absolute Eternal Spirit. Therefore, they are an eternal people. Krochmal cannot ascribe this fact to the special merits or talents of Israel, but only to the working of divine Providence. Nevertheless, living in the material world, the Jews too are subject to the laws of national growth and decay. But when the cycle was complete, the Eternal Spirit which chose Israel has always generated new life and growth.

Krochmal illustrated this thesis in some detail. The first cycle of Jewish history, he held, began with Abraham and ended with the destruction of the First Temple. A new period of growth began with the prophets of the Exile and terminated with the death of Bar Kochba. A third began with the creation of the Mishnah, ending perhaps with the expulsion of the Jews from Spain. He did not apply his pattern to more recent centuries; but we must remember that his writings are fragmentary and incomplete. Yet they have continued to stimulate Jewish thinkers to the present.

Two German rabbis sought more consciously to integrate Jewish teaching with the idealistic philosophy. Solomon Formstecher, Rabbi of Offenbach, has been called the philosopher of the Reform movement. From Schelling, Hegel's predecessor, he derived the idea of God as the World Soul, manifesting His creative power through nature and spirit.

Basically, there are only two religions: the religion of nature or paganism in all its endless forms, and the religion of spirit, or Judaism. Paganism expresses itself in art, in mythology, and in metaphysics, which is a sophisticated version of mythology. Judaism in its pure form is free of all myth, ethical in tone, advancing toward the prophetic goal of world peace and brotherhood.

Formstecher made the first serious attempt at a history of Judaism. In accordance with his idealistic presuppositions, it is not a recital of facts and events, but the account of the unfolding of an idea. Judaism in its earlier stages needed the framework of a national state and later of a legalistic system, within which the idea might develop securely. Moreover, the influence of paganism was so powerful that for centuries Judaism was compelled to compromise with it, and to adopt such mythological elements as the belief in angels and in resurrection. To the fusion of pagan and Jewish elements, Formstecher gave the general name of Cabala, by which he means not only the mystical doctrine of the Middle Ages, but its antecedents from the Bible onward. Gradually, Judaism has been able to discard these pagan accretions, and in lands of enlightenment the national-legal scaffolding is becoming less and less necessary.

The primary task of the Jewish people is to preserve the ideal of independent spirit in its full purity. This truth is too difficult for the pagan world to accept directly. Christianity and Islam are the two missionary agencies of Judaism. They are combinations of Judaism and paganism, by which the ethical values of Judaism have been made palatable to the heathen world. Formstecher saw some evidence that the pagan elements in Christianity are gradually becoming attenuated, and dared to hope for the time when essential Judaism should triumph everywhere and the prophetic dream should be realized.

These ideas were all included in Formstecher's chief work, *The Religion of the Spirit*, published in 1841 when the author was only thirty-three years old. The following year saw the publication of an even larger and more brilliant volume, entitled *The Jewish Philosophy of Religion* by the twenty-seven-year-old Samuel Hirsch. This remarkable work was an attempt to present Judaism from the standpoint of Hegel, and specifically to challenge Hegel's claim that Christianity is the "absolute religion."

Hirsch stressed the centrality of human freedom. It is the power to do right or wrong. Man could not be free if he did not have the possibility of sinning. But while he is able to sin, he is not compelled to do so. It is not necessary for him to yield to the sensual impulses and selfish desires which he shares with all the beings of nature. To submit to such impulses is sin. To acknowledge them as irresistible, to accept the domination of nature over spirit, is idolatry and heathenism. None of the ancient religions and philosophies could bring salvation to mankind because all of them held that man is in bondage to nature and destiny.

A new start for humanity began with Abraham. Under divine guidance he recognized his freedom and broke with the ancestral paganism. Above all, by his willingness to sacrifice his son, Abraham demonstrated that man can rise above natural impulse, that sin is only possible, but not inevitable. This truth was transmitted by an entire people, the descendants of Abraham. But a large group cannot be expected to attain such spiritual heights by its own strivings. Therefore, the truth discovered by Abraham was verified by supernatural revelation at Sinai, and reiterated by the prophets.

Jesus of Nazareth, Hirsch declared, rose to the spiritual level of Abraham and demonstrated the fundamental Jewish truth that man is master of nature by dying innocently on the cross. The Christian religion, however, is a mixture of Jewish and heathen elements. (Hirsch makes no mention of Islam.) Christianity cannot justly be regarded as the absolute religion; it is a means whereby the world is gradually weaned away from enslavement to paganism. The messianic hope can be realized only when men accept the ethical responsibility that goes with liberty.

Hirsch published this extraordinary work, embellished with original interpretations of Biblical and rabbinic passages, while serving as Rabbi in Mendelssohn's home city of Dessau. At the time, he regarded himself as Orthodox. He attacked the Biblical critics, and insisted that the revelation at Sinai was a truly supernatural event. He argued likewise that miracles are possible. Otherwise God Himself would be subject to the laws of nature, and human freedom would be ruled out.

To the question why such miracles as are reported from the past no longer occur, Hirsch replied that the question is based on error. The survival of the Jewish people is a literal miracle. By all the laws of nature and history, the Jews should long since have perished through poverty and persecution. Their continued existence is evidence that Providence still intervenes in human affairs.

Obviously, however, Hirsch's thinking was far from authoritarian, and had nothing in common with that of his namesake, Samson Raphael Hirsch. Soon after his book appeared, Samuel Hirsch had become one of the most extreme modernists. After a few years as Rabbi in Luxemburg, he came to the United States, and for decades preached radical Reform from his pulpit in Philadelphia.

43.

German Judaism Comes
to Equilibrium

1. Frankel and "Positive-Historical Judaism"

IN THE ATTEMPT TO GIVE GREATER DIRECTION AND VIGOR TO THE
Reform movement, three rabbinical conferences were held in the years
1844 to 1846. Geiger was the prime mover and leading spirit in the
undertaking, which brought together a number of the ablest German
rabbis. The conferences debated some of the crucial problems of Reform: the status of women, the revision of the prayers, the observance
of the Sabbath. But though the discussions were scholarly and often
profound, the concrete results were rather meager. The possibilities for
achievement were limited by the differences in outlook among the
participants, and above all by the mixed character of the communities
they served.

The second conference, held at Frankfort in 1845, was marked by
the dramatic appearance of Zecharias Frankel, the Chief Rabbi of Sax-
ony. He had already acquired a distinguished reputation as a scholar,
which was fully justified in subsequent years by his masterly works on
the Septuagint and on rabbinic literature. Frankel was not Orthodox,
but he was deeply troubled by the direction which Reform had taken.
He had published a caustic criticism of the first conference held the
year before in Brunswick; and from the moment he arrived at Frankfort, the other rabbis felt that he was in the opposition.

One of the first items of business was a report on the revision of the prayer book and the place of Hebrew in Jewish worship. Frankel at once demanded a clear statement of basic principles to guide the practical undertakings. For himself, he declared, he stood for "positive-historical Judaism," rooted in the millennial experience of the Jewish people, and independent of the ever changing "spirit of the age." To this, Ludwig Stein, the chairman of the conference, replied that all those present shared the same view. The body clearly did not want to prolong theoretical discussions and proceeded to consider the practical proposals of the committee.

On the third day of the session, a resolution was passed by a narrow margin, to the effect that Hebrew is not absolutely essential for Jewish public worship. This was followed by a unanimous vote that for the present it was advisable to retain Hebrew out of regard for the feelings of the older generation.

Frankel protested vehemently against what he considered a reckless and irreverent decision. For him, Hebrew was a sacred and indispensable element in Jewish life. The word "advisable" in the resolution implied that once the time was ripe, Hebrew could be eliminated altogether. Having expressed his indignation, Frankel withdrew from the conference, to become henceforth an outspoken opponent of Reform. Only one other rabbi followed his example, though a number had expressed the conviction that Hebrew must always be utilized in the synagogue service.

Despite his demand at Frankfort for a clarification of principles, Frankel himself never explained fully what he meant by positive-historical Judaism. (As Stein said, the reformers claimed to stand for just that.) Frankel recognized that the religion had undergone change and development. Though his own researches did not lead him into Biblical criticism, he never explicitly forbade such inquiries. In his great work on the Mishnah, he showed that the oral Torah had been frequently modified as the result of historical circumstances—to the great indignation of the Orthodox, who insisted that the Oral Law, like the written Torah, had been revealed to Moses at Sinai.

But Frankel was reluctant to draw from his studies of historical evolution the consequence that changes and innovations are still permissible. Whatever has been accepted by the Jewish people and hallowed by centuries of observance must not, he insisted, be rejected on rationalistic grounds. He did not exclude the possibility of reforms; but such reforms were acceptable to him only if adopted by the whole people

German Judaism Comes to Equilibrium 295

with the approval of its most responsible leaders. Thus positive-historical Judaism seems to mean that traditional practice must be continued, though without the divine sanctions that previously supported it. The Jewish people itself becomes the ultimate authority. Frankel has therefore been regarded, not without justice, as a forerunner of Jewish nationalism. But whatever the logical difficulties of his position, it won favor in many quarters. Conservative Judaism, as we know it in America today, has borrowed its theoretical basis largely from the school of Frankel.

For years, Geiger had been agitating for the establishment of a "Jewish theological faculty"—preferably as a department of one of the German universities, otherwise as an independent seminary. The latter alternative was made possible in 1847 by the will of a certain Jonas Fränkel of Breslau. Geiger is said to have inspired the bequest; he certainly hoped to head the new institution. But the trustees called Zecharias Frankel to be rector of the *Jüdisches-Theologisches Seminar* of Breslau, which opened its doors in 1854. Though not the first attempt at a modern rabbinical school, it soon became outstanding, and served as a model for many similar institutions.

The curriculum of the Seminary, unlike that of the old y'shivos, was not limited to Talmud and Codes. Students were introduced to the whole range of Jewish history and literature, and to the scientific method of research. They were also required to earn a university degree. Thus Breslau became a distinguished center of Jüdische Wissenschaft. Frankel's conservatism set the tone. Controversial theology was for the most part discreetly avoided. Students and faculty conformed to traditional observance, but full academic freedom prevailed. Frankel's successor as head of the Seminary, the historian Graetz, was one of the most extreme of Biblical critics.

2. Neo-Orthodoxy: S. R. Hirsch and S. D. Luzzatto

Meantime a new kind of Orthodoxy had come to the fore, an Orthodoxy that proposed to reckon with changing conditions instead of turning back to a vanished past. An early exponent of this position was Isaac Bernays, who had been called to Hamburg in 1821 to resist the encroachments of the Temple. Bernays, a man of wide general culture, preached eloquently in German. He did not hesitate to make such changes in the synagogue service as tradition permitted, in order to enhance the dignity and beauty of worship. At the same time he stood uncompromisingly against the admitted heresies of Reform.

His disciple, Samson Raphael Hirsch, achieved a much wider influence, and is generally regarded as the founder of the New Orthodoxy. He was a university graduate; indeed, he and Geiger were fellow students and close friends until the growing divergence of their views drove them apart.

Hirsch's platform was, as he put it, Torah *and* Derech Eretz: Orthodoxy plus secular culture. His espousal of the second element was no mere concession to the need of the time. Between 1846 and 1851 he served as Rabbi in Nikolsburg, the principal city of Moravia, where the old-fashioned Talmudism still was unchallenged. In this environment, Hirsch appeared as a reformer, introducing decorum and beauty into the synagogue service, improving the methods of Jewish education, and stressing secular studies. He met little active opposition, however, because he had given ample evidence both of Talmudic knowledge and of strict piety.

Years before, while Rabbi in Oldenburg, Hirsch had startled the world of German Jewry by publishing *The Nineteen Letters of Ben Uzziel,* an ardent defense of Orthodoxy. (The little book appeared anonymously, and at first many people thought it the work of Bernays.) Unlike previous answers to Reform, the book was not defensive or angry; it breathes positive and truly spiritual piety. Like the reformers, Hirsch emphasized the ethical message of Judaism. Like them, he stressed the centrality of the Bible, without deprecating the importance of the rabbinic writings. Like them, too, he wrote in German and affirmed the close tie between German Jews and their native land. He did not reject the national elements in Judaism but treated them as memories of a distant past and as hopes for a remote and visionary future.

But on the essentials of traditional Judaism he was unyielding. Reform is needed—but not a reform of Judaism. It is the spiritual and moral life of Jews that must be revitalized, through knowledge of the authentic sources of their faith. The reformers made the same basic error as the negativists whom they had sought to convert—the adoption of alien standards. The aim of Judaism is not that of the Enlightenment, to guide the individual to happiness and self-fulfilment. It is not the Greek ideal, mistakenly adopted by Maimonides, of intellectual serenity gained through abstract metaphysical knowledge. The objective of Judaism is the fulfilment of God's will in action.

German Judaism Comes to Equilibrium 297

This purpose leads to the ultimate goal of reconciling all mankind with God.

But to fulfill this consecrated mission, the Jewish people must not weaken themselves by rejecting the distinctive laws of the Torah. The retention of these rites is an indispensable means of maintaining the covenant relationship to God, through which the mission is to be attained. Of course, the mechanical performance of ceremonies does not suffice. Their inner spirit must be understood and experienced; and later on Hirsch undertook to expound in detail the symbolism he discerned in the ceremonial law. But the spirit of the Torah must be expressed through faithful adherence to the letter.

Thus Hirsch, while properly demanding that Judaism be interpreted from within rather than adjusted to some external system, never came fully to grips with the basic problem of revelation. He demanded an act of faith—the acceptance of the written and oral Torah as the literal word of God. But how could a generation reared in the teachings of natural science, historical criticism, and rational philosophy accept this proposition? To this difficulty, Hirsch replied by affirmation and exhortation, but hardly by serious argument.

In 1851 Hirsch returned to Germany as leader of the Orthodox group in Frankfort. Under his vigorous direction, the traditionalists built up their own educational and religious institutions. But the liberal party still remained in the majority. Hirsch therefore led a secessionist movement, which ultimately achieved government approval in 1873. By this decree, Orthodox groups were permitted to withdraw from the general Jewish community and to organize separately, without losing their legal identity as Jews. (This was the sort of recognition which the Reform congregation in Berlin had sought without success.) In Frankfort, Berlin, and a few other cities, the Orthodox party exercised this right. Elsewhere they remained within the official communities, utilizing their influence to prevent any radical change.

In Italy, meanwhile, Jewish tradition found a flaming and heroic champion in Samuel David Luzzatto. Unlike Hirsch, whose voluminous writings are largely polemical and sermonic, Luzzatto was a productive contributor to Jewish Wissenschaft. Through his access to the great Italian libraries, he was able to consult rare Hebrew books and manuscripts, and to make such materials available to his scholarly colleagues in Germany and Galicia. He published many fine medieval Hebrew poems which were previously unknown. He was also a gifted translator and interpreter of the Bible; and he was daring enough to correct some of the apparent errors in the Hebrew text of the prophets and sacred writings—but would take no liberties with the received text of the Torah.

In Italy the tradition of secular culture had never died out among the Jews. Luzzatto took it for granted, neither attacking nor defending its propriety. But in his devotion to what he considered the native Hebraic outlook, he would tolerate no compromise on essential principles. He was not content to limit his attack to the explicit modernism of Geiger. The skeptical tendencies of the nineteenth century were, to Luzzatto, only a recent version of that Greek outlook which was to him the absolute antithesis of Judaism.

Hellenism (or as he preferred to call it, Atticism) glorifies reason, and desires to attain a systematic intellectual grasp of the universe. Judaism is based on the spirit of human compassion, and seeks to help and bless all creatures. There is no real common ground, says Luzzatto, between these two viewpoints. Maimonides and Ibn Ezra made a fundamental error in attempting to harmonize Jewish faith with Greek philosophy. In so doing, they compromised with a force that negates the ideals of the Torah.

Luzzatto justified his hostility toward the Greek spirit by an appeal to history. Hellenic ideals have dominated European civilization. They have achieved magnificent results in science, philosophy, literature, art, and political theory—but they have not produced a humane or happy world. The much vaunted advance of nineteenth century science has only made poverty more sordid and war more terrible—it has not led men forward on the road to brotherhood and peace. Redemption can never come through arrogant intellectualism, but only through humble obedience to the precepts of the Torah, pervaded as they are by tenderness and concern for all God's creatures.

Luzzatto's life was one of endless struggle against poverty and personal sorrow on the one hand, and on the other against the apathy of an Italian Jewish community declining in numbers and spirit. The *Collegio Rabbinico* which he founded in Padua and sustained by his almost single-handed efforts did not survive his death. Another rabbinical seminary was founded in Florence after the unification of Italy.

3. *Liberal Judaism*

While the traditionalist parties in Germany became more articulate and effective, the progressives continued to advocate their viewpoint with considerable vigor. But some of the fire had gone out of the movement. The rabbinical conferences, which had served to focus public attention on the problems of religion, were interrupted after 1846; not until 1868 did the Liberal Rabbis convene again.

At this time a new proposal was heard: a Synod should be established. Judaism, it was argued, does not concentrate authority in the hands of "clergy." The rabbinical meetings had been ineffective, despite the learning and prestige of the participants, just because they were limited to rabbis who could not fully commit their communities. But a Synod made up of outstanding rabbis and laymen, officially delegated by their several communities, might have the strength to bring greater order, discipline, and effectiveness into Jewish religious life.

The enthusiastic proponents of the Synod should have been warned by the failure of Berab's attempt to reconstitute a central authority, to say nothing of the history of the Napoleonic Sanhedrin; but many indulged in grandiose hopes. Since the call for the Synod came from Reform leaders, it was at once attacked by the Orthodox, none of whom attended its first meeting, held at Leipzig in 1869. But some of the Conservatives made an appearance. Though most of the delegates were German, representatives came likewise from Austria, Hungary, Galicia, Bohemia, and Rumania, from western Europe including England, even from the United States and the Virgin Islands. The body chose an outstanding layman as presiding officer—Professor Moritz Lazarus, a well-known philosopher and psychologist, learned in Jewish lore and deeply religious in spirit.* The entire gathering was a distinguished one, and it set to work enthusiastically on the problems of Jewish education and worship.

But basic disagreements between Liberals and Conservatives compelled the Synod to move slowly and limited its accomplishment. Many of the attendants were not the accredited representatives of communities and participated only as individuals; and even those communities which had sent official delegates had restricted their power to act. Finally, no permanent organization was set up to implement by a continuing program the decisions at which the Synod arrived. As a result enthusiasm cooled quickly. The second gathering of the Synod, at Augsburg, in 1871, was smaller in numbers and made up chiefly of Reform stalwarts. It approved a number of changes in marriage laws,

---

* Lazarus' writings include *The Ethics of Judaism*—a work permeated by the spirit of Kant.

mitigated the severity of Sabbath regulations, and considered among other subjects how to strengthen the observance of Chanuko. (For now that Jews were more assimilated to the Gentile world and its customs, Christmas observance was beginning to appear in Jewish homes.) Despite such concrete achievements, the delegates were plainly discouraged; and the Synod was never called into session again.

Geiger meantime had become Rabbi of Frankfort in 1863. In 1870 the Berlin community, now predominantly Liberal, called him as its spiritual leader. And here at last he realized his lifelong dream of establishing a Liberal Seminary. Under his presidency, the *Hochschule für die Wissenschaft des Judentums* was opened in 1870. It was organized in complete independence of any congregational or community control, and was not officially committed to Reform Judaism. Full freedom of thought and expression were guaranteed to the faculty and students, so that liberal spirits found it a congenial haven. Geiger, however, died at the age of sixty-four, just two years after the establishment of the Hochschule.

In 1873, an Orthodox *Rabbinerseminar* was also opened in Berlin under the leadership of Esriel Hildesheimer, on whom the mantle of Samson Raphael Hirsch had fallen. Hildesheimer, like Hirsch, had served for a while in the East (in this case, in Hungary) where his advocacy of secular education and modern methods had called forth indignant protest from the older generation. But it was only in such a reactionary milieu that he appeared to be a reformer; for both in doctrine and observance he was uncompromisingly traditional. The Rabbinerseminar differed from the Hochschule and the Breslau Seminary by its greater emphasis on Talmud and Codes; and by the more explicit requirement that students and faculty acknowledge in principle and practice the divine authority of the halakah. All three of the German seminaries—and those established in Budapest and Vienna on the Breslau model—were notable centers of productive scholarship.

With the unification of Germany in 1871, the religious life of Germany achieved a rather stable equilibrium. The communities were officially recognized by the government, which taxed all Jews for the support of their religious and philanthropic institutions and exercised a moderate control over the latter, just as was the case with the Christian churches. The educational system also provided for periods of religious training in the public schools, conducted for the children of each religious group by ministers of their own. In south Germany the Jewish communities were predominantly Conservative, in the north they were Liberal. But in synagogue practice, the difference between the two groups was not very great. The organ and choral music were heard in all the Liberal synagogues (but the line of demarcation was not sharply drawn on this point); a few modifications were made in the prayers; and clear liberal concepts were enunciated in the sermons. But the more advanced procedures of the Berlin Reform congregation found little imitation; and the Orthodox seceded formally only in a few large cities. This general set-up continued until the destruction of German Jewry by Hitler.

44.

Under the Heel of the Tsars

1. Tradition

IN THE LAST YEARS OF THE EIGHTEENTH CENTURY, THE ONCE PROUD kingdom of Poland ceased to exist. Its territories and people were partitioned by Prussia, Austria, and Russia, with Russia taking the lion's share. Thus, the most numerous, compact, and intensely Jewish of all Jewish communities passed under the rule of tyrants who had neither the will nor the ability to understand their Jewish subjects, and whose announced intention was to eradicate Judaism from their domains by every available means.

We shall not follow all the political maneuvers and decrees, the acts of cunning and cruelty, the open persecution and ruthless violence by which the rulers of Russia sought to "solve the Jewish problem." But the policies of the tsars were bound not only to wreck the material welfare of Russian Jewry, but also to affect its spiritual development. Since the communities of the West and of Palestine have drawn a great part of their man-power and their inner vitality from the reservoir of east European Jewry, it is evident that the medieval tactics of the tsarist government constitute an important factor in the history of all modern Judaism.

The economic status and civic dignity of the Polish and Lithuanian Jews had already been undermined by the wars and persecutions of previous centuries. Excluded from many occupations previously open to them, they were compelled to turn to petty trading and money-lending. Russian policy restricted the residence of the Jews to areas where they had lived before becoming Russian subjects—that is, to parts of Poland, Lithuania, and the Ukraine. The vast reaches of the empire, to the development of which they could have greatly contributed, were closed to all but a few specially privileged Jews. While the Jewish population grew, the "Pale of Settlement" was actually reduced in extent from time to time by the expulsion of Jews from neighborhoods where they had dwelt for centuries. Insecurity and poverty became steadily worse.

Yet the Jews were generally loyal to their new masters. When Napoleon invaded Russia in 1812, Rabbi Shneur Zalman, the leader of the Lithuanian Chasidim, exerted his great influence to keep Jews from joining the French forces. He knew that a victory by Napoleon would result in an improvement of Jewish civil status; but he feared the rationalistic and irreligious ideas that accompanied the forces of enlightenment and freedom. The tsar might be a tyrant, but he was a champion of Orthodoxy.

The once bitter struggle between the Chasidim and their opponents waned in the nineteenth century. Differences in practice and emphasis did not disappear but were accepted more tolerantly on both sides. The influence of the Vilna Gaon remained potent, especially in Lithuania, where Talmudic studies were cultivated with startling brilliance, and many important works of scholarship were produced.

An unusual product of the Lithuanian school was Rabbi Israel Salanter (1810–1883). Without in the least deprecating the importance of Talmudic learning, he felt that this cold, analytic, intellectual discipline alone could not meet the spiritual needs of Jewry. Yet he could not sanction the facile and undisciplined emotionalism of the Chasidim. He proposed instead a program for training the moral will. He organized circles for the study of ethical and devotional literature (musar), in which the participants were encouraged to practice self-examination and repentance, to help one another by mutual guidance and criticism, and to supplement their study and prayer by assuming social responsibilities. His own saintly life was a great factor in the advance of this "ethical culture" movement.

In 1848 Rabbi Israel caused a sensation in Vilna. A cholera epidemic was raging as the fall holy days approached. Consultation with physicians convinced him that fasting would render the people more susceptible to the disease. He therefore publicly urged the Jews of Vilna to eat on Yom Kippur; and fearful that they would not take his advice, set the example himself by eating on the pulpit of the synagogue! This action was entirely in accordance with the halakah, which provides that the commandments may be suspended when life is in danger; but not all the rabbis had the courage to invoke this provision. Salanter, however, saw no conflict between either humanity and spirituality and strict adherence to the Law. He was anything but a liberal; indeed, he fought uncompromisingly against those modernist trends which were steadily percolating into eastern Europe.

2. Haskalah

The liberal movement in eastern Europe is generally known by the term *haskalah*, the Hebrew equivalent of "enlightenment." As in the West, the movement stemmed from Moses Mendelssohn, whose Bible translation—classic German printed in Hebrew characters—provided Yiddish-speaking Jews with a key to western culture. But Mendelssohn had been involved in another project, the consequences of which he could hardly have anticipated: he helped found the first Hebrew periodical, *HaMeassef* ("The Gatherer"). In his day, there were still many Jews in Germany and eastward who read Hebrew by preference. *The Gatherer* and several other publications that followed sought to present new ideas in the sacred tongue. They offered the reader poetry, fiction, and literary essays translated from modern languages or imitating western models, and informative articles on history, science, philosophy, and education. Mendelssohn may have considered this a temporary expedient: the Jews might be readier to accept modern literature in Hebrew dress, and thus prepare for complete cultural integration into the life around them.

In Germany, the Hebrew periodicals were comparatively short-lived. Their eastern counterparts were more substantial and more influential. The Enlightenment spread first to Austrian Poland (Galicia) where, as we have seen, it stimulated the pioneer efforts of Jewish Wissenschaft. Creative writing in Hebrew likewise attained higher standards in Galicia; the satires of Isaac Erter and Joseph Perl, who ridiculed the ignorance and superstition of the Chasidim, are still readable. After a time, however, the haskalah of Galicia waned. The progressives were completely under the cultural sway of Vienna and Berlin, and (except for scholarly writings) largely abandoned Hebrew as their medium. The traditionalists, especially the Chasidim, became all the more rigid because of the challenge of modernism.

Gradually the haskalah made its way into Russia. Secular studies had not indeed been absolutely banned by the Orthodox. The Vilna Gaon himself had been a student of Hebrew grammar and mathematics; but he considered such accomplishments suitable only for the mature Talmudist. His followers were vehemently opposed to the educational patterns of the West, in which secular studies for the young occupied a major position.

Nevertheless, the new trends could not be barred out. Many Jews learned modern languages, and through them acquired knowledge of western culture. Soon popular books on history, science, geography, and other topics began to appear in Hebrew. Some of the new writings challenged the authority of rabbinism. And in the period when the government was admitting Jews to public schools and even to universities, the more extreme enlighteners (*maskilim*) began to argue that Jews should adopt the Russian language, dress, and social customs.

The most eloquent champion of haskalah was Isaac Baer Levinsohn (1788–1860), who has been called the Russian Mendelssohn. Like the Sage of Berlin, he was a conservative in religious matters, insisting that there is no necessary conflict between faith and reason. Secular knowledge, he argued, had always been highly regarded by the great Jewish teachers of the past; its dissemination, far from weakening Judaism, would strengthen it. Forcefully he supported the program of the maskilim: be a Jew at home and a human being in the world! Like Mendelssohn, Levinsohn stanchly defended the Jew against attacks from without.

Not all the maskilim were so conciliatory toward traditional Judaism. Some, feeling their intellectual oats or stung by the opposition of the Orthodox, caustically attacked the religious authorities. Then the conservative party received the help of an unexpected and unwelcome ally —Tsar Nicholas I.

From his accession in 1825, Nicholas discarded the kindly measures by which his predecessor had tried to win over the Jews, in the hope that they would eventually become Christian. Nicholas sought the same end more directly by heartless brutality. The old restrictions were ruthlessly enforced, and compulsory military service was used as a conversionist device. Young men of military age were inducted into the army for twenty-five-year periods, stationed in remote areas far from all Jewish contacts, offered promotion if they baptized, brutally abused if they rejected the offer. Still more horrible, little boys were kidnapped and thrust into the army, to remain—if they survived hardship and torture—

till they were past middle life. Amazingly, many of these "cantonists," torn from their Jewish moorings at nine and ten, remained faithful to a Judaism they could barely remember, and returned to their home communities when the authorities finally released them.

So cynically cruel a government could obviously not be trusted when it made friendly offers. Yet this fact was plainer to the poor ghetto Jews than it was to the intellectuals. In the early forties, several model Jewish schools were opened with the provisional blessing of the tsar. Dr. Max Lilienthal, a gifted young German Rabbi, who had been principal of such a school in Riga, was invited by the government to undertake a reform of Jewish education, and especially to establish rabbinical seminaries after the western pattern. Lilienthal was thrilled by what seemed to him a chance to render signal service to his people. The maskilim were naturally enthusiastic about the prospect; but Lilienthal even secured the somewhat hesitant backing of Rabbi Isaac, the head of the Volozhin Y'shivo (where the traditions of the Vilna Gaon were faithfully conserved), and of Rabbi Menahem Mendel Shneursohn, the leader of the Lithuanian Chasidim. For a few years, Lilienthal was a glamorous figure among Russian Jews.

But the further he proceeded with his work the more disillusioned he became. The corrupt and malicious government, he saw, had no intention of improving the lot of its Jewish subjects. Its only aim was to hasten their conversion. The masses had rightly recognized that modern education without political and economic rights could only generate a mood of frustration that would lead to the baptismal font. Lilienthal fled the country as if he were a hunted criminal, and found refuge in the free air of the United States.

The government-sponsored rabbinical seminaries opened in due course; but they were sparsely attended while the traditional y'shivos were crowded. Graduates of the official seminaries were foisted upon the communities as "Crown Rabbis," but their function was largely limited to the registration of vital statistics. The people distrusted them (perhaps at times, unfairly), and turned for religious guidance to the unreconstructed traditionalists.

But though the policies of Nicholas sobered the enthusiasm of the maskilim and reinforced Orthodox zeal, interest in modern learning did not cease. A new era of hope began when Alexander II ascended the throne in 1855. Alexander was considered a liberal. He did away with the worst barbarities of his father—the kidnapping of children and the violent effort to abolish the old-fashioned Jewish style of dress.

When he issued his famous ukase freeing the Russian serfs, it was widely expected that his next step would be the emancipation of the Jews. But the liberalism of Alexander was half-hearted, and the much hoped for ukase never appeared. Even before his assassination ushered in a new period of naked persecution, the Jews had become altogether disillusioned over the prospect for freedom and equal rights.

The older haskalah, with its rationalistic and assimilatory tendencies, became more and more discredited. Some of the modernists returned penitently to traditional Judaism; the others largely abandoned the open and bitter attacks they had formerly made on Orthodoxy. The conservatives became more conservative than ever. Y'shivo students were required to confine their studies exclusively to the Talmud and its commentators; the authorities took exception not only to the reading of secular books but even to an interest in Hebrew grammar or the philosophy of Maimonides.

Such rules, of course, were made to be broken, and many a forbidden book was read on the sly. A substantial group of Jewish modernists had come into existence. They could neither return to the simple piety of their fathers nor follow the assimilationist counsels of the early haskalah. Though their religious faith had crumbled, they felt themselves to be loyal and devoted members of the Jewish people. Gradually they developed a secular Jewish philosophy, which with passing decades became more and more explicitly nationalistic.

3. *The Beginnings of Jewish Nationalism*

Nationalism as we know it today is a recent phenomenon. From remotest times, of course, men have felt a special loyalty to the land on which they lived and to those who shared the same language, customs, and traditions. But the central object of these loyalties was almost invariably the ancestral god or gods. The ancient pagans often invested their kings with the attributes of deity; in medieval and early modern Christendom, the king was thought to rule by divine right. Nationality and religion were one and inseparable.

It was much the same in ancient Israel. The king was "the anointed of the Lord." The Maccabean revolt began as a defense of the Jewish religion and an effort to rescue the Temple from the heathen; it led to the reestablishment of an independent state, ruled by priest-kings. After the year 70, the hope of national restoration was expressed in the dream of a rebuilt Temple, and the Messiah, essentially an earthly king, was glorified with spiritual and even supernatural qualities. The reformers in the West could discard these national elements from their thinking and their prayers the more readily, because their antique form made them irrelevant to modern conditions.

Secular nationalism is something new; it flowered in the nineteenth century. It attaches primary importance to the community of soil, blood, and language. Where there is a state church, it tends to become one more department of national culture, committed to the national interest rather than to its own universal ideals. Modern nationalism first arose in western countries which were culturally uniform. Gradually it spread eastward, causing an ever greater restlessness among the welter of peoples who made up the Austro-Hungarian and Russian empires. More and more these peoples resisted the political and cultural domination of their rulers. On the one hand they began to demand independence, or at least political autonomy within the various empires. On the other, they revived their ancestral languages (note, for example, the rebirth of Gaelic in Ireland) and drew on their own background for artistic and literary themes. This same process may be observed today among the long dormant peoples of Asia.

Nationalism has been in large measure a movement for liberation, and a powerful stimulus to cultural creativity. Its danger has been the tendency to make the State a substitute for God. The "national interest" may be regarded as subject to no ethical or religious standards, and criticism identified with treason. Of such nationalistic idolatry, the most horrible examples were Fascist Italy and Nazi Germany; and behind the universalist façade of Communism, a similar worship of the absolute state is just as plainly discernible.

The Russian Empire was made up of innumerable racial, national, linguistic, cultural, and religious elements. During the nineteenth century many of these groups—Poles, Finns, Ukrainians, and others— struggled constantly for cultural and even for political independence. Their national loyalties were only intensified by the effort of the tsars to Russify them. In this environment, the Jews (especially those who were no longer Orthodox) were bound to regard themselves as still another national minority. They were distinguished from their neighbors not only by religious faith and practice, but by language, customs, and cultural patterns. They too began to cherish dreams of freedom and greatness as an independent nationality.

Modern Jewish nationalism, however, began in literature before it manifested itself in life. Its vehicle at the start was not the Yiddish language of the masses, but the Hebrew which had been revived by the maskilim. Hebrew (still a written rather than a spoken language) acquired a modern vocabulary, was gradually freed from slavish dependence on Biblical and rabbinic models, and became a vigorous and effective medium of expression. The subject matter of Hebrew literature also underwent a change. It was no longer an instrument for transmitting western culture to the benighted ghetto dweller, but rather a means of rousing him to an awareness of his own resources and of his opportunities for the future. Creative writing in Hebrew drew on sources from the whole range of Jewish experience. The earliest Hebrew novels dealt with Biblical themes; soon Jewish readers were supplied with more realistic fiction, based on contemporary situations and problems. Poetry and essays were more and more directed toward the stimulation of national pride and courage. The same trends were reflected in several excellent Hebrew periodicals established in eastern Europe about the middle of the century. And these trends began to crystallize in proposals for concrete action—usually involving Palestine.

Jews had always prayed for a return to the Holy Land; but a national rebirth on the sacred soil had been to them a heavenly dream, which only the direct intervention of God could fulfill. The pilgrims who through the centuries had settled in Jerusalem, Safed, and other centers of piety, had been utterly unpolitical; their object had been to acquire merit for themselves and for Israel as a whole, but hardly to rebuild the land or to establish a national beachhead. Frequently they had devoted themselves entirely to pious exercises, while depending for their material support on the philanthropy of their brothers in other lands. During the nineteenth century, however, proposals for Jewish colonization in Palestine were made repeatedly both by Jews and by sympathetic Christians; but they evoked only sporadic interest and had no observable results.

Only the growth of national sentiment among the Russian Jews could produce a movement of vitality and continuity. In 1862 an Orthodox Rabbi named Hirsch Kalischer published an appeal for the establishment of agricultural colonies in Palestine; such activity, he argued, must precede rather than follow the appearance of the Messiah. The same year saw the publication of a fully developed argument for what we now call Zionism, strangely enough from a German Jewish Socialist.* Moses Hess had originally shared the conventional doctrine that the triumph of Socialist principles would spell the end of all religious and racial prejudice. He was disillusioned when he discovered the extent of anti-Semitism *within* the Socialist movement. His book, *Rome and Jerusalem*, argued that the Jews are a nation and must act to restore their national life. Most influential of all the nationalist writers was Perez Smolenskin, whose novels and treatises, as well as his periodical *HaShahar* ("The Dawn"), were all directed to the stimulation of national feeling and ardor among the Jews.

There were even a few attempts in the 1870's to establish agricultural colonies in Palestine; but they had little success. Up to 1880, the one visible result of nationalist effort was the emergence of a new secular Jewish literature. From this time on we must turn not only to the writings of religious teachers, but to novels, poetry, and drama for an understanding of Jewish spiritual development. And this not only in eastern Europe, but more and more throughout the entire Jewish world.

---

* We shall discuss the relations between Judaism and Socialism in a later chapter.

45.

The Golden Land

1. *Beginnings*

SCHOLARS STILL DEBATE THE QUESTION WHETHER COLUMBUS WAS AN
Italian Christian or a Spanish Marrano. (It is ironic that Spanish writers who out of national pride claim Columbus for Spain must insist on
his Jewish origin!) But there is no doubt that his crew included four
Jews, that he used the navigation tables prepared by the Jew, Abraham
Zacuto, and that his enterprise was financed by Abraham Senior, Queen
Isabella's Jewish treasurer. (The pawning of the royal jewels is sheer
legend.) Marranos soon came to the New World, attracted either by
its fabulous treasures or by the hope of liberty, or by both; but the Inquisitors were not far behind, and the fires of the auto da fé blazed in
Mexico and Peru. Recent decades have witnessed the appearance in
Mexico City of a Marrano congregation now largely Indian in stock
and culture; and elsewhere in Latin America there are individuals and
groups who still cling to vaguely remembered remnants of Jewish
practice.

Brazil, originally colonized by the Portuguese, had its share of "New
Christians." When the territory was conquered by the Dutch in the
seventeenth century, some of these Marranos openly returned to Judaism, and were joined by immigrants from Holland. But the Portuguese
soon regained control of their vast colony, and the Jews of Brazil had
to scatter. Twenty-three of the refugees landed at New Amsterdam in
1654, to found what has since become the largest Jewish settlement

in the world. The same year saw the establishment of the still flourishing Jewish community on the island of Curaçao. Within the next few decades, former Marranos from Holland and England found homes in various towns along the Atlantic seaboard, and on several Caribbean islands.

Though individual Jews supported the Tory cause, the majority were ardently committed to the American Revolution. When the British forces under Lord Howe occupied New York, the entire Jewish community under the leadership of their minister, the Rev. Gershom Mendes Seixas, moved to Philadelphia rather than remain under British rule. The establishment of the United States as an independent nation made them full citizens with equal rights before the law. A few discriminatory statutes remained on the law books of certain states; they were an annoyance, but did not seriously impair Jewish status. Many Jews took an active and creditable part in the revolutionary struggle, and rose to prominence in commercial, professional, and public life.

From the start, a new spirit of independence characterized the Jewish group. The settlers in New Amsterdam boldly claimed equal rights and equal obligations as members of the colony; and when their demands were refused by the surly Peter Stuyvesant, they secured them by appeal to his employers, the Dutch West India Company. Though for a time Jews were excluded from some colonies and were subject to legal disabilities in others, there was a general and increasing spirit of tolerance and good will, and Jews were never actively persecuted. They held their heads high, participated in the general life of the community, and felt themselves thoroughly at home on the American scene.

The settlers soon established synagogues. The New Amsterdam congregation, still known as "The Spanish and Portuguese Synagogue," is the mother congregation of American Jewry. The beautiful pre-revolutionary synagogue building in Newport, R. I., the oldest house of Jewish worship on the continent, is now a national monument. The American congregations were, however, radically different in character from those of other times and places. The European synagogue was usually an institution of the organized Jewish community, which embraced all the Jews of a given area and was officially recognized by the secular government. The American synagogue was maintained by an independent congregational body, membership in which was a matter of personal choice. This voluntary character of the American synagogue was not so apparent at the start, when the communities were small, and social pressure readily brought into the synagogue every Jew who did not choose to abandon his faith outright. (There was no other way by which he could obtain kosher meat, provide for the religious education of his children, or be buried in a Jewish cemetery.) But as the community grew in numbers and became less homogeneous in character, and as Jewish organizations of many sorts multiplied, it became evident that the synagogue was now an independent association of those who wished to belong to it.

Moreover, this was the character of all religious institutions in the United States after church establishments were done away with by the Federal and State Constitutions. Membership in a particular religious faith no longer conferred superior status, nor did non-membership impair one's rights. The separation of Church and State is one of the unique achievements of the American Republic. It preserved the State against ecclesiastical domination, and the religious institutions from political interference. It assured all religious groups of equality, and therefore tended to enhance the dignity and prestige of Judaism. The churches and synagogues, independent both financially and spiritually of governmental control, have flourished in American freedom.

Many of the early settlers were exceedingly zealous in their Jewish loyalties. A number of the S'fardic colonists of Newport, for example, discarded the exotic names they had borne as Marranos and adopted Biblical names. But in the genial American atmosphere, such enthusiasm tended to wane. There was considerable intermarriage, especially when trade led Jews into smaller communities where there was no organized Jewish life. Within the synagogues there was a correct orthodox practice, usually in the S'fardic style; but little was done to interpret Judaism in terms of the new American life.

This was particularly due to a dearth of trained leaders—a problem that was to continue far beyond the colonial period. The Jewish settlers had no ordained rabbis, and had to depend on laymen of modest attainments who acted as chazanim, ritual slaughterers, and teachers. A few of these men had real gifts of leadership. Seixas, for example, though his official title was chazan, did not confine his activity to chanting the prayers or teaching the children. He acted as preacher, pastor, and guide to the members of his congregation, and as their representative in civic activities. The pattern he set as chazan-minister was widely followed, and was to have enduring influence in the development of the American rabbinate as a new form of Jewish religious leadership. Perhaps the most eminent of the chazan-ministers was Isaac Leeser, who served in Philadelphia from 1829 to 1868. He produced a highly serviceable English translation of the Bible, which remained the standard Jewish version for many decades; he also edited and translated the prayer book in both S'fardic and Ashk'nazic versions. His weekly periodical, *The Occident*, was the pioneer effort of American Jewish journalism, and helped to stimulate interest in Jewish activity throughout the country.

Meantime—in the 1820's and thereafter—a steadier and more considerable stream of immigration came from Germany and other countries of central Europe. Within a few decades, the character of the American Jewish community had been profoundly changed. Instead of being predominantly S'fardic and English-speaking, it was now overwhelmingly Ashk'nazic; and for a generation, a large part of the newcomers preferred to speak German at home and to hear German spoken in the synagogue. The majority of these immigrants were comparatively untouched by the new trends in European Jewry. They brought with them a simple orthodoxy; few of them had much learning, secular or Hebraic. (The sprinkling of Jewish intellectuals who came to this country after the disappointments of 1848 were often rather indifferent to Jewish values.)

The German Jews entered with keen enthusiasm into the developing democracy of America. The earlier Jewish settlers had lived for the most part in the larger eastern centers where the Tory-Federalist tradition and its social snobbery were strong. The German immigrants spread also through the growing South and Middle West. Many of them began as peddlers, and so came into direct contact with "grass roots." They identified themselves with the new Jacksonian trends, and saw in the spirit and institutions of American life the fulfilment of all their hopes and dreams. Their love for their new home was intensified by the contrast with the reactionary mood of the Germany they had left behind. Thus they were conditioned to respond favorably to the liberal doctrine preached by the spokesmen of Reform who began to arrive in the 1840's.

2. *The Advance of Reform*

The first attempt at Reform in this country occurred in the predominantly S'fardic congregation of Charleston, S. C. In 1824 a group of laymen petitioned the trustees of the synagogue for changes in the service which would make it more comprehensible and appealing; and they referred to the new developments in Germany as a model. When their request was denied, some of them withdrew from the congregation and formed a group of their own; they even drew up a new ritual, largely in English, for the services they conducted. The effort petered out after a few years; but the sentiment for Reform grew within the congregation. The Rev. Gustav Poznanski, a former resident of Hamburg, became minister of the Charleston community in 1836; and with the encouragement he supplied, the liberals soon won a complete victory.

The first congregations founded to foster Reform were Har Sinai of Baltimore (1842) and Emanu-El of New York (1845)—both German-speaking. Meantime, many of the established synagogues—even those that considered themselves strongly traditional—were experimenting with new procedures. When Max Lilienthal fled to this country from Russia, he first served as Rabbi of three German congregations in New York. They were all strictly Orthodox; Lilienthal himself had not yet undergone the change of heart that was to make him a vigorous champion of Reform. Yet, during his brief ministry to this congregational union, he introduced a Confirmation service for girls.

Reform in America, however, remained no more than a trend, expressed in scattered episodes, until the appearance on the scene of Isaac M. Wise (1819–1900). While serving as Rabbi in his native Bohemia, he had rebelled against the malicious anti-Jewish restrictions imposed by the Austrian government; and he had acquired a mystic faith in free America long before he reached its soil. To Wise, the United States was not merely a land where Jews were treated fairly: it was a nation whose institutions were the living embodiment of Jewish ideals. The Federal Constitution was "Mosaism in action." The men of America, freed from the political oppressions and social prejudices of the Old World, had it in their power to build a heaven upon earth. But their efforts must be inspired by religion—by a free, rational, ethical religion. Dogmatic Christianity (whose claims Wise attacked in print with startling bluntness) was unsuitable to the spirit of the age. America needed Judaism—but a Judaism stripped of all obsolete and superstitious elements, so that its rational and humane character would be fully evident. Judaism is not only for those of Jewish descent, but for all the men of the new age.

Wise arrived in America in 1846 and became the Rabbi of the little congregation in Albany, N. Y. The American opportunity was all he had dreamed it would be; but the Jewish religious picture was far from encouraging. Though the communities were growing in numbers and prosperity, they were almost entirely without leadership. The congregations were ignorant and apathetic, and at best concerned only with local problems. A broader vision of American Judaism hardly existed; it was just beginning to emerge in a few struggling periodicals, the best of which was Isaac Leeser's *Occident*.

Wise set as his goal the creation of an organized American Jewish life. Two years after he arrived in the country he published an appeal in *The Occident*, inviting the synagogues to send delegates to a meeting in New York with a view to establishing a national union. Though Leeser warmly seconded the proposal, it met with a feeble response and the projected meeting never convened. Through the years, however, Wise continued to labor for inter-congregational unity. A national federation, he insisted, would provide the basis for another indispensable undertaking—a college to train rabbis and teachers for service on the American scene.

In 1854 Wise was called to Cincinnati; and here he continued to press for a national union from his pulpit and in the columns of his own periodical, *The Israelite*. Despite his outspoken commitment to Reform, he continued to work with the more Orthodox leaders, some of whom (like Leeser) were not intolerant and were prepared to make some modifications within the framework of tradition. At a rabbinical conference held at Cleveland in 1856, Wise assented in the interest of harmony to resolutions strongly affirming the authority of the Bible and the Talmud. This concession angered the more extreme reformers (of whom we shall hear shortly), but did not lead to any concrete results. Early attempts to establish a rabbinical college (by Wise in Cincinnati and by a joint effort of the rabbis in Philadelphia) were unsuccessful.

Wise's labors finally bore fruit in 1873, when the Union of American Hebrew Congregations was established. Its member synagogues were located chiefly in the Middle West and South; all were committed to Reform Judaism. With this organized constituency, Wise was able to launch the Hebrew Union College in 1875; its first graduates were ordained in 1883. Though these agencies were explicitly institutions of Reform, their importance extended far beyond the confines of the Liberal movement. For, as we shall see, they provided both a challenge and a model for the traditional groups.

From the Albany days, Wise had championed a moderate Reform. He had discarded the belief in a personal Messiah and in resurrection, advocated equal rights for women in the synagogue, introduced instrumental music, Confirmation, and other changes in ritual. His independence of spirit had led to conflict within the congregation; eventually his supporters seceded and formed their own synagogue. There for the first time family pews were introduced: previously even Reform congregations had maintained a separate section for women. In Cincinnati this moderate Reform program was continued. Wise's prayer book (which characteristically he called *Minhag America,* the American rite) was an abbreviated version of the old liturgy, with modifications of passages dealing with the Messiah and the resurrection. Wise was a zealous champion of the historical Sabbath. The nineteenth century saw a serious decline in synagogue attendance on Sabbath morning, the principal service of the week, at which a sermon was now customary. Many of the reformers met the situation by preaching at Sunday morning services, which tended to displace Sabbath worship. In 1866 Wise introduced a masterly innovation—a service with an address on Friday night after dinner. Such a service, he rightly perceived, would preserve something of the Sabbath mood and atmosphere which worship on Sunday could not provide. This device has proved to be one of Wise's greatest contributions. In most Reform and Conservative congregations today, the chief service is held on Friday night; and even some Orthodox synagogues now hold Friday night "assemblies."

Wise's preeminence in American Reform was due not only to his great talent for organization, but above all to his ardent, colorful, and tireless personality. He traveled constantly from city to city in the interests of the Union and the College; edited (and largely wrote) the weekly *Israelite*; produced many volumes of history, theology, and even novels and plays; and literally to his dying day taught and inspired the students of the College. Understandably, his published writings have a hasty and tentative character; but they reflect the vigorous and original spirit of the author.

His views on Reform are a curious mixture of the conservative and the progressive. Despite his admiration for Abraham Geiger, Wise was out of sympathy with the evolutionary concept. He vehemently denounced the biological evolutionism of Darwin, which was becoming popular, and flatly rejected the method of Biblical criticism. The Pentateuch, he held, is the basic source of Judaism; and except for a few minor additions, it is the work of Moses. Wise, however, distinguished between the Ten Commandments and the rest of the Torah. The Ten Words are literally a divine revelation, the Torah of God. The rest of the Pentateuch is the Torah of Moses, an inspired application of the divine truth to specific circumstances and conditions. As these conditions have changed, much of this law has lost its validity. Animal sacrifice was indispensable in its time; today we have outgrown it, and it should never be restored. Thus we have the right to modify the forms and ceremonies by which the divine truth is made operative. But the truth itself is changeless and perfect. "Progress" is a matter of scientific and technical advance; but spiritually we are dependent on the revelation vouchsafed to a simpler and nobler age. Progressive Judaism has regained the insights granted to Moses; it has not really passed beyond them.

Secure in this faith, Wise looked to the future with confident optimism. As the nineteenth century drew to a close, he voiced the expectation that Reform Judaism would become the religion of most enlightened Americans within twenty-five years!

We have referred to the more radical group of reformers, who for a generation battled Wise almost as fiercely as they strove with the Orthodox. Their outstanding spokesman was David Einhorn, who had participated in the German rabbinical conferences of 1845 and 1846, and after a few years' ministry in Germany had led the short-lived Reform congregation in Pesth. In 1855 he came to Baltimore as Rabbi of the Har Sinai congregation; and with Samuel Adler of New York and Samuel Hirsch, the Hegelian philosopher who had come to Philadelphia, he led the "eastern" branch of Reform in opposition to Wise and his followers.

An interesting difference between the two groups is that Einhorn and his colleagues continued to preach and write in German long after Wise had adopted English in the pulpit. German cultural activity was in fact a prominent feature of American life in the middle of the nineteenth century; and during the Civil War entire German-speaking regiments fought on the Union side. Thus, the use of German by no means implied isolation from the interests of American life. Einhorn's courageous anti-slavery sermons, though spoken in the German language, aroused such resentment in Baltimore that he was forced to flee the city in the spring of 1861. He continued his ministry in Philadelphia and later in New York.

But the German-speaking Einhorn maintained an intimate tie with German philosophic and cultural trends. His approach to Reform was doctrinaire and consistent, that of Wise more experimental and practical. For a long time Wise sought to find a common ground with the traditionalists, whereas Einhorn boldly emphasized the sharp break between Reform and the past. Without denying the importance of Moses and the centrality of the Decalogue, Einhorn recognized more fully the contribution of the later prophets. He also made a clearer and more consistent distinction between principle and form; the basic task of Reform, he argued, was to correct the confusion between these two elements.

Einhorn upheld with mystical fervor the doctrine of the mission of Israel. He was convinced that the Jewish people had been endowed with exceptional gifts for the performance of their priestly task. This radical reformer strongly opposed intermarriage, since it might—so to speak—dilute the inherited genius of the dedicated people!

More than any of his contemporaries, Einhorn taught and exemplified personal inwardness in religious living. The doctrine he shared with his age was rationalistic; but he presented it with unique emotional fervor and deep spiritual piety. His prayer book, in addition to a selection of traditional material, included a number of original prayers which express his glowing ardor. Many of them have become standard in modern Reform worship.

The early eighties saw a vigorous counter-movement against Reform. Energetic and learned leaders had come to Orthodox congregations; in several Reform congregations, rabbis of a more conservative stamp were able to halt if not to reverse the trend away from tradition. The leading Jewish journals of the east were all hostile to Reform. In 1885 Kaufmann Kohler, the son-in-law of Einhorn and his successor in the pulpit of Temple Beth El, New York, took the initiative of calling a rabbinical conference, which met in Pittsburgh. At this gathering, the breach between the two branches of Reform was largely healed. Though Kohler, the disciple of Einhorn, was the moving spirit of the conference, Wise served as its presiding officer.

The resolutions of this conference (the "Pittsburgh Platform") were long regarded as the authoritative statement of the Reform position. It should be pointed out, however, that these utterances were called forth by a particular situation, and were not intended to provide a complete program for Reform Judaism.

The first resolution recognizes that all religions constitute an attempt to grasp the infinite and to recognize the indwelling of God in man; it affirms, however, that the God-concept of Judaism is the highest attained by the human mind. The second describes the Bible as the record of Israel's consecration to its mission and as the most potent instrument of religious and moral instruction; but it admits that the Bible also reflects the primitive ideas of its own age, which must now be discarded. The third and fourth resolutions state that the Mosaic law was fully applicable only in the preparatory period when the Jewish people lived a national life on their own soil. The laws of dress, diet, and priestly purity are now obsolete and have no authority. Only the moral law, and such ceremonial observances as still elevate and sanctify our lives, are deemed binding. The fifth article sees in the advance of culture and freedom the dawn of the messianic age. It declares that the Jews are no longer a nation, but a religious community; they do not desire to return to Palestine, establish a Jewish state, or restore the sacrificial cult. The sixth paragraph asserts the progressive character of Judaism, but affirms also that continuity with historic past must be maintained. It concedes that Christianity and Islam have helped to advance the Jewish mission, and again expresses the hope that the mission will be speedily accomplished. The seventh resolution upholds the doctrine of spiritual immortality, rejecting the resurrection of the body and the belief in heaven and hell.

These statements were basically the work of Kohler. At the instance of Emil G. Hirsch, the brilliant son of the philosopher, an eighth resolution was adopted, pointing to the economic injustices of modern society, and acknowledging the duty to solve the problem of poverty in the spirit of the Mosaic law. This resolution was approved long before the so-called "social gospel" had become popular or trade unions had achieved respectability.

The Pittsburgh conference clarified the position of Reform, and thereby hastened the division of American Jewry into religious parties. It also stimulated the establishment of a permanent rabbinical organization, which came into existence the same year. The Central Conference of American Rabbis was the third national institution which Wise founded; he served as its president until his death. It, too, has provided a model for the other Jewish religious groups. The rabbinical associations serve as a medium for the exchange of ideas and information, clarify and maintain professional standards, and make provision for the welfare of their members.

One of the early projects of the Central Conference of American Rabbis was the production of a *Union Prayerbook*, which soon replaced the great variety of rituals previously used in American Reform congregations. The *Union Prayerbook* drew heavily on Einhorn's ritual; nevertheless Wise, the champion of unity, immediately introduced it into his own synagogue in place of his *Minhag America*.

The Golden Land 321

3. The Conservative Reaction

By 1880 Reform was probably the dominant version of American Judaism. Even when immigration from eastern Europe vastly increased the numbers of the Orthodox, the newcomers could not immediately exert influence on American Jewish affairs. Yet, before their voice could be heard, a Conservative reaction was already evident.

Many congregations and rabbis (including the old S'fardic synagogues) had maintained an uncompromising orthodoxy and had vocally opposed the new trends. But the lines were not always sharply drawn. Leeser was an outspoken opponent of Reform, yet he worked with Wise in the effort to unify American Jewry; and his saintly successor, Rabbi Sabato Morais, was for a time a supporter of the Hebrew Union College.

The traditionalists were strengthened by the arrival of some distinguished European scholars. The most influential were Benjamin Szold in Baltimore, Marcus Jastrow in Philadelphia, and Alexander Kohut in New York. Szold was the author of a Hebrew commentary on the book of Job; Jastrow and Kohut both compiled monumental dictionaries of the Talmud. None of the three was Orthodox, but all were troubled by what they considered the negative and destructive policies of Reform. They severely criticized the leaders of the Reform movement, and undertook to revitalize Judaism by more moderate methods.

It is difficult today to understand the bitterness of the controversy. Szold, for example, produced a prayer book, afterwards revised with the help of Jastrow, who translated the German prayers into English. This prayer book, still used in some middle-of-the-road congregations, is certainly closer to the traditional liturgy than Einhorn's; yet it is a definite departure from Orthodoxy, omitting many passages such as the petition for the restoration of sacrifice, and adding new prayers. Thus the difference between these Conservatives and the reformers seems to have been one of degree rather than kind.

This was not true of Morais. Though his gentle nature was remote from fanaticism, he was committed to the divine origin and changeless authority of the Torah. The Pittsburgh Platform challenged this basic principle; the Hebrew Union College was plainly an agency of Reform. Morais therefore assumed the leadership of a movement to defend tradition. Under his presidency, the Jewish Theological Seminary was opened in New York City (1886), and it quickly became the rallying point of the Conservatives. The demarcation between Orthodoxy and what we now call Conservative Judaism did not become definite for some years.

46.

The Era of Pogroms

AN ASSASSIN'S BOMB ENDED THE REIGN OF TSAR ALEXANDER II IN
1881; and his half-hearted liberalism was interred with him. His successor, the third Alexander, was a whole-souled devotee of medieval tyranny. If he could not put the clock back, he would try to keep it from moving ahead. The serfs could not be reenslaved nor the industrial development of Russia be checked; but the Jews at least were fair game. A series of violent outbreaks against the Jews occurred in a number of Russian cities; though depicted by the government as spontaneous expressions of popular indignation, they had been carefully planned and were carried out with the connivance of the police and the military. At this time, the word "pogrom" enters the vocabulary of mankind.

A year later, the government promulgated a series of decrees (the "May Laws") designed to make Jewish life in Russia physically and economically untenable. The most trusted adviser of Alexander III stated the objectives of the policy with cynical frankness: "One third of the Jews will emigrate, one third will be baptized, and one third will starve." From 1881 to the Revolution of 1917, the Russian rulers were engaged in an actual war against their Jewish subjects. The pogroms, the repressive laws, the bitter anti-Jewish propaganda, and the ritual murder accusations were the result of top-level planning, intended to divert the bitterness of the oppressed masses against the Jews, and thus preserve the old autocracy.

We shall not examine these matters in their gruesome detail, since our primary concern is with the inner development of Jewish life. But we must note that the situation in Russia was paralleled in other countries of eastern Europe. Rumania had a large Jewish population, mostly poor. The Congress of Berlin (1878), which provided international guarantees of Rumanian independence, had exacted the pledge that all citizens of Rumania should have fair and equal treatment. But the Rumanian rulers evaded their promise by holding that the Jews were not citizens; mob violence was encouraged and official oppression was commonplace. In Galicia (Austrian Poland) the situation of the Jews was likewise unfavorable, and became worse toward the end of the century.

Under these intolerable pressures, the old program of haskalah, with its liberal assimilatory tendencies, was finally abandoned. Orthodoxy took a new lease on life. Many who had flirted with modernism sought inner security in unquestioning piety and strict observance to the Torah. The rabbinic authorities and the Chasidic tsadikim became, if possible, more rigid in their opposition to change.

Those who had gone too far from the old faith to return found hope either in Jewish nationalism or in the socialist labor movement. (Few Jews joined the more extreme revolutionary parties.) Nationalist feeling, which had already found extensive literary expression, now began to assume a more practical form.

In 1882 Dr. Leo Pinsker, who had been an eye-witness of the pogroms, published his startling pamphlet, Auto-Emancipation. Like Hess and Smolenskin, he insisted that the Jews are essentially a national group. They have been at a constant disadvantage because they are scattered and disorganized, and so have been compelled to deal with governments as individuals or separate communities. They have, moreover, made a fundamental error in looking to the governments to confer emancipation upon them. But liberty can never be given, it must always be achieved. The Jews must make themselves a free people. Pinsker hoped that the initiative would be taken by the joint effort of the representative bodies which the Jews of England, France, and Germany had already created. He called for a corporation to finance settlements in an area where the Jews could constitute a majority, but did not insist that this area be in Palestine.

Because of the tragic conditions of the time, Pinsker evoked a more vigorous response than his predecessors. The communities of the West indeed had little sympathy for his viewpoint; but under this leadership, the Russian Jews organized the *Chov'vei Zion* ("Lovers of Zion"), an agency to establish colonies in the Holy Land. The Alliance Israélite Universelle and Baron Edmond de Rothschild had already founded the first agricultural colonies in Palestine; and Russian Jewry provided most of the settlers in these and other pioneer undertakings. But the practical difficulties were great and the immediate results meager and disappointing. Many years were to elapse before the nationalist movement achieved significant successes.

Nor could anyone foresee the ultimate consequences of a quixotic experiment undertaken in 1882 by a man who called himself Eliezer ben Yehudah (his family name was Perelman). Settling with his family in Palestine, he undertook to make Hebrew once more a living tongue. Hitherto, the revival of the language had been chiefly literary. Ben Yehudah contributed much by his lexicographical researches, and by coining hundreds of new words. But above all the example he and his family set of actually speaking Hebrew was to serve as a powerful stimulant both to the rebirth of the language and to the national revival.

* * *

The emergence of the Jewish labor movement occurred more slowly. The Industrial Revolution, in every country where it occurred, brought forth a host of new evils: the exploitation of labor, the employment of women and children in mines and factories, horrible city slums, spiritual degradation. These conditions soon called forth criticism and protest in England, France, and other lands. Men cried out not only against the merciless abuses of the system but against its essential impersonality and sordidness, against the physical and spiritual ugliness that accompanied the building of vast industrial empires. Numerous proposals were made for a more just and humane economic order. Some of the reformers found conscious inspiration for their programs in religious sources. They met with little response, especially from the working people they sought to help. Indeed, the masses reacted slowly to the proposals of the revolutionary Socialism which was ultimately to play so great a role in world history.

The enemies of Socialism have often attacked it as a "Jewish" movement, or even plot. Among the forerunners of the movement was Ferdinand Lasalle, who was a Jew only by birth. This erratic, though brilliant personality, had only a tangential relation to Socialism. The patron saint of the movement, Karl Marx, was also of Jewish descent. He was baptized in childhood, and reared as an unenthusiastic Lutheran.

He seems to have been totally devoid of Jewish sympathies, not to say loyalties; in some of his writings he identifies the Jewish group with the worst aspects of capitalism.

Nor in projecting the socio-economic order of the future did Marx draw at all on the inspiration of the Hebrew prophets, those fiery champions of justice and humanity.* Marx repudiated all ethical and spiritual considerations. His philosophy claimed to be completely objective and scientific, an account not of what ought to be but of what inevitably will be. He borrowed from Hegel the notion that history is the working out of logically irresistible forces; but these forces are not, as Hegel taught, ideas; they are material and economic factors. Marx applied the Darwinian theme of the struggle for survival to social institutions. Capitalism must of its own nature expand until it falls apart— the argument for this conclusion need not detain us here—to be followed by revolution, the dictatorship of the proletariat, and eventually by the classless society of true Communism.

Marx emphasized the primacy of material forces, which in an organized society are called economic. Ethical principles, artistic values, political systems, have no independent existence. They are determined exclusively by the economic process. Culture is a mere by-product of the system of production and distribution.

Religion had to be explained in similar terms. Marx called it "the opiate of the masses." It was invented by priests who are allies of the rich and mighty; its aim is to keep the enslaved multitudes docile and submissive by the appeal to a divine authority and by promises of bliss after death. The salvation of mankind by Socialism, therefore, requires the complete overthrow of religion and its institutions.

Anyone who has read this history can easily decide for himself how little this doctrine has in common with the true Jewish spirit. We shall not follow the fortunes of Marxism as a doctrine or as a movement. It produced results as diverse as the Labor Party of Great Britain and the autocratic regime of the Soviet Union. But one point must be made clear to the American reader.

The laboring classes eventually found in trade unionism an effective instrument for correcting the abuses of industrial capitalism. In America, the trade union has concentrated on specific practical objectives: higher wages, shorter hours, better working conditions. Rarely, and only

---

* In contrast, Henry George, the American social reformer, regarded Moses as the great pioneer of economic justice.

in recent years, has the labor movement entered the field of national politics. In Europe, however, the trade unions have always been the operating agencies of the Socialist party or parties, and the centers of popular Socialist education. This has been true in Great Britain as well as on the continent; and it applies also to the Jewish labor movement, to which we now turn.

Although in western countries, individual Jews were active in trade unions and in the Socialist movement, their numbers were small, and they did not constitute a bloc. It was the persistence of bitter anti-Jewish prejudices within the framework of German Socialism which convinced Moses Hess that the new movement would not of itself solve the Jewish problem, and which led him to write *Rome and Jerusalem*. Only in eastern Europe, where there were large, compact, and cohesive Jewish communities, could a distinctive Jewish labor group appear.

This occurred chiefly in the textile manufacturing cities of Poland, especially Lodz. At first, Jewish workers were slow to enter big mechanized plants, because they did not want to work on the Sabbath. But they gradually yielded to the pressure of "progress" in the form of economic need; the resulting invasion of Sabbath observance was a severe blow to tradition. Jewish workers were often employed and sometimes exploited by Jewish industrialists. The influence which the moneyed group exerted on synagogue affairs prepared the minds of many workers for that hostile attitude toward religion which Marx had aroused. Workers' synagogues began to be replaced by workers' clubs, in which secular studies and Socialist propaganda were substituted for prayer and study of the Torah. The first reported strikes by Jewish workers occurred in the 1870's; but the development of a well-knit organization proceeded slowly, handicapped by the threefold hostility of the government to unions, to Socialists, and to Jews. The *Bund*, the Jewish branch of the Russian Socialist party, was not established until 1897.

Why was such an organization necessary? Socialists have always insisted that the rights and interests of all workers are the same, and that racial and religious differences are utilized by the exploiters of labor to divide and defeat their victims. Socialism itself has always been avowedly cosmopolitan and universalistic. The early Jewish Socialists in eastern Europe were also thoroughly secularistic and assimilationist —convinced that the so-called "Jewish problem" would find its solution in the establishment of a just economic order. In such a society prejudice and persecution would disappear.

But this theory did not fit the realities of the situation in eastern

Europe. The Jewish worker differed too greatly from the Pole in speech, background, and outlook to feel at home in one over-all organization. The Bund asserted that the national-cultural values of Jewish life were just as worthy of respect and of preservation as those of the many other national and linguistic minorities of the Russian Empire. Much to the distaste of some Russian radicals, including a young revolutionary who called himself Lenin, the Bund insisted on remaining a separate entity within the Socialist movement.

Those national-cultural values which the Bundists wanted to retain were not, of course, formally religious. They included chiefly the consciousness of Jewish historical experience, group solidarity in the present, and devotion to the Yiddish language and literature. It was largely, though not entirely, through the labor movement that Yiddish acquired a new dignity. It had been the mother tongue of east European Jews for centuries, but it had not been deemed suitable for serious literature. For the benefit of women and of the unlearned, translations of the Torah, the prayer book, and some other Jewish classics had been provided; and there were manuals for devotion, handbooks of morals, and a few popular story books available for the same public. But Hebrew was the medium of adult writing, religious or secular.

In the nineteenth century, however, voices were heard protesting against that condescension which dismissed Yiddish as a mere "jargon." The 1860's saw the publication of the earlier Yiddish writings of S. I. Abramowitsch, best known by his pen name Mendele the Bookseller (*Mendele Mocher Seforim*). Mendele, who also contributed to the developing Hebrew literature, wrote with satiric humor and homely pathos about the life of simple folk. This vein was developed with tragic power by J. L. Peretz, and with a unique combination of humor and tenderness by Sholom Aleichem. Though none of these outstanding Yiddish authors was directly associated with the labor group, they reflected and intensified that concern with the "little man" which was the very essence of the labor movement. There was a similar connection between the labor group and the developing Yiddish stage, which had its beginnings in the last decades of the nineteenth century.

But though the nationalist and Socialist trends were greatly stimulated by the events of the pogrom years, it was a long while before they led to large consequences. The most immediate, and by no means the least important effect of the persecution, was the flight of Jews from eastern Europe. Though few Jews actually starved and few were baptized (despite the predictions of the persecutor), vast numbers did emigrate. Some stopped in the great cities of central and western Europe. But these countries, with their advanced industrial economy, could not readily assimilate vast numbers of penniless and unskilled refugees; nor were the Jews of Austria, Germany, and France over-eager to receive all these poor relations. A considerable number settled in England. Whitechapel, in the East End of London, became a teeming center of Yiddish-speaking life. The majority, however, were assisted to emigrate to America. The expanding economy of the United States provided room for a great increase in population; and the foreigners found for the most part a hospitable welcome. The great influx from eastern Europe was to have profound consequences for every aspect of American Jewish life.

Part 7.
The Road to the Abyss

47.

Emancipation and Anti-Semitism

1. *Emancipation*

THE YEAR 1870 SAW THE UNIFICATION OF ITALY AND OF GERMANY; under the new constitutions the Jews were granted full citizenship. The rights thus affirmed were well respected in Italy, where, however, the Jewish community was declining in numbers and vitality.

But in Germany, discrimination continued even in official practice. The German Jews made great headway in commerce, the professions, and the arts, and some played a prominent role in Parliamentary politics; but they faced serious and sometimes insuperable obstacles to advancement in the army, the universities, and other branches of government service. Conditions were much the same in Austria-Hungary.

The Jewish position was excellent in France, the Low Countries, and Denmark. Norway, Sweden, and Switzerland, which had long excluded Jewish settlement, repealed their discriminatory laws. And the status of British Jewry was rapidly improving.

The small Anglo-Jewish community which existed even in the days of Cromwell was formally legitimized in 1688. The S'fardic settlers were followed by Ashk'nazim from Germany, Holland, and eastern Europe. Though legally aliens, they soon felt at home in England; their position is said to have improved toward the end of the eighteenth century through the popularity of several Jewish prize fighters. As social prejudices crumbled, the Jews gradually acquired equal rights but only after a long Parliamentary struggle. The last episode centered around

333

Lionel de Rothschild, who had been elected to Parliament but had not been seated because he refused to take his oath of office in the prescribed Christian form. In 1858 he was finally permitted to qualify by a modified form of the oath, which he took on the Hebrew Bible with his head covered.

English Judaism faithfully reflected the conservatism of nineteenth century Britain. The S'fardic and Ashk'nazic communities, though independently organized, were alike in their firm adherence to a decorous Orthodoxy. As the number of the S'fardim declined and the Ashk'nazim rose in wealth and social position, the Chief Rabbi of the Ashk'nazic community acquired a steadily increasing dignity. From 1845 to 1911 this office was held by Marcus Nathan Adler and his son Herman; during this long period they added constantly to the prestige of their position by wise statesmanship, and their successors now bear the proud title "Chief Rabbi of the British Commonwealth of Nations."

Through the efforts of Marcus Adler, Jews' College, affiliated with the University of London, was established in 1855 for the training of Jewish spiritual leaders. It has been a notable center of scholarship. Its graduates, however, do not receive the title of Rabbi unless they qualify for the traditional s'micho by intensive Talmudic studies. Otherwise they are known simply as "ministers" with the honorary title of Reverend. The congregations under the direction of the Chief Rabbi were formally organized into The United Synagogue in 1870.

The West London Synagogue, founded in 1840, was the first departure from the official Orthodoxy. It seems to have been inspired by the desire for a more distinctively British form of worship, as well as by Reform influences from Germany. Though vehemently denounced by the traditionalists, led by Sir Moses Montefiore, the founders of this "Reform synagogue" were in fact extremely moderate in their notions. To this day their service is what American Jews would consider Conservative rather than Reform. This pioneer experiment, however, remained almost unique in England until the twentieth century.

Thus the Jews of western Europe arrived at a gratifying stage of emancipation and integration into the peoples among whom they lived. Even in Germany and Austria-Hungary, where much hostility remained, it was regarded as a temporary survival from a less enlightened age, which the advance of liberalism would soon eradicate.

This process of emancipation saw the rise of a new type of Jewish leadership based on wealth and/or political position, rather than on Jewish learning. In the past, Jewish magnates had indeed exercised considerable power in their communities; but the pressure of wealth had been counterbalanced by the authority of the Torah, vested in the rabbis and upheld by the Gentile government. Moreover, the rich men of the past were usually "court Jews," whose influence depended on the continued personal favor of the ruler they served. They were often hated by the common people, Jews and Christians alike. The new aristocrats, however, derived their prestige among their fellow Jews largely from their importance and popularity in the larger world.

Sir Moses Montefiore in England and Adolphe Crémieux in France were the outstanding examples of this new type of leadership. The first was a very rich and generous man, the second a successful politician in the good sense of the term. Though inclined to dictatorial methods, both were wholeheartedly devoted to Judaism and to the welfare of their fellow Jews. This devotion was fully displayed during the notorious Damascus affair in 1840.

The Jews of Damascus had been accused of ritual murder, and several were tortured to death. The reports were received in the West with grief and anger. Assemblies held in England and France formally authorized Montefiore and Crémieux to intervene. Accompanied by Salomon Munk, the great orientalist, the two leaders went to Alexandria, and secured from the Pasha of Egypt (who at the time ruled Syria) an order for the release of the remaining Jewish prisoners. After Syria had been restored to Turkish rule, they obtained assurances from the sultan that such an outrage would not happen again.

In 1858 the Jewish world was shocked when the papal police kidnapped Edgar Mortara, a Jewish child whose nurse had secretly baptized him. This time neither the Jewish leaders nor the Christian dignitaries whose aid they enlisted could bring about the release of the child to his parents. He was reared as a Catholic and ultimately became a priest. But such events convinced Jews in the Western world that more permanent organization was required for the protection of Jewish rights. The Alliance Israélite Universelle was founded in 1860 with Crémieux as its president, as a direct outgrowth of the Mortara incident. It has concerned itself especially with the much-neglected Jews of North Africa and the Middle East, providing them with greatly needed schooling and vocational training. Similar bodies were set up in the other western countries, independent of the Synagogue, though in no way hostile to the latter. They expressed a sense of solidarity with Jews in less fortunate lands; when they were founded, little need was felt for self-defense at home. It was to these organizations that Pinsker later turned for the support of his plan; but he completely misunderstood the temper of the western leaders. They were animated by a warm philanthropic spirit, and sometimes by religious feeling; but Jewish nationalism was utterly alien to them. Politically, they were devoted to the interests of their respective countries; and sometimes they sought (consciously or unconsciously) to serve the national interests of their own land in backward areas. (The *Alliance* later clashed with the German *Hilfsverein*.)

This period, when many Jews acquired financial and political power, also witnessed a great flowering of Jewish activity in the cultural life of Europe. Science and scholarship, literature, music, drama, medicine, law, and philosophy exercised a powerful attraction on Jews who for centuries had been conditioned to respect intellectual achievement. Contributions by Jews to the advancement of civilization are many, and they did not begin in the nineteenth century. But that century, the era of industrial expansion and scientific progress, of popular education and growing universities, was also the time when Jewish talent and resourcefulness, so long repressed, were given a more adequate opportunity. The results were amazing. Men and women of Jewish birth or descent have in the past century and a half contributed to intellectual, artistic, and spiritual accomplishment out of all proportion to the total number of Jews in the population. Nor does the record take account of gifted individuals whose careers were frustrated by discrimination and prejudice that still had not ceased.

Jews have generally pointed with great pride to this record, but it has its less cheerful side. This has already been indicated by the phrase "of Jewish birth or descent." Some of the most eminent persons on the list were born into families estranged from Judaism, or were themselves baptized in childhood (Felix Mendelssohn, Benjamin Disraeli). Others adopted Christianity in order to advance in their chosen careers, or for some other reason (Heinrich Heine, Karl Landsteiner). Many of them intermarried; others, without formally repudiating their Jewish identity, gradually drifted away from their Jewish moorings. A considerable number have remained Jews only in the ethnic or philanthropic sense, but have shown little concern with their religious heritage. One could, of course, cite instances of men preeminent in their respective fields who maintained undiminished loyalty to their faith and people (Waldemar Haffkine, Irving and Herbert Lehman, Eddie Cantor); but the negative trend is much too strong to overlook.

And it is indeed no accident. For it was precisely the successful and famous Jews who were most exposed to the anti-Jewish reaction which in modern times has been called anti-Semitism.

2. *Anti-Semitism*

Modern anti-Semitism is a complex and many-sided phenomenon. Studies have shown that it is most dangerous in periods of economic depression or national crisis, when a discontented and embittered people seek an object on which they can safely vent their feeling of frustration. It has also been noted that anti-Semitism is an effective weapon of political, economic, and clerical reaction; the enemies of democracy have repeatedly sought to enhance their own power by inflaming the masses against the Jews. Nevertheless, anti-Semitism cannot be adequately explained in economic or political terms; it has "spiritual" roots as well. Moreover, its effects on the Jewish soul have been, if anything, more devastating than its effects on the physical security and material welfare of Jews. That is why the subject belongs to this history of the inner life of Jewry.

Hatred of the Jew in the Western world was cultivated and justified for many centuries on religious grounds; the Jews had rejected the Christian savior; they were held responsible for the crucifixion and were deemed alien to the all-embracing Christian society. During the Middle Ages, this theme was enlarged and embroidered; the Jew was depicted as a diabolic, sub-human creature, delighting in evil and malice. Out of the view that the Jews were children of Satan arose the myth (still persisting in some rural areas) that Jews have horns. Though a particular attack on the Jews may have originated in a scheme to burn the notes of Jewish money-lenders, or in a simple desire for loot, this mythological background was always present.

And such deep emotional tides have continued to ebb and flow even in modern times. But as life became more secular, as national loyalties became more powerful than religious ties, it became necessary to find new rationalizations and new myths to justify the ancient hatred. The very term anti-Semitism is a case in point. The word Semitic properly designates a group of languages, including Hebrew, Aramaic, and Arabic. Ernest Renan, a French savant who had himself abandoned his ancestral Catholicism, was the first to indulge in speculations on the psychological differences between Semitic and Aryan *peoples*, a distinction without scientific basis. The term anti-Semitism derives from Renan's suggestion. Yet anti-Semitism has always been directed exclusively against Jews—never against Arabs, though their speech is Semitic. The religious motivation of Jew-hatred was not indeed abandoned. Adolf Stöcker, for many years court preacher in Berlin, regularly denounced the Jews as a menace to Christianity and to European culture. The ritual murder libel cropped up repeatedly in central as well as in eastern Europe.

It now appeared that bigotry need not be confined to the fundamentalists. The new critical approach to the Bible could likewise be used as a vehicle of anti-Jewish sentiment. Some Christian scholars grossly distorted the ideas of the Hebrew Bible, devising a fictitious contrast between the narrow nationalism, legalism, and vindictiveness of Judaism and the universal warmth and tenderness of Christian love. Others, like the Assyriologist, Friedrich Delitsch, tried to show that the important religious and ethical teachings of the Bible were derived from Assyro-Babylonian sources. The German emperor was much pleased with his argument that the Jews were but second-hand dealers in spiritual truth.

More and more, however, the emphasis was laid on racial rather than on religious differences. A school of writers arose to argue (without rational proof) that a nation must be racially homogeneous, and that the Jews are always an incurably alien and corrupt element in any national group. The Aryan (or Nordic) "race" was invested with all noble and creative qualities. Only such a race can create true art and culture. The biological inheritance, the very blood of the Jew, makes him inherently sly, sensual, and parasitic. Not only does he exploit the nobly simple Aryan—he degrades and demoralizes the latter by his sinister influence.

This theory, proposed in the middle of the nineteenth century by the French Comte de Gobineau, was later elaborated by the Englishman, Houston Stewart Chamberlain. But it had its greatest vogue in Germany, where Chamberlain's bulky volumes appeared long before they found English readers.

For convenience we may note here some more recent manifestations of "intellectual" anti-Semitism. In 1910 Werner Sombart, a German economist and historian, published a widely-read treatise in which he ascribed the creation of modern capitalism to the Jews. In his argument (based on an unreliable, if not unscrupulous manipulation of facts), Sombart stressed the evils of capitalism, though himself no radical. It was not till some years later that the Jews were also held responsible for Communism!

Some distinguished writers of recent years have voiced their disgust with the crude superficiality of modern life; they consider democracy vulgar, and sigh for the faith and authority of the thirteenth century. Some of these writers have identified the Jews with everything cheap and unspiritual in modern life. The best known were Gilbert K. Chesterton and Hilaire Belloc in England, and the American-born poets, Ezra Pound and T. S. Eliot.

But, however deep the intellectual and emotional springs of anti-Semitism, it would not have been so virulent had it not been systematically exploited for political purposes. In Germany it was constantly employed as a weapon against liberal movements; even Bismarck, who largely outgrew his earlier prejudices and on occasion defended Jewish rights, tolerated the anti-Semitism of Stöcker because he found it politically useful. From Germany, the perennial fountain of Jew-hatred, the new anti-Semitism spread eastward, fomenting accusations against Jews and Judaism in Austria-Hungary, and reinforcing the ferocity of the tsarist government.

This poison, so potent in its effects on the soul of Christians, acted on the Jewish spirit also. It proved to be especially toxic in German-speaking lands. The combination of official discrimination and popular ill will made many a Jew feel alien and rejected in the land of his birth.

Worst of all was the dark suspicion in the minds of many Jews that the anti-Semites were right. In former ages the Jew, living in a well-knit community and steeped in his own religious culture, faced the world without shame. He knew that he belonged to the people of the Torah and regarded his oppressors as besotted heathen. But in the modern world, the Jew derived his scale of values from the Gentile environment. He was saturated with German culture, in which hatred of the Jew and Judaism is a constant element; and his often meager Jewish knowledge was an insufficient corrective. Frequently, he became infected with the terrible disease of "Jewish self-hate." Accepting uncritically the prevailing judgment on the Jewish spiritual heritage, he suffered horrible feelings of inferiority and guilt. It was precisely those who were most completely identified with German culture—the eminent and the successful—who suffered most often and most painfully from this ailment. But, though the most dramatic instances of Jewish self-hate were to be found in Germany and Austria, it appeared in milder forms throughout the Western world.

Even loyal and devoted Jews sometimes displayed an unpleasant kind of anxiety, generated by anti-Semitic pressures, which led them to self-justification and self-praise. Books and articles appeared in defense of the Jews and of Judaism; the baseless charges of the anti-Semites were refuted in detail. The contributions of Jews to human betterment were enumerated, and Jewish beliefs and practices explained, not always with forthright dignity, but in the attempt to show that Jews deserve approval rather than ill will.

But anti-Semitism, deeply rooted in the popular consciousness and deftly manipulated by unscrupulous reactionaries, could not be defeated by pamphlets.

48.

The Birth of Political Zionism

IN 1894 IT BECAME KNOWN THAT SOME OFFICER OF THE FRENCH general staff had been selling military secrets to the Germans. The only Jew on the staff was Captain Alfred Dreyfus. His record as a soldier was outstanding; there was no evidence to justify even a faint suspicion of guilt. But since he was a Jew, he was selected as the scapegoat. He was railroaded through a court-martial on trumped up evidence, and condemned to penal servitude on Devil's Island. The actual traitor was long protected against exposure; those who sought to get at the truth were vilified and persecuted. The story of the Dreyfus Affair is more absorbing than any fictional tale of mystery and detection; but it cannot be retold here. It did not end till 1906, when Dreyfus was completely vindicated and restored to his military rank.

The Dreyfus case climaxed years of consistent anti-Semitic agitation in the German pattern, carried on by militarists, monarchists, and clericals hostile to the democratic spirit and institutions of the French Republic. The conviction and public degradation of Dreyfus were marked by a savage outburst of mass Jew-hatred. Dreyfus soon became the symbol of a broader issue: should democracy or reaction gain the upper hand in France? Such stalwart defenders of freedom as Emile Zola and Georges Clemenceau were in the front ranks of the Dreyfusards. The nation was bitterly divided by the conflict. An important consequence of the struggle, and of the final triumph of the liberals, was the separation of Church and State in France.

Ironically, the central figure of the drama seems never to have under-

341

stood its larger meanings. Dreyfus was a vehement French patriot of conservative views; apparently he regarded his conviction as little more than an unfortunate error. Nor did this rather indifferent Jew concern himself with the enormous consequences for Jewish life which his trial set in motion.

One of the journalists who reported the case was the Paris correspondent of the Vienna *Neue Freie Presse*, Theodor Herzl. A brilliant young intellectual of great personal charm, Herzl had been uncertain about his position as a Jew. The burden of anti-Semitism troubled him greatly. He had a fair knowledge of things Jewish and a sentimental fondness for Judaism, but he had been inclined toward assimilation and had even toyed with the notion of a mass conversion of Jews to Christianity. The violent passions of the Paris mob roused him to an entirely new outlook.

In a state of emotional excitement, Herzl dashed off a pamphlet entitled The Jewish State. The Jewish problem, he argued, can be solved only by recognizing that the Jews are a nation—a nation being defined as a group with common enemies. Not assimilation, but national rebirth must be the Jewish policy. The Jews must obtain a homeland, preferably Palestine, guaranteed to them by international treaties. This homeland must be colonized on a very large scale; and even in his first hasty sketch, Herzl revealed his unconscious messianic faith by proposals for an improved and just economic system. The establishment of this Jewish state, he held, will provide a basic solution of the Jewish problem. The economic competition which is the chief stimulus of anti-Semitism will be reduced by the withdrawal of large masses of Jews from the areas where they are now most thickly settled. The pressure on those who remain in the Diaspora will be less heavy and their morale and inner dignity will be strengthened by the very existence of a Jewish state, with its diplomatic representatives in all the capitals of the world.

Herzl supposed that he was throwing out a suggestion which recognized Jewish leaders—the rabbis perhaps—would implement. He was totally unprepared for the excitement and controversy which his pamphlet unleashed. Before long, the Viennese journalist found himself transformed almost against his will into a latter-day prophet and statesman, the active head of a world movement which received the name of Zionism. The Jews of eastern Europe paid him all but messianic honors; his majestic appearance, his dramatic personality, and his acquaintance with the famous men of his time all contributed to the growth of a Herzl legend. But from Germany and Austria westward, his opponents far outnumbered his supporters. For Herzl transformed Jewish nationalism from a comparatively local trend into a proposal that all the world talked about.

This fact largely explains the bitter anti-Zionism of the Jews in the lands of freedom. Herzl's doctrine seemed to them the repudiation of all that they had struggled for—the acceptance of Jews as full citizens of the various countries, differing from other citizens only in religion. The attack on Herzl did not come only from Reform Jews, who years before had eliminated the nationalist-messianic hope from their prayers. Opposition came also from traditionalists who still prayed for the coming of the Son of David and the rebuilding of the Temple. Some Orthodox extremists considered Zionism an impious attempt to "force" the redemption before the time decreed by God. Others condemned Zionism as a secular political effort incompatible with the religious character of Judaism. To most of Herzl's contemporaries, moreover, his proposal seemed utterly fantastic and impractical. In an age when hundreds of thousands were finding asylum in the United States and elsewhere, it seemed foolish to seek a haven in a desolate territory of the crumbling Turkish Empire.

Even the "Lovers of Zion" had their doubts about the new leader. Herzl himself confessed that he would never have written The Jewish State had he known that a nationalist movement already existed; only the supposition that he had discovered something entirely new had emboldened him to present it. The pioneers of the movement were perhaps annoyed that the leadership should pass into the hands of a newcomer who could not write in Hebrew. Moreover they disagreed with him on fundamental policy. Herzl did not want to begin the colonization of Palestine until a charter from the sultan of Turkey should give the Jewish people rights to the land, and until this charter should be ratified by the great powers. He was convinced that if Jewish financiers would grant substantial loans to the shaky Turkish government, the charter could be obtained. But the "Lovers of Zion" wanted to proceed at once with the practical work of colonization, even on the most modest scale.

The most searching criticism of Herzl's doctrine was made by the Hebrew essayist Asher Ginzberg, usually known by his pen name Ahad HaAm (one of the people). Ahad HaAm, indeed, had been equally critical of the practical activities of the Chov'vei Zion. He did not believe that the problem of the Jews was primarily economic and political. They suffer, he argued, not only from external disabilities, but also from moral infirmity. Oppression has undermined their courage, integrity, and self-respect. Emancipation has made these sicknesses worse instead of better by creating "slavery in the midst of freedom."

A revival of the spirit is needed, and this is the only true object of the nationalist renaissance. The majority of the Jews can never find a home in Palestine, either through gradual colonization or through an international charter. Ahad HaAm called for the creation of a Palestinian community outstanding not for numbers but for quality. Living an unhyphenated Jewish existence, working out their own destiny without worrying about what the Gentiles think of them, the members of this community can regain their ethical wholeness more readily. Palestine must become a spiritual center for world Jewry. The influence of the new Hebraic culture and the example of its institutions of learning and social organization would radiate to all the communities of world Jewry and supply a power for their spiritual redemption.

Strangely, Ahad HaAm did not call for a religious revival. He had abandoned Orthodoxy; and he rejected Reform Judaism as essentially negative and assimilationist. Yet he strongly opposed neo-pagan tendencies that were beginning to be expressed in Hebrew literature. The chief influence on his thinking was exerted by such English philosophers as John Stuart Mill and Herbert Spencer, who were cool toward religion but stressed the need of a severe, socially useful code of ethics. Of course, Ahad HaAm could find ample ethical material in the classic sources of Judaism. He was apparently not concerned about the problem of organized worship; Hebrew culture and Jewish morality seemed to him sufficient for the spiritual needs of the people.

Herzl, undeterred by critics within or without the nationalist movement, proceeded with plans for a World Zionist Congress. In August, 1897, in the Swiss city of Basel, the Congress declared its purpose: "to establish for the Jewish people a publicly and legally assured home in Palestine." The phrase "publicly and legally assured" reflects Herzl's position. Nevertheless the delegates from eastern Europe to this and subsequent congresses insisted that, pending the attainment of this larger goal, the practical work of colonization and cultural development should be continued.

The Zionist congresses created a permanent executive body, with Herzl as its head, as well as the financial institutions needed for the movement. Most remarkable is the Jewish National Fund (*Keren Kayemet L'Yisrael*) established in 1901 for the purchase of land in

344 *The Road to the Abyss*

Palestine. Land once acquired by this agency became the permanent possession of the Jewish people. Some of it has been used for public buildings and other large projects; but the greater part has been made available to individuals or collectives for farming. Such tenants and their children may retain possession of their holdings indefinitely as long as they farm the land properly; but they may not sell or mortgage "JNF" land. Thus, a modern and practical expression was given to the Biblical idea (embodied in the law of the Jubilee) that the soil is not to be selfishly exploited without regard for the general good. Moreover, the Jewish National Fund was able to improve areas of swamp or desert land, which no individual could have afforded to reclaim, and thus greatly increase the productivity of Palestine.

Theodor Herzl, still earning his living by newspaper work, set out to obtain the charter. This amateur diplomat interviewed the crowned heads of Europe and the pope, to interest them in his plans. He negotiated at length with the Turkish government; and he tried desperately to persuade Jewish financiers to grant the Turkish loan which might have paid for the charter. He realized that he was viewed with disfavor in many powerful circles; and before the first Zionist congress, he offered to step aside from the leadership in favor of Baron Edmond de Rothschild, the patron of the earliest colonies in Palestine. But the great magnates remained hostile, and Herzl's negotiations led to no practical results.

Meantime, the discussion stirred up by Zionist activity had led to a somewhat different proposal, known as Territorialism. Its most notable spokesman was Israel Zangwill, the Anglo-Jewish novelist and playwright. He argued that any considerable territory available for large-scale settlement would meet the needs of the Jewish people—the homeland did not have to be Palestine. This suggestion was received with interest in British official circles, and at length the English government indicated that it was prepared to open a large part of Uganda (British East Africa) to systematic colonization by Jews.

This proposal was presented by Herzl to the sixth Zionist congress in 1903, with the urgent recommendation that it be accepted, at least (as Max Nordau, one of Herzl's lieutenants, put it) as a "lodging for the night." But the east European bloc, whose constituency was most desperately in need of deliverance, flatly rejected the offer. Palestine alone, they contended, could call forth the dedicated loyalty needed to recreate the Jewish nation.

Less than a year later, Herzl was dead, worn out at the age of forty-four by his tremendous labors. The movement continued, gaining slowly in adherents and in the establishment of new colonies, until the outbreak of the First World War.

Now that the State of Israel is an established reality, it is hard to visualize the days when Zionism was largely a matter of debate—to its opponents a dangerous chimera, to its adherents a messianic dream. Yet even the debate, despite the bitterness it engendered, had positive value. It awakened new interest in all aspects of Jewish life. The severest critics of Zionism had to admit that the movement had stirred flagging Jewish loyalties. It won back to some sort of positive Jewish commitment many who had drifted away from religion or even repudiated it openly. Zionism stimulated the cultivation of Jewish cultural values, and helped to generate a firmer tone of independence and self-reliance—that will to auto-emancipation, for which Pinsker had called.

49.

American Judaism, 1880-1914

1. The Great Immigration

MISS EMMA LAZARUS WAS THE DAUGHTER OF A PROSPEROUS AND cultured S'fardic family. She received the upbringing of a fine New York lady, and wrote genteel poetry which Ralph W. Emerson (among others) had admired. When the Russian Jews fleeing from persecution began arriving in New York in 1882, she tried to serve the refugees; and the experience abruptly transformed both her life and her poetry. The shy, sheltered young woman learned the tragedy and the grandeur of Jewish existence. With this new theme, her poems became more profound and impassioned. Both the Jewish past and the crisis of her own time provided her with stirring subjects. She pleaded for Jewish dignity, courage, and independence. She rejoiced that the United States was a haven for all oppressed peoples, and poured out her American faith in the famous sonnet on the Statue of Liberty. But she also had a vision of Jewish national rebirth which she voiced both in verse and in prose.

Few American Jews experienced such a personal transformation as befell Emma Lazarus; but the American Jewish community as a whole was completely changed by the vast new wave of immigrants. First, as to size. In 1880 there were at most three hundred thousand Jews in the United States. By 1914 there were some three million. In half a century, this country had become the seat of one of the largest Jewish communities in the world.

347

The earlier migrants, though most numerous in the eastern seaboard cities, had spread rather quickly throughout the country, even into the smallest towns. Some of the newcomers likewise scattered to remoter areas, but a much larger proportion remained in the big cities, above all New York. The lower East Side of Manhattan became a congested, often sordid, yet intensely vital center of Jewish living. Similar Yiddish-speaking "ghettos" grew up on a smaller scale in all the metropolitan communities.

The older settlers were a more homogeneous group. They arrived in comparatively small numbers; and though rarely affluent, they were seldom destitute. They were often assisted by relatives or friends who had preceded them to this country; from peddling or clerking for others, they soon progressed to independent business ventures. By 1880 most of them were fairly well established economically, and they had encountered little difficulty in adjusting themselves to American life. Nearly all of them were literate, but few had an advanced education, whether secular or Jewish. They were mostly Orthodox in background; but it is probable that by 1880, the majority of American Jews belonged to Reform congregations.

Many of the later immigrants likewise came in search of better opportunities, and used their savings to bring over relatives and help them establish themselves. But many of the newcomers were literal refugees, victims of terror and pogrom, almost without resources of either money or vocational skill. Meantime, the rapid industrialization of American life made the economic problem of the immigrant far more grim than it had been a few decades earlier.

The existing Jewish community, though somewhat bewildered by this enormous influx (and even at times resentful of it), accepted loyally the enlarged responsibilities it involved. The rather simple philanthropic institutions which till now had sufficed for American Jewry were greatly expanded and improved, to provide both emergency help and long-term guidance. We begin to hear about "Americanization," a new term for a new concept.

The Jews of German extraction, who had a normal share of provincial prejudice, were inclined to view all Yiddish-speaking Jews as an undifferentiated mass. The exact reverse was true. Even in speech they were not alike: the dialects of Yiddish vary considerably. Socially, culturally, and religiously, the newcomers were far from homogeneous. Some hailed from crowded cities like Warsaw and Lodz, others were natives of tiny rural communities. Their educational background was equally diverse. Not a few, including many women, were illiterate. Most could at least read and write Yiddish, and knew enough Hebrew to recite the prayers. But for the first time, America had a large group of Jewish intellectuals—learned Talmudists, writers and readers of the new Hebrew literature, Yiddish authors and journalists, and a sprinkling of "intelligentsia" who spoke Russian by preference. Most of the newcomers were Orthodox, some even from the mystic conventicles of the Chasidim; but there were also devotees of haskalah and advocates of Jewish nationalism. Other Jews brought to this country the doctrines of the emerging socialist labor movement; and there were scattered groups of more extreme radicals. Through the immigration from eastern Europe, American Jewish life acquired a colorful variety and an intensity which it had not possessed before, and which it has retained to the present.

The newcomers soon began to provide for their own religious needs. Few of them joined the old Americanized Orthodox congregations; the synagogues were physically too distant, their members socially and culturally too remote. (The Russian Jews would hardly have recognized the Reform temple as Jewish at all.) Many new congregations sprang up, often around a group from the same town or province. The synagogue for a long time expressed not only religious sentiment but nostalgia for the old country. (This has been true of the religious institutions of every immigrant group in America.) Though the traditional wing included the pre-revolutionary S'fardic synagogues of New York and Philadelphia, American Orthodoxy was to have a distinctly foreign flavor for several generations.

In elementary Jewish education, the eastern influence was also strongly marked. The *m'lamed* (Hebrew tutor) and the *cheder* (privately-owned Hebrew school) flourished, though the teaching standards were often pitifully low and the results unsatisfactory. Larger schools organized with community support and known as Talmud Torahs usually provided better educational facilities. All these institutions operated on week-day afternoons and evenings after the close of the public school session, as well as on Sundays. Nor was advanced education neglected. By 1886 New York had its first y'shivo on the east European model, with Talmud as the central subject of study and Yiddish the language of instruction.

The American public school system, now firmly established in the major centers of Jewish settlement, opened vast opportunities to the young. The children of the immigrants were rapidly Americanized.

American Judaism, 1880–1914 349

Fired by the old Jewish love of learning, many made phenomenal progress. One could compile a long list of distinguished figures in business, the professions and the arts, the entertainment world, and public life, who began life in the Russian pale or in the crowded tenements of the East Side.

But these very opportunities also constituted a problem, for they frequently opened a wide breach between children and their immigrant parents. The latter, living and working among other "greenhorns," had little time or energy to learn the language and customs of the new land. The youngsters often felt estranged from their elders; and impatient of the foreign ways of the latter, they rejected much that they could have learned from them with profit.

Both parents and children tended to confuse the essential values of Judaism with the particular patterns of behavior characteristic of the "old country." Fathers and mothers discovered with bewilderment and sometimes bitterness that they could no longer impose their authority on their independent and rebellious youngsters. The breach was often intensified by the incompetence of Hebrew teachers, and by resentment at having to attend supplementary schools when other children were free to play. As a result, large groups of the second generation drifted away from positive Jewish belief and observance, or even explicitly rejected them.

Under these circumstances, even the moral values of Jewish life were not always effectively transmitted. With the decline of parental authority, some gifted and ambitious children might rise the more rapidly to fame and fortune; but others went astray in the poverty and overcrowding of the slums. For the first time, American Jewry had an appreciable though not disproportionate number of delinquent children and criminals. In time, as we shall see, the children of the drifters found ways to regain their religious heritage.

2. The Jewish Labor Movement

The policies of the Russian government had prevented its Jewish subjects from achieving a sound occupational distribution. Comparatively few of the immigrants had either capital to establish themselves in business or technical skills which fitted them for remunerative employment. The more advanced economy of the United States permitted fewer to go into peddling, and offered smaller returns to those who attempted it. Accustomed for the most part to sedentary occupations in large cities, the Jews were seldom qualified for farm life or for the heavy labor which immigrants from peasant backgrounds contributed to building the railroads and industrial plants of America. Jewish philanthropists created institutions for training young Jews in agriculture and the skilled trades; but such projects could produce results only over a long term of years. Meanwhile, thousands of families had the problem of earning their bread at once.

The needle trades supplied a large part of the answer. A number of the older Jewish settlers were manufacturers of men's or women's clothing; a fair number of the newcomers had worked in the factories of Lodz and Warsaw. Many of the operations could be learned rather quickly; some could be performed in the home. This was the background of the notorious sweatshop system. The highly competitive and seasonal character of these industries made it difficult for even the more conscientious employers to maintain wage standards; and the constant influx of new and desperate immigrants tended to keep pay low. The more resourceful workers would save the minimum sums to purchase a few machines and set themselves up as sub-contractors, exploiting the more recent arrivals as they had been exploited. In a period when government had not yet established standards for working conditions, and the protection of women and children in industry was insufficient, terrible physical and spiritual evils resulted. The efforts of humanitarians and social workers might relieve these evils somewhat, but they could be overcome only by the organized activity of the workers themselves.

The labor unions that eventually achieved a solution to these problems were not officially Jewish agencies. Unlike the European trades unions, with their Socialist orientation and their involvement in political affairs, the Amalgamated Clothing Workers and the International Ladies' Garment Workers were and are unions in the American style, devoted primarily to the practical purpose of obtaining the best possible wage scales and working conditions for their membership. In the last decades of the nineteenth and the opening decades of the twentieth century, these unions were predominantly Jewish in membership. This also applied to a large segment of the Hat and Capmakers Union. The struggle for recognition was a long and bitter one; but it ended at last in constructive and inspiring results.

Today and for many years past strikes in these industries are rare. The unions mentioned are models of labor organization, democratically organized, and free of the graft and racketeering that have plagued some areas of the American labor movement. They have made elaborate provision for the welfare of their membership through housing projects, and educational and recreational programs. Increasingly they have sought to cooperate with the manufacturers for the benefit of all concerned.

The garment industry has played an interesting and little noted role in the advancement of American democracy. Time was when class distinctions were accented by the difference between the fashionable dress of wealthy women and the obviously home-made ginghams and calicoes of the poor. The application of mass production to women's garments (the result of a predominantly Jewish enterprise) has enabled the shop girl and farm woman of today to dress as smartly, if not as expensively, as the daughter of the millionaire.

The garment unions were never exclusively Jewish. For the expression of its Jewish aims, the labor group created special organizations, the best known of which is the Workmen's Circle (*Arbeiter Ring*). It is a fraternal order, maintaining various insurance benefits as well as cultural and social activities. It serves, in fact, as a sort of secularist synagogue; in its schools children are taught Yiddish, Jewish history, and Socialist doctrine, and in its cemeteries members may be buried without formal religious ritual. The Workmen's Circle and other Socialist-Yiddishist bodies were akin in spirit to the Jewish Socialist movement in Europe; especially in the earlier years they were antagonistic both to organized religion and to Jewish nationalism. Their positive Jewish interests were chiefly a love for the Yiddish language and for Jewish "folk culture." The anti-religious sentiment (which at one time expressed itself in banquets and balls on Yom Kippur) has very largely diminished.

Mention should also be made of the Yiddish press which flourished in America for many decades, and of the Yiddish theater, which had a briefer period of vigor. Yiddish journalism was not restricted to the Socialist viewpoint; there were newspapers supporting every ideology from extreme Orthodoxy to out-and-out Communism. The standards of Yiddish journalism have been generally high, and the Yiddish press has in fact served as an effective agency for Americanization.

3. *Conservative Judaism*

During the eighteen eighties, as we saw, an attempt was made by Jastrow, Szold, Kohut, and others to find a middle way between an overly rigid Orthodoxy and an excessively negative Reform. Though these scholars may have checked the extreme tendencies in Reform, they did not create a new movement. Conservative Judaism, as we know it today, emerged in the twentieth century.

The Jewish Theological Seminary, founded by Morais in 1886, had struggled along with limited success. After his death in 1897, the future of the Seminary was even more problematical. Then Jacob H. Schiff, the most influential Jewish layman of the time, took a hand. Though a regular worshipper in a Reform temple, he was sympathetically interested in all phases of Jewish life, and he felt that the teeming Jewish center in New York ought to have a great institution of traditional learning. With the moral and financial backing provided by Schiff and others whom he enlisted, the Seminary was reorganized; and Dr. Solomon Schechter was called as its new president in 1902.

A native of Rumania, Schechter had studied in Vienna, and had won distinction as a scholar while teaching in Cambridge and London. He possessed, beside profound erudition, an extraordinary gift of English style, a brilliant wit, and irresistible charm. He had, moreover, a great appreciation for the emotional and mystical aspects of religion, which had been largely neglected by the cool rationalists of the nineteenth century. He was the first to write sympathetically about Chasidism in English.

It cannot be said that he brought much new light to the problem of revelation and authority, the basic issue between Reform and Orthodoxy. He stressed rather a warm appreciation of all the positive values in historic Judaism—scholarship, piety, traditional observance, the Hebrew language, Zionism—and like Frankel advocated the retention of all those practices that were generally observed by the Jewish people. To describe this consensus, he was fond of using the term "Catholic Israel" (*K'lal Yisrael*); and he hoped (though he did not succeed) to lift the Seminary above party struggle and make it a force for Jewish unity. "In fact," writes one of Schechter's admiring disciples, "he had not a logical system or a philosophy of Judaism, but an immense and romantic love of it."

Under Schechter's leadership, the Seminary quickly became an outstanding center of learning, with a brilliant faculty and one of the greatest Jewish libraries of the world. Curiously, a great part of the financial support and the lay leadership came from Reform Jews. For many years, the chairman of the Board of Trustees was Louis Marshall, a distinguished attorney and an ardent champion of Jewish rights, who served also as president of Temple Emanu-El, a citadel of Reform. The tradition that Reform Jews should lend their substantial support to the Seminary, without attempting to modify its religious position, has continued up to the present.

The disciples of Schechter were prepared to meet a growing need, if not with a complete philosophy, at least with an effective program. Thousands of Jews had outgrown what we might call "immigrant Orthodoxy," but did not feel at home in Reform temples. They were uncomfortable when invited to pray bareheaded and in English, or to listen to music without traditional Jewish quality, often rendered by a Gentile choir. Many were at least sentimentally inclined toward Zionism, and were repelled by the anti-Zionist utterances heard from many Reform pulpits. Moreover, there was frequent social cleavage between them and the older settlers who constituted the leadership in most Reform congregations.

Schechter's disciples brought back to a positive Jewish affiliation thousands who had broken more or less violently with the uncompromising Orthodoxy of their parents. The Conservative synagogue provided a service largely traditional in content and tone, but somewhat shortened and conducted with dignity and good taste. Such modifications as the late Friday night service, the abolition of the separate section for women, Confirmation or Bas Mitzvah for girls, and sometimes the use of the organ were generally adopted. But services were held on the second day of the holidays, men wore the hat and *talis* (fringed prayer-shawl), marriages and funerals were conducted in the traditional manner, intensive Hebrew education was provided for the young, and dietary laws were observed at least at congregational functions and in the household of the rabbi. The Conservative rabbinate has been, almost without exception, ardently Zionist.

The twentieth century has seen a phenomenal growth of this movement. The vagueness of its theological position has proved in many respects a distinct advantage. In some small communities, where the Jewish population has been insufficient to maintain more than one synagogue, the Conservative program has furnished a working compromise. In the big cities, too, Conservative synagogues have become large and influential.

4. *Communal Development*

Until the outbreak of World War I, American Jewish leadership was largely preoccupied with the absorption of the great masses of immigrants and with their physical and social welfare. The first Young Men's Hebrew Association was established in Baltimore in the middle of the nineteenth century, and similar bodies were created in most of the larger cities some decades later. Unlike the YMCA, which had a conscious religious motivation, the YMHA's were designed to provide wholesome recreation for the children of newcomers, and had a markedly philanthropic tone. So did the Jewish settlement houses in the slum areas of the great cities.

But the more far-sighted leaders recognized that the community must concern itself with all groups, not merely the immigrant and the poor. One of the most neglected areas was that of Jewish education. Textbooks and teaching materials suitable for American children hardly existed. The Reform Sunday schools were staffed by well-meaning volunteers, the Hebrew teachers in the traditionalist schools were too often incompetents who could not make a living at anything else. The first step toward solving the problem of teaching personnel was made in Philadelphia, where Gratz College began a program of teacher training in 1897.

The following year a young Palestinian, Samson Benderly, arrived in the United States; his long career was dedicated to the improvement of Jewish education, above all by giving the Jewish teacher professional status together with professional standards. A number of his disciples became specialists in Jewish pedagogy. Some of the larger communities established Bureaus of Education, to assist all types of schools—Reform, traditional, nationalist, Yiddishist—in making their work more effective. It became clear that while varying philosophies of Jewish life would lead to varied curricula, every kind of school needed better personnel and improved methods. For the same reason, several teachers' colleges were established with community-wide support.

Educational and cultural enterprises on the adult level were also fostered. An outstanding instance was the *Jewish Encyclopedia*, the most massive and scholarly undertaking of this sort which had yet appeared in any language (1901–1905). It was produced through the enterprise of Dr. Isidor Singer, and published as a commercial venture. Meantime, the Jewish Publication Society of America, a non-profit agency, had come into existence for the dissemination of Jewish literature in English. It has published both scholarly and popular books, including fiction for adults and children. Its most notable accomplishment was a Bible translation (1917), the work of a distinguished committee of scholars, which has become the generally accepted version of the Bible for English-speaking Jews.

Meantime, anti-Semitic trends appeared from time to time in American life, and caused some concern to Jewish leaders. Moreover, the increasingly numerous, wealthy, and influential American Jewish community was gradually drawn into world Jewish affairs. Even in the nineteenth century, American Jews sought the good offices of our government to intervene on behalf of persecuted Jews abroad—notably in Rumania. For many years the Union of American Hebrew Congregations had a "Board of Delegates," concerned with the protection of the civil rights of Jews here and elsewhere. This body was disbanded in 1925; it was felt that its aims could be better achieved by other agencies in the field which transcended denominational lines and represented the entire Jewish community.

Among these agencies, one of the most important was the B'nai B'rith, a fraternal body, which had gradually acquired considerable prestige on the American scene, and which had established lodges in a number of European countries. It was frequently useful in providing a united front for the defense of Jewish interests in the various communities. In 1913 it created a special branch called the Anti-Defamation League to pursue this work more intensively.

In 1906 the American Jewish Committee was established for similar purposes by a group of wealthy and distinguished laymen. Though these bodies were manned and led by men actively identified with the synagogue, they were independent of any religious body, and were destined later to stimulate the growth of a kind of Jewish secularism.

50.

European Judaism before World War 1

1. *The East*

THE TSARIST GOVERNMENT, BUNGLING, CORRUPT, AND CRUEL, WAS crumbling. In a final effort to retain power, it adopted a systematic policy of anti-Semitism. Thus it was hoped that the resentment of the masses might be diverted from the real authors of their misery. What was surmised in the first two decades of the twentieth century has since been fully documented: the Russian government itself fomented the "spontaneous" outbreaks against the Jews.

Small wonder that this period saw a steady and massive Jewish immigration from Russia. Many of the migrants went to new havens: to Argentina, where extensive agricultural colonies were established under the patronage of Baron Maurice de Hirsch; to Australia; to South Africa, which became a rather vigorous center of both Orthodoxy and Zionism. The majority, however, came to North America, a considerable number to Canada but most to the United States.

Nevertheless, Jewish life in the eastern center continued with hardly diminished vigor. The Orthodox maintained their y'shivos and the Chasidim their pious circles. Yiddish journalism, literature, and drama flourished. Peretz and Sholom Aleichem were still in their heyday, but a new star was rising in the heaven of Yiddish literature—the novelist and playwright Sholem Asch, who was destined to achieve first fame, and later notoriety.

At the same time, Hebrew letters, stimulated by the growth of Zionism, achieved new levels of excellence. We have already mentioned the essayist Ahad HaAm. In poetry, the outstanding figure was Chaim Nachman Bialik, whose nationalist fervor was deeply rooted in traditional experience. Bialik, however, did not glorify the past uncritically. He called for an end of passive submission and the adoption of a more manly, militant attitude toward the world. His terrible poem on the Kishinev massacre voiced a certain contempt for the victims who allowed themselves to be butchered without resistance, and stimulated the formation of Jewish self-defense groups. Bialik's chief rival in Hebrew poetry was Saul Tchernichowsky, a latter-day Hellenist, who translated Greek classics into Hebrew and sought to infuse the bright Greek spirit into his original poems.

This literary activity reflected a growing and dedicated effort to advance the Zionist cause. It was in the East that the partisan differences within the movement were most sharply marked and significant. At the right stood the Mizrachi group, spiritual heirs of Rabbi Kalischer, who combined nationalist sentiment with unswerving Orthodoxy. They envisioned a Jewish state built not on secular principles, but on the positive foundations of Torah. Zionism was to them a means to a larger end; the creation of a national state would not be the messianic redemption but the necessary prelude to it.

The Zionist center party was not completely unified. There were differences between the strict followers of Herzl's political philosophy and the "practical" Zionists; cutting across these lines was the group headed by Ahad HaAm, whose chief emphasis was on the spiritual rebirth of the nation.

At the left were Socialists, who had broken with the majority of Jewish Marxians by espousing Zionism. They were convinced that even under Socialism, the Jewish problem could be solved only if the Jews had a state of their own; but this, they insisted, must be a Socialist commonwealth. Within this group were several contending factions; the most durable was called the *Poale Zion* ("Laborers of Zion").

The main body of Jewish Socialists had organized in 1897 into the Bund, the first Jewish political party in Russia. The Bund took an active part in the unsuccessful revolutionary uprisings at the beginning of the century. As the Bund developed from a small association of Marxian theorists to a mass movement, its spokesmen found themselves champions of a kind of secular nationalism, not indeed demanding an independent Jewish state, but maintaining the right of Jews to cultural autonomy.

During the same years, a theory of "Diaspora nationalism" without Socialist involvement was advanced by the great Russian Jewish historian, Simon Dubnow. Starting out as an advocate of haskalah, he too had abandoned assimilationism as neither possible nor justifiable. His demands, however, were more modest than those of either the Bundists or the Zionists. He sought the abolition of restrictive and discriminatory laws and practices, and the recognition of the Jews as a national minority within the framework of the empire, with the right to preserve their own languages, customs, and cultural values. But the political party he established for these purposes never gained the support of large numbers.

Russia was not the only land where Jews were oppressed. When Austria-Hungary, with liberal intent, granted more local autonomy to its Polish subjects, the result was disastrous for the Jews who dwelt among them. Polish national sentiment found an outlet in persecution, which sent thousands of Galician Jews fleeing westward. As for Rumania, the case of Rabbi Moses Gaster will serve as sufficient illustration. An encyclopedic Jewish scholar, he was also one of the foremost authorities on Rumanian literature and folklore. But when he dared to protest against the oppressive anti-Jewish policies of the government, his contributions to the culture of his native land were disregarded. He was expelled from the country in 1885, and spent the rest of his long and productive life as the leader of the S'fardic community of England.

2. Germany

The twentieth century saw the beginning of a German-Jewish renaissance which came to its glorious climax between the two world wars. Not that the negative tendencies disappeared from German and Austrian Jewry. Baptism and intermarriage were wide-spread and many distinguished figures were crippled by Jewish self-hate. But there was an unmistakable revival of positive trends. The Liberal congregations and the Liberal rabbinate formed national bodies to strengthen their movement, creating a new (and rather conservative) prayer book, and other literature for their purpose.

In 1905 a young Liberal Rabbi named Leo Baeck published a short book called *The Essence of Judaism;* it made a profound impression that was to grow with the years. Like his predecessors, Baeck stressed the ethical and spiritual aspects of Judaism, and assigned a secondary place to ceremonial. But the tone of his work was new. The discussion of ritual was brief and came at the very end of the work. The emphasis on spiritual and ethical values was more truly prophetic, less relaxed and optimistic. The confident faith in progress was replaced by a sense of the arduous and tragic character of Jewish destiny. Universalism was no longer identified with patriotic service to the state. With uncanny foresight, Baeck stressed the opposition between Judaism which insists on the freedom of the individual conscience and the absolute demands of the deified state: for the totalitarian outlook was already foreshadowed by Prussianism.

The most notable figure in the spiritual life of German Jewry before the great war was the philosopher, Hermann Cohen, one of the leading figures in the revival of Kantianism. The rigorous critical analysis of concepts on which Kant had insisted was now resumed with the instruments of modern mathematics and logic; a thoroughgoing rationalism was combined with that austere and unbending ethical spirit which was also characteristic of the old master. Cohen's earlier works set forth a highly abstract and universalistic monotheism, in which the existence of God serves a logical rather than a religious purpose. God is the link between the external logical world of pure reason and the internal ethical world of pure will. Put differently, the fulfilment of ethical purpose is only possible in a material world which truly exists, and in which ethical purposes are capable of being advanced. If the world in which we seem to live were a transitory and unstable dream, true ethical conduct would not be possible. God, in Cohen's earlier system, is the Guarantor that we are not thus deceived, that there is a stable universe within which we can carry forward our ethical striving. Religion differs from philosophy only in approach, not in subject matter.

Cohen himself, however, was not satisfied with these abstractions. Despite his world-wide fame as founder of the "Marburg School" of Neo-Kantianism, he sought an expression of his views that would do fuller justice to both his deep religious feelings and his ardent Jewish loyalties. For Cohen came from a warmly observant background and had studied at the Breslau Seminary. Jewish ritual practices were an essential part of his life. While yet professor at Marburg, he was lecturing at the Hochschule in Berlin; and after retiring from his university post, he devoted his last years entirely to Jewish teaching.

As we might expect, Cohen's thinking was largely akin to that of the Liberal school. He stressed the ethical, prophetic, and universal values of Judaism, and was strongly anti-Zionist. But he was not content with a mild doctrinaire liberalism. In his devotion to the prophetic doctrine of justice, he supported the practical program (though not the Marxian theory) of the Socialist movement. He adopted the Reform concept of the messianic age in a new dynamic version. To Cohen, the golden age of the future is not a fixed goal which can be attained or even approximated. The messianic age must always be in the future. It is the affirmation of man's unlimited freedom to advance toward ever-higher spiritual levels.

Cohen had a unique and deeply religious approach to the perennial problem of suffering. We should regard all misfortune as a double moral challenge. My own suffering should be accepted as a punishment, not for any particular sin, but for all the shortcomings of my life. Adversity should summon me to repentance and improvement. But I must not draw the same conclusion from the suffering of others. My fellow man's pain should lead me to no inferences about his sinfulness, but only to concern with his need, and to such sympathetic and brotherly service as will relieve him. Thus, both one's own sorrows and those of others should lead to moral and spiritual growth.

Despite his outspoken universalism, Cohen differed with many Reform Jews in emphasizing the importance of ritual, which he regarded as a powerful instrument for sanctifying life and its tasks. He likewise advocated the retention of Hebrew as the holy tongue, though deprecating its revival for secular uses. In one respect only he vigorously urged a departure from traditional custom. Through thousands of years, Jews had buried their dead; Cohen, however, urged the practice of cremation, not because it is "modern" or sanitary, but for religious reasons. Burial is associated with the old belief in bodily resurrection; cremation, he argued, would underline the conviction that with death we have no further use for the outworn husk, and that immortality is spiritual.

An important agency which united elements of eastern and western Jewry was the Agudath Israel, organized in 1912 as the instrument of right wing Orthodoxy. It was called forth in particular by defeats suffered by the Mizrachi group within Zionism. The more radical Orthodox withdrew from the Zionist movement altogether, repelled not only by its failure to respond to their wishes but by its secular and worldly character. Among their aims was the resettlement of the Holy Land by individuals and groups dedicated to the scrupulous observance of the Torah. In addition, the Agudah sought in a variety of ways to strengthen Orthodoxy in the various countries of Europe. Its constituents were by no means homogeneous. Westernized pietists from Frankfort were linked with Chasidim and rabbinists from the east. Even among the German Agudists, there were sharp differences of opinion as to how far they should cooperate with the non-Orthodox, for example in communities where the Liberal group were in the majority. The Agudath Israel has survived all the storms of the past forty years, and still remains the world agency of right wing Orthodoxy.

3. England

The rather sluggish religious life of British Jewry also experienced a quickening in the twentieth century through the rise of a distinctive Liberal movement. It was the work of three unusual personalities, none of them rabbis, but possessed of gifts and equipment unusual today in laymen.

Claude G. Montefiore, descendant of a famous family and provided with every advantage wealth could supply, had originally hoped to be rabbi of the Reform Synagogue in London, and had pursued intensive studies in Germany with that end in view. Even after he decided not to enter the rabbinate, he continued his scholarly interests; and his voluminous writings include important works on the Bible, the New Testament, and rabbinic literature. But his concern was always with the living problems of religion, and this concern is evident in his studies of the past as well as in his books and articles on current issues. In his earlier years, under the influence of Benjamin Jowett of Cambridge, his viewpoint was close to Unitarianism, and he was particularly interested in those elements of the teaching of Jesus which might supplement or correct the Jewish inheritance. In Germany Montefiore met the brilliant Solomon Schechter, whom he brought to England to tutor him in Rabbinics, and whose career at Cambridge he helped to advance. While Schechter did not make Montefiore a traditionalist, his influence led his pupil and patron to a greater appreciation of Talmudic literature, and to a more moderate and positive Jewish position.

The second figure in the movement was Israel Abrahams, son of an Orthodox rabbi, who succeeded Schechter as Reader in Rabbinics at Cambridge. A gentle soul and charming litterateur, his career was devoted largely to spreading the knowledge of Jewish culture in its manifold variety. The two friends edited twenty volumes of the *Jewish Quarterly Review* (the deficits of which were paid out of Montefiore's pocket), devoted both to scholarly studies and to serious discussions of current problems.*

Here, and in his independent books, Montefiore concerned himself with the basic questions of Jewish religion. He found the mild English Orthodoxy of his time unsuitable both because of its unwillingness to face the challenge of modern thought and because of its lack of dynamic fervor. Matters were equally static in the Reform Synagogue of West London. Montefiore began to appeal for a "liberal" Judaism, which should meet both the intellectual and emotional needs of modern men. In substance, what he proposed was little different from the Reform Judaism which had developed in the United States; Montefiore's writings, however, possess a unique quality, due to the straightforward earnestness and deep personal faith of the author.

Meantime, the Hon. Lily Montagu (whose father, Lord Swaythling, was one of the pillars of the United Synagogue) found in this liberal Jewish faith the answer to her own spiritual strivings and the cause to which she was to devote her life. Though her outspoken championship of the liberal position led to a break with her father, she refused to compromise; and it was largely through her dynamic and insistent drive that Montefiore and Abrahams organized the Jewish Religious Union, which developed into the first Liberal synagogue in London (1902). Gradually the idea of Liberal Judaism, well advertised by the indignant opposition of the Conservatives, won wider acceptance; Liberal synagogues were established in various parts of greater London, in other British cities, and more recently in Dublin.

Most of the rabbinical leaders of these English Liberal congregations have been (until recently) graduates of the American Hebrew Union College. While making good use of the publications of American Reform, the Liberal Jews of England have also produced some valuable educational materials, as well as a prayer book of their own. Like the early American reformers, the Liberal congregations of England have been strongly anti-nationalist. Yet it is worth noting that for a number of years, an ardent Zionist was "assistant rabbi" of the London Liberal Synagogue, and that Montefiore (a true liberal) carefully protected his freedom of utterance on the subject.

---

* Since 1910 it has been sponsored by Dropsie College (Philadelphia) as a purely learned journal.

After the First World War, Miss Montagu inspired the establishment of the World Union for Progressive Judaism. This organization brought together the Liberal bodies of England and Germany, the smaller Liberal units of the Continent, the Union of American Hebrew Congregations, and the Central Conference of American Rabbis, into a loose federation. In addition to sponsoring meetings for the discussion of common problems, the World Union has provided assistance to Liberal groups in countries where the movement is just getting started.

The challenge of the Liberal movement has proved beneficial to the traditional congregations of England as well. "Competition" has stirred them to make their worship and preaching more vital, to organize youth groups, and to expand their programs.

51.

The Effects of the First World War

1. *Europe*

THE SUMMER OF 1914 REVEALED THE FATAL DEFECTS OF WESTERN
civilization. The lust for power—economic, political, military—shattered
the external veneer of culture. The optimistic faith in progress crashed
as the most advanced material civilization ever known used its skill to
produce more efficient machines for slaughter. The First World War
was the most terrible mankind had ever known, not merely because of
its vast extent, but because of the cold savagery with which it was
fought—and yet it was to prove only the prelude to a still more dreadful
conflict a few years later. It is difficult to estimate the full effects of the
catastrophe on the souls of mankind, because we cannot be sure to
what extent the moral decline was the result of the war, and to what
extent it was the cause of the war.

But there can be no question as to the impact of the war upon the
Jewish people. The tragedy is beyond all measure. By an ominous coincidence, the hostilities began on the Ninth of Ov, the anniversary of
the destruction of the Temple, and the most sorrowful day in the Jewish calendar.

On the Eastern Front, the largest and most concentrated Jewish
population in the world was caught between two great armies. The
Russian government, alarmed by military reverses, accused the Polish

Jews of pro-German sympathies; later they were victimized by the German invaders. A few years after, they were persecuted both by the Poles and the Russian Bolsheviks.

But precisely in this time of greatest need, the avenues of escape to the West were virtually closed. The war interrupted the steady flow of immigrants. Shortly after the fighting ended, the United States and other western lands hastily adopted laws restricting immigration to a minimum. This policy was justified on the grounds that a large influx of poverty-stricken refugees would increase unemployment and depress wages. But the rise of a narrow chauvinistic nationalism had much to do with this legislation.

The tsarist tyranny was overthrown. Poland and Lithuania, reconstituted as independent nations, now held the bulk of the "Russian" Jews. About two million Jews remained in Russian territory. After a brief democratic interlude, they passed under the control of a Communist dictatorship which has endured until the present.

In 1919 a "White Russian" army attempted to overthrow the Bolsheviks. It failed in this undertaking; but in one respect it revived the glories of the old regime. The White Russians massacred more than a hundred thousand Ukrainian Jews. It is painful to recall that this expedition was supported by the United States and other allied nations.

The Communists, on the other hand, claimed to be dedicated to the equality of all men, and condemned anti-Semitism as counter-revolutionary. But their practical program was hardly philo-Semitic. For under the old order, the many restrictions on Jewish employment had forced a great proportion of Jews into peddling and petty trading. These unfortunates were now classified as ex-capitalists, and subjected to the degradations and disabilities visited upon the exploiters of labor.

Communism, moreover, was militantly anti-religious. Judaism was subjected to the same attack as other faiths. Its teachers and spokesmen were persecuted, its adherents penalized. Atheism was taught in the public schools; all sorts of restrictions hampered those who wished to provide religious instruction for their children. Only professed atheists were eligible for admission to the Communist Party, the new aristocracy. For a time there was a special "Jewish" section of the party, which displayed excessive zeal in repressing Jewish religious observance, like the medieval apostates in their day.

Zionism was outlawed and its advocates liquidated. It was not merely that Zionism was "imperialistic" and "capitalistic," since it had British support; the monolithic Communist state could not tolerate any loyalty except blind loyalty to itself. The use of Hebrew, whether for religious or secular purposes, was frowned upon. Yiddish, however, was recognized as an official language where the Jewish population was dense.

To offset the appeal of Palestine, the Soviet government cooperated in an effort to establish Jewish farm colonies in the Crimea (financed with funds provided by American Jews), and set aside an immense area in eastern Siberia (called Biro-Bijan) as the site of a proposed Jewish Soviet Republic. But despite much propaganda fanfare, Biro-Bijan never really got beyond the stage of talk.

Thus this large and once creative segment of the Jewish people was cut off from contact with fellow Jews, subjected to the regimentation of Soviet life, denied the free exercise of its religion, forbidden to express its nationalist aspirations. The fact that some of the Communist leaders were of Jewish birth was no comfort to loyal Jews: it simply meant that some of their oppressors were doubly hostile to them. It was small compensation that overt expression of anti-Semitism was now forbidden by law. For the Communist government itself was above this law, and did not hesitate to persecute Jews when the leaders found it expedient.

2. Palestine

In November, 1917, the British government issued the Balfour Declaration, officially endorsing the project of a Jewish National Home in Palestine. This action was no doubt called forth by a combination of motives. In part, it was an expression of gratitude to Dr. Chaim Weizmann, whose chemical researches had greatly aided the allied war effort, and who was already a commanding figure in world Zionism. In part, no doubt, it was aimed at winning the support of Jews in areas controlled by the Central Powers, whose defeat was already in sight. But there were also more generous considerations. Great Britain had repeatedly demonstrated its friendly interest in Jewish welfare. In those days of Wilsonian idealism, many people hoped to create a new world of justice and peace, in which age-old wrongs would be righted. The Balfour Declaration was cautiously drawn to make plain that the rights of non-Jews in Palestine and of Jews in other lands should not be prejudiced by the establishment of a Jewish state. Yet while the British government was publicizing this decision, its agents in the Near East were quietly making commitments to Arab leaders which seemed to be in conflict with the Balfour Declaration.

The proposal for a Zionist state was ratified by all the allied powers, including the United States. A "Jewish Legion" fought under Allenby against the Turks. After the war, the predominantly Arab portions of the Turkish Empire, including Palestine, were detached from Turkey for immediate or eventual independence. Those which were not yet deemed ready for self-government were temporarily mandated to western powers by the League of Nations. The mandate for Palestine was entrusted to Great Britain, and the Balfour Declaration was one of the terms of the mandate.

A tremendous expansion both of Zionist activity and Zionist spirit was bound to follow. The Jewish population of Palestine, which had declined during the war, began to grow rapidly. The spirit of the pioneers was more assured: an independent state was no longer a distant dream, but an achievable goal. The fighting was barely over and the land still desolate when the Hebrew University was founded in Jerusalem—a vivid testimony to the strength of the Jewish hope and its essentially spiritual character.

Jewish opposition to Zionism became less vehement. The endorsement of the movement by the British and American governments relieved the apprehension that Jewish nationalism would impair the civil rights of Jews in those countries. Even more decisive was the practical consideration: the western lands no longer offered refuge to multitudes of Jews desperately seeking to escape. Palestine alone could be a home to substantial numbers. Consequently, even those Jews who still vigorously rejected the theory of Jewish nationalism grew warmer in support of efforts to settle their brothers upon the ancestral soil.

3. United States

American Jewry felt the impact of World War I long before the United States entered the conflict. When the campaign on the eastern front brought disaster to the Polish Jews, their fellow Jews in this country soon recognized that they must provide help on a large scale. A body was established for Jewish War Relief, and large funds were raised. But it soon became evident that the plight of European Jewry was no temporary emergency. Jewish War Relief was transformed into a more permanent agency, the American Jewish Joint Distribution Committee. At this juncture, American Jewry came of age and assumed for the first time a commanding role in world Jewish affairs.

The Joint Distribution Committee has a unique place in Jewish history. It is perhaps the only project on which all American Jews have fully united. It has carried on relief activities on a wider scale, and has collected and expended larger sums than any Jewish philanthropic body. Indeed, there is little to compare with it in the entire history of humanitarian service. The work of the Joint has been administered by extraordinarily competent and devoted social workers, who wisely utilized, wherever possible, the existing community institutions of those whom they served. After the close of the war, the JDC carried on an extensive program of economic reconstruction, health services, and support for religious and cultural institutions among the Jews of eastern Europe; later it was to sustain the victims of Hitler. For two generations of European Jews, the word "Joint" has been a symbol of deliverance and hope.

An entirely new task faced American Jews when their country entered the war—to provide for the religious and social needs of Jews in the armed forces. During the Civil War Jews had obtained the right, against considerable opposition, to have their own chaplains. (Isaac M. Wise took a leading role in this struggle.) But after 1865, the military establishment of the United States was small, and relatively few Jews sought a career in the army or navy, so that no special provision could be made for them. During the skirmish with Mexico in 1917, chaplaincy service for Jewish troops on the border was provided by a single rabbi, through an arrangement between the War Department and the Central Conference of American Rabbis.

Now for the first time, vast numbers of citizens were to be in uniform. The Chaplains Corps had to be greatly enlarged and a great program of social and recreational service was to be set up in the training camps and overseas, financed and staffed on a voluntary basis. The Jews had to participate in all these efforts.

President Wilson was well informed about the Jewish scene, and knew that no American Jewish body was sufficiently inclusive and representative to meet the double need of providing chaplains and participating in the recreational program. At his request, a number of outstanding leaders, representing the various interests and viewpoints of American Jewry, came together and created the National Jewish Welfare Board, to deal with all matters involving Jews in the armed services.

Under the auspices of the Jewish Welfare Board, some twenty-six commissioned chaplains served with the American forces in this country and overseas. Most of them were from the Reform group; their services, however, were available to all Jews in uniform, and wherever possible

The Effects of the First World War 369

to non-Jews as well. All three divisions of American Judaism were represented on the committee which approved their qualifications for services; this committee also created a prayer book for military use, which included both the traditional prayers and selections from the *Union Prayerbook.*

The Jewish Welfare Board likewise set up recreation centers, and provided personnel to administer them. For this purpose it drew largely on the staffs of the YMHA's and Jewish Community Centers, which at this period were growing in numbers and effectiveness. Special arrangements were made from year to year to enable all the men in the armed forces to celebrate the Jewish holidays—especially, to participate in the Passover Seder (ceremonial meal).

With the close of the First World War and the return of the bulk of servicemen to civilian life, the work for which the Jewish Welfare Board was established shrank to a minimum. Jewish chaplains and other workers remained on duty only at a few key installations. While continuing to administer this small program, the Jewish Welfare Board now utilized its large and effective organization for another purpose. It became the national agency of the growing community center movement.

The American Jews realized more and more that they must concern themselves also with the political effects of the war. The issuance of the Balfour Declaration and the collapse of Russia meant that the fate of millions of Jews would have to be decided at the peace table. The American Jewish community, now large and prosperous, part of the nation that had become the leader of the democratic world, was obligated to work for the political as well as for the physical welfare of world Jewry.

But how were the American Jews to formulate and express their position on these issues? The Joint Distribution Committee, on the pattern of the Red Cross, had properly avoided any political involvement. The functi s of the Jewish Welfare Board were also sharply delimited. These were the only organizations that might reasonably claim to represent all American Jews. The most significant services in defense of Jewish rights had been performed by the American Jewish Committee. But this agency, despite its admirable record, represented a relatively small moneyed group, chiefly of German-Jewish extraction and Reform affiliation, and unanimously non-Zionist. The large masses of east European Jews were no longer inarticulate immigrants; more and more they were demanding a voice in the management of Jewish affairs.

Their sympathies were largely, if not predominantly, with the Zionist cause.

Almost from the outbreak of the war, proposals were heard for the creation of an American Jewish Congress, democratically elected, to deal with problems growing out of the conflict. These proposals touched off a long and bitter controversy in which the Zionist groups championed the Congress plan and the American Jewish Committee opposed it. A compromise was finally reached in 1916. The Committee agreed to participate in the Congress subject to several stipulations, the most important of which was that the Congress should not be a permanent body. After dealing with problems arising out of the peace, it was to disband. Some three hundred thousand persons took part in balloting for delegates; the national organizations were to be represented directly.

Before the Congress could meet, the United States was at war. The delegates elected in 1916 did not assemble until 1918, on the very eve of the Peace Conference. Despite all the prior wrangling, the participants in the American Jewish Congress worked together surprisingly well. They agreed on a statement of principles, and appointed a strong delegation to represent American Jewry at Versailles. Due in no small part to the arguments of this delegation, the allied leaders wrote into the treaties provisions to guarantee the rights of all minorities in the various countries of eastern Europe. That these clauses would prove ineffective could not yet be foreseen.

52.

The Last Glories of European Jewry

1. Germany

THE GERMAN-JEWISH COMMUNITY IN ITS LATER YEARS PRESENTS A maze of contradictions. Nowhere had Jews acquired so commanding a role in national culture as in the German lands. On this score, the Nazis were not wrong as to the facts, though they distorted their meaning. Jewish scientists, writers, musicians, artists, journalists, were among the chief contributors to the great German cultural tradition, which would have been in decline without them. For example, eleven of the thirty-eight Germans and three of the six Austrians who received a Nobel prize prior to 1933 were Jews or of Jewish extraction.

Yet, only the pathological imagination of the Nazi could see in this phenomenon the "Judaization" of German culture. There were some artists and writers whose work clearly reflected their Jewish origins and interests; but they were in the minority. Many of these creative spirits were remote from their Jewish background or indifferent to it. Not a few shared the anti-Semitism so deeply rooted in German life.

Intermarriage, baptism, and other assimilationist phenomena were common in Germany. But the situation was very different from that in Italy, where the Jewish group had also declined in numbers and vitality. Among the Italians anti-Jewish feeling was almost non-existent, and the process of assimilation was calm and gradual. In German lands, assimilationism had a certain convulsive quality, and Jewish self-hate took on sensational and at times almost majestic traits. It may be studied, for example, in Jakob Wassermann, the famous novelist, who felt himself in spirit deeply akin to the German people, yet hopelessly rejected by them; who bore his Jewish identity almost as an affliction, and bitterly resented the implication that the "oriental hordes" of east European Jewry had a claim on him. Yet, Wassermann was passionately devoted to the prophetic ideals of truth and humanity, and warred against the callousness of heart which our mechanistic civilization has generated. Several of the most beautiful characters in his novels are Jews. Wassermann was to end his days in lonely exile.

Even more complex was the case of Walther Rathenau, one of the most gifted and noble men who ever lived. This great engineer and industrialist was the prophet of a fairer kind of society and a freer kind of man than capitalism had produced or socialism proposed. His efficient mobilization of German raw materials in 1914 prevented the defeat of the Central Powers early in the war; and as foreign minister of the Weimar Republic he contributed greatly to the rehabilitation of Germany as member of the family of nations. But Rathenau had been deeply infected with the racist doctrines; and even after he realized that they were nonsensical, he was still emotionally under their spell. He identified his practical commercial talents with the Jewish side of his nature; his lofty idealism was the German aspect of his character! Rathenau had been offered a diplomatic career in pre-war days on condition that he be baptized; he refused, not out of Jewish loyalty, but because he would not assent to an unjust and prejudiced policy. In his later years he began to draw somewhat closer to the Jewish people and to Judaism; but the process never was completed. A bullet from the pistol of a blonde, blue eyed Nordic, of the type he had always admired, ended his career.

Yet the same country which saw such sensational examples of Jewish disloyalty was also the seat of an incomparable positive Jewish activity. The religious, cultural, and philanthropic institutions of German Jewry were models. The rebirth of Jewish spiritual vitality described in a previous chapter continued in the post-war period with even greater distinction, even though economic depression made it doubly hard to maintain institutions and to publish books and periodicals. Gifted artists created new forms of synagogue architecture and liturgical music. The intellectual standards of the rabbinate were high, the scholarly level of the seminaries on a par with the brightest days of Geiger and

The Last Glories of European Jewry 373

Frankel. German Orthodoxy produced sturdy champions, who played a leading role in the Agudath Israel; and the German Liberals were among the vigorous spirits who founded the World Union for Progressive Judaism.

Two religious thinkers, in particular, exercised a great influence. Martin Buber had risen to prominence even before the First World War. In contrast to Hermann Cohen, the champion of rationalism, Buber was the spokesman of the mystical spirit.

His grandfather, Salomon Buber of Lemberg, had been a wealthy lumber merchant, who devoted his leisure to rabbinic scholarship. His outlook was that of the Galician haskalah. Martin Buber, however, outgrew his grandfather's influence at an early age, and was attracted to the Chasidim, among whom he actually lived for a time. Among his earliest publications are collections of the sayings and tales of the great Chasidic masters, retold in magnificent German. Buber did not attempt to copy the externals of Chasidism—he is the most sophisticated of moderns—but his spirit was profoundly influenced by the Chasidic way of life.

Buber insists that Judaism is not merely to be understood; a *concept* of God is not adequate for religion. Judaism must be experienced directly; it is the confrontation of God by the individual soul. Religion is not talk about God; it is the saying of "Thou" to God.

As Buber was deeply touched by the mystic piety of the Chasidim, he was also impressed by their relationship to one another and to their rebbe. They were not parts of a mechanically organized system but members of one family. In this relationship Buber found the hint for the establishment of a true society. In our ordinary dealings with others, we regard them as objects. We deal with them (even when we want to help) much as we deal with any mechanical tool or instrument. We must learn to view each personality, not as an "it," but as a "thou."

The same kind of thinking governs Buber's concept of the Jewish people. They are not merely the adherents of a certain doctrine, but the heirs of a continuing experience which is stamped on their very flesh and blood. (Here Buber's language must not be taken too literally; he is not a racist.) The loyal Jew is one who relives, not only intellectually, but with every fiber of his being, the experience of the Jewish people. Buber became an active but unconventional Zionist; to him Zionism was not just a political program but a means of spiritual rebirth.

Buber, for many years a professor at the University of Frankfort, is the one contemporary Jewish religious thinker who has exerted a marked influence on Christian theology. First on the Continent, later in England and America, Protestant thought has moved away from liberalism and rationalism to a more conservative, "existentialist" approach. Buber's little book *I and Thou* has been much read by Christians, and seems to have contributed to this development.

In 1913 Franz Rosenzweig, a young Jew from the city of Cassel, decided to be baptized. The brilliant son of a wealthy, cultured family, he had received a sketchy and half-hearted Jewish training. Convinced by his studies in philosophy that a religious commitment is indispensable, he prepared to adopt the Christian faith so closely bound up with German culture. But he proposed to enter the church through Judaism, and went to Berlin to spend the High Holy Days in a small synagogue of east European Jews. There he underwent a decisive experience: he concluded that he could find his spiritual home within Judaism. He began to work intensively with Cohen and others; during the World War he continued his studies even while serving as an officer on the eastern front. The postal cards he wrote to his mother were later collected to form the first part of the *Star of Redemption,* the difficult and profound philosophic work which he completed after his return.

The book shows the influence of Søren Kierkegaard and other nineteenth-century Christian thinkers. It turns away from the intellectualism of idealistic philosophy to the "existential" problems of the living and suffering individual. The highest truth, Rosenzweig holds, is not discovered by academic reflection; it is proved true by living it. God is not to be argued about; He must be made manifest as the creative and redemptive power in the life of the individual. Judaism, which proclaimed this truth, is the Star of Redemption. But from the star emanate the rays of Christianity, by which the light is made manifest to the still pagan world. (This view reminds us of Samuel Hirsch, the exponent of that Hegelianism which Rosenzweig opposed.)

Rosenzweig was not Orthodox. He held, in accordance with his basic doctrine, that one should observe those customs and ceremonies which he could personally adopt and make his own; but in fact, the Rosenzweig home was completely traditional. Rosenzweig's most notable contribution, however, was not his personal philosophy, but the institution he created—the Free Jewish House of Study in Frankfort. It was a unique school of adult education. In a fresh and unacademic way,

Rosenzweig and his associates began to study and teach the classic literature of Judaism, and to interpret problems of the present from the Jewish viewpoint. This movement was particularly effective in winning back to Judaism many marginal Jews who started from a situation similar to that of Rosenzweig.

A fruitful career was suddenly cut short by a mysterious illness which in about a year completely paralyzed the brilliant young penitent, robbing him even of speech. But he confounded medical science by living on for seven years, communicating with the world by rudimentary signals which he and his devoted wife were able to work out. He and Buber began a new translation of the Bible into German, designed to convey the sense and flavor of the original Hebrew more fully. He painfully dictated letters and articles; and his silent influence was still exerted to an amazing degree. As a personality he contributed perhaps more than any other to the magnificent efflorescence of German Judaism in the decades before Adolf Hitler destroyed it.

2. The East

It was carefully specified in the peace treaties that the newly independent nations should accord full rights to the various minorities they included. For almost none of these nations was a homogeneous cultural and linguistic unit. Poland, for example, included among its citizens Polish-speaking Catholics, Ruthenians who spoke a Russian dialect and belonged to the Orthodox church, German-speaking Lutherans, and Jews whose usual language was Yiddish. Each of these groups, according to the program set forth in the treaties, was to be recognized as a legitimate national grouping within the larger framework of the state. Each minority would have its representatives in the Parliament, and its own state-supported schools and community institutions. Such an arrangement was not entirely new. It had been practiced to some extent in the old Austro-Hungarian Empire, and an analogy may be found in the Canadian province of Quebec, which maintains separate school systems for French Catholics and English-speaking Protestants. The significant departure, however, was the insistence by the framers of the peace treaties that equal rights and privileges should be accorded to *all* the minorities.

In practice, the only nation that lived up to its commitments in these matters was Czechoslovakia. Oddly enough, the Jews in this country had been chiefly German-speaking, and were closer culturally to the German minority than to the Czech majority. Though this fact caused some minor resentments, the Jews enjoyed full equality in the Czecho-slovakia of Masaryk and Beneš. Prague, famous as a center of Jewish life and learning in the ghetto period, continued this honorable tradition until the country was swallowed up, first by the Nazis, later by the Communists. Among the notable figures of Prague Jewry were two remarkable novelists, Max Brod and his friend, Franz Kafka. Brod's literary career was marked by a steady progress toward a positive Jewish commitment; one of his best-known novels deals with David Reubeni. Kafka, a sensitive and frustrated personality, achieved little recognition during his short life, but has now become one of the most famous and influential figures in world literature. His enigmatic, dream-like novels and stories have been the subject of much discussion; among the issues still debated is their inner relationship to Judaism.

Elsewhere in eastern Europe, Jewish life between the two world wars was gloomy and filled with forebodings of worse things to come. Though the League of Nations had a permanent commission to see that minority rights were respected, it proved unable to secure compliance with the treaty obligations. Jews found themselves the objects of economic, educational, vocational, and political discrimination by the governments themselves; and when outbreaks of anti-Semitic violence occurred, the Jews received little protection, and might even be arrested and condemned as the inciters of disorder. Though the "Joint" expended millions of dollars for the economic rehabilitation of the Jews of Poland, Rumania, and other countries, the results were never really encouraging, and in the end proved completely futile. Talmudic and Chasidic orthodoxy, scholarship, and creative writing in Yiddish and Hebrew, socialist effort and Zionist activity were still vigorous within the several divisions of Jewry; but nothing radically new could be expected of a community whose chief aim was flight. The growth of the Jewish population in Palestine was due largely to the migration of Jews from eastern Europe. Their number would have been far greater had it not been for the British restrictions on the entrance of Jews into Palestine, and for the lack of funds to assist immigration.

53.

Progress in Palestine

THE HISTORY OF PALESTINE BETWEEN THE BALFOUR DECLARATION
and the establishment of the State of Israel involves complicated economic, sociological, and political factors. We shall note here only developments that were significant for the inner life of Palestinian Jewry.

We begin with the people themselves. Palestine had a pre-Zionist
population drawn from almost every quarter of the globe. Jews tended
to form little communities based on country of origin, and to perpetu-
ate their cultural and religious differences. The varying customs and
traditional melodies of Persian, Bokharan, Iraqi (Babylonian) and
Yemenite Jews, as well as the more familiar divisions of S'fardim and
Ashk'nazim, could all be studied in the little synagogues of Jerusalem's
"Old City." Karaite and Chasidic circles were also to be found there.
Many east European Jews, supported by charity, continued to live their
old lives in y'shivos and other institutions, speaking Yiddish and wearing the old Polish garb.

Agricultural colonies, though begun in the 1880's, multiplied but
slowly. In some cases, Jewish landowners operated their farms with
Arab labor. A handful of idealists from Russia, who dedicated themselves to actual work on the soil, struggled for many years against heavy
odds. This newer type of pioneer (chalutz) became less exceptional
during the early decades of the twentieth century; after 1918, such men
and women transformed both the outward appearance of the country
and its inner spirit.

A minority of the newcomers were Orthodox. Most of them were committed to secular Zionism and to Socialism. Both their Socialism and their nationalism were pervaded by intense and sacrificial faith, which was certainly spiritual, though not formally religious. These were the workers who transformed the malarial swamps of the Valley of Jezreel into the most productive farmland of the country, who cleared and irrigated stony wastes, and planted millions of trees on eroded hillsides. Many of them died as martyrs for the redemption of the land.

Their sacrifice was the more notable because they were not all penniless proletarians, with no alternative but hard labor. A large proportion of them were intellectuals who had arrived at two basic convictions. First, that the inner and outer problems of Jewish life could be solved only through national rebirth. Second, that this rebirth and all its blessings could be brought about only through a radical change in the occupational pattern of Jews. Their position as middlemen (whether merchant princes or peddlers made no difference) was basically unsound. Physical labor, above all on the soil, production for use instead of distribution for profit—these would heal both the land and the soul of the people. The socialism of the chalutzim was no mere economic theory; it had profound moral and even mystical implications.

The great apostle of this doctrine, Aaron David Gordon, was certainly influenced by Tolstoy even more than by Marx. Though remote from the customary religious traditions of Judaism, he was always preoccupied with spiritual values, to be expressed through a better society. Gordon was one of the founders of Degania (established in 1909), the first of the collective colonies which became more and more numerous after 1918.

These collectives (*k'vutzot* or *kibbutzim*) are established on land of the Jewish National Fund, with their initial equipment provided by the Palestine Foundation Fund. Each colony is an independent, democratically governed entity. Membership is voluntary; a member may withdraw at any time, or he may be asked to leave if the others feel that he is not adapted to community living. Aside from personal belongings, everything is owned jointly. If a member takes a job outside the farm, his earnings are paid into the community treasury. Meals are cooked in one kitchen and served in a community dining room. Children are cared for in a community nursery, and spend only leisure hours with their parents. The women not needed in the kitchen or nursery are thus available for farm work. Many of the collectives supplement agriculture by establishing factories and other enterprises. As they prosper, they are able to provide greater comfort for their members, advanced education for the more talented children, even financial assistance to families of members still left in Europe. But the collective principle remains in force; members have little personal privacy, and are constantly subject to social discipline.

In other settlements, the collective principle is applied less vigorously. A familiar form is the *moshav*, in which each farmer cultivates his own plot, but machinery is owned jointly and produce is marketed by a cooperative. These ventures, too, have been supported by the Jewish National Fund and the Palestine Foundation Fund. Of course, many persons came to the country with some capital of their own to invest in farm property.

By 1920, the various labor groups had formed the *Histadrut HaOvedim* or General Labor Federation, which soon became a tremendous power in the land. This one big union includes industrial, agricultural, and even white collar workers. It has established cooperative marketing agencies, a complete health insurance system, homes for the care of the aged and other dependents, and educational institutions. Its membership included workers of the Orthodox group who soon established kibbutzim of their own. Because of its avowed Zionist aims, the Histadrut did not accept Arab members, but it worked to improve relationships with the Arabs and to raise the labor standards of the latter. It soon gained control of the *HaShomer*, an old association for self-defense, out of which *Haganah*—a better organized semi-military body—later developed.

Many groups remained outside the growing Labor Party. They included the members of the Agudath Israel, who wished to build a purely religious non-Zionist settlement; the more conservative elements of the Mizrachi party; the relatively small number of General Zionists, who were opposed to Socialism—and the Revisionists. This last group was headed by Vladimir Jabotinsky, an accomplished linguist and orator and a dynamic personality, who had taken the initiative in forming the Jewish Legion during World War I. The chief feature of his policy was its aggressive and militant quality. He opposed any compromise with the Arabs who were steadily becoming more hostile; and he urged an intransigent attitude in dealing with the British who were yielding more and more to Arab demands.

At the opposite pole from the swaggering Revisionists was a little group which sought to create peace and brotherhood with the Arabs through the establishment of a bi-national state in Palestine. Judah Leon Magnes—who began his career as an American Reform Rabbi and was for many years Chancellor of the Hebrew University—was the dedicated spokesman of this position, which was supported by Martin Buber and other choice spirits. But British policy tended to discourage the moderate Arabs who might have been drawn into such an undertaking, and both Jewish and Arab nationalism became more and more inflammatory.

Meantime, the World Zionist movement was growing from day to day. All the parties we have mentioned (and their innumerable subdivisions) were represented in the Diaspora and had their spokesmen in the Zionist Congresses. Outside Palestine, the General Zionists were by far the most numerous group. Most of the parties agreed in attempting to win the friendship of the Arabs, and in cooperating with the mandatory power. Because of their opposition to these policies, the Revisionists were forced out of the Zionist Organization in 1935.

By 1929 the former opponents of Zionism in the West had become convinced that their old attitude must be modified. The condition of east European Jewry was worse than ever. The anti-Jewish policies of the Polish government and the hostility of the people had largely nullified the effect of millions spent by the Joint Distribution Committee for economic rehabilitation. The Jewish agricultural colonies established by the Soviet government with funds provided by Julius Rosenwald were proving an experiment of dubious value. Only a negligible number could immigrate to the free countries. Palestine was the one hopeful area for Jewish settlement.

Louis Marshall became the spokesman of wealthy Jews in the United States, Great Britain, and Germany, who had always held aloof from Zionism. He was extraordinarily qualified for this purpose, not merely as a successful lawyer and man of affairs, but because of his unique personal qualities. American born, reared in the Reform tradition, he had acquired a broad and inclusive approach to Jewish life. He had been for many years the lay head of the Conservative Jewish Theological Seminary. As president of the American Jewish Committee, he had defended Jewish rights with bold forcefulness. He had even learned Yiddish, so that he might better understand the thought and outlook of the masses.

Mr. Marshall entered into negotiations with Dr. Weizmann, the head of the World Zionist Organization, and in the summer of 1929 the enlarged Jewish Agency for Palestine was created. It was to include a number of non-Zionists along with the leaders of the World Zionist Organization. Without committing themselves to the nationalist philosophy, the non-Zionists were thus to have a share in the practical work of financing and administering the settlement of Jews in Palestine. No doubt some of them also hoped to influence the Palestinian economy along more conservative lines. The non-Zionists did not succeed in mitigating either the Zionist or the socialist ardor of the settlers they were assisting. Nevertheless, they remained in the Jewish Agency, especially since the Hitler persecution soon made ideological discussion pointless.

The relationship of Palestine Jewry to the Arab world and to Great Britain became ever more tense. The mandate, it should be remembered, envisioned the establishment of a Jewish National Home. The Arab leaders, moreover, had approved this proposal when the peace treaties were signed. But advancing Palestinian Jewry came into conflict with the growing spirit of nationalism among the Arabs. The Arab population of Palestine was also increasing. Improved sanitary and medical services, introduced by the Jews, were lowering the death rate; moreover, many Arabs entered Palestine from neighboring countries, attracted by better wages and working conditions. A number of the leading Arabs favored cooperation with the Jews; but there were many champions of opposition and violence. British officialdom generally favored the latter, and worked steadily to whittle down the promises of the Balfour Declaration.

The thinly settled territory east of the Jordan, which had been part of Palestine through most of recorded history, was detached by a British administrative decision, and built into a new Arab state, from which Jewish settlers were barred. Haj Amin Al-Husseini, an unscrupulous adventurer, was made Grand Mufti of Jerusalem through British support, after the Arabs themselves had rejected him at the polls. His official religious position made it easier for him to launch a policy of terror, directed in part against the Jews but even more against his opponents among the Arabs of Palestine.

There were serious outbreaks against the Jews in 1921, and worse ones in 1929, just after the formation of the Jewish Agency; British efforts to control the rioting were half-hearted. Repeated inquiries and investigations by British-appointed commissions invariably proposed the curtailment of Jewish rights in the land. This process culminated in the "White Paper" of 1939, which in effect repudiated the Balfour Declaration, and was denounced by the Mandates Commission of the League of Nations.

Though the British failed to protect the Jews of Palestine against Arab violence, they outlawed Haganah, the Jewish self-defense organization. Nevertheless it became an increasingly effective military force. To the eternal credit of the Palestinian Jews, it is to be recorded that through the chronic terror of the 1930's they consistently followed the program of self-restraint (*havlagah*): they used their weapons only for self-defense, avoiding both aggression and retaliation.

Despite all their problems of rehabilitating the soil, settling immigrants, and protecting themselves against Arab enemies and British "defenders," they devoted themselves also to cultural advancement. Hebrew became in every sense a living language. Nurseries and kindergartens were set up so that the children of newcomers would promptly learn to speak the national tongue. Newspapers and magazines flourished, and an extraordinary number of books were published, both original works and translations from many languages. The Hebrew University quickly became an outstanding center of learning, and several other institutions for technical education and research grew in size and accomplishment. The theater and other arts were vigorous and lively.

In formal religion, however, there was little advance. A highly static orthodoxy was its only expression. The pioneers, heirs of the most advanced western culture, conditioned by their Marxian training to view all religion with suspicion, were confirmed in their anti-clerical prejudices by the spokesmen of a rigid, medieval dogmatism. The celebration of the festivals continued, but in a new vein. Much of the traditional religious spirit disappeared, and the festivals acquired more of a folk-character.

The situation was complicated by a religio-legal problem. The Turkish government had never established a general law concerning marriage, divorce, and inheritance. In these matters, its citizens were subject to the religious law of the group to which they belonged. For Jews, such questions were decided according to Talmudic law and administered by the chief rabbinate. The British authorities inherited and continued this system; they could hardly have done anything else. But the result was to confer substantial power on a group of men who had little understanding or sympathy for the majority of those with whom they had to deal. The antagonism between the "religious" forces and the secularists was thus intensified.

From 1921 to 1935, Chief Rabbi Abraham Isaac Kook stood at the head of the Orthodox community. An inspiring personality and a profound religious thinker, he sought to interpret some of the insights of the Cabala in terms relevant to modern life. Rabbi Kook had a cer-

54.

American Judaism, 1918-1932

THE JEWS OF THE UNITED STATES EMERGED FROM WORLD WAR I AS the leaders of all Jewry. They had numbers, wealth, and political influence, and they rapidly acquired a sense of their own responsibilities.

But for several decades, this sense of obligation was manifested chiefly in fund-raising and organizational activity. There was not much spiritual progress. The war boom which affected the entire American economy was felt especially by the Jews, so largely engaged in commercial enterprises. After the brief depression of the early twenties, the new expansion that culminated in 1929 caught up all Americans, the Jews with them, in an orgy of materialistic optimism.

The same people who built lavish homes and country clubs also embarked on public spirited enterprises. Magnificent synagogues, community centers, and philanthropic institutions were built and heavily mortgaged. The depression of the thirties was to leave many of these institutions crippled by debt.

A number of new congregations were established, especially in the growing suburban areas. But more rapid progress was made by the Jewish center movement. It still retained something of the philanthropic character that had led the wealthy to assist the early YMHA's, but more and more the center was becoming a genuine community agency. It provided a neutral meeting ground for Jews of varying religious or non-religious viewpoints, who—especially in the light of the war experiences and the increase of anti-Semitism—were recognizing more and more the need of cooperation. Few activities of the center had a positive Jewish character. Its chief function was to provide facilities for athletics, dances, socials, and club activities. (Some of the clubs had specifically Jewish interests.) There was also a "cultural" aspect to the center program: music, dramatics, debating, and classes in Hebrew, Yiddish, literature, and current events. Most centers had a lecture forum which dealt chiefly with general issues of current interest; one or two evenings would be devoted to Jewish themes. Chanuko and Purim entertainments were generally provided; on Sabbaths and festivals the center was closed. A summer camp for children was often conducted.

In general, the center helped foster Jewish group loyalty, but rarely contributed much to the inner Jewish consciousness of those it served. Some of the center staff members, though able administrators and group leaders, were indifferent or even hostile to religious values. The relationship of the center to the synagogues often proved a difficult and delicate problem. The center which enlarged its Jewish program might be criticized for competing with the synagogue; if it omitted such features, it might be accused of being un-Jewish and secular.

A number of congregations tried to meet this difficulty by establishing "synagogue centers," in which the athletic, recreational, and general cultural activities of the center were combined with the religious program of the synagogue. Such synagogue centers are found in all three groups of American Jewry, though chiefly in the Conservative wing. They have hardly achieved their basic aim. All the centers, whether or not under synagogue auspices, have served a useful purpose by providing necessary and welcome facilities. But the presence of a gymnasium and swimming pool in the same plant as the synagogue sanctuary has not proved an inducement to worship. The National Jewish Welfare Board greatly extended its Jewish Center Division during these decades, providing personnel, advice, and program materials for existing centers, and stimulating the establishment of centers in many new communities.

The upheavals of the war and post-war period caused an increase of anti-Semitism in the United States. Not directly related to this was the problem of discrimination against Jews in colleges, universities, and professional schools which appeared at this time. For now Jews were seeking higher education and professional training in considerable numbers; and since Jewish population was concentrated in the large eastern cities, the eastern colleges and universities in particular had a sizable increase in the number of applications from Jews. When they began to set quotas for Jewish students, their example was widely followed throughout the country. Such restrictions were not practiced in state and municipal colleges; some of the institutions directly under church control were more generous in their treatment both of Jewish students and Jewish instructors than many "non-sectarian" universities.

The increase in anti-Jewish activity at home and the continuing problems of Jews in other countries demanded more intensive effort by the agencies for self-defense. Up to this point the American Jewish Committee had done most of the political and juridical work; the Anti-Defamation League of B'nai B'rith—as its name suggested—was largely concerned with correcting or preventing misrepresentation or caricature of the Jew in the press, and on the stage and screen. The more militant forces, strongly Zionist in spirit, which had demanded the calling of the American Jewish Congress, still felt the need of an agency of their own. In 1922 the Congress, which had ceased to exist in accordance with the previous agreement, was reorganized. No longer the representative body of all American Israel, it was now the defense agency of the Zionist groups.

Succeeding decades have witnessed a complicated and often badly-confused situation. The steady rise of anti-Semitism in the United States compelled American Jews to more vigorous action to protect themselves and their brothers in other lands. Both self-interest and loyalty led them to raise large sums for defense. This defense effort was not entirely negative. The twentieth century had seen the rise of extensive interfaith activity, aimed at the reduction of religious and racial prejudices and the increase of good will among all groups. The spread of anti-Semitism drew the best elements of the Christian community into such efforts.

The trouble arose out of the question: Who was to represent the Jews in all these undertakings? Though the three large agencies were doing most of the work in this field, many other groups were also involved. Competition and duplication were inevitable. On several occasions there was public controversy within the American Jewish community as to the best method of dealing with some danger. These problems have not been overcome to the present. Not only have they delayed progress toward American Jewish unity; because of the competitive situation, the question of self-defense has been overstressed to the detriment of the more positive values in Jewish life.

Jews in the larger cities had organized federations of their charitable agencies early in the twentieth century, to simplify fund-raising and conduct philanthropic affairs more effectively. These Jewish federations served as a model for the organization in most American cities of a "Community Chest," to finance all local charities—Catholic, Protestant, Jewish, and non-sectarian. The Community Chest movement spread rapidly between the two world wars, and the Jewish philanthropic agencies cooperated wholeheartedly in supporting this trend.

But the Jews were called on to assist many causes which could not be included in Community Chests—overseas relief, Palestine, and the maintenance of many national Jewish institutions and agencies. There was a natural tendency to consolidate these efforts, and so Jewish welfare funds were created for the support of all causes which were not served by the local Community Chest.

The vast New York Jewish community, too big and shapeless for effective organization, was the exception to these trends. New York City has never had a Community Chest, nor has New York Jewry a welfare fund. It has indeed a great Federation of Jewish Philanthropies which currently maintains 116 admirable institutions; but there are dozens of other Jewish philanthropic and health agencies which have never joined "Federation."

Meantime, Zionist sentiment and activity were steadily growing. Hadassah, the women's Zionist body founded in 1912 by Henrietta Szold (the gifted daughter of the Baltimore Rabbi), had become one of the most vital of Jewish women's organizations. Its monumental work for public health and child welfare in Palestine attracted to its membership many women who were not committed to the nationalist idea; yet Hadassah is likewise the official women's section of the Zionist Organization of America.

The Jewish National Fund and the Palestine Foundation Fund united for fund-raising purposes to form the United Palestine Appeal. This body engaged in many communities in a struggle with the Joint Distribution Committee over the apportionment of funds raised for overseas needs. The supporters of the JDC, which had been receiving the largest part of the sums collected, pointed to the far broader area and the larger number of persons served by the "Joint," and deprecated the use of community funds for "political" purposes. The Zionists pressed for a larger share because their work was not merely palliative but constructive. Gradually, the pressure of the American Jewish community brought the two causes together, first in combined local drives (especially where there was a welfare fund), and ultimately (1939) in the United Jewish Appeal.

With the establishment of the enlarged Jewish Agency under the aegis of the greatly respected Louis Marshall, anti-Zionist sentiment gradually waned. But it was only in 1935 that the Central Conference of American Rabbis (followed in 1937 by the Union of American Hebrew Congregations) repealed a long-standing anti-Zionist resolution. Both bodies henceforth took a neutral position on the question.

All these developments—the community center movement, the extension of defense work, the advance of Zionism, the expanded philanthropic programs professionally administered, and the emergence of a large-scale fund-raising as a regular department of Jewish life—imparted an increasingly secular tone to the American Jewish scene. A body of Jewish professional workers grew up, well trained for their specialized tasks, but often with little Jewish knowledge and sometimes lacking in sympathy for the inner values of Jewish life. It was generally assumed that the synagogues were obligated to provide man-power and moral support for all community enterprises; but interest in the synagogue and its maintenance was regarded as a matter of individual conscience or inclination.

The new undertakings drew heavily upon the resources of American Jewish lay leadership. Even those who were personally loyal to their religion were inclined to devote more time and energy, and to contribute more substantially to causes that seemed most urgent and inclusive. But there was now a considerable number of prosperous Jews so affected by the materialism of the times and so far gone in assimilation that they were no longer interested in Judaism for themselves. They might lend their money and talents to fight anti-Semitism, or to maintain charitable agencies that would protect the good name of Jewry; their Jewishness was (in both senses of the term) disinterested. Thus it happened that in some large cities, important institutions were directed by wealthy assimilationists and staffed by professionals with left-wing sympathies; positive Jewish values—for example, the religious training of children in the care of these agencies—were neglected. Nevertheless, several important religious accomplishments date from this period.

The Jewish Institute of Religion was founded in 1922 by Dr. Stephen S. Wise, the best-known and perhaps most controversial personality on the American Jewish scene. The son of a Hungarian-born Reform Rabbi, Wise had been privately ordained. His superb oratory quickly won him fame and distinction. He refused to accept a call to Temple Emanu-El of New York unless he could be assured of absolute freedom to discuss any and all topics from the pulpit, an assurance that was not given. Shortly thereafter (1906) he established the Free Synagogue, and for several decades drew vast crowds to his Sunday morning services in Carnegie Hall. He was both admired and condemned for his forthright championship of labor in some of the great industrial conflicts and for his direct involvement in the struggle against the corruption of New York's Tammany Hall. He was a fiery Zionist, a leader in the movement for the American Jewish Congress, and president of the reorganized Congress.

Though anything but a traditionalist, Wise was critical of what he considered the separatist and sectarian tendencies of the Reform movement. The Seminary he proposed to create was to stress Jewish unity. Like the Berlin Hochschule, it would not be committed officially to the Reform viewpoint, but would train men also for the Conservative and Orthodox pulpits. And in fact, a minority of the graduates of the Institute are serving as Conservative and Orthodox rabbis.

Dr. Wise clearly wanted to prepare students for the Liberal rabbinate in a warmly Zionist atmosphere. By this time the College in Cincinnati had already graduated many ardent Zionists, but the institution itself, as represented by President Kaufmann Kohler and most of its faculty, was still unsympathetic to the nationalist philosophy.

Most of the graduates of the Jewish Institute of Religion (the first ordination was in 1926) joined the Central Conference of American Rabbis, and have played an honorable role in the Reform rabbinate. The existence of the Institute must also have been a stimulus to activity and progress in the Cincinnati seminary. But obviously, the two institutions and their graduates were bound to be in competition, with results that were frequently troublesome. Repeated efforts were made to merge the two seminaries, but they did not bear fruit until many years later.

The year 1924 saw the start of another constructive undertaking— the Hillel Foundation. American Jewry had been slow to make provision for the Jewish needs of college students. The Menorah Society was founded at Harvard in the early nineties, and gradually grew into the Intercollegiate Menorah Association; its interests were chiefly intellectual and esthetic, and it was committed to no positive position on either Jewish religion or Jewish nationalism. Nor was it equipped to supply adult leadership for its various chapters. Its chief accomplishment was the publication of the *Menorah Journal,* a periodical of first-rate literary standards. But it had little effective impact on the average undergraduate. In a good many colleges, Zionist student groups were formed, but by their nature they could only reach a limited segment.

The Hillel Foundation was inspired by a Christian professor at the University of Illinois, Edward Chauncey Baldwin. He was appalled at the situation of several thousand Jewish students in the university, most of whom had neither knowledge in or interest concerning their Jewish background. Some of them even concealed or denied their Jewish origin. This situation Baldwin rightly ascribed to neglect by the organized Jewish community. He turned to Benjamin Frankel, a rabbinical student who was part-time minister to the little congregation in Urbana, and urged some activity comparable to that provided by the Newman Clubs and the Wesley Foundations. Upon graduating from the Hebrew Union College, Frankel persuaded the B'nai B'rith to sponsor the undertaking. The Hillel Foundation established at the University of Illinois was so successful that the program was extended to other universities, and soon Hillel was a national institution.

The Hillel program is one of inclusive Jewish activity under full-time professional (usually rabbinical) direction. It provides religious services, both traditional and Reform, classes and discussion groups, a variety of social functions, special interest projects such as dramatics, and personal counseling. It is an old story that religious loyalties often weaken or break under the impact of college experience; Hillel, like the parallel Protestant and Catholic agencies, has been able to counteract this tendency in considerable degree. The training it provides has equipped many young people for leadership in their own Jewish communities after graduation. In addition, Hillel has frequently raised the status of the Jewish group on the campus, which often suffered in the past because it had no voice, and because of the negative attitudes of many Jewish students. The proposal to establish a Hillel Foundation in a particular college or university has sometimes been opposed at the start by Jewish students (and oddly enough, by Jewish fraternities) on the ground that it would segregate and "ghettoize" them. In practice, the effect has been just the opposite.

Today, Hillel has over seventy foundations with full-time directors, and many more counselorships at colleges with smaller Jewish enrollment. The sponsorship of this undertaking, incidentally, gave new life to the B'nai B'rith.

Another achievement of the period seemed at the time to be of minor importance—the foundation of the Synagogue Council of America. Dr. Abram Simon had been serving as president of the Central Conference of American Rabbis; he brought together representatives of the congregational and rabbinical bodies of Orthodox, Conservative, and Reform Judaism, and persuaded them to create this rather loose federation. The objects were to stress the religious interpretation of Jewish life and to speak for a united Judaism about issues on which all groups agreed. The undertaking was plainly hazardous. Not only were there important differences of belief and practice between the groups, but long-standing suspicions and antagonisms had to be overcome. The constitution of the Council, therefore, gave unlimited veto power to each of the six constituents. Nevertheless, it was a hopeful thing that these divergent religious groups should enter into a formal agreement. Through the years they have been able to cooperate on many projects. In particular, the Synagogue Council has been an effective means of presenting a united Jewish position on many questions before the Gentile world.

55.

The Greatest Tragedy

THE EVENTS WE MUST NOW CONSIDER CERTAINLY CONSTITUTE THE greatest disaster that ever befell the Jewish people. But they were also a spiritual tragedy for mankind—perhaps the worst moral failure in the history of humanity.

Jew-hatred had been endemic in German lands since the Crusades. After the First World War, a proud and prosperous nation found itself humiliated and impoverished, and therefore needed a scapegoat all the more. Rising anti-Semitism fed on the fact that a few Jews achieved high office in the Weimar Republic. These resentments were carefully cultivated by the great industrialists, who saw in anti-Semitic nationalism a weapon against the power of organized labor, as well as against the growing trend toward Communism.

Thus, the chief ingredients of National Socialism—chauvinism, economic reaction, and racist anti-Semitism—were all well developed before Adolf Hitler appeared on the scene. And yet his movement was something new; a deliberate and radical repudiation of religion, morality, and humanity. It released and glorified the savagery within man. It equipped the modern barbarian with all the instruments of an advanced technical civilization, so that tyranny became far more efficient, and destruction infinitely greater and more horrible.

This barbarism was imposed by force upon the very agencies of civilization. Academic freedom and intellectual honesty were outlawed from the once great German universities. Objective science was rejected as "Jewish," and professors and students alike had to subscribe to the

393

racist doctrine. Legal decisions were no longer rendered in accordance with precedent nor did evidence have to be weighed seriously; verdicts were determined in advance by the political bosses. The press, the radio, the schools, the youth organizations, were coordinated for propaganda purposes, and no dissenting voice was tolerated. The churches were ordered to join the chorus, and most of them did so. But here the success of the Nazis was incomplete. The only overt opposition to Hitler came from religious leaders, some of whom suffered severe persecution for their outspokenness.

Three groups in particular were singled out as victims. The rights of women were severely curtailed. No longer were they to have careers of their own. They were to be household drudges, and to bear soldiers for the state. The labor unions were destroyed, and their leaders liquidated. But overshadowing all else was the relentlessly insane attack on the Jews.

Many people had thought that Hitler's anti-Semitism was merely a political device. He was seeking popularity by blaming all Germany's ills on the Jews; once he came into power, and with power assumed responsibility, he would adopt more moderate policies. The Nazis themselves fostered such thinking outside Germany, where they were already building a great propaganda machine.

In fact, Hitler meant all that he said on this subject. Anti-Semitism was absolutely basic to Nazism. For the Jews were a symbol of all that the Nazis sought to destroy—intelligence, morality, religion, peace. Perhaps the greatest offense of the Jews was that they had produced Jesus. Christianity, with its message of compassion and sacrifice, had grown out of Jewish roots. Now that the doctrine of a Universal Father was to be replaced by the worship of the Absolute State rooted in blood and soil, and the ethics of brotherhood and love by the Teutonic virtues of animal courage and utter ruthlessness, it was necessary to destroy the Jews physically, and to overwhelm them and their ideals with every kind of degradation and shame. And since it is not easy for a whole nation that has been trained (however imperfectly) in moral and religious principles to abandon them overnight, the Nazis projected upon the Jews those very vices which they themselves cultivated and cherished. The Jews, Hitler proclaimed, are dishonest, treacherous, lustful, and cruel.

The Nazi campaign against the Jews was carefully planned and proceeded with horrible logic, order, and thoroughness. There was a brief, triumphant outburst of violence; selected victims were tortured and put to death. Thereafter more systematic and deliberate methods were pursued. The Jews were deprived of citizenship, removed from public office, excluded from the professions, and barred from educational and cultural institutions. Their elimination from the commercial and industrial life of the nation was slower; Jewish executives and technicians were tolerated until they could be replaced by reasonably competent substitutes, lest the shaky economy of the country suffer still more. The medieval Jew-badge was introduced, Jewish-owned stores were marked as such, Jewish children still in the public schools were subjected to mental torment. The Nazis understood that their ultimate objective— the complete extermination of the Jews—could not be achieved unless they first crushed the morale of their victims, steadily and remorselessly extinguishing courage and hope.

German Jewry was stunned by the swift march of events. Those who saw the realities most clearly fled the country if they could find a haven; thousands brought to other lands the rich intellectual, spiritual, and practical resources the Nazis had despised. Many who had the opportunity to leave, however, decided to wait and see. Older folk especially were convinced that this was but a passing convulsion and that Germany would regain her sanity. Those who remained by choice or necessity closed ranks firmly.

At the behest of the rulers, the Jews established an over-all national body, to regulate their internal affairs and to represent them in dealings with the government. Parallel to this was an organization to provide relief for the growing numbers who were deprived of a livelihood and victimized by fines and confiscations. Both these agencies were headed by Rabbi Leo Baeck. A Liberal Rabbi and a non-Zionist, he rightly enjoyed the confidence of all groups in German Jewry. Despite repeated arrests and threats of death, he bore himself with unflagging courage and dignity, and his inspiring example helped to sustain the morale of his people. For the eve of Yom Kippur, 1936, Dr. Baeck composed a prayer to be read in all German synagogues, containing the sentence, "We bow our heads before God and stand erect before men." The Gestapo forbade it to be read; but the congregations knew the content of the prayer and were strengthened by its message.

Dr. Baeck received many offers of posts in England and America, but despite the dangers of his position, he declined all the invitations. As long, he said, as there are Jews left in Germany, it is my duty to remain with them and to give them what spiritual support I can provide.

For several years the Jews of Germany maintained their own theaters, concerts, and publications. Many who had previously been indifferent to Judaism or estranged from it now returned to their religious and cultural heritage. Courses in adult Jewish studies multiplied, and excellent handbooks of Jewish information appeared. Zionist sentiment, naturally, grew by leaps and bounds. Many of those once hostile to Jewish nationalism turned to it in desperation when they found themselves rejected by the Germany they had loved so well. But the *Jüdische Rundschau*, organ of the German Zionists, spoke for all parties in its famous editorial headed, "Wear it with pride—the yellow badge!"

This regrouping of Jewish forces was, however, only a temporary episode. Time was running out. A minor Nazi official in Paris was murdered by a hysterical young Jew—an incident in which the Germans themselves may have connived. This was the signal for a nation-wide orgy of destruction, in which nearly all the synagogues of Germany were burned, and Torah scrolls trampled in the streets (November 9-10, 1938). When Austria and Czechoslovakia were annexed, swift measures were taken against refugees from Germany, and the native Jews received comparable treatment. When the Second World War began, the program of extermination was ready to start.

World Jewry reacted swiftly to these terrible events. Meetings of anguished protest were held in many western lands. The Joint Distribution Committee at once began to provide funds both for the relief of the needy and the maintenance of the institutions of German Jewry. The Jewish Agency and the allied Zionist bodies labored to bring refugees to Palestine. Thousands of American Jews provided the necessary guarantees for relatives and friends, and even for complete strangers, so that they might be permitted to enter the United States. American officials were generally helpful, as far as the rigid immigration laws allowed.

How did the world at large react to the Nazi revolutions? Many voices were raised in eloquent protest against the new German barbarism. Some Christian agencies, notably the American Friends Service Committee, gave concrete expression to their sympathy. But these manifestations were overbalanced by the great growth of anti-Semitism, stimulated and in part financed from Berlin. The world was still in the grip of economic depression, and at such times minorities are always in jeopardy.

Between the out-and-out anti-Semites and the consistent Christians, there was a large group of respectable people who "did not approve" of the Nazi excesses, but still hoped to do business with Hitler. After all, they felt Nazism was anti-Communist. They were the same people who had been impressed by Italian Fascism (Mussolini had made the Italian trains run on time)! The western governments, apparently, did not consider that they might properly deny recognition and break off trade relations with a government that persecuted its own law-abiding nationals. The policy of appeasement adopted by Baldwin and Chamberlain was a betrayal of moral decency which in a few years proved to be disastrous for Britain.

The League of Nations established a commission on refugees, with the great American James G. MacDonald as High Commissioner; but he was not given either the financial or the political means to accomplish anything important for those he was called to serve. Almost the only funds at his disposal were those provided by the American Jewish Joint Distribution Committee. He finally resigned his post in protest against the failure of the nations to recognize their responsibility. An inter-governmental conference on refugees held at Evian, France, in 1938, produced nothing but rhetoric. The situation of the German Jews was growing more and more plainly hopeless, yet no nation was willing to modify its immigration laws; and Great Britain had stipulated in advance that Palestine must not even be discussed.

The moral flabbiness of the democracies in the face of the Nazi challenge is tragic evidence of how little the ideals of the Bible had permeated even those peoples who professed to guide their lives by the revealed teachings of the Jewish prophets. The Second World War cannot be blamed exclusively on Hitler. The governments which surrendered principle for temporary advantage and which, to achieve "peace for our time," abandoned the Jews and the Czechs to the barbarians, must share in the guilt and shame.

In 1939 Hitler invaded Poland, and the fate of European Jewry was sealed.

56.

The Greatest Tragedy— Second Phase

IN 1938 HITLER NEGOTIATED A NON-AGGRESSION PACT WITH HIS SWORN enemies, the Russian Communists. Confident that the great power to the east would not trouble him, he moved against Poland, and the Second World War began. It was the most horrible conflict in man's history, not only because of its global extent, but because of its unequaled savagery. The systematic bombing of cities with high explosives, later with atom bombs, erased the distinction between fighting men and civilian populace, and made women and children regular targets of battle.

Once the war had started, the Nazis no longer needed to consider the not-so-sensitive conscience of the western powers, and could deal as they pleased with the Jews of Germany, Austria, and Czechoslovakia. But the number of their potential victims soon swelled enormously as Poland, Rumania, Hungary, Yugoslavia, and Greece fell before German arms or submitted passively to the Nazi rulers. And the once free Jewries of France, the Low Countries, Denmark, and Norway were trapped as the Blitzkrieg swept over these lands. Now the Gestapo had millions of Jews to destroy.

The program of extermination was set in motion rapidly. In parts of Poland Jews were forced to dig mass graves and then were machinegunned. Few of the Poles seemed to mind. In Holland, Belgium, and Denmark, the Christian populace was not so callous; Jews were therefore rounded up and deported to concentration camps in Germany and Poland for torture or liquidation.

In these camps every form of physical and mental torment was elaborated with appalling ingenuity. Thousand of Jews died of slow starvation, exposure, and disease. Living human beings were subjected to fiendish "medical experiments." Able-bodied men were assigned to slave labor projects and literally worked to death; young women were exploited for the amusement of the master race. Dachau, Buchenwald, and Bergen-Belsen are names of unforgettable infamy.

Part of the program was the spiritual degradation of the victims, so that their physical destruction could be more readily consummated. Everything was done to humiliate and terrorize the Jews. Some broke under the treatment and became spies and traitors against their own. Leaders were forced to collaborate in the arrest and ultimate destruction of their people. The Jews in their turn tried to sustain group morale by conducting schools, religious services, and programs of lectures and music even in the camps, and especially in the ghettos of eastern Europe, where numbers made the process of extermination somewhat slower.

The Nazi leaders became impatient at these delays. So great factories were built near the Polish towns of Maidanek and Oswiecim (Ausschwitz), where mass production methods could be applied to the gassing of great numbers of victims. Hundreds of thousands of men, women, and children were done to death for the crime of being born Jews. Soap was manufactured from their corpses.

Stunned and confused, most of the Jews went to their death without fighting. But a substantial minority engaged in active resistance. In France, for example, Jews joined with other Frenchmen in the Maquis underground which fought the Nazis and the Vichy collaborationists. But in the East, Jews were not always welcomed by the "Partisans." As the infamous Warsaw ghetto was being emptied of its masses, the most aggressive elements—the Zionists and the left-wing radicals—eventually made common cause and determined on a last-ditch stand against the Nazis. They had difficulty in obtaining even a small and insufficient supply of weapons from the Polish underground. The "Battle of the Warsaw Ghetto" began on April 19, 1943, and lasted for nearly a month. The heroic defenders knew from the start that they could not win; but they fought to the end with gallant courage. In their death they bore testimony to a faith that pervaded the Jewish masses even when they did not have the means of physical resistance. This faith was expressed in a Yiddish song widely sung in the ghettos and death camps:

> "Never say that you walk the last road;
> The leaden skies foretell a bluer day.
> Our longed-for hour will yet come;
> Our marching footsteps will proclaim: We are here." *

Under Mussolini, Italian Fascism had not been anti-Semitic. The dwindling Jewish community had offered no opposition to his regime; some Jews even held important posts in the Black Shirt party. Mussolini had expressed sympathy for Zionism; and Jabotinsky had argued that Jews outside Italy should not alienate a friend by attacking Fascism. But as the Italian dictator became more and more the captive and underling of Hitler, he was forced to adopt his master's racial policy. The Italians had little taste for persecution and did not cooperate very well; in the latter days of the war, the Germans treated Italy virtually as a conquered nation, and themselves carried out the program of exterminating Jews.

The Nazi invasion of Russia involved new Jewish tragedy; for the greater part of Russian Jewry lived in the western part of the Soviet Union. Though the fate of these Jews could be readily foreseen, the Communist leaders made no effort to evacuate Jews from the invaded areas. The native Ukrainians willingly cooperated with the Nazis in rounding up and destroying Jews.

There were, of course, many individual cases in which Christians hid and sheltered Jews, sometimes at great personal sacrifice. Such instances were, however, highly exceptional in Germany and eastward. It was different in Holland, Belgium, and Denmark, where many distinguished leaders and large masses of the people made common cause with the Jews. Early in the occupation period, the Jews of Antwerp were ordered to wear the Jew badge, whereupon many Christians also placed the yellow circle on their clothing. Countless acts of courageous humanity were performed by the Dutch. The Danes helped hundreds of Jews to escape in small boats; they made their way across the Baltic to Sweden, where they were received with decency and kindliness.

The Jews of England and America received the news of the holocaust at first with incredulity, then with mounting horror. They raised

---

* The author, Hirsch Glick, was murdered in a concentration camp.

large sums for relief, but most of the victims were now beyond their help. A small but steady stream of refugees made their way across Spain and Portugal to Lisbon. The Fascist rulers of Spain were not relentless, and the Portuguese dictator, Salazar, was sympathetic. The "Joint" maintained its Lisbon office throughout the war, enabling those who were stranded to keep body and soul together, and facilitating the immigration of such as could obtain visas to North or South American countries. Other bands trekked all the way across Russia and Siberia to ports on the Pacific. Shanghai had been open to refugees throughout the Hitler period; thousands were caught when the Japanese invaded China and remained there in a precarious state till the end of the war in the Far East. Switzerland and Liechtenstein provided safe havens for limited numbers.

The Jews of Palestine, more than any other group, were directly involved in the efforts at rescue. For a long time, escape from the Balkan countries was not entirely cut off. But few of those who escaped could enter Palestine legally; and Great Britain stubbornly refused to relax its decrees. A fair number were nevertheless smuggled into the land of Israel.

In 1943 thirty-two young Palestinian volunteers parachuted into the Balkans for the purpose of working with the resistance fighters there. The British arranged the operation in the interest of specific military objectives; but the parachutists had permission to do what they could for the rescue of Jews. The actual accomplishments of the little band were not very great; but some of its members have become undying names among the heroes and martyrs of Israel. The most famous was the young poetess, Hanna Senesch. A beautiful and gifted girl of twenty-three, she was betrayed to the Nazis shortly after reentering her native Hungary, and was shot as a spy. A few days before her execution, Hanna wrote this little poem (in Hebrew):

"Blessed is the match that is consumed in kindling flame.
Blessed is the flame that burns in the secret fastness of
the heart.
Blessed are the hearts with strength to cease their beating
for honor's sake.
Blessed is the match that is consumed in kindling flame."

The events we have thus briefly and inadequately sketched are of decisive importance for all the future history of Judaism. No religion can be studied apart from the fate of those who profess it. In 1939 the Jews of the world numbered at most 18,000,000. Before the end of World War II, 6,000,000 Jewish souls had been destroyed. The Jews were not, indeed, the only victims of the war; but no other people lost a third of its numbers. Nor was the future growth of any other people blighted by the systematic butchery of its children. Yet this appalling loss of human resources was only part of the tragedy. Jewish life for a thousand years had been centered in Europe and had been endlessly fruitful there. Now European Jewry is gone. The great Polish Jewish community, rich in tradition, creative and vibrant, survives only in lifeless fragments. German Jewry, so productive of cultural values, consists today of a few thousand old or aging folk, largely intermarried. The survivors in western Europe are only a small fraction of once substantial communities. What is left of Hungarian and Rumanian Jewry, locked behind the Iron Curtain, awaits seemingly inevitable doom, in part through disintegration, in part through the growth of Soviet anti-Semitism.

The Jews of the world have become keenly aware that they themselves must solve what is called the "Jewish problem," if it is to be solved at all. The great democracies of the West, for all their hostility to totalitarianism, have not understood—or else have refused to reckon seriously with—the crucial position of world Jewry in the struggle against all tyranny. Prior to the outbreak of World War II, the western powers contented themselves with guarded expressions of sympathy; yet, as we have seen, they did little or nothing to defend or rescue the first victims of the power that nearly overwhelmed them all. And when the war was ended, they found themselves incapable of dealing with the problem of the homeless survivors of the Nazi horror. The United States would not alter its immigration law; Britain became more rather than less rigid in its stand on Palestine. Thus, for years after the end of hostilities, thousands of Jews remained in German concentration camps—better fed and kindly treated, but with no place to go and no prospects for the foreseeable future. When these camps were finally emptied, it was because of Jewish action and not by the decision of the great powers.

The Jews who lived in the western democracies, and who participated fully in the war, suffered no impairment in their civil or social status. To the contrary, they felt themselves in every sense part of the nations to which they belonged. But they recognized that the moral claims of persecuted or homeless Jews would hardly be acknowledged by the free governments. Mild sympathy and occasional assistance might be forthcoming. But the Jews themselves would have to provide the answer to Jewish needs.

The result was a considerable strengthening of Jewish loyalties. Many who had apparently forgotten that they were Jews were aroused by Hitler at least to participate in work for relief and self-defense. In many cases, however, a more significant awakening occurred. Thousands began to consider seriously the nature of Jewish destiny, to seek more Jewish knowledge for themselves and their children, and to ponder the values of Jewish religious faith. This revival has continued to the present, and we shall explore it more fully in our last chapters. But it is a rebirth dearly bought.

Part 8.

Problems and Opportunities

Part 8.

Problems and Opportunities

57.

The State of Israel

IN PREVIOUS CHAPTERS WE HAVE NOTED THE STEADY RETREAT OF THE British government from the clear commitments of the Balfour Declaration and the Palestine Mandate. It is a curious and tragic story of moral failure, which never yielded even temporary advantage. The first stage of this process culminated in the vicious White Paper of 1939, which proposed to restrict Jewish immigration to Palestine for a few years, then terminate it altogether. Thus Palestine would be the one country in the world to bar Jewish immigrants just because they were Jews! This decree was denounced as illegal by the Mandates Commission of the League of Nations; but the League was moribund, and during a war period, any action could be justified on grounds of emergency.

British officialdom clung to the letter of the White Paper through the darkest days of Hitler persecution and the war years, turning away shiploads of desperate refugees, and dealing severely with all who attempted to enter the country without permission. Some were deported to the island of Mauritius in the Indian Ocean; others were interned behind barbed wire on Cyprus. Scant attention was paid, however, to the constant infiltration of Arabs over the land borders of the country.

This appeasement of the Arab terrorists yielded no profit. The Grand Mufti, the creature of the British colonial administration, spent the war years in Berlin, broadcasting pro-Axis propaganda to the Arab world. He was later arrested as a war criminal, but he was never brought to trial; and he was so carelessly guarded that he was able to escape to

Egypt and continue his operations there. Iraq, which had become independent after a period of training under a British mandate, attempted to enter the war on the side of the Nazis; allied military intervention put a less openly hostile government in control. During the North African campaign, the Egyptians did nothing to defend their own country against Rommel's invasion.

The Jews of Palestine, on the other hand, made a substantial contribution to the allied war effort in the production of materials, the care of casualties in the new hospitals, and in actual fighting men. This time, however, the British forbade the organization of a Jewish legion and actually limited the number of Jewish volunteers they would accept. They also carefully avoided public acknowledgment of Palestinian services to the allied cause.

These discriminatory policies, inaugurated by the reactionary governments of Baldwin and Chamberlain, had been severely criticized by Winston Churchill. But when this avowed Zionist became prime minister, the enforcement of the White Paper continued without change. At the close of the war, the British Labor Party came into power; but its leaders promptly forgot their indignant criticisms of Palestine policy and outdid the Conservatives in cynical ruthlessness.

The end of fighting left thousands of homeless Jews in the German camps, doomed to an indefinite exile. Their numbers were swelled by refugees from Poland, where a new wave of pogroms had broken out. American Military Government and the United States Army (together with the ever-present "Joint") did whatever they could to alleviate the physical and mental misery of the stateless Jews. Individuals who could qualify for visas might immigrate westward; a thin trickle of legal immigrants and a more substantial number of "illegals" went to Palestine. But the majority had to wait, with no prospects for a solution of their problems, while months dragged on to years. This situation added to the anguish of world Jewry and the mounting rage of the Palestinians.

These political circumstances explain the internal developments in Palestine. Except for the Revisionist minority, the Jews of the Holy Land had tried hard to cooperate with the mandatory power, but to no avail. British policy encouraged the Arabs to increasing violence; the Jews found themselves literally at war. Haganah, though forced to operate underground, became a highly trained and resourceful organization. It avoided aggressive action, but fought off many Arab attacks; and it had an elaborate system for bringing in illegals into the land. It built up reserves of arms and ammunition, despite severe punitive action by the British whenever such stores were discovered. With rare exceptions, Haganah followed the rule of havlagah or self-restraint.

But there was an increasing number who were no longer capable of patience or discretion. Some had suffered at first hand under the Nazis, or were the sole survivors of entire families and communities. Many had relatives or friends languishing in the European camps or detained behind barbed wire on Cyprus. There seemed to be no prospect of bringing them to freedom and constructive life. Unable to bear the strain any longer, the extremists in Palestine launched a program of terror, reviving in contemporary form the methods of the Zealots and Sicarii. Their principal agency was called the *Irgun Zevai Leumi* (National Military Organization); it included many of the old Revisionists. A small independent group of fanatics was known as the Stern Gang.

Like their ancient prototypes, the terrorist groups included persons of different character. Some, no doubt, were anti-social individuals who welcomed an excuse for violence. Some were sensitive idealists, convinced that they were serving a holy cause, and prepared to make every sacrifice for it.

The indiscriminate acts of bombing and assassination which they committed were repudiated with horror by most of the Jews of Palestine. They cannot be justified. But no small part of the blame for the appearance—so long delayed—of such desperate bands in a people known for its patience and its aversion to bloodshed must be placed upon the colonial administrators and upon the successive British cabinets who sacrificed principle to policy.

Meantime, the victorious Allies had made a new attempt at creating an international body to establish and maintain peace—the United Nations. To this new body Great Britain reported its increasing dissatisfaction with the situation in Palestine, and its desire to give up the mandate. In November, 1947, the General Assembly of the UN adopted a resolution on Palestine. It recommended the termination of the mandate and the partition of Palestine into Jewish and Arab states (this solution had been proposed by the British in 1937, but nothing had been done about it). Jerusalem, containing the holy places of all three major faiths, was to become a separate international area.

This decision was hailed with delight by world Jewry, even though the hoped-for Jewish state was to include only a fraction of the area once envisioned. At least, the resolution proposed definite action. But Britain did nothing to carry out its terms. She merely delivered repeated warnings that she would soon abandon the mandate and remove her officials and troops from the country. In the interim, the British military tried systematically to disarm the Jews of Palestine, though the Arab states had refused to accept the UN's decision, and had announced their intention to destroy a Jewish state. It seems plain that British Foreign Minister Ernest Bevin, the architect of his nation's policy, expected and perhaps hoped that the Jewish National Home would be wiped out.

But these expectations did not come to pass. On May 14, 1948, almost at the moment of the departure of the British from the country, a "National Council" met in Tel Aviv and proclaimed the establishment of a Jewish State, henceforth to be known as Israel. The veteran Zionist leader, Chaim Weizmann, was made president of the provisional government; David Ben-Gurion, leader of the Labor Party, became prime minister. President Truman, by-passing the State Department bureaucrats, many of whom were sympathetic to the British chicanery, at once announced American recognition of the new state. This action added greatly to the morale and prestige of the Israeli leaders, and facilitated Israel's admission to the United Nations.

But almost at once an attack was launched from the north, south, and east by Syria, Lebanon, Iraq, Jordan, and Egypt. They had been provided with British arms; the Jordan Legion, trained and led by a former British officer, was almost the only Arab unit that was effective in the field. Haganah, now the army of Israel, had to depend largely on primitive weapons of home manufacture, and on what could be smuggled into the country from outside, chiefly from Czechoslovakia.

But the Israeli forces, greatly outnumbered and poorly equipped, possessed a morale that was unbeatable. Fired by the devotion to the national ideal which must be realized at once or abandoned forever, fully aware that defeat might mean the massacre of all the Jews of Palestine, young men and women (and older ones, too) fought with incredible courage and resourcefulness. When the UN finally achieved a truce, the Arab armies had sustained crushing defeats both in the north and south. As a result, the borders of the Jewish State extend somewhat farther than was proposed in the original UN plan. The only Arab success was won by the Jordan troops who obtained a firm grip on the eastern part of Jerusalem, including the Old City, the Hebrew University, and the Hadassah Hospital.

The Arab states refused to take even preliminary steps toward a peace conference, despite repeated expressions by the Israeli government that it was ready to cooperate in such an effort. Every device was utilized to impede Israel's economic development. But the State of Israel made amazing progress. It has a stable democratic government, a well-organized military and a tolerably effective civil service.

Despite serious economic difficulties, greatly increased by the need to maintain large armed forces and by the cessation of trade with its neighbors, the State at once adopted the policy of opening its doors to unlimited Jewish immigration. The concentration camps, which had presented too great a problem for the mightiest world powers, were swiftly emptied by the action of this one little state. Thousands of refugees came in from lands behind the Iron Curtain and from the various Arab countries, where the Jewish position had become increasingly precarious. When the State of Israel was founded in 1948, it had a Jewish population of 650,000; by 1967 the number of Jewish citizens exceeded 2,300,000.

To provide housing and jobs, and even to feed these newcomers, most of them destitute, produced almost intolerable strains on the economy of the State. All citizens had to accept a regime of rigid austerity, but all were agreed that there was no other choice. By 1952 the difficulties had become so great that laws were reluctantly adopted to slow down and regulate immigration. As the economy progressed—with the development of both light and heavy industry and with the great expansion of tourism—rationing and other controls could be discontinued and the restrictions on immigration relaxed. According to the "Law of Return," Jews entering the country to settle permanently become citizens at once, without having to go through the usual long and complicated procedures of naturalization. Despite American official displeasure, the national capital was moved from Tel Aviv to Jerusalem in 1950.

Throughout the world, Jews reacted to these events with pride, joy, and thanksgiving. Many who were neither orthodox nor mystical were awed at the fulfilment after so many thousand years of ancient Biblical prophecies. The fact that Jews had taken their fate into their own hands and that they had proved able fighters made a great impression on many non-Jews and Jews alike. It is a sad commentary on the spiritual level of our times that success in battle won more esteem for Israel than the many creative achievements of Palestinian Jewry.

The Jews of the West, especially in the United States, rallied wholeheartedly to the support of the great new undertaking. Many individuals possessing technical and industrial skills aided Israel's economic advancement. Every legitimate effort was made to secure support from the American government. And the sums raised by the United Jewish Appeal in the last decade, chiefly for the assistance of Israel and its new immigrants, are the greatest ever contributed to any cause in the entire history of human philanthropy. The rebirth of a nation after a lapse of over two thousand years was something new in the experience of mankind.

58.

American Judaism, 1932-1945

THE RATHER INDIFFERENT COMPLACENCY THAT MARKED AMERICAN Jewish life in the days of "stock market prosperity" was rudely shattered. The onset of economic depression found many communities in serious trouble because of heavy indebtedness on synagogue and center buildings; hard work and real sacrifice were now demanded if Jewish institutions were to survive and the good name of the community was to be maintained.

This shock was followed by the far more terrible blow of Hitler's rise to power and the persecution of German Jewry. American Jews reacted with stunned incredulity, then with grief and rage, not unmixed with fear. Meetings and demonstrations of protest against Nazism, in which distinguished Christian leaders took part, served at least as an outlet for these emotions.

The Joint Distribution Committee, whose collections had dwindled during the depression years despite great needs in eastern Europe, was given substantial funds for the assistance of the suddenly impoverished Jews of Germany. An immediate effort was made to get as many as possible out of Hitler's clutches. The first refugees to arrive were almost lionized as martyrs of the faith. Later, when refugees had become a commonplace, they sometimes encountered the familiar prejudice of the old settler for the newcomer.

The German emigrés formed a distinctive ingredient in the American community. As a rule, immigrants are drawn from the lower strata of society; they are fitted for hard physical labor, and come to a new

413

land in hope of better opportunities. The newcomers from Germany, however, were mostly well-educated middle-class people, many of whom had been persons of consequence and distinction; now they were suddenly stripped of material security and of prestige, uprooted, and reduced to an obscure and inferior status. Some of those who got out of Germany soon enough were able to rescue some of their capital, or to transfer profitable industrial processes to this country. Leaders in science and the arts—Albert Einstein, the actress Elisabeth Bergner, and the composer Kurt Weil, for example—were able to continue their careers in America with comparatively little difficulty. Physicians and others with special technical skills gradually established themselves. But many a successful business man or prominent lawyer could count himself lucky, under depression conditions, to get a job as a clerk or salesman. The psychological adjustments were as difficult as the economic adjustments.

The American Jews established new agencies to help the newcomers find homes, provide vocational guidance and retraining, and assist them in adjustment to the new surroundings. In the large cities, especially New York, the German Jews formed colonies, with synagogues, clubs, and publications of their own. Many of the earlier arrivals rendered devoted service to those who came here later. But even in New York large numbers preferred to affiliate themselves directly with the institutions of American Jewish life. It is probable that no group of immigrants has Americanized itself so quickly. In part this was due to their high educational level—many of the emigrés already knew English—in part to the violent rupture of their ties with the old country.

The German refugees have made a remarkable contribution to American life. The talents and energies which Hitler had rejected were put to good use, if not in the depression years, then a little later. Only the states of New York and Illinois permitted refugee physicians to practice before they had completed the lengthy process of naturalization; but these physicians brought higher medical standards to many a country town, and helped to relieve the shortage of doctors during the war period. In the war itself, many of the younger men were especially useful because of their knowledge of the German language, social conditions, and psychology.

The newcomers also constituted a valuable addition to Jewish life in America. A few of them were extreme assimilationists. But the loyal majority were for the most part better informed and more traditional in practice than their American co-religionists. Scholars, rabbis, and writers of distinction enriched American Jewish culture. In particular, the standards of synagogue music were noticeably raised when cantors, organists, and composers of stature entered the service of American congregations. The German emigrés provided a valuable reinforcement to all kinds of synagogues, Orthodox, Conservative, and Reform.

The Jewish consciousness of American Jews was greatly stimulated by the need of helping their fellow Jews here and abroad. But this revival of loyalty was joined to a new concern for their own status and security. They recognized that what had happened in Germany was no isolated and exceptional episode. Nazism was a world movement, and its repercussions were soon felt in all the countries of the West. Most of the German-American organizations (in which many Jews had been active) were captured by pro-Nazi groups, and native anti-Semitism became a serious menace. Vicious anti-Jewish libels flooded the mails and were peddled by street corner orators. Synagogues were defaced, and actual physical violence was not unknown. Anti-Semitic addresses were broadcast to a huge radio audience by Charles Coughlin, a Catholic priest. Shortly before Pearl Harbor, Charles Lindbergh (once the darling of the American people) accused the Jews and the Roosevelt administration of trying to drag this country into war.

American Jews had long been aware of anti-Semitism, and had talked about it a great deal. But their thinking on the subject was usually superficial. They regarded Jew-hatred as a survival of old prejudices, due chiefly to ignorance. Many of them felt that it was caused largely by the irritating behavior of Jews—of course, other Jews. Now they were forced to recognize the existence of political, economic, and psychological factors which they could not control, and whose intensity was greater than they had ever remotely suspected. Many American Jews were close to panic.

Their fears were sometimes exploited by the defense organizations in their drives for financial support, yet the danger was real enough. A vigorous counter-attack was launched against the anti-Semites. The subversive character and alien affiliations of the Jew-baiters were uncovered. Jewish agencies joined in every effort to strengthen the democratic spirit, and worked closely with many Christians who were deeply disturbed by the growth of anti-Semitism.

Nevertheless, a strong isolationist movement persisted in the United States until the attack on Pearl Harbor, and this movement had a strong anti-Semitic coloring. When the Axis powers forced

America into war, organized anti-Semitism had to retreat. Some of its spokesmen were arrested as enemy agents, the rest became more circumspect.

The awakening of Jewish consciousness was thus motivated in part by fear, but it had positive aspects as well. Zionism became much more popular. There was an increasing impatience with the ideological conflicts and organizational rivalries dividing American Jewry, and a steady demand for unity. Many drifters joined synagogues for the first time; and Jewish parents—if only as a sort of prophylactic against prejudice and its psychological dangers—were providing in far greater numbers for the Jewish education of their children.

An important phenomenon of this period was the growth of local Jewish community councils. It was clear that in so troubled a time, cases of real or alleged discrimination and outbreaks of open anti-Semitism should not be dealt with by individuals or small groups acting on their own. Those who were dissatisfied with the wrangles of the national defense agencies saw no need to repeat these controversies on the local level; they proposed to deal with their problems of public relations on a community-wide basis, and with all groups in the community participating. The Community Councils have generally included all the synagogues, as well as Jewish organizations and clubs of the most varied character. By this means, elements in the communities which formerly had no contact have become acquainted with each other, and have learned to work together. In the larger cities, the councils soon acquired professional staff. In addition to conducting programs of community relations, some of the councils have also concerned themselves with Jewish education and other internal affairs. They have often sponsored the establishment of a Jewish welfare fund. Only in the vast sprawling New York area was this new procedure ineffective. There is a vigorous Community Council in Brooklyn (seat of the largest Jewish population in the world); but it cannot exert the discipline possible in smaller communities, and it has no counterpart in the rest of New York.

The American defense program was expanding rapidly long before Pearl Harbor. Along with other religious groups, the Jews had to provide a steadily growing service to those in the armed forces, and the pace was stepped up rapidly after we were forced into war. The Jewish Welfare Board, in the field since World War 1, quickly expanded its facilities. This time, the recreational work was coordinated with that of other bodies through the United Service Organizations (USO).

The share of the Welfare Board in this operation has been widely praised.

At the same time, the program of chaplaincy was developed on a far greater scale than ever before. In the First World War, the total number of Jewish chaplains in the American armed forces was twenty-six; during the Second World War it rose to three hundred and ten. (This in addition to the large number of civilian rabbis who served camps near their own communities.) As in the previous war, the initiative was taken by Reform rabbis, who at the start constituted the majority of the Jewish chaplains; but the Conservative and Orthodox groups gradually increased the extent of their participation. Many from all three groups rendered distinguished service; a number died while on duty. Special veneration is accorded the memory of Alexander Goode, one of the "Four Chaplains" who gave up their life-belts to others when the troop-ship "Dorchester" was torpedoed in the North Atlantic.

All told, about half a million American Jews were in the armed forces during the war. An unexpected by-product of this experience was a revival of interest in Jewish values. Thousands of these young people came from the great metropolitan centers where their environment had been predominantly Jewish. Now for the first time they had to adjust themselves to steady and intimate contact with non-Jews, some of them hostile or prejudiced; and they were compelled to start thinking about the meaning of their identity as Jews. But they were ill prepared for this task. Their Jewish education had been meager and insufficient; their notions about Judaism were vague and often distorted. They might identify it with a preference for certain types of delicatessen (which the JWB tried hard to provide for them), or the importance of wearing a hat or performing some other ceremonial detail, without any grasp of its meaning. By attending the intelligible services conducted by the chaplains, participating in discussions, and receiving personal guidance and counseling, many of them gained their first insight into the real nature of Judaism and its relevance to their own lives.

This experience helped prepare the way for the revival of Judaism which has taken place in the United States since the close of World War II.

59.

Israel Today

BUT THERE ARE SOME REALITIES WHICH WILL NOT BE CHANGED quickly. Europe, which was the central area of Jewish living for over a thousand years, is so no longer. Only broken fragments remain of its once great Jewish communities. Jewish life today is focused in two major centers—North America and Israel. Though substantial Jewish communities are found in many parts of the world, it is in Israel and the United States that the decisive development of Judaism will take place during the next decades. These two great communities, moreover, are linked by many strong ties.

* * *

The most urgent problems of the new State of Israel are economic and political. The development of a country so long neglected and abused would be in any case difficult; but it has been made far more complex by two factors, one forced upon the people and one chosen by them. The unremitting hostility of the Arab countries disrupts the normal processes of international commerce, and compels Israel to maintain a large and expensive military establishment. And the will of the Israelis to admit to the land all Jews who desire to emigrate has imposed a heavy burden in providing the newcomers with housing, food, and jobs. Despite the large financial aid furnished by Jews in other lands, especially the United States, all this would have been impossible had not the Israelis been ready to accept a regimen of the most severe self-denial. Characteristically, this struggling nation provides all its children between the ages of five and fourteen with free compulsory education—a standard found elsewhere only in a few of the most prosperous countries. And parents make many sacrifices to give their children the advantages of secondary schooling.

But these problems are bound up with many spiritual factors. The new immigrants are very different from the pioneers who created the State. The latter came to the land voluntarily, imbued with the Zionist ideal, and prepared to make many sacrifices for its attainment. The more recent comers have fled to Israel chiefly because they have no other haven; many are physically and spiritually handicapped by their experience of persecution and war, and are poorly prepared for either the privileges or the responsibilities of democracy. Moreover, the dominant groups have till now been European in origin and modern in outlook. The influx of hundreds of thousands from the countries of North Africa and the Near East has created many difficulties. Few of these people understood modern concepts of industrial efficiency, hygiene, or political freedom. Illiteracy and superstition are common among them; some have been impaired morally by the degrading conditions under which they were forced to live in such countries as Morocco and Persia. On the other hand, the positive values which many brought with them as their heritage have been threatened by contact with the dynamic material culture of the West. Their patriarchal family life, their folk-song and handicrafts, their simple piety, tend to disappear under the heavy pressures of a new way of life. Social cleavage between oriental and western Jews has been inevitable, and has generated considerable friction. The most responsible leaders of Israel are seeking a way to integrate the eastern Jews into Israeli life and still preserve the distinctive cultural elements they can contribute.

Nearly all the oriental Jews are nominally Orthodox, a large proportion of them deeply pious. This fact has intensified the religious conflicts that trouble the State. For religion in Israel, as in so many other countries, is directly involved in political affairs. The government includes a Ministry of Religion, which has admirably protected the interests of the Christian, Moslem, and other religious minorities in the country. It has been less successful in dealing with Judaism.

The term "religious" is in modern Israel applied almost exclusively to the embattled Orthodox who constitute a considerable and vigorous minority. They are, indeed, somewhat divided; they range from the Orthodox labor group, in whose kibbutzim the ideals of cooperative living are combined with traditional piety, to the small group of fanatics who call themselves the *N'turei Karto* (guardians of the city, i.e., Jerusalem), and who have refused to recognize the legitimacy of the (secular) Israel government. But most of the Orthodox groups work together as a political bloc (such religious political parties are not uncommon on the European continent) and have been able to exert a good deal of influence.

This is due in part to the situation, inherited from the past, whereby marriage, divorce, and other family matters are administered by each religious group for its own adherents. All Jews are subject in these concerns to the direction of the chief rabbinate. Civil marriage does not exist; intermarriage is thus impossible. Persons who have been divorced in other countries may be denied the right of remarriage if the religious authorities consider the auspices under which they were divorced insufficiently pious.

The power of the Orthodox has been further enhanced by the peculiar political situation in Israel. No party has ever had a clear majority in Parliament; consequently it has been necessary to govern by coalition cabinets. The religious bloc, in return for support of the government's foreign policy of cooperation with the West, has been able to exact a good many concessions. Busses do not run on Sabbath in Jerusalem and Tel Aviv; the importing of non-kosher meat is forbidden, and Orthodox Jewesses are exempt from the compulsory military service required of both sexes. (They render various forms of civilian service instead.)

The majority of the Israelis consider themselves non-religious. Even those who are not influenced by the Marxian traditions of the dominant labor group think of their Jewishness in national rather than religious terms. They are resentful of what they consider an unjustified intrusion into their personal liberties by aggressive Orthodoxy, and are repelled by the obscurantism and medievalism of many spokesmen of religion.

Moreover, the leaders of organized religion offer them little in a positive way. In no other country except the Soviet lands has the synagogue so little connection with the actual life of the people. The rabbis are not leaders and ministers but officials. Military chaplains supervise *kashrus* (observance of dietary laws), but rarely interest themselves in the personal concerns and aspirations of the young men and women in the services.

Newer versions of Judaism have slowly made progress. The first "liberal" congregations, established by German Jews, following the traditional liturgy, but with preaching in the modern spirit, made little impression on the general Israeli public. But there were small groups, conscious of a spiritual lack, which sought new ways through fellowship, discussion, and prayer. Starting in 1958, the World Union for Progressive Judaism has sponsored new congregations, which presently number seven; their spiritual leaders include Americans, Germans, a Yemenite, and a native Israeli.

These progressive congregations have suffered considerable harrassment from the Orthodox, who sought to deny them the use of public halls for their services. The progressive rabbis are not authorized to officiate at marriages. More serious, the progressive congregations do not receive the government subventions which are granted to Orthodox synagogues. (In a socialist state it is difficult to maintain religious institutions without such aid.) These groups must therefore depend on help from the United States; but even so, sacrificial devotion by both rabbis and laymen is indispensable—and present.

The progressive cause is also furthered by the Leo Baeck School of Haifa, which fosters a modernist religious approach; its secondary department is under the aegis of the World Union. The Hebrew Union College Biblical and Archeological School in Jerusalem —completed in 1963 after a long battle against Orthodox hostility— is another outpost of the progressive movement; its chapel services attract many Israelis. The Jewish Theological Seminary of America has also established a study program in Israel for its students and graduates.

It is chiefly the religious situation which accounts for the fact that Israel has no written constitution. The traditionalists insist that a new constitution is unnecessary—what better constitution can Jews have than the Torah? Any new laws that are required should be framed in harmony with the letter and spirit of divine revelation.

The argument must be viewed seriously. The Bible has been a basic source for the law of western democracies. Moreover, some portions of Talmudic-rabbinic law have continued to develop over the centuries, and have unique merits of their own. To discard all this for a new code would seem the wanton rejection of a precious heritage. On the other hand, the proposal of the Orthodox implies a union of Church and State (to use western terms) and would leave many important legal institutions permanently in the hands of a clerical caste. Understandably, the leaders of Israel, hounded by the problems of defense and of economic survival, have avoided a constitutional convention.

The official religious leaders have indeed recognized that new conditions require changes, adaptations, and innovations in the halakah. The traditional system, as we have seen, makes provision for such changes; though Orthodox authorities in recent centuries have generally been timid about exercising their powers for this purpose. But obviously, modern conditions require public utility services to operate continuously, even on the Sabbath. The chief rabbinate has also relaxed somewhat the ban on autopsy, hitherto forbidden on the basis of old laws against mutilating a corpse.

Such concessions have been thus far piecemeal, reluctant, and not altogether consistent. The need for a more thoroughgoing and systematic restudy and revision of the law has led to a bolder suggestion —that the Sanhedrin be revived in accordance with the proposals of Rabbi Jacob Berab. Some of the proponents of this scheme hope to reestablish the authority of an enlarged rabbinic legal system within the Jewish State, and to secure the acceptance of the Sanhedrin as the supreme Jewish tribunal even for the Diaspora. Others think of the Sanhedrin an academy rather than as an actual high court. Such suggestions, though enthusiastically welcomed in some quarters, have not received unanimous support even in Orthodox Jewry, and have been sharply challenged by the non-Orthodox groups.

While religion in its official and formal aspect is sharply sundered from the life of a large part of the people of Israel, there is no lack of concern for spiritual values. Much contemporary Hebrew poetry is suffused with reverence and aspiration, often stimulated by the new contact with the world of outdoor nature. The Bible is systematically studied in the schools; it is read on the radio; and it has provided the inspiration for many new literary productions. There is wide popular interest in Jewish history, in the exploration of the land and the excavation of ancient sites. Leading figures at the University (Martin Buber, who died in 1965, was perhaps the best known) have powerfully championed the religious viewpoint.

But religion is more than doctrine or observance: it is a way of life. When we speak of spiritual values in modern Israel, we must take account of the great sacrifices by which a new home has been provided for the homeless. We cannot overlook the attempts to build an economy in which there shall be less competition and more cooperation, or the extraordinarily progressive health, educational and social services which are provided for all the people.

These benefits are shared by the non-Jewish—chiefly Arab—citizens of Israel, presently numbering nearly 300,000. The latter enjoy full civic rights; there are several Arabs in the Parliament, and a considerable number in the civil service. Israel is the only country in the Near East where all Arab children receive free schooling.

This brings us to the much discussed problem of the Arab refugees. At the outbreak of the war, the Arab leaders called on all Arabs living in Israeli territory to flee, warning them that if they remained they would be persecuted by the Jews and would be regarded as traitors by their fellow Arabs. Thousands responded to this call, expecting rich rewards in land and plunder after the victory of the Arab armies.

But many remained. Some, chiefly adherents of the Druse religion, fought with the armies of Israel. Most of the Israeli Arabs seem reasonably contented with their situation. But the Israeli government, arguing that those who fled had demonstrated their hostility to the new state, has refused to let them return, and has utilized the land and dwellings they abandoned to accommodate some of the new Jewish immigrants. The Arab refugees remain in camps located in areas adjacent to Israel, and have been maintained by United Nations funds supplied chiefly by the United States.

Critics of Israel have severely condemned the new state for this policy, which has indeed caused many an Israeli qualms of conscience. The government has indicated its readiness to do its share in solving the problem of the refugees as part of a program of establishing peaceful relations with the Arab world. (It cannot be separated, for example, from the problem of Jews who formerly resided, or still reside, in Arab lands, and who have been deprived of their property and their civil rights.) But the Arab nations have stubbornly refused to enter into any negotiations with the new state. They have chosen to make political capital of their unfortunate brothers, rather than help them build a new life. The refugees, numbering nearly 800,000, could be resettled in vast areas of the Arab countries that still await development: Israel has absorbed an equal number of Jews in a much smaller territory. But neither the Arab governments nor the wealthy Arabs of Cairo and Bagdad have shown the will to attempt a creative solution; it is easier to abuse and threaten the Israelis.

60.

In Many Lands

ORGANIZED JEWISH LIFE IS TO BE FOUND IN NEARLY ALL THE CIVILIZED areas of the globe except eastern Asia. Some of the communities, however, have long been cut off from contact with the main-stream of Jewish experience, and have only a marginal relation to Jewish life. Such are the little colony of the Samaritans, the Sabbatian crypto-Jews of Turkey, and small groups in the remote mountain country of North Africa.

Somewhat more numerous are the Falashas, the black-skinned Jews of Ethiopia, who became known to world Jewry through reports of Christian missionaries in the nineteenth century. They trace their descent from the servants of Solomon who returned with the Queen of Sheba, the legendary ancestress of the Ethiopian royal family. But scholars think that they probably came to Ethiopia by way of Arabia, where there were ancient Jewish settlements. Their religious traditions are unmistakably Jewish, but include many unique features. Some of their customs recall the reports of Eldad the Danite concerning the "ten lost tribes." Ties have been established with the Falashas by Jews of Europe and America, and more recently by those of Israel.

Another unusual group, called Beni (for B'ne) Israel, are centered around Bombay; they are descendants, according to their tradition, of Jews shipwrecked on the Indian coast. When they first became known to European Jewry, they knew little Hebrew and were culturally more Hindu than Jewish. Chiefly through the interest of settlers from Bagdad, they have been educated to a more familiar version of Judaism. Recently, they have shown interest in the Liberal movement. Small communities may also be found in other parts of the vast Indian sub-continent, but their religious life is sluggish.

The groups we have mentioned are at least partly of Jewish descent; but we must take note of others that are completely Gentile in origin.

There has been a recurrent tendency in Christian circles to move back from the New Testament toward the Old. The Puritans began their weekly rest day on Saturday evening; one English sect adopted so many Old Testament customs, including circumcision, that their critics called them Jews. The Seventh Day Baptists and the Seventh Day Adventists, fundamentalist Christians in belief, observe the Saturday Sabbath most strictly; the latter abstain from the eating of meats forbidden by the Torah.

A similar movement in nineteenth-century Russia led to more radical results. Some of these Sabbath observers rejected Christianity altogether, and declared themselves Jews in name and fact. Often they had great difficulty in learning the standard practices of Judaism; for they lived in the interior of Russia, far from the Pale of Settlement, and rarely had contact with born Jews.

How then, did they come to adopt Judaism? Chiefly, it seems, through study of the Bible. Many of those who read the Scriptures during the long winter evenings concluded that the New Testament was not the fulfilment of Old Testament prophecy, and centered their allegiance on the Hebrew Bible alone. The new converts did their best to enter into relations with established Jewish communities, in order to regularize their conversion and to receive authoritative guidance.

We do not know how many of the Judaizers survive behind the Iron Curtain. But a fair number had previously settled in Palestine and are integrated into the Israeli community. A notable Hebrew poetess of the past generation was the Russian-born convert, Elisheva.

This is the only instance in modern times of a mass conversion to Judaism. There are, however, smaller convert communities. Early in this century, several farm families near Lincoln, Nebraska, became Jews. A larger group originated in San Nicandro, in southern Italy, when one of its inhabitants, crippled by a serious accident, began to study the Bible to while away his long hours of enforced idleness. Under his guidance most of the village adopted Judaism, and were formally converted after World War ii; since his death, they have emigrated as a community to Israel.

Negro synagogues exist in New York, Brooklyn, and Cleveland.

Some of their members claim to be of Falasha origin, but predominantly these congregations consist of American negroes; they were founded in part out of a desire to reclaim a lost African heritage. The forms of worship used in the Negro synagogues are largely Orthodox, with some distinctive customs not found elsewhere. These groups have provided their own leadership, and up to the present have had little contact with the organized American Jewish community.

* * *

For nearly a thousand years, Europe was the central area of Jewish life and religion. Since the Nazi Holocaust, it presents a bleak and discouraging picture. The Jews of the Soviet Union, numbering two and a half million, seem to have no Jewish future. They suffer not only from the general antireligious policies but from special discrimination, much of it officially directed. Jews, many of whom once occupied important political and managerial positions, have now been largely eliminated from the higher offices. In the last years of Stalin they endured actual persecution; and "de-Stalinization" has brought only limited relief. Zionism has always been proscribed since it implied a loyalty to something other than the Soviet regime; now, with the Russian support of Arab aggression against Israel, the position of Soviet Jews has become ever more difficult.

The government has given many evidences of malice. It has prevented or delayed shipments of prayer books and other religious articles, and of Passover food, to Jews in Soviet lands; and it has maintained spies and informers within the surviving synagogues. Actually the feeble and leaderless Orthodoxy can offer little to Jews who are products of the Communist educational system. Yet a sense of Jewish identity remains, strengthened rather than diminished by the continuing anti-Jewish policies. Its most remarkable manifestation occurs each year on the eve of Simchas Torah, when thousands of young people assemble inside and outside the Great Synagogue of Moscow and dance for hours. But considering their lack of Jewish knowledge and of opportunities for practical commitment to people and faith, one wonders how long such gestures of resistance can continue.

In the different satellite countries conditions vary, and in each land they are subject to change. Thus in Poland, where the fragments of Jewish population (25,000 where once there were two million) were for some years fairly secure, attacks on "Zionism" have lately become more frequent and vehement. ("Zionism" is now the term of abuse for anything Jewish.) Jews suffered real persecution in Czechoslovakia in the Stalinist period. During the liberal era that followed, their lot improved. Elaborate plans were made to celebrate the thousandth anniversary of the Jewish community of Prague; when Russian troops occupied the country, the preparations stopped. In Rumania there were periods when Jews were allowed to migrate to Israel (though compelled to leave all their property behind) and other periods when the gates were closed and Zionist activity was punished. At present, Rumania is one of the friendlier satellite countries; tourism between Rumania and Israel is officially encouraged. The Hungarian Communists have not seriously interfered with Jewish communal and religious life, and the Rabbinical Seminary in Budapest has more than a dozen students.

But nowhere under Communism can Judaism really flourish.

The Jews who remain in Germany and Austria are few in numbers and feeble of spirit.

In the Low Countries, France, and Italy there has been a modest revival of Jewish life for those who escaped destruction. It has been a struggle against many handicaps—small numbers, lack of trained leaders, and poverty. Nazi influence has in some cases left a residue of anti-Jewish feeling; Christianity has made considerable inroads. Catholic families and institutions which rescued a good many French and Italian Jews (especially children) from massacre have sometimes influenced their beneficiaries to enter the Christian church. The most sensational instance was that of the former Chief Rabbi of Rome. Despite the difficulties, the Jews of western Europe, with some help from the United States, are making a valiant effort to maintain their religious existence. The dominant form is a moderate traditionalism; but there are strong Liberal congregations in Paris and Amsterdam, and smaller groups in Brussels and several Dutch cities.

Swedish Jewry has survived intact, and most of the Danish Jews are home again. These small communities continue to follow the pattern of German Liberal Judaism; most of their rabbis were German trained. In Madrid a small congregation, which for some years conducted services unobtrusively under the stringent regulations imposed by the State Church, has now been able to dedicate a building of its own.

The British Jews suffered along with their fellow Englishmen from the blitz and the post-war depression; but they rapidly rebuilt a vigorous community life. One of the most impressive achievements of the traditional community is the publication by the Soncino Press—a private venture—of a complete English translation of the Talmud, and of other Jewish classics. The Orthodox group, however, was badly shaken by heresy proceedings against one of its most learned younger leaders, Rabbi Louis Jacobs. Dr. Jacobs, who was to have become Principal of Jews' College, was denied this post and later removed from his rabbinical charge because of mildly modernist opinions. The Chief Rabbi was able to assert his authority and to make the United Synagogue a bastion of dogmatic Orthodoxy, further to the right than it had ever been before.

The progressive movement has gone forward in England, despite the passing of its most eminent figures, Claude Montefiore, Leo Baeck, and Lily Montagu. In the past its growth had been hampered by the division between "Reform" congregations associated with the West London Synagogue and the "Liberal" group (p. 363). Though the liturgy of the Reform group was somewhat closer to tradition, there was no serious disagreement on principle between the two parties. Today personal and organizational rivalries have subsided; and the Leo Baeck College for the training of rabbis is being jointly maintained.

In the British Dominions, Jewish religious life strikingly resembles that in the home country. The principal cities of Australia and the Union of South Africa have substantial Jewish communities whose members are prosperous and respected. The original congregations maintain the tradition of British Orthodoxy, but there is a strong Liberal movement which has not only served its own adherents but has provided a wholesome challenge to the traditionalists.

The progress of Reform has been particularly sensational in South Africa, where it was unknown until 1933. Both Orthodox and Liberal groups there are ardently Zionist. But the future of this currently flourishing community is tied to the uncertain future of the whole country, with its abnormal economy and its tragic racial antagonisms.

Despite the close ties between Canada and the United States, the Jewish scene in Canada is quite different from that in this country. Montreal has an old S'fardic congregation; but otherwise the Canadian Jewish community is almost entirely of east European origin and relatively recent beginnings. It is strongly traditional, but the line between Orthodoxy and Conservatism is not so clearly drawn as in the United States. Reform congregations, some large and well established, exist in Montreal, Toronto, Hamilton, and Vancouver.

For self-defense and public relations, the Canadian Jewish Congress operates effectively for all Jews of the Dominion.

* * *

The earliest Jewish settlement in the Western Hemisphere was in Brazil. Yet organized Jewish life in Latin America is relatively new. In most cases, the "founding fathers" were from eastern Europe; they were followed by S'fardim from the eastern Mediterranean area, and since 1933 by refugees from the Hitler terror. These elements have remained largely distinct, especially in the larger centers.

Today, the Jews of Argentina constitute the fifth largest Jewish community in the world. It dates only from the final decade of the nineteenth century, when the Jewish Colonization Association, with large funds supplied by Baron Maurice de Hirsch, established a number of agricultural settlements for Russian emigrants. These farm colonies still exist, and some have been quite successful. But the bulk of Argentinian Jewry is concentrated in Buenos Aires.

As early as 1894, the Jews of this city established a burial society, the *Chevra Kedusha Ashkenazi.** This body (which for some years owned the one Jewish cemetery in the area) soon became an agency to promote unity and maintain standards of Jewish life. In the early decades of this century, it waged a successful battle against a few Jews who had defamed the name of Jewry by participating in the white slave traffic, then centered in Buenos Aires. Eventually, the Chevra Kedusha developed into a full-fledged kehillah or community organization, which supervises the leading philanthropic, educational and social activities of the community. Up to the present, however, the

* More correctly, Chevra Kadisha (Aramaic for "holy society"), the traditional name for a group that arranged funerals.

S'fardic congregations and the more recent settlers from central Europe are not part of the kehillah.

Yiddish is widely spoken among the Latin-American Jews, and Buenos Aires is today perhaps the chief center of Yiddish publishing. Even authors who live in New York find it advantageous to bring out their books in Argentina, where printing costs are lower and an extensive reading public is at hand.

The Latin-American Jews have been much interested in Zionism and in the progress of Israel. Their religious life, however, has been rather feeble and ineffective. This may be due in part to the tone of the environment; for in many areas of Latin America, Catholicism, though unchallenged, has not been very ardent. The chief difficulty, however, has been lack of leadership. Many of the smaller communities have no rabbi; and the religious leaders in the larger centers, trained in the European tradition, are not always equal to the challenge of an entirely new situation.

American Jewry, meantime, preoccupied with the needs of Europe and Israel, and with its own problems, has shown little concern with its neighbors in the south. Since their status is reasonably secure and they do not need financial aid, they have been left almost altogether to their own resources. The Jewish Welfare Board has been giving some guidance in the organization of community centers, to meet the needs of youth. Progressive congregations now exist in Buenos Aires, where both the Reform and the Conservative movements have provided rabbis, and in São Paulo; and there are small, struggling groups elsewhere. Mexico City has a well-organized community, which has established admirable educational and social facilities. But a significant religious revival among Latin American Jews is not yet in sight.

* * *

Through the centuries there have been considerable Jewish communities in North Africa and in the lands of western Asia from Turkey to Yemen (South Arabia). In earlier times they were great centers of Jewish thought and activity, but in recent years they have produced little of importance for our story. The high cultural level of Turkish Jewry, due to the influx of exiles from Spain, gradually declined with the decay of the Ottoman Empire. For other Middle

Eastern lands, the golden age of Jewish expression was still further in the past.

The Jews of Morocco and of Persia have long suffered cruel and degrading oppression, and in many other Moslem lands they have been handicapped by discrimination, poverty, and ignorance. From time to time, such outbursts as the Damascus affair have threatened their security.

When Algeria became virtually a part of France during the nineteenth century, the French Jews under the vigorous leadership of Crémieux waged a successful fight to secure equal rights for the Algerian Jews. The latter soon adopted the speech and cultural outlook of Frenchmen.

The Alliance Israélite Universelle has been the one agency of European Jewry that concerned itself seriously with the Jews of the Middle East. Its schools have stressed hygiene and vocational guidance; though they have tried to conserve the religious interests of their students, they have naturally enough been suspect in the eyes of the ultra-Orthodox.

Jewish religion in all these countries has followed the oriental-S'fardic tradition, sometimes in rather debased forms. There has been much superstition and obscurantism, though in many places a high standard of Hebrew knowledge for men has been maintained. Western cultural influences permeated these communities in varying degrees, but rarely affected religion. On the other hand, there are some interesting and beautiful customs found only in this area. The Jews of Morocco and those of the Caucasus, for example, enact a dramatization of the Exodus during their Seder service.

The growing spirit of nationalism in the countries of North Africa was bound to have disastrous consequences for their Jewish inhabitants. This spirit was often tinged with Moslem fanaticism; moreover, many Jews had ties with the European communities against which the North Africans were revolting. Sympathy for the Arab nations aligned against Israel added to the danger; in 1967 a number of Jews were killed by mobs in Libya angered at the outcome of the Six-Day War.

But by that time the mass exodus of North African Jewry had already occurred. Most of the Algerian Jews, being French citizens, resettled in mainland France, as did many others from Tunisia and Morocco. Large numbers were impoverished; and the Joint

Distribution Committee liberally assisted the French Jewish community in helping the newcomers find homes and employment. Most of those who did not go to France migrated to Israel. The Jewish population of Libya, Algeria, Tunisia, and Morocco, which in 1950 had amounted to more than half a million, dropped to less than 65,000 in 1968. At the same time, the French Jewish population rose from about 235,000 to some 535,000. These additions have resulted not only in greater bulk, but also more vitality, among the rather listless members of the French Jewish community.

Oriental Judaism could be studied in a high degree of "purity" among the Jews of Yemen, who for centuries were virtually isolated from contacts with the outside world. Even in the days of Maimonides they were a remote and secluded body; and for precisely that reason they turned to him for help when beset by a variety of problems, including persecution by their rulers and the claims of a messianic pretender. The great philosopher replied to their inquiries in his famous *Epistle to Yemen,* and his memory has always been specially venerated among the Yemenites.

Until recently, their life still retained the medieval pattern. The Jews were skilled and diligent craftsmen, living with moral dignity and simple piety. Though Arabic was their spoken tongue, they all knew Hebrew well. Their synagogue service was conducted in unison, without a leader or cantor; and their teachers and scholars were unsalaried volunteers. Most of the women, however, remained illiterate. They were married off at an early age, and polygamy was not uncommon.

Constant oppression, varied by outbreaks of more vigorous persecution, was their lot throughout history. Already in the nineteenth century, the more venturesome spirits among them began to migrate to Palestine, and the numbers increased as the rebuilding of the homeland progressed. Meantime, conditions in Yemen became more and more desperate for those who remained. In 1949 authorities in Israel, representatives of the Joint Distribution Committee, and the Yemenite leaders came to a decision. The whole community was to be transferred to Israel. The Yemenites abandoned their homes (and most of their possessions went in taxes and tolls) and made their painful way to the British protectorate of Aden. Thence they were flown ("Operation Magic Carpet") to Israel, to the number of nearly forty thousand.

In Many Lands

61.

American Judaism Today

1. *Divisive Forces*

THE STORY OF AMERICAN JEWRY IN THE LAST DECADE IS ONE OF growth and progress. The American Jewish community has attained a level of material well-being, prestige, and influence unparalleled in all Jewish history. It has borne honorably the responsibility to world Jewry which its favorable position requires, and it has made considerable strides toward cultural and spiritual maturity. But to avoid overstress on the positive and often exciting aspects of American Jewish life, it is advisable to report at the outset the dissensions and confusions that still plague it.

In part, the conflicts are due to serious differences of principle; but to a great extent they are simply an inheritance from the chaos of earlier generations with their group antagonisms and organizational rivalries. Large numbers of Jews, especially in the metropolitan centers, have no clearly-defined relationship to the basic institutions of Judaism. Many are ignorant of Jewish beliefs, values, and practices; and their rapid rise to prosperity has often produced distortions of outlook and behavior, such as the lavish Bar Mitzvah celebration. Communal self-discipline is far from adequate. All this has made it difficult to resolve the ideological and organizational controversies.

The old debate over Zionism, which had waned between the two world wars, flared up again in the 1940's. It was plain that at the end of the war, the nations would have to make important decisions regarding the future of Palestine. American Jewry was now overwhelmingly pro-Zionist. This was true also of the Reform group, although its agencies remained officially neutral. But there was still an irreconcilable anti-Zionist minority which sought some means of voicing its opposition.

The American Council for Judaism was formed by a group of rabbis who held that the neutrality rule of the Central Conference had been violated, and who wanted to stress the universalistic doctrine of Reform Judaism. But the organization soon became a predominantly lay organization dedicated to all-out attack on Jewish nationalism. Many of its founders withdrew in disappointment over its negative spirit. The spokesmen of the Council fought the proposal for a Jewish state in Palestine; and since the State of Israel has become a reality, they have continued angrily to challenge the alleged attempt of Zionists to dominate American Jewish affairs in the interest of a "foreign power." Understandably, the American Council for Judaism has drawn upon itself the bitter condemnation of every element in Jewish life. Though most of its membership is drawn from the Reform group, it has no official ties with the agencies of Reform, and has repeatedly attacked the educational program and publications of the Union of American Hebrew Congregations. But it has been compelled by the logic of its own position to foster some positive religious program. A few congregations and schools have formally adopted its philosophy, and it is publishing materials for elementary and adult education.

The American Council for Judaism was launched shortly before the first meeting of the American Jewish Conference. The latter was an attempt to provide a united voice for American Jewry on the problems of peace and post-war reconstruction—to do, in short, what the original American Jewish Congress had done after World War I. Again, the Zionist leadership took the initiative; again the American Jewish Committee insisted on various limitations to the scope and power of the new body. The local elections were bitterly contested, and the Conference assembled in a stridently emotional mood (August, 1943).

Palestine was the one important issue at this gathering. The American Jewish Committee presented a moderate resolution in the hope of achieving unanimity: it denounced the British White Paper, called for greatly increased immigration into Palestine, and proposed that the ultimate status of the country be determined later by international agreement. But the Zionists insisted on a resolution calling for the immediate creation of a Jewish state, which they carried by a large majority. Shortly thereafter, the American Jewish Committee withdrew from the Conference; other bodies (such as the National Council of Jewish Women and the Union of American Hebrew Congregations), which abstained from voting on the resolution, remained as members.

But interest in the Conference waned once the Zionists had achieved their propaganda objective. The prospect of a strong inclusive body representing all (or nearly all) of American Jewry seemed to threaten the prestige and importance of existing agencies. Moreover, the local community councils were demanding a larger share in policy making within the framework of the American Jewish Conference. And so the body, which had become an embarrassment to some of its original sponsors, went out of existence in 1949.

There has also been considerable conflict, competition, and duplication in the work of the several agencies for Jewish defense. In an effort to reduce such difficulties, they formed the National Community Relations Advisory Council (NCRAC); but when this joint body attempted a far-reaching redistribution of functions among its constituents, reactions were violent, and several of the largest agencies withdrew from membership for some years. The breach has since been healed, but American Jews continue to defend their rights on a competitive basis.

2. *The American Jewish Renaissance*

Since the close of the Second World War, an extraordinary revival of Judaism has taken place in America. We are still too close to the movement to judge how profound or decisive it is, but the fact is beyond question. The rapidly mounting number of congregations, the growth of synagogue membership, the increased participation in many types of Jewish activity, the enlarged enrollment in Jewish schools, provide clear evidence. The attitude of Jews toward their Jewish identity has recognizably changed. Negative and assimilatory tendencies have not disappeared, but the counter-trend toward a more affirmative view of Judaism has become much more vigorous.

Many reasons for this upswing can be adduced. The Hitler persecution and the rise of world-wide anti-Semitism awakened Jewish self-consciousness among the indifferent. The rosy trust of many young intellectuals (Gentile and Jewish) that the Soviet experiment would lead to the salvation of mankind ended in disillusionment. The rise of the State of Israel and its successful War of Independence stimulated Jewish morale. The experience of many young Jews in the armed forces and their contact with the chaplains gave them new insights into the meaningfulness of Judaism. Meantime, the synagogue youth programs, the Zionist groups, the Hillel Foundations, and other similar efforts gradually produced a nucleus of men and women equipped for the tasks of leadership. Moreover, religious values have become increasingly important in all American life, and this trend was also bound to have an impact on American Jews.

Past events and current conditions dovetailed amazingly to produce a revival of Jewish life. For American Jewry is becoming more and more a homogeneous group. Once preponderantly immigrant, it is today overwhelmingly native-born and educated. A high percentage of American Jews are college graduates. They are not preoccupied any longer with problems of Americanization, or worried about acceptance. Overt anti-Semitism is at a low ebb, and vocational discrimination (though it still exists) is lessening. On the other hand, the new generation is keenly aware of its great responsibility for Jewish welfare throughout the world. For all these reasons, young people have been led to inquire seriously into the meaning of their own life as Jews. They recognize the need to interpret Jewish experience to their own children, and in this process have often gained a new appreciation of the value of Judaism for themselves. The typical pattern of America, in which each generation had less Jewish knowledge and weaker Jewish loyalties than the previous generation, is becoming less typical. Many young parents who in their own childhood had no significant Jewish experiences are now sending their children to religious schools and introducing ceremonial observances in their homes.

This process has been enormously hastened by an external factor— the rapid movement of Jewish population from the large cities into the surrounding suburban areas. For a generation, it was chiefly the well-to-do who bought country homes and became commuters. But after the Second World War, middle and low cost suburban developments developed rapidly, attracting chiefly young couples with children of school age.

Moving from the amorphous big-city environment into relatively small settlements, the newcomers have quickly acquired a sense of community. And wherever Jews have arrived in appreciable numbers, a Sunday school or Hebrew school, and soon after a congregation have sprung up. The new congregations have served as social centers (a role entirely within the tradition of the historical synagogue); but they have also been the means of reintroducing a whole generation to meaningful worship and study. Part of the leadership has come from young people trained in the established synagogues; but the new congregations have quickly drawn into activity many who were previously estranged from (and even hostile to) Jewish religious values. Their interest in the content of Judaism has been enhanced by the adventure of building something new, by the opportunity for action and leadership, and the freedom to experiment and create, so often denied younger people in congregations where the "old timers" dominate. This trend has been carefully guided and encouraged by the national synagogue unions; but the growth of new synagogues has been the expression of a felt need, and often of a spontaneous demand.

The older congregations have likewise expanded their activities. Adult education, through organized courses, and through such methods as clubs for young married couples and parents' workshops, has made some headway. Much attention has been given to a program for youth beyond the age of Bar Mitzvah or Confirmation. Synagogue youth groups, which were once content to arrange social gatherings, are now seriously concerned with the whole range of Jewish religious interests. The national synagogue unions have done much to elevate standards of youth work. Conferences and institutes held at summer camps have proved especially useful for awakening interest and stimulating the mood of worship.

A generation ago, Jewish intellectuals—university people, writers, artists—were more often than not estranged from or even hostile toward matters Jewish. And those who dabbled in Jewish interests often cultivated a private Judaism remote from the realities of organized Jewish life. Today, many of the best-known figures in the intellectual and artistic life of the United States are actively engaged in rediscovering their Jewish roots, and some are distinguished leaders of the Jewish renaissance.

There are now Jewish architects who specialize in synagogue architecture. There has never been a unique style for synagogue buildings, and the contemporary synagogues plainly reflect the severe functional approach of our day. But whereas nineteenth-century American synagogues were often routine copies of church structures, with the spiritually meaningless six-pointed star as the distinctive item of decoration, the newer synagogues are being planned with greater insight into the specific needs of Jewish congregations, and with much more serious effort to utilize significant symbolism in structure and ornament.

Synagogue music likewise has been greatly improved. Much of the music performed in Reform temples was a commonplace imitation of nineteenth-century German and Italian styles, whether composed by Jews or by Gentile organists; and the chazanim of Orthodox and Conservative congregations were often lacking both in musical taste and in knowledge of the authentic Jewish traditions. The situation has been remedied through research in Jewish musicology and through the creative work of contemporary composers.

Some of these are specialists in synagogue music, but such international figures as Ernest Bloch and Darius Milhaud have also produced compositions for use in Jewish worship.

In all these fields, American Jewish culture has been enriched by the contribution of exiles from central Europe. And the creative work of Israelis both in the graphic arts and in music has aroused much interest among American Jews.

Another sign of the times is the rapprochement between the Jewish labor group and the religious forces. The old antagonisms have dwindled, and there is increasing cooperation and good will between parties once hostile. The diminishing importance of Yiddish on the American scene has perhaps led the former Yiddish-Socialist group to seek some other positive Jewish content for its adherents; the labor group is much less "proletarian" in the prosperous America of the post-New Deal period; the interest of synagogue organizations and especially of rabbinic bodies in problems of social justice has won the respect of many who once regarded religion as a tool of social reaction. And since no group is more violently anti-Communist than the Socialists, the struggle against Soviet influences has tended to establish a friendlier tie with the representatives of religion.

The secularizing tendency in community institutions seems also to be on the wane. Child care agencies, for example, are taking greater interest in providing Jewish education and religious observance for their charges. More chaplaincies are being provided for Jewish hospitals, homes for the aged, and other institutions. In New York an extensive chaplaincy program conducted by the New York Board of Rabbis is now financed by "Federation"; it includes provision for training rabbis and rabbinical students in the techniques of institutional ministration.

The national agencies for defense and social welfare are stressing the importance of a "positive Jewish outlook"; and Jewish education, in one form or another, has been included in the program of almost every national Jewish body. It is being recognized more and more that technical skill is not sufficient to qualify a worker to serve in a Jewish social service agency or community center; and opportunities are now provided such workers to acquire more adequate knowledge of "Jewish content."

A novel departure in this period was the establishment of Brandeis University at Waltham, Mass. (1948). Unlike Yeshivah University, it is not a denominational institution, but a non-sectarian university established and financed by Jews. It has an excellent Department of Jewish Studies, but it does not attempt to indoctrinate its students with a particular viewpoint, and no distinction of race or religion is made in the admission of students or the appointment of professors. During the same years, there has been considerable expansion of an older institution, the Dropsie College in Philadelphia, established for graduate study and research in Hebrew and related fields of learning. It too has no denominational commitments.

In short, it has become clear that the establishment of the State of Israel marks a turning point for American Jewry no less than for the oppressed communities of the Old World. For the present, indeed, American Jews must continue to raise funds and to engage in political effort on behalf of those who are still persecuted and of the State that is still insufficiently strong. But these activities are no longer enough to provide a meaningful Jewish life for the American Jew; and barring a world catastrophe, their importance will lessen in the future.

The very existence of a Jewish State, to which those who regard themselves as Jews by nationality may migrate, points up the challenge to those who chose to remain in other countries. Why need they remain Jews any longer? And in what sense shall they continue to be Jews? To such questions the Jews of the United States have been responding with a renewed affirmation of religious loyalty.

62.

American Judaism Today

(continued)

1. *Orthodoxy*

ORTHODOX, CONSERVATIVE, AND REFORM JUDAISM, FROM THE STAND-point of religious leaders and agencies, have sharply distinguished doctrines and correspondingly divergent programs. Such distinctions are not nearly so clear to the individual layman or even to the individual congregation. The distance between Orthodoxy and Reform is considerable and generally recognized; it is harder to distinguish between right-wing Conservatism and Orthodoxy on one hand, and between left-wing Conservatism and Reform on the other. Individuals may join a congregation because of its accessibility, its attractive building, the personality of the rabbi, or the prestige of its members, rather than on purely ideological grounds. Not infrequently, an individual maintains membership in more than one synagogue for sentimental reasons or because he wants to support all communal institutions.

Within each of the three main divisions there is considerable variety of outlook and practice. Thus, the Orthodox category includes the pre-Revolutionary congregations of New York and Philadelphia with their old S'fardic traditions, and also the Chasidic bodies which frown on the adoption of western dress and on secular education. Neither of these extremes, however, is typical of American Orthodoxy. Most of the traditional congregations have a central or east European background, but are now largely Americanized. Indeed, a substantial segment of their membership is American born. Modern methods of administration, greater decorum in the service, English sermons, increased activities for women's groups, progressive pedagogy, and provision for the Hebrew education of girls are now commonplace. The rabbis of these synagogues are college graduates, and, like their Reform and Conservative colleagues, perform the pastoral duties of an American minister.

A large percentage of these rabbis are graduates of the great New York Yeshivah named after Rabbi Isaac Elhanan Spektor, the Rabbi of Kovno at the end of the nineteenth century, who was famed for his liberal interpretations of the halakah. In recent decades, the Yeshivah established a Teachers' Institute, and then an undergraduate college of arts and sciences. Yeshivah College was the first general academic institution established under Jewish auspices in the United States. Like other denominational colleges, it aims to provide a higher education permeated by explicitly religious attitudes and ideals. More recently, the institution has been rechartered as Yeshivah University; a School of Medicine and an undergraduate college for women have now been established.

Less ambitious in scope but equally modern in spirit is the Hebrew Theological College of Chicago. It, too, provides some instruction in secular subjects, as well as training in the traditional rabbinic disciplines. There are a number of other y'shivos, however, chiefly in the New York area, which follow the east European models more closely. Secular education is admitted only to the extent that the law of the state demands, and Yiddish is the language of instruction for Jewish subjects. The sponsors of such institutions look askance at the more progressive elements of the Orthodox community, and they have a fairly large following.

The Americanized synagogues, to the number of over seven hundred, constitute the Union of Orthodox Jewish Congregations, and their spiritual leaders generally belong to the Rabbinical Council of America. These bodies cooperate with the corresponding agencies of Conservative and Reform Judaism through the Synagogue Council of America and the NCRAC. The Yiddish-speaking rabbis maintain an older organization, the *Aggudas HoRabbonim,* which claims exclusive authority in matters of Jewish law, and rarely collaborates with any other group, even though it be Orthodox.

A striking change in the American Jewish scene is the multiplication of Jewish Day Schools (sometimes called *Y'shivos K'tanos* and, inaccurately, Jewish parochial schools). This trend reflects not only a more confident and aggressive Orthodoxy but also general dissatisfaction with the state of Hebrew education in this country. The supplementary Hebrew schools have not achieved as much as was hoped. Meeting in the late afternoons, they impose an added burden on children already tired from the public school session and eager for play outdoors. For this reason, many of their pupils resent Hebrew study and even acquire a distaste for Judaism; in any case, most of them drop out as soon as they are Bar Mitzvah. Thus, educators have sought a solution in a school where Hebrew and secular subjects would be part of a single curriculum, and where full-time employment for Hebrew teachers would facilitate the improvement of pedagogic standards.

Schools of this sort have existed for years in the larger cities, but now, strikingly, they have spread to many smaller communities, where there is considerably more day-to-day contact between Gentiles and Jews.

The advantages of the day school are obvious. It makes possible an intensive program of Hebrew studies, an opportunity that leads some non-Orthodox parents to enroll their children. It engenders strong Jewish loyalties, and avoids the conflicts that arise from the specifically Christian teachings and practices often included in public school curricula. On the other hand, the enrichment derived from living and working with children of varying cultural and religious backgrounds is necessarily lost. Despite the expansion of the Hebrew day school movement, the overwhelming majority of American Jewish children attend the public schools.

Clearly, Orthodox Judaism has been much affected by the conditions and spirit of American life. The last decade has witnessed the emergence of a small but distinguished group of Orthodox thinkers who are thoroughly at home in modern science and philosophy and who are trying to reformulate traditional doctrines in terms of the contemporary social and intellectual scene. Some of them are much admired in non-Orthodox circles; within their own group, their influence has been limited.

Orthodox Jewry has, in fact, suffered a good deal from internal divisions. Despite its general emphasis on authority, it has not yet succeeded in establishing effective authority even in practical affairs. The question of kashrus is particularly vexing. The observant housewife must rely on the fitness of meat sold in local kosher markets. It is therefore necessary to provide for the licensing of slaughterers and the regular inspection of stores selling kosher products. This supervision should make kosher meat a little more costly than non-kosher meat of the same grade; but in practice, kosher meats are often unreasonably expensive. Lack of community discipline has thus far made it impossible to control profiteering; sometimes there is even doubt whether meat sold as kosher is so in fact. Factional disputes, and personal or organizational rivalries among rabbis have compounded the difficulties. In many localities, however, the situation has been relieved by the establishment of kashrus boards, sponsored jointly by a number of congregations, and frequently including representatives of the Conservative group.

It is evident that Orthodoxy has sustained considerable losses in the last few generations. The membership of Reform and Conservative synagogues has been drawn from erstwhile Orthodox Jews, or from the unsynagogued whose families were once Orthodox. There is, nevertheless, no reason to think that Orthodoxy will disappear. Many people require the kind of religion that affirms a fixed and changeless doctrine and maintains definite rules and regulations. For them, Orthodoxy is not confinement but support; they prefer its reassuring certainties to the hazards of liberalism. Their numbers seem presently to be growing.

2. The Conservative and Reconstructionist Movements

Conservative Judaism made rapid strides during the twentieth century. Its success is readily understood. It met the needs of thousands of Jews who were not Orthodox, but for various reasons (already mentioned) could not accept the prevailing versions of Reform. Many people were attracted to the Conservative synagogue because it provided workable compromises. It was a meeting ground for traditionalists who were not strictly Orthodox and for modernists who loved the old forms. To many, the wearing of a hat during worship seemed a more vital issue than the doctrine of revelation.

Nevertheless, as the American Jewish community has become more homogeneous socially and culturally, and as its laymen have matured intellectually, questions of fundamental principle are emerging more sharply. The Conservative movement will have to reckon increasingly with theological problems.

The most trenchant criticism has, in fact, come from within. Dr. Mordecai M. Kaplan, a graduate of the Jewish Theological Seminary and a leading member of its faculty, has been the spokesman of the opposition and indeed the leader of a new movement.

For Professor Kaplan was dissatisfied with all current formulations of Jewish doctrine. Neo-Orthodoxy, in his opinion, has not seriously faced the challenge of modern ideas. Reform deserves credit for having done so, but Kaplan cannot accept the solution it offers. The prime error of Reform, he holds, was to reduce Judaism to the dimensions of a mere church or sect, denying or minimizing the national element in Jewish life. Secular nationalism, on the other hand, has not accorded to the religious values of Judaism the central importance they rightfully claim. As for Conservative Judaism, it is not a philosophy, but an uneasy partnership between the right wing of Reform and the left wing of Orthodoxy.

Kaplan has therefore called for a reconstruction of Jewish life, and the movement he has headed is known as Reconstructionism. Fundamental to this approach is the view that Judaism is a civilization. In this civilization, religion is the central and indispensable element, but not the only element. Ethnic, legal, linguistic, literary, and artistic values are also important. Nationalism and religion are both essential to a complete Jewish philosophy and a complete Jewish life. The American Jew must share in two civilizations, the American and the Jewish; and the culture of contemporary Israel is part of the Jewish civilization.

Kaplan is more explicit in his modernism than most of the Conservative leaders. He bluntly rejects all supernaturalism, and denies that the Torah is of literal divine origin. The ceremonial laws are "folkways." They are a valuable part of the Jewish civilization and must not be lightly discarded; but they are not absolutely binding. The dietary laws, for example, should be observed in the home where they help to create a Jewish consciousness; but they need not be kept so strictly on the outside, in view of the exigencies of modern life.

Like the reformers, Kaplan rejects the belief in miracles, the personal Messiah, and the resurrection. But he goes beyond them in denying the doctrine of the election of Israel. To hold that one people was "chosen" from among all others appears to him unreasonable and chauvinistic. We may say only that Israel has a "vocation," and that every other people likewise has its distinctive role in world history, determined by its qualifications and experiences. Kaplan's treatment of the God idea is also quite extreme. In his writings, God is the name for the totality of factors that make for human fulfillment; He is hardly a self-existent Being.

The Reconstructionist leader has been admittedly much influenced by the American pragmatist philosopher, John Dewey. His theoretical formulation is bound up with a practical program. The basic unit in American life should not be the congregation but the "organic community." For the congregation is a religious body (and a sectarian one at that), whereas Judaism is more than a religion. Moreover, many individuals today are affirmatively Jewish but are not practicing religionists. Membership in the local community should therefore be open to everyone who wants to identify himself as a Jew. The inclusive community, democratically governed, should provide for the philanthropic, educational, Zionist, and religious needs of all its component elements; and it should cooperate with similar bodies in building the organized national Jewish community. Kaplan sees in the Jewish community centers and community councils the initial stages in the creation of an "organic" community.

The clarity and courage with which Dr. Kaplan has maintained his views have won him many loyal followers within the Conservative and Reform groups, particularly among rabbis. Several congregations have identified themselves as Reconstructionist. But for a good many years, the movement did not seek to establish institutions paralleling those of the three major sects. It sought rather to influence thinking among all groups in Jewry, and the Reconstructionist Fellowship cut across the usual lines. Among many publications of the movement is a prayer book, traditional in form and style, but modernist in content. More recently, however, there has been a trend toward institutional consolidation. In 1969 the Reconstructionist Rabbinical College was opened in Philadelphia. Its students are expected to supplement their rabbinical training by obtaining doctorates from secular universities.

The leaders of the Conservative movement have had to reckon with the challenge of Reconstructionism. The thinking of Professor Kaplan has had an influence on many who have not fully adopted his position. An official prayer book for Conservative use has now appeared which contains a number of significant departures from traditional wording. (Previously, Conservative synagogues utilized a variety of rituals, prepared by individual rabbis.) A considerable segment of the Conservative rabbinate, including the leaders of the Seminary, seem to have reacted to the modernist trend by a more vigorous affirmation of traditional authority. Discussion has centered largely around problems of Jewish law. The group just mentioned seeks to maintain the structure of the halakah and to make such changes as are necessary within the traditional framework. An example is the recent proposal to change the wording of the k'subo or marriage contract by which the bride and groom agree that they will take counsel with a rabbi if they encounter difficulties in their married life, and if necessary submit their problems for adjudication by a rabbinical court. But other Conservative leaders insist that a bolder and more independent approach to Jewish law and observance is necessary for any realistic program: though they make plain that they wish to avoid the "mistakes" of Reform.

Despite these disagreements, there is a fair degree of uniformity in the practice of Conservative synagogues. In personal and family life, the extent of religious observance varies greatly among Conservative Jews, as it does among those affiliated with the other religious groups. One cannot safely draw inferences as to the actual practice of the individual Jew from the kind of synagogue to which he belongs.

3. Reform

Time was when Reform occupied a privileged place in American Jewish life. Except in a few eastern cities, the Reform temple was the oldest congregation in the community, its members were the most affluent and influential, and its rabbi uniquely qualified to represent Judaism before the general public. This situation has now changed greatly. In many cities, the size, wealth, and prestige of the Reform group have been eclipsed by the traditionalists; and in most places there are Conservative and Orthodox rabbis well fitted to play a leading role in civic affairs. Reform, meanwhile, has acquired a far broader outlook, and its leaders have done much to advance the cause of Jewish unity. The establishment of the Synagogue Council of America and of many local community councils was due to the initiative of Reform Jews.

There has been a vigorous tendency within Reform to reemphasize traditional values, the Hebrew language, and ceremonial observance. This fact has been variously explained. A great many Jews stemming from east European Orthodox backgrounds have joined Reform congregations and have become Reform rabbis. The more recent comers from the Liberal congregations of Germany likewise held fast to many traditional observances. Zionism has become influential within Reform, and the establishment of Israel heightened the Jewish consciousness everywhere. Contemporary Protestantism has also become more hospitable to ritualistic tendencies. No doubt all these factors have been involved. Yet the inner logic of the situation would probably have produced this traditionalist movement in any case.

At the start, when Reform was struggling against Orthodox rigidity, it had to battle the dominant ritualism and insist that ceremony was not of primary importance. Many people who joined the Reform movement experienced a sense of liberation and joyous release in being able to discard with good conscience regulations that they felt to be outworn and wearisome. But this gratification could not be transmitted to their children and grandchildren. The latter found no inspiration in not doing what they had never been forced to do! Only something positive could stir them; and for this purpose, theological and ethical generalities, no matter how sublime, were not enough. Children, especially, it was found, were not likely to develop a love for Judaism unless it was made vivid for them through meaningful and enjoyable observances.

The problem of Christmas, so widely celebrated in secularized form among Jews, provided a challenge and starting point. Children were encouraged in the religious school to light the Chanuko candles at home, and to ask for presents at the Jewish rather than the Christian festival. What had been a relatively minor occasion in the Jewish calendar now took on larger importance. The Friday evening Kiddush, the family Seder, and other holiday celebrations have gradually been brought back into homes from which they had been absent for several generations.

Reform Jewish education has become more professional and intensive. The Commission on Jewish Education (jointly sponsored by the Union of American Hebrew Congregations and the Central Conference of American Rabbis) has pioneered in the production of first-rate textbooks and other teaching materials. Its program includes provision for all age groups, from pre-school toddlers to adults. The publications of the Commission have been widely used in the schools of both Reform and traditional congregations, and have stimulated the production of better teaching materials by the Conservative and Orthodox groups.

Many Reform synagogues now conduct week-day sessions in addition to the Sunday school—thus facilitating more intensive Hebrew instruction, supplementary activities in dramatics and arts and crafts, and training for Confirmation. The age of Confirmation has been generally raised to fifteen or sixteen; pupils benefit by the additional years of instruction, and are more mature when they participate in the ceremony. An increasingly effective youth program keeps a large proportion of religious school graduates in touch with synagogue life through the critical teen-age years. Many congregations provide a full high school course. Whereas, formerly the Sunday school was conducted in basement rooms by volunteer teachers, the new synagogue buildings provide splendid physical facilities for education; and the percentage of the temple budget devoted to the religious school has everywhere steadily risen.

Worship in the Reform synagogue has taken on a more characteristically Jewish flavor by the restoration of some traditional customs and the utilization of distinctively Jewish music. The cantor, who had disappeared from all but a few Reform synagogues, is again becoming a familiar functionary. Most Reform rabbis wear a gown in the pulpit, many a talis, some a pulpit hat.

Some Reform Jews have been distressed by these tendencies which they condemn as "a return to Orthodoxy." For the same reason, these trends have been observed with hope by spokesmen of tradition. But such an interpretation is hardly justified. There has never been complete uniformity in Reform practice; some synagogues belonging to the Union of American Hebrew Congregations have been more traditional, some quite radical in liturgical matters. Nor are the newer trends in any sense a movement toward authoritarianism. The traditional customs have been revived in considerably modified form, and there has likewise been much experiment with ceremonies that have no precedent in the Jewish past. The objective has not been to restore the synagogue procedures of an earlier generation but to make modern worship more varied and inspiring.

All this is well illustrated by the most recent revision of the *Union Prayerbook*. It contains traditional materials not found in earlier editions, but also many new prayers and meditations concerned with present-day life. To avoid monotony, variant forms of service for the different Sabbaths of the month and for week-day worship have been provided. The prayer book includes a new ritual for the kindling of Sabbath candles at the Friday night service, generally performed by one of the women of the congregation. Such traditional customs as the procession of scrolls for the Rejoicing of the Law and a memorial service for the last day of Passover are restored, but much changed in form.

A joint committee of the Union and Central Conference is engaged in continuing experimentation with ceremonies for synagogue and home. It has published much new material and has encouraged the production of handsome ceremonial objects.

Several important events affecting the structure of Liberal Judaism in the United States must be recorded. Shortly before his death in 1949, Dr. Stephen S. Wise took the first steps which have since led to the legal merger of the Jewish Institute of Religion and the Hebrew Union College. The united College-Institute maintains the Cincinnati and New York schools as well as a branch in Los Angeles. The New York center now includes the School of Religious Education, which trains teachers and educational directors, and the School of Sacred Music. The latter prepares cantor-educators qualified to meet the needs of American congregations. Its graduates are bringing the cantorial style and Jewish traditional melody back to synagogues where these elements had long been absent. The School of Sacred Music, moreover, is officially committed to training cantors not only for Reform but also for traditional congregations. Among the activities of the Cincinnati school is an active program of graduate study for Christian scholars, which has proceeded most successfully.

Clearly, Reform Judaism is taking a broader view of its function in Jewish life. In the same way, it was more than a mere administrative change when the Union of American Hebrew Congregations moved its national headquarters to New York City. Previously, they had been located in Cincinnati, simply because Isaac M. Wise had lived there. But since the bulk of American Jewry is concentrated on the Atlantic seaboard, and since most national Jewish bodies have their principal offices in New York, it was deemed important that the Union also should have its administrative leaders in the teeming center of American Jewish life. The impressive building where national offices are located, known as "The House of Living Judaism," serves not only a utilitarian but also a symbolic purpose.

Reform, then, which during the early decades of the twentieth century had been relatively static, is growing in numbers and in the intensity of both local and national programs. It has achieved notable success in winning back to Judaism many who were previously unaffiliated and indifferent. Recently, voices have been heard calling for advance on still another front. Judaism, they point out, was once a missionary religion, and abandoned its activity in this field only under duress. The time has come, it is argued, to resume this function, and to bring the message of Judaism more vigorously to the millions of non-Jews who today have no church affiliation. It is held that Reform Judaism is uniquely adapted to this purpose. These suggestions have thus far produced little practical result. To most Reform Jews, even to many rabbis, the idea of proselytizing is strange and even disturbing. But these proposals are being more and more generally discussed and may in time bear unexpected fruit.

63.

The Six-Day War and Its Aftermath

THE WAR OF LIBERATION ENDED NOT WITH PEACE, BUT WITH AN uneasy truce, supervised year after year by UN forces. The Arab nations refused to recognize Israel's existence and would enter into no negotiations looking toward peace. Their spokesmen plainly stated their intention some day to resume hostilities and to destroy Israel. Organized terrorist groups—some based in Jordan, others in Sinai and the Gaza Strip under Egyptian control—struck repeatedly at Israeli settlements, killing and destroying. The great powers paid little attention to these continuing acts of aggression but grew stern and moralistic when the government of Israel instituted reprisals.

In 1966 Egypt nationalized the Suez Canal—previously under joint British and French control—and denied its use to any ship under any flag bound to or from an Israeli port. In October of that year, Israeli forces attacked and destroyed the terrorist bases in the Sinai Peninsula; and French and British troops moved in to regain control of the Canal. But the Soviet Union threatened to intervene, and the Eisenhower Administration was unwilling to take any risks, adding its pressure upon the British and French. When these powers withdrew, Israel had to do the same. But the UN settlement, which guaranteed ships of all nations the use of the Suez Canal, was disregarded by Egypt. Israel, however, continued to have access to the Red Sea through her port at Elath.

Subsequently, the Soviet Union expanded its influence in the Middle East, and Communist hostility to the State of Israel became increasingly vocal and abusive. By 1967 the Arab forces, provided with Soviet arms and instructed by Soviet experts, were deemed ready. Egypt demanded the immediate removal of UN truce forces, and Secretary-General U Thant acceded to the demand with what must be called indecent haste. The Straits of Tiran, through which all shipping to and from Elath had to pass, were closed by Egypt. As Egyptian and Syrian armies massed on the borders of Israel, the Arab press and radio announced in shrillest tones the plans for the massacre of all Israelis. Representations before the UN Security Council that war was imminent were ridiculed by the Russians, who were clearly prepared to veto any action that would stop their Arab puppets.

In a situation of mortal danger, Israel struck first. The Egyptian and Syrian airfields, and the planes they served, were wiped out in a single day. The fighting ended in six days with the total rout of the Egyptian and Syrian forces. The Israeli army had control of all Sinai, and of the east bank of the Suez Canal. It also captured the Golan Heights, from which the Syrians had previously rained down artillery fire on Israeli settlements along the Sea of Galilee. Had not political prudence dictated otherwise, the Israelis could have occupied Cairo and Damascus.

With a little more caution, Jordan would have fared better. Forces in East Jerusalem began firing on the New City only one day before the Egyptian collapse. The Israelis refrained from using artillery against the Old City, with its many holy places; but they had soon captured it, and thereafter occupied the entire area west of the Jordan—the most productive part of the Kingdom of Jordan.

Indescribable enthusiasm was evoked among Jews throughout the world by the reunification of Jerusalem. For the first time since 1948, Jews could visit the Western Wall (called by non-Jews the Wailing Wall, it is part of the outer masonry of Herod's Temple). Not only the Orthodox, who had previously frequented this place of sacred associations, but many hard-bitten unbelievers found themselves deeply moved by the experience. The enthusiasm was tempered by sadness. Many historic synagogues in the Old City, as well as the Jewish cemetery on the Mount of Olives, had been ruthlessly desecrated, and the Hebrew University buildings on Mount Scopus were dilapidated.

The astonishing victory of the Israeli forces transformed the mood of world Jewry from extreme anxiety to limitless joy and pride. In the United States, contributions came to the United Jewish Appeal in such record numbers and amounts, that volunteers had to be called for to record and acknowledge them; and many Jewish intellectuals who had hitherto been detached and critical toward the Jewish State were startled by the intensity of their "visceral" reactions.

The general public in the Americas (and in most noncommunist countries elsewhere) was strongly pro-Israel. But this was not the case with the Christian churches. The Vatican expressed disquiet that the "holy places" should be in Jewish hands—it had never complained about their being in Moslem hands—though the Christian shrines in Nazareth had been admittedly well protected by Israel and despite the desecration of Jewish "holy places" by the Jordanians. Church bodies in the United States issued ambiguous statements which evidenced hostility to Israel, and some prominent Protestant clerics followed the communist line and branded Israel as the aggressor. A distinguished few spoke out bodily on behalf of a center of democracy in the Middle East threatened by the Arab–Soviet coalition. These negative reactions within official Christendom caused some interruptions and difficulties in the Jewish–Christian dialogue, which previously had been making excellent progress.

Jewish leaders were quick to remind their constituents that the end of the Six-Day War did not mean the end of danger to Israel. The Soviet Union and its satellites denounced the "aggression" of Israel before the UN in vicious terms, and the rearming of the Arab states began almost at once. Perhaps most shocking to the Jewish world was the action of the French president, General Charles de Gaulle, who suddenly aligned himself with the Arab–communist bloc. France has refused to deliver to Israel war planes already ordered and paid for, nor has it returned the monies received for them! The French Rothschilds responded to de Gaulle's action by publishing results of a poll proving that French public opinion was strongly on the side of Israel.

Up to the present, the situation is one of continuing crisis. There are artillery duels across the Suez Canal (which remains closed to all traffic) and the Jordan River, and raids across the borders; terrorists have set off bombs in Jerusalem and elsewhere. Terrorists also attacked Israeli commercial planes at Athens and Zurich. The pitiful remnants of Jewry in Iraq, Egypt, and North Africa have been victimized by officials and by mobs venting their frustration at humiliating military defeat. All these barbarities have been officially disregarded by the UN, despite open admission by the Arab governments that they are harboring and supporting the terrorists; yet acts of reprisal by Israel have been severely condemned by the international community, including on occasion the United States.

The will of the Israeli people to survive and the will of world Jewry to support them have not changed.

64.

An Age of Anxiety

THE PERIOD FOLLOWING WORLD WAR II WAS MARKED BY AN IN-
creasing acceptance of Jews and Judaism on the American scene.
Overt anti-Semitism was at a low ebb, confined to a lunatic fringe.
Many occupations where Jews had previously experienced severe
discrimination—engineering, for example, and university teaching
—were now open to all qualified applicants.

In literature and the arts Jews were outstanding in numbers
and distinction. More important, much of their work was explicitly
Jewish in content. Novels and plays about Jews and Jewish experience won both popular and critical acclaim. One of the most
successful of Broadway musicals was based on stories by the Yiddish
author Sholom Aleichem about poor Jews in tsarist Russia. The
American Jewish writers were not invariably flattering in their
depiction of Jews or conventionally pious in their treatment of
Judaism. Their accounts ranged from the sentimental and the
traditional, through the satirical and critical, to the obscene and
defamatory. Yet all these writers were affirming their own Jewish
identity and apparently finding in their Jewishness a means of
contributing something distinctive to American culture. The public,
Jewish and non-Jewish, was interested in what they had to say.
Even Jewish radio and television comedians—in an age when the
old-fashioned dialect comedian was all but extinct—found occasion
to speak of Jewish observances, mores, and cookery—sometimes
in good taste, sometimes with vulgarity.

These changes of relationship between Jews and Gentiles in America, and indeed throughout the western world, were also mirrored in new relationships between the Christian churches and the institutions of Judaism. Not that interfaith activity and good-will movements were a novelty. But they had previously been conducted for the most part by the more explicitly liberal elements in both Jewish and Christian communities. From time to time, Protestant, Catholic, and Jewish bodies also cooperated in efforts for civic betterment and social progress. But wholehearted inter-faith endeavor had been hampered, on the one hand, by the con-versionist aims of some Protestant groups, and on the other, by the reluctance of most Catholic bishops to allow either clergy or laity to involve themselves very far in such activity.

A marked shift of attitudes became manifest after John xxiii ascended the papal throne and convoked the Second Vatican Coun-cil. Though he became Pope when he was advanced in years, he brought a new spirit of youth and adventure into the ancient Roman Church. The Vatican Council, under his leadership, de-voted much effort to rethinking Catholic attitudes toward non-Catholic Christians and toward non-Christian religions. Prominent in its agenda was a restatement of the Catholic attitude toward the Jews.

The history of this episode is too complicated to be told here in detail. From the Jewish side, it was marred by the overeagerness of some Jewish organizations to advise and influence members of the Council and to claim credit for positive results—as well as by over-effusive and perhaps premature expressions of gratitude for an act of justice centuries overdue. On the Catholic side, the proposals of the more liberal churchmen were resisted by clerical reaction-aries, especially by bishops from Arab countries. The statement finally adopted, after Pope John had died and been succeeded by the more conservative Paul vi, was less forthright than the original draft and contained less than many Jews had hoped for. There was, for example, no word of regret for the sufferings endured by Jews for centuries at the hands of the Church and its leaders. But the statement did reject the notion that all Jews for all time are guilty of "deicide"; and it called for the revision of liturgical or educational materials that might encourage anti-Semitism.

An Age of Anxiety 455

The practical results of all this in the United States were striking. Catholics now took the initiative in arranging dialogues with Protestants and Jews concerning both theological and social issues. The assistance of non-Catholics was sought in the revision of teaching materials. Priests and nuns appeared frequently before Jewish and Protestant bodies—sometimes even in pulpits—and laymen, including students, who had previously been discouraged from attending non-Catholic services, were permitted and even encouraged to learn at first hand about other religions. These trends tended also to stimulate more interfaith activity between Protestants and Jews.

This same period has also witnessed a wave of interest, and of creativeness, in the field of Jewish theology. This is not a popular movement; the great mass of Jews, even of those active in synagogue life, have not been greatly affected by it. But it has challenged a considerable number of earnest and thoughtful people, including many Jews in academic life—especially in the fields of philosophy and religion—as well as rabbis and seminary professors.

All formulations of Jewish theology in our age have been deeply affected by the tragic events of World War II and the destruction of European Jewry. Those terrible years demolished the easy optimism of many liberal thinkers by revealing man's frightening capacities for evil. (Such considerations had been urged a generation earlier by such Christian thinkers as Karl Barth; no doubt, too, Freudian psychology, with its generally pessimistic view of human nature, was thought to support older notions of "original sin.")

Thus, many recent Jewish writers on religion have espoused some form of religious existentialism, drawing upon Martin Buber and Franz Rosenzweig, upon such Christian thinkers as Barth and Reinhold Niebuhr, and upon the father of existentialism, the nineteenth-century Danish author Søren Kierkegaard. The Jewish thinkers in question, dissatisfied with the rationalism and moralism of liberal formulations, are concerned not with reflection *about* God but rather with a direct encounter *of* God. They see in the Bible a record of such encounters, even though they are not literalists and do not reject the findings of Bible criticism. However fragmentary and inadequate the reporting, they hold, the evidence of a divine–human encounter is unmistakable. There follows—as with Rosenzweig—a tendency to stress traditional observance, even among those associated with the Reform movement. Other existentialist thinkers, affiliated with Conservative and Orthodox Judaism, stress even more the fulfillment of the *mizvos*.

Those who continued to support a liberal theological position had likewise to take into consideration the tragic experiences of the Jewish people—and indeed of all mankind. The relaxed expectation of a messianic age soon to arrive through the steady operation of the forces of progress had to be discarded. The complexity of man's nature, his range of power for both evil and good, had to be appraised more realistically. This change appeared in the thinking of Leo Baeck—perhaps the most notable of liberal Jewish theologians—long before Hitler. Baeck stressed the fact that Judaism contains a mystical as well as an ethical component. Mystery and commandment supplement and interpenetrate each other. Moreover, by his heroic leadership of German Jewry throughout the Hitler years, his insistence on remaining with his people when opportunities for escape were still open to him, and his indomitable bearing even in the concentration camp, he fulfilled the existentialist demand that truth be made evident not merely by logical argument, but by whole-souled action. Baeck's last book, begun during the last days of German Jewry, continued on scraps of paper in the concentration camp, and completed just before his death at the age of 83, was significantly entitled *This People Israel: The Meaning of Jewish Existence.*

A third trend which has continued to exert some influence is that of religious naturalism, as expounded by Mordecai M. Kaplan and others. The Reconstructionist movement, while rejecting the literalism and supernaturalism of Orthodoxy, has not promulgated an official theology. Holding that religious pluralism is legitimate and inevitable within the Jewish community, Reconstructionists have not attempted to impose credal uniformity even upon themselves. But many of the Reconstructionist spokesmen have taught a naturalistic doctrine, accepting the description of reality provided by the sciences as the most reliable available to us, and so arriving at a rather abstract and impersonal God-concept.

Much more extreme is a small group of radical theologians, the Jewish counterpart to the Christian exponents of "the death of

God." Several of the Jewish representatives of this viewpoint are preoccupied with the Nazi Holocaust, which to them indicates that God is either nonexistent or inaccessible. How this radical theology is to be distinguished from simple rejection of all positive religious values is not entirely clear: Auschwitz would seem to make faith in man at least as difficult as faith in a living God. Yet there is, no doubt, significance in the attempt of these thinkers to find some religious values even within their bleak, atheistic world view.

American Jews have regarded themselves as defenders and supporters of their fellow Jews, wherever the latter were in need or in danger. They have been deeply concerned about the State of Israel and its people. But recently they have had to give more thought to their own situation, in terms both of physical and political security and of inner soundness.

Anti-Semitism, after nearly twenty years of virtual quiescence, has become a much more open and serious phenomenon. This change has been directly connected with social disorder in the United States, aroused chiefly by the increasingly vehement demand of Negroes for legal and economic equality and by opposition to American involvement in Vietnam.

Jews, of course, are not all alike in their opinions and their prejudices. But it seems clear that in the struggle by black Americans for civil rights, they received proportionately far more support from Jews than from the white population as a whole. Many Jewish religious and defense agencies spoke up vigorously for Negro demands; and individual Jews were among the outstanding participants in the civil rights effort, both in providing funds and in personal activity, sometimes at the risk of real physical danger. In the South several synagogues were bombed by white racists, and hate literature linked the Negro revolt to "Jewish communism."

Nevertheless, Jews began to find themselves singled out as special targets of hatred in the black community, especially on the part of extremist militant groups. There were many reasons for this. Anti-Semitism was a convenient device for black rabble rousers, as it had been for Hitler and so many others; it was fortified by the fundamentalist Christian background of many Negroes and by their emotional need to find a scapegoat for their ills.

But there were also more specific causes. Many of the black

ghettos were once Jewish neighborhoods. (Perhaps this phenomenon has repeated itself so often because—unlike some of the white Gentile groups—Jews did not employ violence and terror to prevent blacks from moving into their areas.) As a result, a relatively high number of Jewish landlords and merchants remained in these neighborhoods after the Negroes moved in. Some of them doubtless exploited black tenants and customers, and this contributed to the picture of the Jew as enemy of the black man. In New York City dissatisfaction with the public schools was compounded by the fact that a high proportion of teachers and supervisors are Jewish; in some instances, literally terroristic methods were used to force Jews out of their positions so that they might be replaced by Negroes. Nor can communist influences be ruled out: witness statements from extremist groups that "white" Israelis have been massacring "black" Arabs in the Middle East. During riots in the black ghettos, many of the stores that were looted and burned were those of Jews, whose marginal enterprises were completely wiped out.

These events have not reduced the anti-Jewish attitudes of right-wing whites. They have created something of a Jewish backlash, the extent of which is hard to determine. Official Jewish bodies, while denouncing black anti-Semitism, have insisted that Jews must continue to support the effort for civil rights, economic equality, and antipoverty measures. But in any case, recent occurrences have produced a serious emotional upheaval in American Jewry. The problems, both social and spiritual, are far from resolution.

At the same time, the American Jewish community has been confronted with serious questions as to its own inner soundness and its prospects for survival. These questions emerge from the attitudes of Jewish youth, especially of college students.

The 1960's have witnessed a deep generation gap in almost every sector of American urban and suburban life. (It is less manifest in conservative rural areas.) The phenomenon includes a failure of communication between parents and children, and a repudiation by the latter of many of the life-patterns and standards of their elders. This runs from the rejection of conventional habits of dress and personal cleanliness to advocacy of the use of drugs and of

An Age of Anxiety 459

virtually unrestricted sexual freedom. It has also included vehement criticism—by no means unjustified, let it be said—of the materialism and emptiness of much of middle-class living.

This is not the place for an extended analysis of this youthful revolt, which has its counterparts in nations as different as Sweden, the Soviet Union, and—prior to the Six-Day War—Israel. What is important for our purpose is that the alienation of youth, marked throughout the United States, has been especially common among Jews. It has been estimated that, at the height of the short-lived "hippie" movement, twenty-five percent of the dropouts who gathered in San Francisco were Jewish youngsters. And among the radicals of the New Left, who have been engaged in disruptive activities on university campuses, a disproportionately large number are from Jewish families. This fact has not been overlooked by reactionaries who seek to block even salutary change.

The young rebels of every stamp, opposed to the Vietnam war and the power of the military–industrial complex, critical of the mechanization of life and of the cult of success, see themselves as genuine idealists; and we might interpret the wide participation by Jews in these movements as evidence of the intense idealism of Jewish youth. But the young rebels rarely acknowledge any connection between their attitudes and either traditional or prophetic Judaism. Most of them identify Jewish religion with their parents and with the Establishment and want nothing to do with it. In cases of black–Jewish confrontation, some young Jews have identified themselves with the blacks against the Jews—to the extent that the militant young blacks would tolerate their participation. The more extreme Jewish leftists have even swallowed the myth of Israeli aggression against the Arabs. Though they proclaim their solidarity with all victims of injustice and oppression, they have been silent about the oppression of Jews in Soviet Russia and about the terror suffered by Jews still living in Arab countries. Evidently they are not free from a sort of Jewish self-hate; it differs from the variety found in pre-Hitler Germany in that it is not generated by an anti-Semitic environment—something which few of these young people have ever experienced.

All this has evoked deep concern among mature and responsible Jews. It has revealed the ineffectiveness of Jewish education in

America, which has not adequately inspired loyalty and commitment to the Jewish people and to Judaism. The generation born after the Holocaust finds difficulty in believing that it really happened. Many of its members feel little attachment to the lackluster Jewish life which they have witnessed—with its imposing but poorly attended synagogues, big *Bar Mitzvah* parties, constant fund raising, scramble for prestige, and lack of deep moral concern.

There are, of course, many loyal and enthusiastic young Jews. But the inner and outer threats to Jewish life in America are serious. The outcome cannot be forecast. Things cannot remain indefinitely in their present state: they must either get worse or get better, perhaps both. But the whole history contained in this volume argues against any hasty defeatism.

At Parting

The end of the book is not the end of the story. By the time this volume is off the press, there may be new developments in Jewish life that will require recording. Judaism, after four thousand years, is still intensely vital. The gloomy forebodings of Moritz Steinschneider who, nearly a century ago, assumed that nothing remained except to chronicle the creative achievements of a vanished past, have not been justified. Both Jewish nationalism and Jewish religion have flowered again; Hebrew is reborn; a great Jewish literature in many languages and many-sided artistic productions have enriched Jewish culture; Jewish ethical and social idealism has affected the march of world events; new forms of Jewish organization and institutional life have appeared. The bloodiest pages in all Jewish history have been written; but the Jewish people, though gravely wounded, has not been defeated.

There is much that is disquieting and disturbing in present-day Jewish life. There are no easy guarantees of a glorious future in Israel or in the United States or anywhere else. But there are certainly possibilities and opportunities for the attainment of such a glorious future. Whether they will be realized depends largely on the will of Jews themselves. But perhaps not only on them. Despite the frustrations and difficulties that arise from circumstances they cannot control, as well as from their own inner weaknesses and failings, many Jews are sustained by a faith which the story of their great adventure seems to justify, the faith embodied in the ancient words:

> "I, the Lord, change not;
> And ye, O sons of Jacob, are not consumed."

Book List

THIS IS NOT a comprehensive bibliography nor a guide to the sources, but simply an aid to those who want to pursue further reading.

Bible quotations in this work are from *The Holy Scriptures,* Jewish Publication Society, Philadelphia, 1917, the version used by most English-speaking Jews.

The hymn on p. 136, translated by Israel Zangwill, is from *The Service of the Synagogue,* Routledge and Kegan Paul, London, 1906.

The poems on p. 156 are respectively from *Selected Religious Poems of Solomon ibn Gabirol,* translated by Israel Zangwill (1923) and *Selected Poems of Jehudah HaLevi* (1924). The poem on p. 400 was translated by Marie Syrkin and is cited from her *Blessed Is the Match* (1947). These poems are reprinted by permission of the Jewish Publication Society.

In the ensuing list, JPS—Jewish Publication Society, Philadelphia; UAHC—Union of American Hebrew Congregations, New York City.

GENERAL REFERENCE WORKS

FINKELSTEIN, LOUIS (ed.), *The Jews: Their History, Culture, and Religion.* 4 vols. JPS, 1949. (Fourth, enlarged ed., 3 vols., Schocken Paperbacks, 1970).

Jewish Encyclopedia, The. 12 vols. Funk and Wagnalls, New York, 1901–1905. (Reprint ed., Ktav Publishing House).

Jewish People—Past and Present, The. 4 vols. Central Yiddish Culture Organization, New York, 1946–1955.

Universal Jewish Encyclopedia, The. 10 vols. New York, 1939–1943.

HISTORY OF THE JEWS

GRAYZEL, S., *A History of the Jews.* JPS, 1947.

ROTH, C., *A Bird's-Eye View of Jewish History.* Revised ed. UAHC, 1954. (Also appeared under the title *History of the Jews.* Schocken Paperback, 1961; revised ed., 1970).

JEWISH LITERATURE

FLEG, E., *The Jewish Anthology.* Behrman House, 1940.

GLATZER, N. N., *A Jewish Reader.* Schocken Books, 1961. (Schocken Paperback, 1961).

RELIGIOUS IDEAS

BAECK, L., *The Essence of Judaism.* Schocken Books, 1948. (Schocken Paperback, 1961).

KOHLER, K., *Jewish Theology.* Macmillan, 1918.

SCHECHTER, S., *Studies in Judaism.* 3 series. JPS, 1896, 1908, 1924.

CUSTOMS AND OBSERVANCES

SCHAUSS, H., *The Jewish Festivals.* UAHC, 1938. Also appeared under the title *Guide to the Jewish Holy Days.* (Schocken Paperback, 1961). ———, *The Lifetime of a Jew.* UAHC, 1950.

WORSHIP

FREEHOF, S. B., *The Small Sanctuary.* UAHC, 1942.

Chapters 1-11

BAMBERGER, B. J., *The Bible: A Modern Jewish Approach.* Hillel Little Books, 1955. (Enlarged ed. Schocken Paperback, 1963).

COHON, B. D., *The Prophets: Their Personalities and Teachings.* Scribner, 1939.

FREEHOF, S. B., *Preface to Scripture.* UAHC, 1950.

KAUFMANN, Y., *The Religion of Israel.* University of Chicago Press, 1960.

Chapters 12-13

BICKERMAN, E., *From Ezra to the Last of the Maccabees.* Schocken Books, 1962. (Schocken Paperback, 1962).

HERFORD, R. T., *The Pharisees.* Macmillan, 1924.

TORREY, C. C., *The Apocryphal Literature.* Yale University Press, 1945.

Chapter 15

BENTWICH, N., *Hellenism.* JPS, 1920.

Chapter 16

KLAUSNER, J., *Jesus of Nazareth.* Macmillan, 1925.

SANDMEL, S., *A Jewish Understanding of the New Testament.* Hebrew Union College Press, 1956.

Chapters 17-21

MOORE, G. F., *Judaism in the First Centuries of the Christian Era.* 3 vols. Harvard University Press, 1927–1930.

SCHECHTER, S., *Some Aspects of Rabbinic Theology*. Macmillan, 1909. (Also appeared under the title *Aspects of Rabbinic Theology*. Schocken Paperback, 1961).

Chapters 25-27

GUTMANN, J., *Philosophies of Judaism*. Holt, Rinehart & Winston, 1963.

HUSIK, I., *A History of Medieval Jewish Philosophy*. Macmillan, 1916.

Chapters 29 and 33-35

SCHOLEM, G. G., *Major Trends in Jewish Mysticism*. Revised ed. Schocken Books, 1946. (Schocken Paperback, 1961).

SCHOLEM, G. G., ed. *Zohar, The Book of Splendor*. Schocken Books, 1949. (Schocken Paperback, 1963).

BUBER, M., *Ten Rungs*. Schocken Books, 1947. (Schocken Paperback, 1962).

Chapters 39, 41, etc.

PHILIPSON, D., *The Reform Movement in Judaism*. Revised ed. Macmillan, 1931.

Chapters 41-56

BERGMAN, S. H., *Faith and Reason*. Schocken Books, 1961. (Schocken Paperback, 1963).

ELBOGEN, I., *A Century of Jewish Life*. JPS, 1944.

GLATZER, N. N., *Franz Rosenzweig: Life and Thought*. Schocken Books, 1953. (Schocken Paperback, 1961).

GUTMANN, J., *Philosophies of Judaism*. Holt, Rinehart & Winston, 1963.

KAPLAN, M. M., *Purpose and Meaning of Jewish Existence*. Jewish Reconstructionist Press, 1964. (The major portion of this book deals with Hermann Cohen's exposition of Judaism as a rational religion).

Chapters 47 and 55-56

HAY, MALCOLM, *The Foot of Pride*. Beacon Press, Boston, 1950. (Also appeared under the title *Europe and the Jews*. Beacon Paperback, 1963).

Chapters 48, 53, 57

AHAD HA'AM, *Nationalism and the Jewish Ethic*. Schocken Books, 1962.

Book List 465

BUBER, M., *Israel and the World*. Schocken Books, 1948. (Revised ed. Schocken Paperback, 1963).

LEARSI, R. (pseud.), *Fulfillment: the Epic Story of Zionism*. World Publishing Co., 1951.

HERTZBERG, A., *The Zionist Idea*. Meridian—JPS Paperback, 1960.

Chapter 62

HESCHEL, A., *Israel: An Echo of Eternity*. Farrar, Straus & Giroux, 1968. (Noonday Paperback, 1969).

———, *Man Is Not Alone: A Philosophy of Religion*. JPS, 1951. (Harper & Row Paperback, 1968).

KAPLAN, M. M. *Judaism as a Civilization*. Reconstructionist Press, 1957. (Schocken Paperback, 1967).

Notes

IN GENERAL, documentation has not been given; it may be found in the standard works listed in the Bibliography. The notes below concern statements in the text which depart somewhat from the traditional or conventional account, and will guide the inquiring student to a more detailed treatment.

The opening chapters present—albeit somewhat skeptically—a critical position which many scholars regard as somewhat old-fashioned. This is because the author is even more skeptical about newer fashions in the field.

Chapter 1, p. 9. See Ezekiel 40:1, and Morgenstern, *Hebrew Union College Annual*, Vol. 1 (1924), pp. 22 ff.

Chapter 4, p. 22. Isaiah 22:1-14; Buttenwieser, *The Prophets of Israel*, pp. 254 ff.

Chapter 7, p. 38. Following Buttenwieser, "Where Did Deutero-Isaiah Live?" in *Journal of Biblical Literature*, Vol. 38, pp. 94 ff. But many scholars believe that he lived in Babylonia.

———, p. 40. Morgenstern, *As a Mighty Stream*, p. 272.

Chapter 18, p. 111. Lauterbach, "Midrash and Mishnah," *Rabbinic Essays*, pp. 163 ff.

Chapter 23, p. 143. Nemoy, "Early Karaism," *Jewish Quarterly Review*, Vol. 40 (1950), pp. 307 ff.

Chapter 27, p. 176. On the correct text of this Mishnah, see Zeitlin in *Jewish Quarterly Review*, Vol. 31 (1940–41), p. 312, citing Yer. Peah 16b.

Index

Anti-Semitism, 52, 85f., 311, 337ff., 341ff., 356f., 381, 386f., 393-403, 415f., 426f. *See* Persecutions.

Apocalyptic Writings, 70-75, 126, 128, 198, 203; gaonic, 146

Apocrypha, 115, 213, 277

Apologetics, against Hivi al-Balkhi, 148; against Karaites, 145, 148; against Christianity, 117, 145, 166, 177, 258f., 316. *See* Disputations.

Arabia, Jews in, 139, 424. *See* Yemenite Jews.

Arabic writings (Jewish), 141, 148, 157, 162f., 179, 190, 277; translation into Hebrew, 180

Arabs, 139ff., 161; in Spain, 154ff.; modern, 367f., 378, 380ff., 407ff., 430f.; in Israel, 422f.; refugees, 423. *See* Arabia, Egypt, Spain, Syria.

Aramaic, 92, 114, 157

Argentina, 357, 428

Asceticism, Talmud on, 126; Karaite, 144; 200, 236; Chasidic view, 244f.

Asch, Sholem, 358

Asher ben Yehiel, 196

Ashi, Rav, 133

Ashk'nazim (Central European Jews), 154, 194, 214, 229, 315, 333f., 378. *See* S'fardim.

Assimilation, 262, 266f., 301, 307f., 336f., 359f., 372f., 389, 434. *See* Converts to Christianity, Intermarriage.

Assyria, 13, 17, 20ff., 30

Atonement, Day of, *see* Yom Kippur.

Attributes, *see* God, idea of.

Australia, 357, 427

Austria, 219, 267, 305, 339, 342, 359, 396, 398, 426. *See* Bohemia, Galicia, Germany, Hungary, Moravia.

Authority, of kings, 13ff., 68f.; of high priest, 40, 77; of Pharisaic-Rabbinic leaders, 80, 113ff., 187ff.; of tradition, 108, 280; of charity collectors, 119; of the communities, 186, 234; of Bible and Talmud, 317; of the rich, 334f. *See* Ban,

Chief Rabbi, Gaon, Halakah, Nagid, Nasi, Ordination, Rabbi, Sanhedrin, Torah, Exilarch.

Autopsy, 422

Avicebron, *see* Gabirol, Solomon ibn.

Azriel ben Solomon, 202

b

Baal Shem Tov, Israel (Besht), 243f., 253

Babylonia, ancient, 5, 33ff., 38 (459), 40, 42, 79, 84; Chaldean rulers of, 30, 33, 36; Jews in, 33ff., 38, 131ff., 137ff., 143ff., 147ff.; divergences from Palestinian custom, 132, 147, 153f., 234; modern (Iraq), 378, 410, 431

Babylonian Religion, *Shapatum*, 9; laws and myths, 52f.

Bachya ibn Pakuda, 162, 173

Baeck, Leo, 359f., 395

Bagdad, 137, 143, 153

Baldwin, Edward Chauncey, 391

Balfour Declaration, 367, 382f.

Baltimore, 316, 319, 322, 355

Ban, 113, 181, 187, 224f., 247

Bar Kochba, 104, 111, 114, 228

Bar Mitzvah (coming of age), 194, 230,·271, 432. *Bas Mitzvah*, 354. *See* Confirmation.

Belgium, *see* Netherlands.

Benderly, Samson, 355

Ben-Gurion, David, 410

Ben Meir, 147

Ben Yehudah, Eliezer, 326

Berab, Jacob, 233ff., 300, 422

Berlin, 258, 260, 267ff., 274f., 301, 338, 360, 375; Reform congregation of, 283f., 298

Bernays, Isaac, 296f.

Besht, *see* Baal Shem Tov, Israel.

Bialik, Chaim Nachman, 358

Bible, Formation of, Torah, 44f.; prophets, 63; completion, 115

Bible Commentators, Karaite, 145; Saadia, 148; in N. Africa, 153; in Spain, 157; in Provence, 179; Rashi,

189f.; Nachmanides, 202; Abrabanel, 216; in Germany, 260. *See also* Gikatilla, Moses ibn; Ibn Ezra, Abraham; Kimchi family; Lyra, Nicholas de.
Bible, Hebrew text, 135f.
Bible Translations, Greek (Septuagint), 85, 92, 135, 277; Aramaic (Targum), 114; Arabic, 148; German, 191, 260, 305, 376; English, 191, 315, 356; other, 277
Biblical Criticism, 6f., 277, 280f., 295f., 338; in medieval Spain, 157; Spinoza's, 225; I. M. Wise on, 318f.; Pittsburgh platform on, 320f.
Biro-Bijan, 367
BLOCH, ERNEST, 249, 437
B'nai B'rith, 356, 387, 391
Bohemia, 300, 316. *See* Austria, Czechoslovakia.
Bokharan Jews, 378
BONAPARTE, JEROME, 264, 266, 268
BONAPARTE, NAPOLEON, 264ff., 266, 304
Brandeis University, 438
Brazil, 312, 428
Breslau, 283, 296, 301
BROD, MAX, 377
Brooklyn, 416, 426
BUBER, MARTIN, 374f., 381, 422
Buenos Aires, 428
Bund, 328f., 358f. *See* Socialism.

C

Cabala, 147, 173, 181, 198-208, 212, 225, 231, 235ff., 239f., 243, 291, 383f.
Calendar, development of, 8f., 46, 114; mathematically computed, 132; controversy over, 147
Canaanite Religion, 11f., 54f.
Canada, 357, 427f.
Cantor, *see* Chazan.
Capital Punishment, 122
Caucasus, Jews of, 430
Central Conference of American

Rabbis, 321, 364, 369, 389f., 392, 433, 446, 448
Chaldeans, *see* Babylonia.
Chalutzim (Pioneers), 378f.
Chanuko (Dedication), 68, 301, 386, 446
Chaplains, in American forces, 369f., 417, 435; in civilian institutions, 437; in Israel, 421
Charity, *see* Philanthropy.
Charleston, S. C., 315f.
Chasidim (pious), ancient, 67, 77, 79
Chasidim, medieval, 200f.
Chasidim, modern, 243ff., 304f., 307, 325, 349, 353, 362, 378, 439; Buber and, 374
Chazan, caretaker, 80; cantor, 188, 196, 437, 447ff.; chazan-minister, 313ff.
Chazars, 170f.
Chief Rabbi, medieval, 187; of Jerusalem, 235; of France, 265; of British Commonwealth, 334; of Palestine, 383f.; of Rome, 427; of Westphalia, 279
Chilul haShem (profanation of the name), 128. *See* Kiddush haShem.
CHORIN, AARON, 279
Chosen People, *see* Israel, Election of.
Chov'vei Zion (Lovers of Zion), 325, 343
Christian Church, preserved old Jewish writings, 74, 92, 115; councils of, 125, 218f.; Maimonides' works denounced to, 181; pressure on Jews, 186, 192f.; reaction to Nazism, 394, 396. *See* Chuetas; Church and State; Counter-Reformation; Crusades; Disputations; Ghetto; Marranos; Mortara, E.; Persecutions; Reformation.
Christianity, on Satan, 74, 201; grew out of Pharisaism, 76, 82; rise of, 94ff.; Jewish influences on, 114, 127, 161, 191, 212f., 219, 374f., 425; on celibacy, 121, 126; and Islam, 139ff.; Jewish thinkers on, 145, 159, 291f., 316, 321, 375;

DAVID, 12ff.; family of, 21; descendant of Ruth, 48; Exilarchs claim descent from, 131, 137; 157. See Messiah.
DAVID BEN ZAKKAI, 147f.
Dead Sea Scrolls, 81
Defense Organizations, in Russia, 358; in Canada, 428; in U.S.A., 356. See American Jewish Committee, American Jewish Conference, American Jewish Congress, Anti-Defamation League, B'nai B'rith, Community Councils, N.C.R.A.C.
DE HIRSCH, MAURICE, 357, 428
Deism, 257f.
DEL MEDIGO, ELIJAH, 213
Democracy, of the Synagogue, 46; Pharisaic movement, 77ff.; of the Rabbis, 112, 131; of Jewish communities, 187; "delay of prayers," 188; Council of Four Lands, 230f.; of early Chasidism, 243ff.; American and Jewish, 316; garment industry, 352; of Palestine collectives, 379f.; of State of Israel, 411
Denmark, see Scandinavia.
Derech Eretz (manners), 128, 297
Deuteronomic Reformation, 27ff.
Deuteronomy, Book of, 27ff., 53
Diaspora, 83f.; holiday observance in, 132; no ordination in, 234; viewed as blessing, 282
Dietary Laws, 93, 108, 122f., 354, 420f., 442; Maimonides on, 168; research on, 277; Kaplan on, 443
Disputations, 182ff., 242, 244
Divorce, see Marriage and Divorce.
Dönmeh (Crypto-Jews), 240, 424
DREYFUS, ALFRED, 341f.
Dropsie College, 363, 438
Dublin, 363
DUBNOW, SIMON, 359

ℓ

Ecclesiastes, see Koheleth.
Education, Adult, in the synagogue, 46, 80, 112f.; Kallah Assemblies,

133; in Germany, 274f., 375, 396, 399; in Russia, 305ff.; in Israel, 380; in U.S., 385, 436
Education, Elementary, 60, 77; in medieval communities, 188; in Amsterdam, 225; in Poland, 230, 376; in Germany, 260, 267f., 271; in U.S., 314, 349f., 352, 354f., 416, 433, 435ff., 440, 446f.; of Alliance Israélite, 335, 429f.; in Israel, 383, 422; Yemenite, 430
Education, Higher, 386f. See Brandeis University, Dropsie College, Hebrew University, Hillel Foundation, Rabbinical Seminaries, Science of Judaism, Yeshiva University, Y'shivos.
Egypt, ancient, 5, 7, 20ff., 30; Ptolemaic, 65f.; Jews residing in, 84ff., 155, 186; modern, 335, 408, 410
Egyptian Religion, 53f.
EINHORN, DAVID, 319f.
EINSTEIN, ALBERT, 414
ELAZAR B. AZARIAH, 112
ELDAD THE DANITE, 138, 424
ELIJAH (prophet), 13, 15, 202
ELIJAH BEN SOLOMON (Vilna Gaon), 246f., 273, 304, 306f.
ELISHEVA, 425
Emanation, 203ff. See S'firos.
EMDEN, JACOB, 242, 273
England, 193, 217, 226f., 300, 313, 330, 333ff., 359, 362ff., 427; British policy on Palestine, 367f., 382ff., 397, 407ff.
Enlightenment, 257f., 267, 272, 287, 297. See Haskalah.
En Sof (The Infinite God), 203f., 225, 235. See God, Idea of.
Essenes, 81, 95, 102
Esther, Book of, 63
Ethics, Prophetic, 14f., 17f., 21, 46f., 70f.; of Torah, 28, 43f., 53, 86, 192f.; of Proverbs, 6of.; Pharisaic-Rabbinic, 80, 109, 117-123, 125, 127ff.; Essene, 81; of Jesus, 98f.; of ghetto period, 220f.; of Spinoza, 226; of Luria, 236; of Chasidism,

gued by Abraham b. David, 179f.;
of Plotinus, 203; in Cabala, 203f.;
of Spinoza, 225f.; Sabbatian, 241;
Chasidic, 246; deist, 257; of Kant,
288; idealistic, 289ff.; in Reform,
320; of Cohen, 360; of Buber, 374;
of Kaplan, 444. *See* En-Sof, S'firos,
YHWH.
"Golden Rule," 43, 79
GOODE, ALEXANDER, 417
GORDON, A. D., 379
GRAETZ, HEINRICH, 274, 296
Greece, 216, 398
Greek Influence, in Palestine, 62,
65ff., 77; in Alexandria, 85ff.; in
Middle Ages, 141, 157f., 160ff.; in
modern times, 358; opposition to,
172, 299
GRÉGOIRE, ABBE, 263

h

Hadassah, 388
Haganah (militia), 380, 382, 408
Haggadah, see Aggadah.
HAGGAI, 40
HAI GAON, 149, 155
Halakah (Law), 98, 111, 130; defini-
tion, 117; provisions of, 118ff.,
132, 189, 220; Karaite and Tal-
mudic, 144; responsa on, 138, 148;
codification of, 157ff., 196, 221f.;
proposals to revitalize, 234f.; Con-
servative Judaism on, 445; in mod-
ern Palestine, 383f., 420ff. *See*
Calendar, Commandments, Cus-
toms, Law, Marriage and Divorce,
Ritual, Torah.
Hamburg, 242; Temple, 269ff., 285,
296
Hammurabi, Code of, 52f.
HASDAI IBN SHAPRUT, 170
Haskalah (Enlightenment), 305ff.,
325. *See* Enlightenment.
Hasmoneans, 67ff., 73, 76
HAYYUJ, JUDAH IBN, 157
Hebraists, Christian, 212, 219, 276
Hebrew Grammar, 145, 148, 157, 212

Hebrew Language, 11, 43, 54, 92,
145, 155ff., 180, 212ff., 274, 376;
prayer in Hebrew, 295, 361, 445;
modern revival of, 305ff., 310,
326, 358, 383; Communist opposi-
tion to, 367
Hebrew Poetry (Post-Biblical), in
Palestine, 136; in Spain, 155ff.; in
Italy, 213, 241; modern, 358, 401,
422, 425
Hebrew Union College, *see* Rabbini-
cal Seminaries.
Hebrew University, 368, 381, 383,
410, 422
HEINE, HEINRICH, 124, 275, 284
Hellenists, *see* Greek Influence.
HEROD, 76f.
HERZL, THEODOR, 342ff.
HESS, MOSES, 311, 328
High Priest, 40, 46; under the Syri-
ans, 66; Hasmonean, 77; presided
over Sanhedrin, 80
HILDESHEIMER, ESRIEL, 301
HILLEL THE ELDER, 79f., 103f.,
109f., 131
HILLEL (*Nasi*), 132
HILLEL (Rabbi), 125
Hillel Foundation, 390f., 435
HIRSCH, EMIL G., 321
HIRSCH, SAMSON RAPHAEL, 293,
297f., 301, 441
HIRSCH, SAMUEL, 292f., 319, 375
Histadrut HaOvedim (Labor Union),
380
HIVI AL-BALKHI, 148
HOLDHEIM, SAMUEL, 283f.
Holland, *see* Netherlands.
HOSEA, 18ff., 23, 109
Humor, Jewish, 222
Hungary, 247, 285f., 301, 319, 398,
426
Hymns, 136, 146, 178, 214, 236, 268

i

IBN EZRA, ABRAHAM, 179, 225, 273,
299
Idolatry, 10, 38, 45

k

l

m

Marriage and Divorce, Biblical law, 108f.; polygamy, 119, 189, 264, 430; in *halakah*, 119f., 189; marriage and duty, 121; in Modern Israel, 383, 420. *See* Women, Status of; Intermarriage.

Marriage Contract, 119f., 445

MARSHALL, LOUIS, 354, 381f., 389

Martyrs & Martyrdom, of Maccabean period, 67, 72, 79; of Hadrianic persecution, 115; ideal of, 128, 165; medieval, 194; in Poland, 231. *See* Kiddush haShem, Persecutions.

MARX, KARL, 326f.

Massoretes, 136

MATTATHIAS, 67

MEIR, RABBI, 115

MEIR OF ROTHENBURG, 189, 196

MENASSEH BEN ISRAEL, 226

MENDELE MOCHER SEFORIM, 329

MENDELSSOHN, MOSES, 253, 258ff., 263, 287, 305f.

Menorah Society, 390f.

Messiah, 39, 70f., 95, 102, 129, 146, 242, 309, 343; denied by R. Hillel, 125; Maimonides on, 159, 177; Nachmanides on, 183; in Cabala, 206; Menasseh ben Israel on, 226f.; Luria on, 235; rejection of personal, 269f., 281, 317f., 443; Kalischer on, 310

Messianic Age, Isaiah on, 22f.; Reform view, 281f., 321; Cohen on, 361

Messianic Claimants, Theudas, 95; Bar Kochba, 104; oriental, 145f., 430; David Reubeni, Solomon Molcho, 238; Sabbatai Zevi, 239ff.; Jacob ··Frank, 242. *See* Jesus of Nazareth.

Mexico, 217, 312, 369

Midrash, Method of Interpretation, 110f., 144, 157, 190; literature, 126, 135f., 190, 202, 275

Milhaud, Darius, 437

MIRABEAU, COUNT, 263

Miracles, Belief in, 6, 148, 245, 248; S. Hirsch on, 293; M. M. Kaplan on, 443

Mishnah, 115f., 133, 176, 233; on repentance, 127

Misnagdim (opponents), 247ff.

Mizrachi (Orthodox Zionist Party), 358, 361, 380

MODENA, LEO DE, 227

MOHAMMED, 139ff., 177

MOLCHO, SOLOMON, 238

Monogamy, *see* Marriage and Divorce.

MONTAGU, LILY, 363f.

MONTEFIORE, CLAUDE G., 362f.

MONTEFIORE, MOSES, 334f.

MORAIS, SABATO, 322f., 353

Moravia, 279, 297

Morocco, *see* Africa, North.

MORTARA, EDGAR, 335

MORTEIRA, SAUL, 224f.

MOSCATO, JUDAH, 213

MOSES, 5, 7f., 26, 45, 48, 53, 107, 110, 157, 168, 177, 234, 318ff., 327

MOSES DE LEON, 202

MOSES BEN MAIMON (Maimonides), 155, 162, 207; code of, 158f.; philosophy of, 168f.; creed of, 176ff.; opposition to, 179ff., 249, 297, 299, 308; *Nagid*, 186f.; influence on Spinoza, 225; on ordination, 234; and Yemen, 430

MOSES BEN NACHMAN (Nachmanides), 181f., 183, 202

Moshav, *see* Collective Colonies.

MUNK, SALOMON, 335

Musar (Ethics), *see* Ethical Writings, Salanter.

Music, Synagogue, 196, 244, 317, 354, 415, 437. *See* Organ, Chazan.

Mysticism, in Philo, 91f.; rabbinic, 126; gaonic, 146f.; in Gabirol, 173; Cabala, 199ff., 235ff.; Chasidism, 243ff.; in Buber, 374

N

NACHMANIDES, *see* Moses ben Nachman.

Nagid (Prince), 186f.

Philanthropy, in Torah, 28, 118; in Proverbs, 61; Jesus on, 99; rabbinic laws on, 119; in medieval communities, 188, 192; in Amsterdam, 225; modern Jewish philanthropies, 325, 335f., 347f., 357, 368ff., 385, 387f., 395, 411ff., 429ff., 437f. *See* Community Chest, Jewish National Fund, Joint Distribution Committee, United Jewish Appeal, Welfare Funds.

Philistines, 12, 21

Philo, 89ff., 97, 198, 213, 277

Philosophers, Gentile, pre-Socratic, 87f.; Plato, 88f., 160, 163; Voltaire, 145; Stoics, 160; Aristotle, 163ff., 172f.; Thomas Aquinas, 165, 174, 211; neo-Platonists, 173; Albert the Great, 174; Duns Scotus, 174; Plotinus, 203; Enlightenment thinkers, 257; Kant, 287f., 300, 360; Hegel, 289f., 292, 375; Schelling, 291; Mill, 344; Spencer, 344; Dewey, 444

Philosophy, Greek and Hellenistic, 87ff., 203; medieval scholastic, 148, 160-184, 191, 225; controversy over teaching philosophy, 178ff., 196, 213; of Spinoza, 225f.; of Mendelssohn, 258f.; Kantian and idealistic, 287ff., 360f.; philosophy of history, 290; Ahad HaAm, 344; existential, 374ff. *See* Philosophers, Gentile; Abrabanel; Abraham ibn David; Albo; Allegorical Interpretation; Azriel ben Solomon; Bachya; Cabala; Buber; Cohen, H.; Crescas; Ethics; Evil, Problem of; Formstecher; Freedom of Will; Gabirol; God, Idea of; Hirsch, Samuel; ibn Ezra; Judah HaLevi; Kaplan; Krochmal; Lazarus, M.; Levi ben Gershom; Maimon, S.; Moses b. Maimon; Philo; Revelation; Rosenzweig; Saadia; Steinheim; Tibbon.

Pilpul (Casuistry), 229f., 244, 246

PINSKER, LEO, 325f., 335f., 346

Pittsburgh Platform, 320f.

Piyyutim, see Hymns.

Poland, 229ff., 239, 242ff., 288, 303ff., 328, 365ff., 376f., 381, 397ff., 426. *See* Galicia, Russia.

Polygamy, *see* Marriage and Divorce.

Portugal, 154, 187, 216f., 312, 401

Prague, 274, 377

Prayer, 46, 80; standard, 113f.; texts, 129, 174, 395; of intercession, 194f.; private, 195; in Cabala, 206; Chasidic view, 244; for return to Palestine, 269f.; language of, 280, 295. *See* Hymns, *Kaddish,* Prayer Book, Psalms, *Sh'ma.*

Prayer Book, 138, 148, 214; Reform prayer books, 269, 316, 318, 320ff., 370, 447; research on, 277; revision of, 294; translation, 315; military, 370; Conservative, 444; Reconstructionist, 444

Preaching, 80f., 114, 130, 213, 227; modern, 269; Zunz on, 275f. *See* Aggadah, Midrash.

Predestination, *see* Freedom of Will.

Priestly Code, 43ff.

Priests, 12, 26; Zadokite, 35, 45f.; Scribes, 60; Hasmonean family, 67; Sadducean party, 77ff.; Reform view, 321. *See* High Priest, Sadducees, Sacrifices.

Printing, 214

Progress, belief in, 257f., 282, 319

Prophets and Prophecy, 14f., 16-25, 26ff., 33ff., 38ff., 40, 46f., 49, 64; decline of, 47; and apocalypse, 70ff.; view of Aristotelians, 166; of HaLevi, 171f.; in creed, 177; of Einhorn, 320. *See* Amos, Elijah, Haggai, Hosea, Isaiah, Jeremiah, Jonah, Moses, Nathan, Samuel, Zechariah.

Prosbol (legal device), 79

Proselytes, *see* Converts to Judaism.

Provence, 178f., 202

Proverbs, Book of, 54, 60f., 115

Psalms, 59f.,-91, 156, 198

Pumbeditha, 131, 137, 149

Purim (Feast of Lots), 63, 213, 386

q

Quorum (for worship), 110, 219

r

RAB (Abba Areka), 131
Rabbi, title, 107; ancient, 112; local
judge, 137; professional status,
187f.; in Poland, 230; ordination,
234; Chasidic, 245; decline of rabbinic dignity, 275; in central Europe, 282; "Crown R.," 307; in
U.S., 314, 440; in England, 334,
363f.; in Israel, 421. See Central
Conference of American Rabbis,
Chief Rabbi, Rabbinical Confer-
ences, Rabbinical Seminaries, Tsa-
dik, Y'shivos.
Rabbinical Conferences, German, 283,
294f., 300, 319; at Cleveland, 317;
at Pittsburgh, 320f. See Aggudas
HoRabbonim, Central Conference
of American Rabbis, Rabbinical
Council of America.
Rabbinical Council of America, 440
Rabbinical Seminaries, 276; German,
296, 301, 360, 373; Italian, 299;
Russian, 307; American, 317f., 322,
353f., 363, 381, 389ff., 440, 448.
See Y'shivos.
RABINA, 133
Racial Doctrine, 338, 373, 393ff.
RAPPOPORT, SALOMON J., 274
RASHI (Rabbi Solomon Yizchaki),
189ff., 275
RATHENAU, WALTER, 373
Rationalism, medieval, 161ff.; criti-
cism of, 170ff.; of the Enlighten-
ment, 257ff., 270, 316, 360
Reconstructionism, 442ff.
Reformation, Protestant, 144, 218f.
Reform Judaism, 154, 224; in Ger-
many, 267ff., 279ff., 291, 293ff.,
300f.; in Moravia, 279; in Hungary,
285f.; in U.S., 315ff., 348, 353f.,
370, 389f., 417, 442ff., 445ff.; in
England, 334, 362ff.; in Canada,

427f. See Central Conference of
American Rabbis, Liberal Judaism,
Union of American Hebrew Con-
gregations, World Union for Pro-
gressive Judaism.
Refugees, German, 413ff., 428
Reincarnation and Transmigration,
235f., 241. See Immortality.
Renaissance, European, 211ff., 221
Repentance, see T'shuvo.
Responsa, 137f., 141, 148, 277
Resurrection, 72, 79, 96f., 110, 125,
177, 179, 317f., 361, 443; Maimon-
ides on, 168; Mishnah on, 176. See
Immortality.
REUBENI, DAVID, 238, 377
REUCHLIN, JOHANNES, 212
Revelation, medieval views, 163,
165ff., 170ff., 177, 257; Mendels-
sohn on, 260; Geiger on, 280f.;
Steinheim on, 288f.; S. Hirsch on,
292; S. R. Hirsch on, 298; I. M.
Wise on, 318f.; Reform view, 320f.
See Prophets and Prophecy, Sinai,
Torah.
Revisionists, 380, 408
Revolution, American, 258, 263, 313
Revolution, French, 258, 263f.
Revolution, Industrial, 255, 261,
326ff.
Revolution of 1848, 285, 315
Reward and Punishment, 10; prophetic view, 16ff., 21f.; in Deut.,
29f.; in Ezekiel, 36; in Job, 61f.;
in apocalypse, 72; in rabbinic
thought, 125, 127; in medieval
thought, 177f. See Evil, Problem
of; "Eye for Eye"; Immortality.
RIESSER, GABRIEL, 284f.
Ritual, prophetic view, 17f., 24; Ezekiel on, 35; rabbinic view, 117f.,
172; in Cabala, 206f.; Mendelssohn
on, 260; Reform views, 267f., 281,
321, 360, 445ff.; S. R. Hirsch on,
298; H. Cohen on, 361; Rosenzweig on, 375; Kaplan on, 443. See
Commandments, Customs, Sacrifices.

Sicarii, see Zealots.
Simchas Torah (Rejoicing over the Torah), 132, 448
SIMEON BEN GAMALIEL, 113
SIMEON BEN JOHAI, 202
SIMON, ABRAM, 392
SIMON THE HASMONEAN, 68
Sin, Forgiveness of, 18f., 44, 126f., 361. See T'shuvo, Yom Kippur.
Sin, Original, 96f., 126
Sinai, Revelation at, 5, 7, 9, 111, 167, 171, 292f. See Revelation.
SINGER, ISIDOR, 355
Slaughtering, Ritual, 123. See Dietary Laws, Shochet.
SMOLENSKIN, PERETZ, 311
Socialism, 310f., 326ff., 358f., 361, 379f.
SOLOMON, KING, 12, 60, 62
SOLOMON BEN ADRET, 182, 188
Solomon, Wisdom of (book), 88f., 115
Spain, Arab, 138, 153-178; Christian, 172, 178ff., 187, 196, 202ff., 214ff., 312, 401, 427. See S'fardim.
SPEKTOR, ISAAC ELHANAN, 440
SPINOZA, BARUCH, 174, 224ff.
STEIN, LUDWIG, 295
STEINHEIM, SOLOMON L., 288f.
STEINSCHNEIDER, MORITZ, 277
Suffering, Problem of, see Evil, Problem of.
Sukos (Feast of Tabernacles), 9, 43, 78
Superstition, 159, 194, 201, 248f.
Sura, 131, 137, 147
Switzerland, 258f., 333, 344, 401
Sybilline Oracles, 86
Synagogue, origin, 36, 45f.; organization, 80f., 103, 112ff.; in Alexandria, 85; medieval, 188; Reform temples, 268ff.; in U.S., 313ff., 349, 354, 386, 390, 436f., 439f.; workers', 328; in England, 334; architecture of, 373, 436f.; in Israel, 378, 421; burning of, 396; Yemenite, 430. See Community Organization, Temple.

Synagogue Center, 386
Synagogue Council of America, 392, 440, 445
Synod, 300f.
Syria, Seleucid, 66f.; Damascus affair, 335; modern, 410, 431
SZOLD, BENJAMIN, 322
SZOLD, HENRIETTA, 388

t

Tabernacles, Feast of, see Sukos.
Takonos (ordinances), 109, 189. See Marriage Contract, Prosbol.
Talis (prayer-shawl), 354, 447
Talmud, 107ff., 133f., 137f.; attacks on, 133f., 183, 212, 242; commentaries on, 153, 190; parody on, 213; rejected by "Friends of Reform," 270; English translation, 427
Talmud, Palestinian, 130f., 158, 246
Tannaim (teachers of Mishnah), 115, 234
Targum, see Bible Translations.
TCHERNICHOWSKY, SAUL, 358
Tel Aviv, 410, 420
Temple, of Solomon, 12, 22, 33; Ezekiel's plan for, 35; restoration of, 40, 45; Second, 49; Psalms sung in, 60; defiled and rededicated, 67f.; rebuilt by Herod, 77; Jewish temples in Egypt, 84, 95; supported by Diaspora Jews, 84, 95; destroyed, 103; memorial of, 194; temple as name for synagogue, 269f.
"Ten Lost Tribes," 20, 33, 138, 238
Territorialism, 345
T'filo, see Prayers.
Tibbon family, 180
Tiberias, 228, 233
TIKTIN, S. A., 283
Tolerance, of Gamaliel, 96; of Rabbinic Judaism, 125; of Chazars, 171
Torah, 5f., 26-32; presented by Ezra, 43ff.; final editing, 44f.; love of, 59; Pharisaic and Sadducean views, 77f.; Paul on, 97; interpretation of,

108ff.; public reading of, 113f., 132, 188, 194; rabbinic view, 117ff., 125; divine origin, 176f., 225; in Chasidism, 246; I. M. Wise on, 318; and State of Israel, 421; Kaplan on, 443. See Bible, Halakah, Law, Revelation.
Torah, Oral, 78, 108ff., 140, 143ff., 269; Frankel on, 295
TRUMAN, HARRY S., 410
Tsadik (Saint), 245f.
T'shuvo (repentance), 126, 244
T'shuvo (responsum), 138
Turkey, 239ff., 335, 343, 345, 368, 383, 424; Karaites in, 145; Spanish exiles in, 216, 227ff., 429

U

Uganda, 345
Ukraine, 229, 304, 366, 400. See Russia.
Union of American Hebrew Congregations, 317f., 356, 364, 389, 433f., 446ff.
Union of Orthodox Congregations, 440
United Jewish Appeal, 388f., 411f.
United Nations, 409f., 423
United States, 263, 271, 285f., 300, 313ff., 343, 347ff., 368ff., 385ff., 413ff., 432-449
United Synagogue of America, 444
United Synagogue (British), 334, 363
Universalism, 17f., 21ff., 35, 38ff., 44, 48ff., 125f., 213, 259, 281f., 291ff., 297f., 316, 319f., 360f.
Usury, see Interest.

V

Venice, 214, 219, 227, 238
Vilna, 246, 304
Vilna Gaon, see Elijah ben Solomon

W

Warsaw, 348, 351; battle of Warsaw Ghetto, 399f.

WASSERMANN, JAKOB, 373
Weeks, Feast of, see Shovuos.
WEIZMANN, CHAIM, 367, 381f., 410
Welfare Funds, 388f., 416
West Indies, 300, 313
Westphalia, Kingdom of, 264, 266, 268; duchy of, 279
WILSON, WOODROW, 369
Wisdom Literature, 60ff.
WISE, ISAAC M., 316f., 369
WISE, STEPHEN S., 389f.
Wissenschaft des Judentums, see Science of Judaism.
Women, Status of, in Reform, 271, 294, 317; in Conservative Judaism, 354; in Israel, 420; in Yemen, 430; in modern Orthodoxy, 440. See Marriage and Divorce, Confirmation.
Workmen's Circle, 352
World Union for Progressive Judaism, 364, 374, 429

Y

Yemenite Jews, 378, 430f.
Yeshivah University, 438, 440
YHWH, 7ff., 12, 26, 61; pronunciation restricted, 45. See God, Idea of.
Yiddish (Judeo-German), 221, 229, 259, 310, 348f., 367, 437, 440; literature in, 247, 329, 348, 352, 357, 400, 428
Yizkor (memorial prayer), 195
Yom Kippur (Day of Atonement), 46, 50, 127, 195, 304f., 395
YMHA, 355, 370, 385. See Community Center.
Youth Groups (synagogue), 436, 447
Y'shivos (academies), Jabneh, 103f., 111f.; Babylonian, 131, 137f., 187; Russian, 307, 357; American, 349, 440; in Palestine, 378. See Rabbinical Seminaries, Yeshivah University.
Yugoslavia, 398, 426.